BOLLINGEN SERIES LIX · 2

PAUL FRIEDLÄNDER

PLATO

2

THE DIALOGUES
First Period

TRANSLATED FROM THE GERMAN
BY HANS MEYERHOFF

BOLLINGEN SERIES LIX

PANTHEON BOOKS

THIS IS THE SECOND OF THREE VOLUMES
CONSTITUTING THE FIFTY-NINTH PUBLICATION
IN A SERIES SPONSORED AND PUBLISHED BY
BOLLINGEN FOUNDATION

Originally published in German as
Platon, II: *Die Platonischen Schriften, Erste Periode*
(2nd edition) by W. de Gruyter & Co., Berlin, 1957.

For this translation, the notes have been considerably corrected and suplemented; the text has been revised to a lesser extent. The volume will correspond to the 3rd German edition, which is in press. —P. F.

LIBRARY OF CONGRESS CATALOGUE CARD NO. 57–11126
MANUFACTURED IN THE UNITED STATES OF AMERICA
DESIGNED BY ANDOR BRAUN

Translator's Preface

In translating this volume, I have had the benefit of working from an English version previously prepared by Professor Bayard Q. Morgan.

Completion of this translation of *Plato* (volume 2) by Paul Friedländer coincides with the author's eightieth birthday. This is a happy occasion to dedicate my own efforts as a translator to the man who wrote it.

H. M.

Los Angeles, California
March 21, 1962

Table of Contents

PART III
SELF-PORTRAIT AND DISGUISES OF THE PHILOSOPHER

PART IV
"THE *LOGOS* TAKES A STAND"

FIRST PERIOD

PART I

Protagoras and the Main Body of
Aporetic Dialogues in Search of a Definition
Arete – Philia – Kalon

ONE

Protagoras

S OCRATES joins some people who remain a shadowy group. An anonymous Somebody is their spokesman. He alludes to Socrates' affection for Alkibiades, but only in social and sensual terms. Socrates replies jocularly in the same tone. Again, it is superficial curiosity that prompts the nameless interlocutor to inquire about the meeting between Socrates and Protagoras. For if this were a matter of serious interest, he would know about the arrival of the famous man by now, three days later. The young and eager Hippokrates had heard of it the previous evening; Socrates knew about it still earlier (310B).

Thus, the frame of the dialogue provides an initial approach to the main topic. It also alludes to something more essential, for there is the paradoxical turn that Alkibiades, the beautiful, must take second place to Protagoras who is more beautiful, because wisdom is beautiful. This irony points to a genuine gradation in the scale of values. It is not Alkibiades himself who occupies a lower rank; it is rather the passionate love of beauty that is on a lower (and preparatory) level as compared with the still more passionate love of "wisdom." Thus, the erotic byplay on the surface has a deeper meaning. The theme of the dialogue will be education, or, more specifically, the contrast between sophistic and Socratic education. For Plato, this contrast involves the basic fact that Socrates—and only he—educates through the power of *Eros*. Playfully as the theme of love is introduced, this is the only passage in the dialogue where it is made explicit. When Socrates gives credit to Alkibiades for having "come to his aid" (309B), he anticipates what is to happen later in the main body of the dia-

5

logue. In terms of the progress of thought, Alkibiades' interventions are mere interludes. In terms of the philosophical drama as a whole, however, these interventions take place at crucial points when the conversation threatens to disintegrate, and they save it from collapse (336B, 348B). In this mixed company, there is a tacit understanding between Socrates and Alkibiades, his disciple; it is expressed in the common will to keep the philosophical dialogue alive. The basis of this understanding becomes apparent in the frame conversation, if we perceive the deeper layers beneath the surface talk about love in social and sensual terms.

In the prelude to the dialogue, the beginning of the report by Socrates, curiosity develops into a passionate impulse: young Hippokrates awakens Socrates during the night because he is eager to receive instruction in "wisdom" from Protagoras. Socrates, replying amiably, soon takes command and compels the overenthusiastic young man to confess that he does not know what he is talking about (313c 2). This helps to clarify the issue and conveys the point that something of great human significance is at stake. The subject of knowledge already had come up in the introductory conversation in connection with the name of Protagoras. Now we distinguish between two kinds of knowledge: first, technical-vocational instruction, as in the case of the physician or sculptor, designed to teach the practice of a skill (ἐπὶ τέχνῃ), and second, human (or cultural) education (ἐπὶ παιδείᾳ), designed to make the pupil into a person in his own right, different from the teacher.

The Sophist, evidently, aims at the second and higher kind of education. But what is a Sophist? This is a question that still occupies a central place in the late dialogue, the *Sophist*; it is a question invariably linked with the search for the philosopher. The name "Sophist" suggests *sophia*, knowledge or wisdom. But there is no knowledge unless we can say knowledge "of what." Moreover, it will not do to restrict (as young Hippokrates does) the knowledge of the Sophist to the art of rhetoric and public speech. For again Socrates asks: speech "about what"? There is no answer to this "what" in the case of the Sophist. Perhaps he lacks an object (τί) of knowledge. A figure of speech makes it clear that we are dealing with a dangerous being (κίνδυνος, 313Α 2, 314Α 2). The Sophist is a merchant, or peddler, of goods for spiritual nourishment and consumption. (The same image recurs in the late dialogue—*Sophist* 223c *et seq.*—and Plato's charge, often repeated elsewhere, that the Sophist takes money for his teaching points in the same direction.) One must be a physician of the soul (περὶ τὴν ψυχὴν ἰατρικός, 313Ε 2) to know something about the value of these goods, especially since, unlike ordinary food, they cannot be tested by experts before they are consumed. Hippokrates, of course, does not realize that such a physician of the soul is here at work; nor does he become aware of the fact when Socrates invites him to come along and see these wise men who are "older," hence more experienced, than "we young people." But the reader witnesses the meaning of Socratic (as against sophistic) education in action. The main body of the dialogue will show Socrates in a fighting spirit. Here, after an introductory glimpse of him as the loving man, we encounter Socrates as the educator.

I have tried to show elsewhere[1] not only how space and time clarify the course of events, but also how they have a symbolic meaning that runs parallel to the progress of thought in the philosophical universe of discourse. Here we may note briefly the cramped sleeping quarters where one person is sitting and another lying down, then the spacious court where the two are walking up and down engaged in conversation, and, finally, the darkness of the night and the growing light that coincides with a kind of intellectual dawn.

A narrative interlude takes us from here to the beginning of the actual discussion with Protagoras. Socrates and Hippokrates are on their way to the house of Kallias. We do not learn anything about the subject of their conversation, but we see that they remain outside the house until the *logos* has run its course. A Socratic conversation must not be "incomplete" (ἀτελής). The Sophist breaks off wherever he likes. This difference is later repeated in the debate with Protagoras. It is also shown in the *Gorgias* when Kallikles declines to answer, and Socrates urges him not to desert the *logos* and leave it "incomplete" (505D).[2] In the *Protagoras*, the distinction between Sophists and Socrates

INTERLUDE
314C–316A

appears in a peculiarly iridescent light in the scene with the door-keeper who refuses to admit the two newcomers because he does not like the Sophists. Socrates persuades the reluctant eunuch to let them in because "we are not Sophists"—thus distinguishing himself, for the benefit of the reader, from those for whom he does not wish to be mistaken.

Inside the house, we meet the participants in the drama before the action itself gets under way. The facetious form is taken from the review of the dead in the *Odyssey*: "Thereafter I saw. . . . Tantalus I beheld. . . ." But there is more beneath the surface. That Socrates, like Odysseus, is also standing at the threshold of Hades, that he is the only one who is truly alive, whereas the others are "shades"—it would be strange if these thoughts came to us had Plato not so intended.[3]

There are three groups. In the front hall Protagoras is walking up and down with associates and disciples. Hippias is sitting in the hall to the rear, lecturing ex cathedra "apparently" about na-ture and astronomy. Prodikos is lying in a dark chamber; he is sickly and speaks only in a muffled murmur. Whether this picture contains biographical information need not concern us. What we see are typical attitudes (as in a painting by Marées) which de-part progressively from those of a Socratic dialogue, eventually descending into a murky, stagnant mode. We should recall, in contrast, that Socrates got up and walked about in the court, in the open air, when he began his questioning of Hippokrates before daybreak.

The pleasure we derive from this rich scene must not keep us from inquiring into the meaning of the details, especially those that concern the secondary figures. Kallias, the host, walks beside Protagoras. He is the typical busybody, or weather vane, in in-tellectual affairs, similar to the "associates" in the introductory frame of the dialogue, but with this difference: while they are entirely receptive, he is an active participant. Even this lowest level of a purely social interest is needed to get the conversation started, if only informally. Later, when the conversation threatens to fall apart, it is Kallias who tries to put it together again by seizing the hand and the cloak of Socrates (335CD). The *logos*, to be sure, needs stronger support; besides, when the conflict breaks out, Kallias—by virtue of his own nature—tends to be on the side of Protagoras. The sons of Perikles, half brothers of Kallias, follow on the scene. They are always (as they are here) witnesses to the thesis that *"arete* cannot be taught" (319E). Charmides walks on one wing. He represents the noblest type of Athenian youth in search of *arete*. His name evokes the dialogue, *Charmides*, in which Plato deals with the virtue of *sophrosyne*. (Perhaps Plato had planned or even written the *Charmides* at this time in order to develop a partial aspect of the problem discussed in the *Protagoras*.) On the other wing marches Antimoiros. The only non-Athenian present, he has come to study with Protagoras for the sake of receiving technical instruction (ἐπὶ τέχνῃ), not for the sake of *paideia*. Here the distinction alluded to in the preliminary conversation reappears; later it will become a matter of importance in the distinction between technical knowledge (ἔντεχνος σοφία) and political *arete* (319C, 321D). Protagoras presumably teaches both, whereas Socratic education is focused steadfastly upon a single goal. Behind Protagoras walk a train of nameless followers whom he, another Orpheus, attracts by the "magic of his voice" (κατὰ τὴν φωνὴν κεκηλημένοι). Socrates himself admits later (328D) that he is "spellbound" by the performance of the man. This is a dangerous magic, far removed from the genuine attraction and education exercised by the *logos* and not by the voice, by Socrates and not by Protagoras.

Gathered around Hippias and Prodikos are persons we know mainly from the *Symposium*. It is difficult to say whether they have any special meaning here. Disregarding differences in kind and status, we may be reminded of Balzac's *Comédie humaine*, where we also find the same people who play a principal role in one volume assigned to the background in another.

Socrates, too, has his following. Alkibiades and Kritias follow him—by chance, as it were; but this is a chance arrangement designed by a poet, for, as we know, together with Charmides, both men later are of greatest importance in politics. That "Socrates the Sophist" was executed "because he educated Kritias" was a popular view for decades after the event (Aischines I 173). It is common knowledge also that, after the death of Socrates, there was an agitated literary debate about his relationship with the

politically subversive Alkibiades.[4] Thus, the reader who understands these implications realizes that, as far as Socrates is concerned, more is at stake than "academic" philosophy: the search
for *arete* involves the nature of the state. In this respect Socrates
(316c 1) and Protagoras (319A 1) agree with each other, as
much as they disagree about the deeper meaning of this proposition. After the introductory frame of the dialogue, we look forward with excitement to Alkibiades. He will come to the aid of
the *logos* in distress. Although for him the conflict is primarily a
trial of strength, he reflects the radiance of Socrates; yet he is
without the latter's depth, and thus in him the master's irony
becomes straightforward obviousness (336D). There is a peculiar
contrast between the followers of Socrates and the disciples of the
Sophists. Socrates' following is arranged with less design; superficially it appears to be an accidental grouping. Its intent, however, is quite different. He is not a teacher, says Socrates in the
Apology (19D); i.e., in the sense of the Sophists he is not a
teacher. Yet Hippokrates comes to consult him and Alkibiades
takes his side.

MAIN
DIALOGUE
316A–362A

The structure of the main dialogue presents an interplay of
sophistic and dialectic sections.

First Sophistic Section

I
316A–317E

Socrates introduces the young Hippokrates to Protagoras and
soon elicits an *epideixis*, "exhibition." This form of discourse
makes its appearance here all the more noticeably because, in
the first polite exchange, Protagoras used the word "conversation" (διαλεχθῆναι, 316B 3), and Socrates in replying left it open
how this "conversation" (διαλέγεσθαι, 316c 3) was to be conducted
—as if the manner of speaking were self-understood. The reader
must be startled, therefore, when Protagoras launches into a long
speech, the opposite of conversing, and at the end even suggests
"going on" (317c 5). In content the Sophist's speech is an
encomium of his art which Protagoras associates with the most
illustrious names in history. He singles himself out from his
predecessors as the only one who, despite the dangers entailed,
openly declares his profession. "I admit to being a Sophist—
i.e., a teacher of wisdom—and to being an educator of men"

(317B 4). A dangerous calling—it is what Socrates (only with more justification) might say about himself, yet he would never boast (317BC) that he had taken proper precautions against the dangers inherent in practicing such a profession. To be an educator of men: Socrates might, with a different emphasis, use these same words except for the fact that he would reject any claim concerning "education" as understood by the men in this circle. Here arises the tension that leads to the collision. But before the conflict breaks out, Socrates proposes that Prodikos and Hippias also be brought into the conversation. He does this to flatter the vanity of Protagoras (317CD), but there is further significance in his move. Socrates is the single individual confronting the many. It is the encounter with Socrates that gives to this group of different men the common label "Sophists." Thus, it is Socrates through whom Plato creates a united, hostile front.

First Dialectic Section

As soon as the conversation is resumed—as if there had been no *epideixis* at all (318A; cf. 316BC)—Socrates puts the decisive question. Protagoras claims to educate; his pupils are to become "better" men: better "at what"? (τί; εἰς τί; περὶ τοῦ;) It is the same question that he previously raised in the cross-examination of Hippokrates (311B). Here it occurs in a different and more advanced context, because it involves the notion of "becoming better," i.e., a relationship to the good. In responding to this situation, Protagoras distinguishes his teaching from that of other Sophists. He claims to teach not any particular, specialized skill (τέχνη), but "good counsel" (εὐβουλία) in personal affairs and in the state. This concept of *euboulia* in the political sense plays an important part in the *Alcibiades* (125E); in the *Republic* (428B), Socrates likens it to the concept of *sophia* which is the characteristic of the ruling class. Protagoras and Socrates seem, then, to be quite close in their views; in fact, we do violence to the distinctions of merit observed by Plato if we lump all Sophists together as nothing but bad men. In their commitment to education they stand above the popular view of their profession as represented by Meletos in the *Apology* (24C *et seq.*) and by Anytos in the *Meno* (92E): that education is anybody's (hence, nobody's) business and that it corresponds to learning Greek, i.e., to a process of nature.[5] In some respects Protagoras, who pursues a "political" objective, is closer to Socrates than the other Sophists concerned with teaching technical lessons only. Yet, in the end, it is by being measured against the figure of Socrates that the differences among the Sophists are made to disappear and that what, at first, seems closest to him proves to be an empty shell.[6]

Socrates sets out to clarify the objective of education. Protagoras must have in mind the "art of politics"; he must wish to educate men into being "good citizens." This process of clarifying the other person's meaning so that cross-examination can begin is a characteristic movement in the early dialogues and a characteristic function of Socrates in these dialogues. In this particular case, he expresses his doubts immediately. He does not believe that "virtue is teachable," and the question whether or not virtue can be taught is the touchstone by which the claim of the Sophist is tested.

This is not, as it may sound today, the banal theme of a high-school essay. It is the vital question of the age.[7] *Arete* is the goal passionately pursued by the political man. Now here is a person who claims he can procure this "good" for us through his teaching. But can it be taught at all? Is education possible—not technical instruction, about which there is no doubt because it may be observed everywhere, but education for the sake of *arete*? Socrates advances two arguments against the thesis that *arete* can be taught. First, the Greeks always listen to experts when they debate technical matters in the Assembly, but when they debate general matters of government and administration, they listen indiscriminately to everybody. The second argument expands on the (by now familiar) distinction between vocational training and education in the sense of *paideia*. The great statesmen—Perikles is the example nearest at hand—provide proper instruction for their sons, it is true, but their own *arete* they do not pass on. This argument reflects, as the first argument probably does also, the widespread popular discussion on the exciting question of education.[8] Thus, Plato's Socrates here becomes the spokesman (apparently or actually) for the view that denies the possibility of education and therefore goes against those who claim to be professional educators. Nobody will believe that this is Plato's ultimate and serious judgment of the matter, although the customary conception of irony—i.e., the mere exchange of a yes for a no—also fails to do justice to the situation's complex shadings.[9] For the time being, however, it is enough to see that Socrates opens the game with standard moves.

Second Sophistic Section

Protagoras must feel that his very existence is at stake. We do not fail to see that, behind the urbane mask, for him the question is: To be or not to be? He replies, as befits him, with an impressive speech in which he reaches his heights and, at the same time, his limits. First he tells a myth about the creation of man; then he weaves arguments together into a long discourse, throughout addressing Socrates repeatedly and specifically. Socrates would not make such a speech; he would not begin with a myth. That this is not a matter of "mere form" will be shown later when the difference between the two modes of discourse leads to the break between the rhetorician and the dialectician (334E et seq.).

III
320C–328D

The myth itself is discussed elsewhere.[10] The most important thing is to distinguish between technical knowledge (ἔντεχνος σοφία), which Prometheus brought to men and distributed among them individually, and the art of politics, which Zeus bestowed upon mankind in general. This distinction runs through the dialogue from the prelude on and is now brought out in the dimension of myth. "Right and reverence" (δίκη καὶ αἰδώς), or "political virtue," are gifts of the highest god and must extend throughout the body politic if states are to rest on firm foundations.[11]

III 1
320C–323A

A series of arguments follows. Whereas Socrates (representing the common, antisophistic view) had concluded that this kind of virtue because universally distributed was not a subject for "teaching," Protagoras seeks to prove the opposite by citing the function of punishment. Its function, he says, is to educate people in what is right or just. And whereas Socrates—again going along with the popular view, at least to this extent—justified his doubts about the teachability of virtue by citing as evi-

III 2
323A–328D

dence that the sons of great statesmen do not resemble their fathers, Protagoras now refutes this argument by appealing to the innate differences in human nature. He concludes, first, with a reprimand of the haughty spirit (τρυφή) in Socrates, who denies that education is possible; next, with a bow to the others in the crowd, since everybody is promoted to the status of an educator according to his ability; finally, with a eulogy of himself set apart from the others by his superior ability—and with a farewell reference to his fee.

This is *epideixis*, not conversation, myth, not *logos*; and myth is presented first, superficially, concealing rather than clarifying. Although these are anti-Socratic features, it would be against the spirit of Plato to reject them totally. The myth of the origin of man—today it might be called "cultural philosophy"—brings to life a distinction that is thoroughly Socratic, as the preliminary conversation has shown. There are two different paths of education: becoming a good citizen is altogether different from receiving instruction in some technical or vocational skill. The activities of the carpenter or husbandman are basically different from the "sound judgment" of the good citizen; the exercise of one's vocation does not bring "good counsel" and "wisdom" into the affairs of the city. (This is said again explicitly in *Republic* IV 428BC.) Yet, on the other hand, Plato often associates the art of politics with the arts and crafts in general (e.g. *Gorgias* 490B *et seq.*; *Statesman* 279A *et seq.*) in order to show that politics must first be raised to the level of expertness taken for granted in the crafts. Protagoras is not capable of making this move. When he concludes by saying that political *arete* must proceed by way of justice and *sophrosyne* and that this *arete* must dwell within the body politic to make a *polis* possible, we have then to look forward to the problem's development and solution in the *Republic*. Political *arete*, extending as it does through the whole body politic, is different certainly from technical specialization. But to assume that everybody has all of this *arete* would mean to overlook the differences in human nature. The Herakleitean tension between justice and knowledge supports the structure of the state only in so far as each class, in analogy with the crafts, "does its own work" (this is "justice") and only in so far as all classes converge upon the primacy of knowledge (this is *sophrosyne*). Here we are dealing with an early work; besides, it is the Sophist who is speaking. These facts notwithstanding, we may still recognize in this passage a first approach to the final solution.

Upon the myth follows *logos*. When, in the proof that virtue is teachable (323c–324D), Protagoras argues that political virtue "does not derive from nature, but is acquired by instruction and effort" (323c), he is pursuing the same objective as Socrates. This is evident at the end of the dialogue where Socrates subscribes to the very same view. And Plato's dialectics is based essentially upon the same conviction. Even the argument justifying this thesis is Platonic: the function of punishment is to improve the offender, i.e., to educate him. It is this view that provides the dimension of depth in the *Gorgias*; and, with literal allusions to the speech of Protagoras, Plato still argues in the *Laws* (934AB) against the view that punishment is retribution for a past offense and in favor of the view that its function is to change conduct in the future.[12] If Protagoras had knowledge instead of belief, however, he would not in the end shift to the opposite side. Moreover, his view of punishment is entirely compatible with that expressed by Meletos in the *Apology* (24D *et seq.*): the law educates and the judges do, too; in short, everybody educates—except the educator. What Protagoras lacks is the basic Socratic and Platonic insight that political *arete* can be taught—more precisely, that it hovers in ironic tension between teachability and nonteachability —because it is a form of knowledge and because knowledge is directed toward a specific mode of being.

Toward the end, Protagoras attacks the argument derived from the evidence of statesmen and their incompetent sons in a far-ranging discourse based upon both principle and experience. He pinpoints the question that resolves the *aporia* (ἐν τούτῳ λύεται ἡ ἀπορία). "Is there or is there not some one thing in which all citizens must share, if there is to be a state at all?" This "one thing," *arete*, a unity as opposed to the multiplicity of technical endeavors, a unity also as against the multiplicity of justice, moderation, and piety: this "one thing" exists. It is universally recognized and human conduct is based upon it, as is shown in the justification of punishment. It is unthinkable, therefore, that

III 2a
323A–324D

III 2b
324D–328D

statesmen would not educate their sons in *arete*. When he states
these majestic propositions, Protagoras is closer to Socrates and
Plato than at any other time. Unity within and above multiplicity
is the characteristic aspect of Plato's world-view. The unity of
arete is the view that animates all the early dialogues up to the
Republic; it is the goal the *Protagoras* moves toward but does
not ever attain.

Socrates later takes this as his line of departure (329c), only
he must ask about it specifically (329cd): for him this "unity"
cannot be clear. Moreover, the principle of unity, i.e., the element of knowledge in the Socratic sense, is lacking. For Protagoras, *arete* is something empirically given. Its nature (or "what-
ness") is not questioned. Thus, his is a moving plea, but he does
not perceive clearly what he is pleading for. This, indeed, is the
source of the intellectual comedy; when Socrates sets out to prove
the principle of unity, Protagoras will offer every possible resistance to the same thesis which here he is emphatically asserting.

Besides, there is a system of education, Protagoras continues.
Thus, why should *arete* not be teachable? Here again we are
close to Plato's own domain. The spiritual order of a system of
education is envisaged—for example, that of Athens as it ought
to be—and the integrating concept advanced by Protagoras, applicable to every individual phase of education, is that the pupil
"should become as good (or perfect) as possible" (ὡς βέλτιστον
γενέσθαι). For Protagoras, musical and gymnastic education follow each other much as in the *Republic* (376E), where this combination is said to have been "invented a long time ago." We
note in particular the spiritual effects ascribed to musical training.
Rhythm and harmony penetrate the soul and appease it; the goal
of musical education is *eurhythmy* and integration (εὐαρμοστία)
of the soul. This will be said again in the *Republic*, in almost
the same words (*Protagoras* 326B; *Republic* 400D, 401D, 410CD,
522A).

What, then, is missing in this Platonic Protagoras? His commitment to the principle of "becoming as good as possible" lacks
clarity (as did the principle of unity and *arete*) with regard to
being good "at what." Thus, this type of education lacks a clear
objective. Even for Protagoras, to be sure, gymnastics does not

have a purely physical function; its purpose is to make the improved body serve the power of the mind, which is the good thing in man (326B). This view is more advanced than the common opinion (*Republic* 410c), which assigns gymnastics to the body and music to the soul. Thus, Protagoras is on his way to Socrates in search of the foundations for a body politic, but he can never attain the heights of Socrates, according to whom both educational disciplines exist for the sake of the soul, i.e., for the sake of true human perfection. In the *Republic*, musical education is a preliminary stage that prepares the soul to receive the *logos* as its kindred spirit (402A). The *Protagoras* is deeply disappointing in this respect, for as soon as we have learned that the aim of education is "to make the soul more rhythmical and harmonious," this objective is subordinated to something else on a much lower level: "usefulness in what we say and do" (ἵνα εὐρυθμότεροι καὶ εὐαρμοστότεροι γιγνόμενοι χρήσιμοι ὦσιν εἰς τὸ λέγειν τε καὶ πράττειν, 326B 3). Here it is most evident how little Protagoras knows about a scale of values; he lacks any reference to an absolute standard or even the urge to seek one.

Protagoras at last states his solution to the *aporia*. If great statesmen do not bequeath their wisdom to their children, this is because human beings differ in their talents or capacities. Just and unjust are not absolute concepts, and, as compared with the savage, even the unjust men of our society are just. Everybody is a teacher of *arete*, which we learn as we do our native tongue. There are only relative differences in the skill of teaching *arete*; as far as he himself is concerned, Protagoras claims only to have developed an especially high degree of talent on this relative scale. It is obvious that he lacks an absolute, or cognitive, standard. What he presents is nothing but a naturalistic or relativistic theory that ultimately deprives him of his own claim, his sorry attempt to defend it notwithstanding. If everybody is able to teach *paideia*, nobody does. Protagoras, without noticing it, has reached the position held by his opponent. The proposition that education resembles the learning of one's native tongue (ἑλληνίζειν) derives, of course, from the stock in trade of those who think that true education is superfluous or impossible.

Plato himself recognizes the validity of the argument from

nature (*Republic* 414D *et seq.*). He correlates class membership in society with the admixture of metals whether precious or not so precious. But beyond these foundations in nature, there is something altogether different—knowledge and teaching. Thus, the basic flaw of the Protagorean system is its failure to account for knowledge and the realm of being that corresponds to it. While the relativism of Protagoras blurs all boundaries, Socrates keeps his mind fixed unshakably upon *arete* as something that is not simply inherent in the biological sphere, like the learning of one's mother tongue, but transcends this dimension.

Second Dialectic Section

IV
328D–334A
IV 1
328D–330B

Socrates is "enchanted" by the *epideixis*, which has indeed a profound effect. Moreover, he is now convinced that "there is a human endeavor by which good men acquire goodness." This sudden change of mind makes us suspect the seriousness of his initial doubt. At the same time, his ironic description of how he had expected Protagoras to go on talking and the image of the struck gong to which he compares the eloquent speeches of the rhetoricians convey his criticism of the sophistic—as opposed to the "dialogical"—mode of discourse. "Dialogical" discourse, as we know from the conversation with Hippokrates, achieves "completion" by its very nature; the sophistic type goes on without aim or limits.

A Socratic or "dialogical" section follows. Socrates begins with a "small"—i.e., the decisive—point (328E 4). Plato made Protagoras speak emphatically on behalf of the unity of *arete*, thus focusing upon a central thesis of Plato's own philosophy. This unity that Protagoras merely proposed, but did not clarify, is now examined by Socrates. Does unity mean complete identity so that the different "virtues" are nothing but different names for one "virtue"?[13] Or does it mean the unity of the parts of a piece of gold? Or is it the unity of the parts of a face (ὥσπερ προσώπου), the unity of an organism? Perhaps there is some truth in each of these analogies. Perhaps they even indicate different gradations within the idea of unity. May we not say that complete identity would be the appropriate expression for *arete* as conceived by Socrates—and by him only? Protagoras adopts the third possibility (the unity of a face), again making a choice that is meaningful and close to Plato's own. For when the relationship of the "political virtues" is clarified, in the *Republic*, it turns out to be a system composed of parts that are different from each other yet inherently integrated in a higher unity. The Sophist has hit upon the truth but only accidentally, for he does not understand the Socratic analogies. This is shown immediately in what follows. Almost in the same breath, he asserts that it is possible to possess one virtue but not another—as if the parts of a face did not form an organic unity.[14] Thus, the continuation resumes the comic theme. Protagoras is incapable of defending the unity of *arete*; Socrates proves it against his opponent's resistance. What he proves, to be sure—with a peculiarly iridescent irony, hard to grasp—is an exaggerated form of unity, unity as strict identity, and, to make matters worse, his proof employs egregious fallacies. He almost succeeds in this project when the conversation breaks off.

First, Socrates "proves" that justice and piety are identical. "Or something very similar" are his words at the end (331B), or "almost the same" (333B). Evidently things are not quite in order. Justice is something just and piety is something pious— that will do. But to say that since, according to Protagoras, justice and piety differ, and that therefore to be just is not to be pious or to be pious is not to be just—that is a grave fallacy. The next step is even worse: if to be just is not to be pious, then it must be something impious, or, conversely, piety must be something that is unjust. Thus, the inference that Socrates draws from this artificially constructed piece of nonsense is made worthless: the complete identity of piety and justice. Let us add at once that it is superior to the relativistic talk in which the baffled Sophist indulges: "somehow" (τι, 331D 2; ἀμῇ γέ πῃ, 331D 3, 7; ἔστιν ὅπῃ, 331D 4) everything is both like and unlike everything else.

Next, Socrates "proves" the identity of *sophrosyne*, sound mind or temperance, and *sophia*, wisdom or knowledge. This is done by showing that they both are opposed to "thoughtless" or "foolish" behavior (ἀφροσύνη). Each thing, the argument goes on, has only one opposite; if two things have the same opposite, they must be identical. Here we note first that the two "virtues"

IV 2
330B–334A
IV 2a
330B–332A

IV 2b
332A–333B

are not examined carefully, but are treated like stereotypes. This makes it easy to find the same opposite for both. Second, and more important, "opposite" is construed as exclusive, as a contrary in the sense of contradiction. That this is a conscious deception on the part of Socrates—or an exercise in logic for the reader—he shows by offering a correcting alternative: either the thesis that every thing has only one contrary must be false or else it must be false to say that the virtues form a unity "as the parts of a face." We should expect Protagoras to choose the former as a way of saving his initial thesis, and to recognize the logical fallacy. But he does not find his way out of this dilemma, and so it happens that Socrates proves the unity, not in the sense of organic unity, but in the sense of identity. It is left to the reader to discover the mistake in this logical exercise and to think for himself about how unity is to be conceived.[15]

IV 2c
333B–334A

Finally, it is to be shown that the four concepts now joined into two pairs are one and the same. This proof does not develop, however, because Protagoras refuses to co-operate. He breaks off—not because he sees through these fallacies, but precisely because he does not. He has a vague feeling (333E), nevertheless, that in probing the *logos* Socrates also "probes and tests him who answers" (333c 7–9). Protagoras breaks away—not into the open, but into the thickets of his own relativism and the looseness of Sophistic verbiage as he holds forth about the relativity of the useful and the diverse multiplicity (ποικίλον, 334B 6) of what is good.

We must look at the matter in detail. Is it possible to do wrong and, at the same time, to be of sound mind, temperate and wise (σωφρονεῖν, εὖ φρονεῖν)? This is Socrates' question (333D), and suddenly we realize that, behind the play with concepts, this is the decisive question of life itself. It is the theme of the *Gorgias* and the *Republic*; and in the background looms the thesis of the tyrant that violence is the highest intelligence. We must note Protagoras' own position on this point. Many people, he says, think it is possible to combine doing wrong with "sound mind," but he does not. Thus, he differs from the many.[16] (This again points toward the road that leads to Socrates.) When Protagoras agrees to represent the opinion of the many in the course

of the conversation, however, we must ask ourselves whether
he would not have done so in earnest as well. The many believe
that it is indeed possible to have a "sound mind" and to do
wrong, provided that wrongdoing leads to success (εἰ εὖ πράτ-
τουσιν ἀδικοῦντες). This is the key to Socrates' question whether
the good means what is useful or advantageous. Again, Protagoras seems to differ from the utilitarianism of the many, since
he asserts that the good is good even if it is not useful. He is not
serious about defending this thesis and at once evades Socrates.
He loses himself in mere talk instead of submitting to a critical
examination.

The question raised by Socrates is complex. On the one hand,
Plato often seems to take it for granted, without any proof, that
"the good"—or "the beautiful"—is identical with the advantageous (*Gorgias* 499D; *Republic* 457B). Yet, on the other hand,
he is always aware of the danger of relativism implicit in the
concept of the useful. The portrait of Protagoras here is proof
of this danger: he is wrecked by this relativism. Thus, the equation between the good and the useful (or beneficial) may drag
the concept of the good down into the realm of the relative, or
it may raise the concept of utility into the realm of the absolute.
If we were clear about the good as something absolute, the discussion of the problem, which here remains fragmentary, would
be continued to the point where "justice" and "sound mind" are
also seen as inseparable because both are based upon knowledge
and, ultimately, upon the knowledge of the good as the highest
form of being.

Crisis

Protagoras loses himself in mere talk. He evades the probing   v
power of Socrates, now even with regard to the proper form of   334A–338E
his discourse. When Socrates protests against his manner of
making speeches, the Sophist is annoyed and withdraws. Socrates
states that, forgetful as he is, he cannot follow—or make—long
speeches. Behind this ironic mask, the dialectician, defender of a
dialogical method of inquiry (who "cannot do otherwise"), challenges the principle repugnant to him. When he intimates having heard that Protagoras is capable of speaking both at extreme

length and with supreme brevity (334E)—Gorgias makes the same claim for himself, almost in the same words, in the dialogue named after him (449BC)—he is indicating that a Jack-of-all-trades does not consider any formal principle as necessarily binding. The threat of seeing the conversation break down mobilizes all who are interested in seeing it continued. Kallias, the host, represents the type of man interested in nothing but the pleasure of entertainment. In the name of Protagoras, he makes a suggestion that is quite impossible: let everybody conduct the conversation in his own way. This would of course destroy the possibility of a genuine exchange. Alkibiades, impetuous as he is, can only look upon the conflict as a contest of strength that must be settled by an admission of defeat. He does not understand the *logos*, which has its own law and must not be "deserted." Attracted by the inner strength of Socrates, however, he strongly defends the Socratic principle of the dialogue and clearly perceives the defect in Protagoras: the man refuses to "give an account" of himself (336c).

Kallias and Alkibiades merely restate the conflict; they do not remove it. Kritias, as a politician, mobilizes what is left of the neutral forces in order to prevent complete disruption.[17] The various speakers do not have much to offer in their pleas for harmony. Prodikos displays his well-known skills of semantics. Hippias warms up the somewhat stale antithesis of nature and convention. He tries to blunt the differences with a eulogy of Athens as "the sacred shrine of wisdom" and with praises of the house of Kallias. Hippias' suggestion that they appoint a referee shows that he, too, sees the whole encounter as strictly a contest. Socrates knows that the *logos* has its own rules which are not set by any referee. By means of a proposal as clever as it is relevant, he succeeds in renewing the conversation and in making the "dialogical" principle prevail: Protagoras is to assume the leadership in questioning.

This animated scene usually is called an "interlude," and rightly so, if the progress of ideas is the only criterion of significance. In the philosophical drama itself, however, the passage is something quite different. It is the first outbreak of the struggle between Socrates and the Sophists over the proper form of discourse. This is not a matter of "mere form," but indeed a basic condition for philosophy in general. In the end, the dialogical principle prevails. But the victory is as yet incomplete. Only the form of discourse will be Socratic, not the substance. Protagoras will be in charge of the conversation. This will be decisive for the outcome of the discussion that follows because only the dialectician knows how to handle the instrument of the dialogue.

Third Sophistic Section

Thus, what occurs next is a new sophistic section beginning with the discussion of a poem by Simonides.[18] In principle, the Socratic way of conducting a discussion is recognized. But the content is un-Socratic and sophistic. This is a rhetorical debate about a poetic work with a finished structure of its own, not a dialectical inquiry into a problem whose content directs the course of the conversation. Socrates later will state the distinction as follows (347E *et seq.*): the interpretation of a poem cannot yield any final truth, because we cannot question the poet—this is the same objection that Socrates raises against books in general and against long speeches—whereas the true dialogue tests both the truth and those who seek it. The lack of truth in poetic interpretations is also shown in another respect. There is but *one* true *logos*, whereas a poem may have many interpretations. Protagoras has an interpretation of his own; Socrates suggests three different interpretations; and Hippias agrees reluctantly to dispense with the fine speech he was contemplating (347A).

It is not an accident that Plato makes Protagoras choose a poem by Simonides, for "unlike the earlier poets, Simonides—animated, critical, and militant—is fond of spirited discussions" (H. Fränkel). There is a distant kinship between Simonides and the debating Sophists. Yet when Protagoras claims that the poem deals with the subject under discussion, the obvious objection is that it does indeed deal with *arete* but not with the questions of whether it is "teachable" and whether it is "one." Nor does the Sophist do anything except practice his wit at the expense of the defenseless poet by showing that the latter contradicts himself. What Simonides says at the outset, he later forgets, we are told, so that he rejects his own view when it is ad-

VI
338E–347A

vanced by somebody else. It is delightful how Protagoras describes his own behavior! There follow the amusing counter-
thrusts by Socrates. First, he uses the semantic skill (or verbal
legerdemain) of Prodikos. He does this so successfully, in fact,
that he wins Prodikos over by adopting the latter's technique.
Socrates beats one Sophist, as it were, with the weapons of the
other, thus displaying his superiority even on sophistic grounds.
When Protagoras protests the use of this method, Socrates employs the same tactics again and even more delightfully. Instead
of making careful distinctions in the meaning of words, he now
mixes them up (χαλεπόν and κακόν), turning the technique of
Prodikos into its opposite. Prodikos remains convinced, nevertheless, that it is his own hobbyhorse which Socrates is now
riding in the spirit of the old Simonides. The result is true to the
method employed: "It is bad when one is good." But when Protagoras objects again, Socrates shows that he does not take this
game seriously. Instead, he embarks upon his third sally, a formal
lecture as a model for interpreting the poem. Appropriating the
form of the long speech, he now presents a systematic interpretation far superior to the critical and incomplete hairsplitting
previously practiced by Protagoras.

Protagoras had begun to play his role in the dialogue by invoking such illustrious names as Homer and Orpheus as predecessors in his art of rhetoric (316D). Socrates now begins his
interpretation by looking back upon the origins of philosophy.
These origins, he explains—with obvious pleasure at the implicit paradox—are to be found in the institutions of Sparta and
Crete; the earliest philosophical documents are the sayings of
the Seven Sages (this is not too farfetched); and the poem of
Simonides is based upon one of these sayings (this is quite
right). Following this historical introduction, the exegesis itself,
as opposed to that of Protagoras, undertakes to encompass "the
whole outline (τὸν τύπον τὸν ὅλον) and aim (τὴν βούλησιν)" of
the poem. This breadth of design goes together with an almost
philological attention to such details as the grammatical function
of the particle μέν and the stylistic pattern of hyperbaton.

Just the same, the Socratic interpretation is as arbitrary as the
sophistic and even surpasses it, in fact, in the consistency with

which the speaker misinterprets the text for his own purpose.
To become a good man, says Socrates, is the difficult thing, i.e.,
to prove oneself as such in action. *To be* a good man, always and
unchangeably, is altogether impossible. This is the privilege of
the gods. Thus, the contrast is the difference between human
striving and divine perfection (344BC). Proper care and hence
"faring well" (εὐπραγία) in the case of the physician, as in the
case of any other expert, depends upon learning and study (μάθη-
σις). Only a man who has become an expert can fail (κακὸς γίγνεσθαι); a layman without experience cannot. The argument moves,
as always in Plato, from the expert to the "good man" in general.
The latter also may become bad and thus fare badly (κακὴ πρᾶξις);
this occurs when he is deprived of knowledge, but only then
(345B). Finally, the Socratic thesis that "nobody will do wrong
willingly" is elicited from the poem. This view obviously is connected, in substance, with the previous analysis, but it is all the
more striking because Socrates can impress this meaning upon
the poem only by doing violence to it, combining the words
falsely. The interpretation as a whole reflects features of Plato's
ontology and is a brief sketch of what is called the Socratic ethics
of knowledge. The attentive reader realizes that he is introduced
here to a doctrine of essential significance[19] even though it is
concealed by a sophistic method and by a capriciously deceptive
interpretation. But there is more. In the last Socratic-dialectic
section (328D–334A), the conversation fell apart because the
knowledge of the good was lacking. In this epideictic-sophistic
section, i.e., in a non-Socratic context, however, Plato most
amusingly makes us see the essential link between knowledge
and the good (upward to the divine good), whose lack precipi-
tated the crisis in the conversation.

Third Dialectic Section

After Socrates had finished, the sophistic flow of words might
have continued; even Hippias offers to make a speech. But instead, the "dialogical" energy reasserts itself, first, characteristically, in Alkibiades who, as if guarding an advanced post, recalls
the participants to the principle of the dialogue. Socrates joins in
sharply criticizing the poem's interpretation that he just deliv-

VII
347A–360E
VII 1
347A–349A

ered so brilliantly. He proposes resuming the discussion where it broke off (348A). Socrates alone has his eyes fixed on the *logos* and its demands, whereas the others are satisfied to score a verbal triumph or indulge in indiscriminate talk. Against the last resistance put up by Protagoras, Socrates prevails—with the help of Alkibiades and the others who, without understanding the principle in its depth, let themselves be carried along by Socrates and his superior guidance.

VII 2
349A–349D Socrates goes back to the old question of how we should conceive the unity of the different "virtues." We recall that Protagoras rejected unity in the sense of identity and asserted that it was analogous to the organic unity of "the parts of a face." We recall further that Socrates proceeded to prove a sense of unity in an extreme and exaggerated form, employing obvious logical fallacies, and that Protagoras, at his wits' end, deserted the *logos* before it was completed. Now the struggle has abated. Protagoras has acknowledged the unity of the four virtues—justice, piety, temperance, and wisdom. They are "very similar." We note that he does not concede identity and that Socrates does not pursue this point either. Thus, the question of how this unity is to be achieved is now treated—in a Socratic-Platonic, i.e., undogmatic, manner—somewhat nonchalantly as compared with the earlier question of whether there is unity at all. For we encounter a new problem: what about the fifth virtue, courage? Protagoras asserts that it is altogether different (πάνυ πολὺ δια-φέρον) from the others, so that it might be possible to exhibit courage of the highest degree without possessing any other virtue. He is restating a popular view,[20] not realizing that in doing so he has abandoned his own thesis of the organic unity of all virtues.

Again, we could look upon this problem in purely conceptual terms, but it is necessary to keep in mind that the question at stake is how to live and how to educate. Thus, the discussion has a different objective. Courage, the "manly virtue" (ἀνδρεία), although most easily mistaken for a purely biological value or even for its excess (i.e., for δεινότης or θαρραλέον), still is indispensable to human and social existence: this virtue must be integrated with the other powers operating in social life.[21] Because this is the hardest task, it is put last. Protagoras is made spokesman for the popular view, which is inconsistent, so that the Socratic principle may prevail in the course of refuting this view. The integration is achieved in the *Republic*: to separate courage from the other virtues would mean to break up the structure of the state and the individual soul.

Yet, strangely enough, at the end of the *Statesman* we learn about a polarity in human beings, who differ according to the degree to which either "courage" (ἀνδρεία) or "self-discipline" (κοσμιότης) predominates in their nature. The true statesman must know how to combine these polar opposites into the unity of the state. Did Plato, then, later subscribe to a view that he is refuting here in the final section of the *Protagoras*? Certainly not. The very contrast, as a matter of fact, clarifies the meaning of the Protagorean thesis and its refutation. According to the *Statesman*, there are two human types: one is "sharp" (ὀξύς), the other "moderate" (σώφρων, ἡσυχαῖος). The latter type, in particular, reminding us of the definition of *sophrosyne* that is refuted in the *Charmides*, shows clearly that we are dealing not with virtues in the moral or political sense, but with natural dispositions in man. We see, then, what is at stake in the final section of the *Protagoras*. A naturalistic conception of man is to be overcome by a moral and political conception. Man is not simply a product of nature; he is a product of education developing natural dispositions.

Let us be clear about the strategy Socrates employs to put across the thesis of unity. For him courage must be a form of knowledge. This is clearly the target of his initial move (350D). The most direct route to the goal would then run somewhat as follows. Courage as a virtue must be distinguished from natural daring or boldness. The latter is the raw material, without form or "beauty." Courage is the "form" made out of this material. What forms it? *Episteme*—i.e., not practical, specialized knowledge, but knowledge of the essential nature of man.

It is not characteristic of Socrates to proceed in such a straight-forward fashion. Besides, how would Protagoras understand this knowledge as conceived by Socrates? Thus, while keeping his objective in mind, Socrates goes quite astray in pursuing it. In-

VII 3
349E–350c

stead of distinguishing between courage and natural daring—as he does in the *Laches*—he throws them together and causes a confusion that is felt strongly by the attentive reader. *Arete* is something "beautiful," a form of human perfection.[22] Daring or boldness is at times nothing but a form of madness. What we need is to distinguish, not fuse, the two. Socrates does allude next to the element of "knowledge," but he does not pursue its real meaning. Instead, he refers only to the lower, practical levels of knowledge as in the case of the diver, the horseman, or the peltast. We feel that to have courage, *episteme* is needed; again we are led astray, however, for it remains to be seen what kind of *episteme* is needed.

VII 4
350c–351b

Protagoras launches a counterattack against the weaknesses in his opponent's position.[23] First, he points out that the sentence, "The courageous are daring or confident," cannot simply be converted; but he does not know what to do with this logical point. Second, he makes the correct distinction between nature (φύσις) and knowledge (ἐπιστήμη). Yet how little he knows about the nature of knowledge he shows by aligning daring (or physical power) with knowledge, and courage with natural disposition; again, by aligning "bravery" and "madness" with *episteme* and "proper upbringing" (εὐτροφία) with *physis*. It is impossible to confuse matters worse. By these means—Socrates leading us astray like a will-o'-the-wisp, and Protagoras vainly trying to find his way out of the confusion—Plato sets the reader his own task.

VII 5
351b–360e

Socrates now makes the final thrust. Courage is a form of knowing (σοφία); it is not possible to be both ignorant and courageous. The unity of the virtues is preserved on the foundation of "knowledge." The Sophist concedes defeat. How devious —and sophistic—are the paths by which Socrates achieves his objective.

VII 5a
351b–352d

To begin with, he puts two questions to Protagoras. First, does "good" simply mean to live pleasurably—apart from the consequences? Protagoras hesitates to say yes. Pleasure, he insists, is "good" only if it is pleasure in what is beautiful. This is a type of "hedonism" of which Plato always approved. But here Socrates' intention is to exclude the good and the beautiful as

intrinsic values and to reduce the good to what is pleasant or
agreeable as such. This was never Plato's view, "variously as
he expressed himself on the subject of pleasure" (*varie et multi-
formiter de voluptate disseruit*, Gellius VIII 5) and much as he
acknowledged, especially in later years, the factor of pleasure in
the ledger of life as opposed to an overstrict rigorism. In the
Laws (V 733E *et seq.*), he weighs the forms of life according to
the quantities of pleasure present in them. This is said to be the
"human" measurement and serves to complement the "divine"
standard which preceded it and without which the human scale
would not be permissible.[24] In the dialogue named for him, Protagoras replies that it seems "safer" to distinguish between the
good and the pleasant—not only for the purpose of the present
discussion, but for life in general. This reply shows that a decision of highest significance is at stake, but the word "safer"
(ἀσφαλέστερον) also indicates that it is uncertain whether Protagoras will remain firm on the side of Socrates.

The second question (352B) is, what is your attitude to
knowledge? Do you believe, as most people do, that it is always
the weaker part compared with such emotions as pleasure and
pain? Again, a matter of highest significance is at stake: whether
human life should and must be governed by the passions or by
the mind. On this issue Socrates makes a quick and clear decision
in which Protagoras concurs. When the latter intimates, however,
that he must accept the Socratic view for the sake of professional
honor, we may doubt that his choice is based on true insight. In
making Protagoras admit that there is a good that is the ultimate standard and that knowledge has power, Socrates thereby
has defined his own domain, as it were, from which he can look
down upon the plane of the "many." He has drawn Protagoras—
for the moment, at least—away from the many, who despise
episteme. Soon Socrates will push him back into the world of the
many from whom the Sophist cannot set himself apart perma-
nently.

What does it mean, to succumb to pleasure or to be weaker
than pleasure (ἡδονῆς ἥττων εἶναι)? What does this comparative
judgment signify? That is the crucial question. For Socrates—
and for Protagoras at the moment—there is good and there is

VII 5b
352D–357E

episteme, in addition to pleasure; and it is through *episteme* that the good is known and prevails. How do the many, who reduce good and evil to pleasure and pain, explain the phenomenon that we succumb to pleasure? They can do so only by saying that pleasure competes with pleasure, pain with pain, a nearby thing with something distant, a present thing with something in the future—in short, by comparing, weighing, and measuring. For they do not recognize a standard of the good by which pleasures could be measured, nor do they recognize knowledge which might have power over the passions. Yet, in so far as they weigh and measure quantities of pleasure and pain, they need an art or a science of measurement. Thus, even on their own terms, they must acknowledge that there is a science over and above pleasure and pain. On their own terms, furthermore, "to succumb to pleasure" means to make a mistake in calculating the maximum quantity of pleasure, and this is the greatest folly: ignorance.

The implication is clear without being made explicit: if even on the level of the many we agree that only knowledge can decide (whenever a decision is called for), how much more certain are we on a different level where we acknowledge "the good" as a firm standard and where we have a genuine art of measurement, *episteme.*

We might take another step if we look back from the perspective of Plato's late works (*Philebus* 55E; *Statesman* 283C *et seq.*). At this time, when measuring and counting have become still more important for Plato than in his early phase, he is firmly committed to an "art of measurement" (the same words as in the *Protagoras*). This art now deals not with pleasure and pain, but with magnitude, excess, and deficiency. It deals, in fact, with anything of which there is number and measure. We know what the word "measure" means in Greek life and for Plato. Thus, it would be difficult to overlook, in the *Protagoras,* a hint at the genuine and pure art of measurement when we read: "What kind of art, or branch of knowledge, it is we shall investigate later" (357B).[25]

VII 5c
357E–358B
Before the strategy of Socrates brings the question about courage to a decision on the ground where he is in control, we note another interlude, brief, but effective and important. After Soc-

rates has proved that even the "many" cannot dispense with knowledge, he concludes by reproaching them; they fail to send their sons to professional teachers, Protagoras, Hippias, or Prodikos, as if there were no such thing as teaching and learning (ὡς οὐ διδακτοῦ ὄντος). The reproach is meant quite seriously, if only for a moment, even though the ironic reference to fees removes some of its sting. Similarly, in the *Laches* (180c, 200d), in the *Theages* (127e *et seq.*), and in the *Theaetetus* (151b), Plato's Socrates sends some youths who are not suited to receive instruction from him to Damon, Prodikos, and "other wise men." There is, to be sure, a deep irony in this referral, but this need not mean that Socrates is not serious as well. He did believe that for many youths this kind of education was better than his own or none at all. No matter how we read these iridescent ambiguities, one thing is clear: the Sophists assent enthusiastically. They are so delighted, in fact, that they lose their own wits and clever heads. For what happens now is quite odd. Socrates says, "You agree then that the pleasant and the good are the same," and they all assent. But why? Did not Protagoras just repudiate this thesis? And, in the last discussion conducted by Socrates alongside Protagoras, was not the point precisely to refute the view of the many, who do not see the difference between what is good and what is pleasant? It takes a mere flattery to catch the Sophists off guard and push them back to the level of the many. On the side of such dubious allies, Socrates now delivers his final thrust against Protagoras (359a). It remains to be seen whether the latter can hold his ground.

The subject, then, is "courage." But what happens to courage if we adopt the hedonistic thesis of the many? If pleasure and pain are the only criteria, nobody will qualify as a courageous man in the accepted sense of going out to meet a dangerous situation, i.e., something that arouses the opposite of pleasure. Conversely, both the courageous and the cowardly will pursue what excites their pleasure. In other words, the distinction between the courageous and the cowardly seems to be eliminated (359d).

Protagoras will not let himself be argued out of this difference, and rightly so. But since he is no longer firm in his attitude

vii 5d
358b–360e

toward the hedonistic thesis (ὡμολόγηται γοῦν, 360A 3), it is not hard for Socrates to wrest from him the admission that, if the coward is cowardly, he avoids what is pleasant. And this is possible only because of ignorance, since everybody desires the pleasant. Conversely, if the foolhardy display a kind of bravery that is reprehensible, they seek something that must be painful. Again, this is possible only because of ignorance. Thus, even for those who reduce good and evil to nothing but pleasure and pain, the distinction between courageous and cowardly action—if it is not to be abolished altogether—must rest on knowledge and ignorance. This is not knowledge in the Socratic sense. His kind of knowledge deriving from God is far off. In the context of the controversy with Protagoras, this is a knowledge, or ignorance, of what is to be feared (δεινόν). This is enough, however, to show the many—and Protagoras is now one of them—that courage cannot be divorced from the other virtues as something different. Another thought remains unspoken: this conclusion will be all the more valid if we see it as only Socrates can see it at present and as he has intimated mostly in the disguise of a poetic exegesis. To that end, however, the discussion must move to a different level. From the hedonistic level where knowledge applies to what is practically useful or, ultimately, to what is pleasant, we must move to the Socratic level where the form of the good is the measure of all things and where knowledge means the knowledge of this good. We might also say: *hedone* must be raised to the level of *eudaemonia*.

CONCLUSION
360E–362A

The end of the dialogue leads back to the beginning. The motif-like revival of the myth of Prometheus serves as a reminder and as a cyclical closure. It is crucial to see clearly the reversal in the positions of the two partners. The "outcome of the conversation" (361A 4) is now stated as if it were a person speaking through Socrates (as the *logos* speaks elsewhere). Socrates pulls the threads of the conversation to their conclusion. He himself, he explains, is now defending the view that there is knowledge of *arete* and hence that it is teachable, whereas in the beginning he doubted whether such teaching was possible. Protagoras, he goes on, is now bent upon denying that there is such knowledge and hence rejects the view that virtue is teachable. What does this change of front signify? In the case of Protagoras the meaning is clear.[26] He has not thought through the subject of *arete* nor lived with its reality; he does not see where Socrates is going and how much support he would find by following him. As a Sophist he is against the unity upon which (by his own admission and according to Socrates) the knowability of virtue depends. He had already surrendered his own position that virtue is teachable—this was actually a form of self-surrender—when he claimed that, to a certain extent, "everybody" was a "teacher of virtue" (327E). His collapse is complete when he lets himself be pushed into the kind of hedonism whose dangers he first recognized.[27]

For Socrates the reversal has quite a different meaning.[28] To begin with, it is an ironic strategy. By advancing a radically opposite thesis he lures the opponent from his position—in order to occupy it himself. But this way of looking at the issue is still too simple. Above all, we must not think that the initial thesis advanced by Socrates is "merely ironic," i.e., not serious at all, or that the final thesis is not ironic, i.e., quite serious. Irony is not the opposite of seriousness; it is the Socratic form of the *esprit de sérieux*, and it is not a mask that Socrates could put on or off at will. Thus, the ironic shift in his position conceals the peculiar nature of the problem of *paideia*, which we can only touch upon briefly.

Socrates takes up the popular view that virtue is not teachable. This view was a challenge to professional educators, a plea for freedom from any obligation, and an expression of hostility toward any system of education in general.[29] Socrates, too, is opposed to the claims of those who parade as educators, but for the altogether different reason that their education is inadequate. Let them teach a technical skill (*techne*) and take pay for it. But when they claim, as in the words of Protagoras, that they can help the pupil attain the higher good of political *arete*, and when they sell as a kind of commodity what can only be bestowed as a free gift, Socrates must challenge them for the sake of preserving the higher rank of *arete*. Similarly, he objects in the *Apology* (19DE) to being mistaken for one of those "who educate men and take pay for it."

In a deeper sense, however, the matter is quite different, for Socrates *is* the teacher. *Arete*, to be sure, is not teachable in the customary sense of transferring factual material or content "from the full to the empty" (*Symposium* 175D). But does not a new sense of teaching emerge here, a Socratic-Platonic *agoge* and *anagoge*? Plato himself would not be living if he did not believe in the possibility of *paideia*. For this reason, he later used to cut short discussion of the problems raised in the course of this dialogue. He always took the side of the "teachability of virtue," not as a dogma, but as a basis for any discussion on the subject, as well as a challenge to the enemies of any binding order in society "who say there is no education and who are ready to cut a person to pieces who holds the opposite view" (*Republic* 488B). In the *Euthydemus* (282c), Socrates asks whether "wisdom" is teachable or whether it develops automatically as a part of human nature. Delighted when his interlocutor concedes that it is teachable, he confesses that this admission relieves him of conducting "a long inquiry." This indicates how complex the problem is and how much is left unsaid in such a brief formulation.

As a matter of fact, when Plato has reached his heights, he is fully aware of the hidden complexities and difficulties. In the *Meno* (99E 6) he recognizes a kind of "virtue" acquired by "divine dispensation"; it is below virtue in the proper sense as founded upon knowledge. According to the myth in the *Republic* (III 415A), differences in human nature are due to various admixtures of gold, silver, iron, or copper. These facts of *physis* put limits upon teaching. Thus, we must censure only the pure forms of naturalism and relativism that are advanced here by Protagoras (326E *et seq.*) and by Alkibiades in the dialogue named after him. But one can educate, or lead toward knowledge, only a person upon whom nature has bestowed the necessary capacities and a sense of "kinship" with the subject.[30] We also know that this intellectual guidance leads the pupil to a point where a spark is kindled (or is not) and where, in the presence of the *Arrheton*, even the *logos* is inadequate as a guide.[31] These are the limiting conditions to which "teaching" is subject. Although we cannot prove that Plato had perceived the ultimate limits when he wrote the *Protagoras*, perhaps we catch a glimpse of them when Socrates says that, formerly, he had not believed

"that there is a human endeavor (εἶναι ἀνθρωπίνην ἐπιμέλειαν) by
which good men acquire their goodness" (328E). We have a
right to take every word seriously, and if, for the moment, we
put the emphasis upon the word "human," it is difficult to overlook the background of the more-than-human, particularly since
we find the same hint in the *Laches* (196A).

The final section ends with an explicit challenge that indicates
the previous discussion and progress of the dialogue were strictly
preliminary and conditional. The question, What is *arete* itself?,
must be clarified first, for then we might see more clearly whether
or not it can be taught. Thus, in the end, we have come back to
the old Socratic question, "What is . . . ?" Did Plato have an
answer to this at the time of the *Protagoras*? The reader is shown
part of the way. We have seen unity, unity within multiplicity,
and we have seen knowledge as something beyond specialized
know-how, but we do not as yet know what this *episteme* is or
its true object. Perhaps we may guess that the object of *episteme*
is this very unity—the unity of powers and capacities inherent in
man as natural dispositions and developed and formed by education and culture. When Plato, who depicts Socrates never "as
he is in himself" but always as he is alive in Plato, makes Protagoras comment upon the youth of his partner and predict his
future fame in the field of philosophy (361E), we may suspect
that the Socrates in Plato was more mature than he is shown
to be.

Socrates takes his leave. He really must be off. He reminds
us of what he had said earlier (335c); he has an appointment to
keep. Does this not suggest that what has been going on here is
not the most important thing for him? Does he not indeed have
in mind something that is far more important than the refutation
of sophistic claims, namely, his own work of *paideia* as he had
embarked upon it in the preliminary conversation with Hippokrates? Perhaps the playful concluding line of the dialogue, "I
stayed to oblige Kallias, the beautiful," also reminds us, not by
accident, of the very beginning and the playful talk there about
Alkibiades, the beautiful. Beauty and love—they always belong
together in Plato. Here they flash up ironically at the extreme
horizons of the dialogue.

Must we still say what the dialogue is all about? Some have

concentrated upon the struggle between Socrates and the Sophists as the heart of the matter, or just upon the aspect of satirical
comedy; others have concentrated upon the conflict of methods;
and still others upon the aspects of Plato's dialectics and ethics
that are incorporated in this work.[32] We must not forget the
basic principle that Plato always is creating a world of his own,
in each dialogue and in the whole body of his work, and that this
dialogue, the richest among his early works, cannot be grasped
by isolating a single element and making it the basis for an interpretation of the whole. There is, to be sure, the struggle
against the Sophists waged with every weapon, including satire.
This is more than a struggle against hostile forces, for these
forces are also assigned their proper place in the cosmos that is
here taking shape. Nor is Socrates simply fighting against anti-
Socratic modes of education. He is himself at work as an educator,
in the beginning and not only then. There is a conflict of methods,
to be sure, but this conflict also clarifies matters of substance.
Above all, we must not lose sight, in the midst of the abundant
details, of the goal that Socrates keeps steadily before his eyes,
the roundabout and deceptive bypaths notwithstanding. If we
say he is seeking the one in the many, or "being," or knowledge,
we say the same thing in different ways. When we hear him
insist, in the end, that we must first inquire into the nature of
virtue itself, this is the same thing again; and we realize that
we are in the very midst of such an inquiry.

In the group of aporetic dialogues in search of a definition, this
problem is attacked in each case from a specific point of view.
The final answer is found in the system of virtues characteristic
of the good society as depicted in the *Republic*—although this
answer is not conclusive either. Looking back upon the *Protagoras*
from the perspective of the *Republic*, we can see something else.
We find at work, in this early dialogue, important (perhaps the
most important) forces that later will go into the building of the
state; only the ground plan and over-all blueprint are still missing. *Arete* is conceived from the outset in the political sense: a
first attempt is made to integrate the different intellectual and
moral capacities of man into a unitary structure with political
intent. Socratic *paideia* or guidance is beginning to emerge as

having a unique status. We may even discern what is to become the core of the structure of the ideal state, hidden here by Plato's ironic artistry in layers that are not strictly Socratic[33]: when, for example, if only in the myth of the Sophist, we find Zeus bestowing political virtue upon mankind, or when, if only in the Socratic interpretation of a poem, we catch a glimpse of the divine good as eternal being.

A final point that we must not overlook brings Socrates back to the myth of Prometheus (361D). He sides with Prometheus against Epimetheus: "I spend my time on all these matters as a means of taking forethought (προμηθούμενος) for my whole life." Thus, care for one's own existence runs through and transcends the series of clashes and conceptual definitions. Since Socrates himself alludes to this existential theme, there is no reason not to read the *Protagoras* in this light. We shall find a corresponding note at the end of the *Laches* and the *Euthyphro*. Concern for the self in the existential sense is an integral part of the group of early works known as the aporetic dialogues.

TWO

Laches

THE SIMPLE action of this dialogue in which fathers consult Socrates about the education of their sons and the simple
inquiry, a search for the definition of "courage," the manly virtue, contrast with the relatively large number of participants.
In addition to Socrates, there are the two fathers, Lysimachos
and Melesias, with their sons, then the two generals, Laches
and Nikias, without their sons. In the *Theages*, Plato is satisfied
with one father and his son; in the *Charmides*, with a youth and
his older friend; in the *Lysis*, with two boys and their admirers.
Here he might have been content with Nikias and Laches together with their sons, who would then have to be somewhat
older. But the abundance of persons permits degrees of affinity
with Socrates as well as a greater conceptual differentiation.

I
178A–189D
On the lowest level are the many. Their main principle is "to
let the young do as they like" (179A). There are no representatives of this view in the dialogue itself. Lysimachos and Melesias
are on the next higher level. Taught by their own experience
of not having received an education from their famous fathers,
they have the best intentions—but also a very low degree of
insight—in that they wish to see "renewed in their sons along
with the names (Aristeides and Thoukydides) the fame of the
grandfathers." Somebody has told them that "fighting with
weapons" is the proper subject of instruction. (This skill is
hardly superior to that of the juggler; not by accident it is practiced, along with sophistry, by the pair of clever brothers in the
Euthydemus.) The two fathers here have no idea that Socrates
might be able to advise them, although Lysimachos comes from

the same deme, Alopeke, and even has family ties with Socrates
(180c–e). He just vaguely hints that the young have praised
Socrates highly. That is the only contact between Socrates and
these strangers in spirit.

Nikias and Laches represent a higher level, closer to Socrates.
They are men of ability who care about their sons and do not
share the lack of concern shown by other famous fathers. Laches
is surprised that Socrates was not consulted at once on the matter
of education. Nikias stresses the fact that Socrates had secured
the well-known music master Damon as a teacher for Nikias'
son (180cd). Moreover, Nikias seems to know that Socrates is
more than a consultant: he would be the right teacher himself,
if only he were willing (200c). (This qualifying condition is
discussed as a problem in the *Theages*.) Closest to Socrates, for
the moment at least, seem to be the boys, even though they join
in the dialogue only with an enthusiastic, "Yes, that is he"
(181a). As they all unite in paying homage to Socrates, and
Laches, the general, even praises his qualities as a soldier, the
topic of conversation is introduced—*courage*.

Even Lysimachos now knows to whom he should address his
question,[1] and at this point, Socrates secretly takes the lead. To
begin with, however, he turns the conversation over to the two
generals, reserving the right to express his own views later.
Thus, we are not yet on the Socratic level. What we hear are the
experiences of two specialists with regard to technical matters.
They contradict each other in their judgment as to whether fighting with weapons is a useful subject of instruction. The two have
in common that they are not capable of recognizing the general
principle involved. As military men they can envisage courage
only in the context of war, to which they subordinate all education in a dangerously one-sided view. When Nikias uses the two
words "bold" and "courageous" (θαρραλεώτερον καὶ ἀνδρειότερον,
182c) as if they were the same, and when Laches makes a similar
remark (184b), we realize that there is as yet no attempt to
distinguish between natural capacity and moral form (virtue).
This is a distinction at which Socrates is clearly aiming in the
last part of the *Protagoras*.

Lysimachos asks that Socrates decide between the opposing

views presented; he is trying to drag him down to the lowlands
of their conversation. Instead, Socrates pulls the discussion up
to his own level, where it is not a matter of majority vote and
where the word *episteme* is heard for the first time, if only in the
sense of technical, professional knowledge (184E 8). To emphasize the new element introduced here, Plato draws Melesias into
the conversation and has Nikias show some resistance (185c):
as if everybody knew what the talk was all about—about fighting
with weapons, of course! Yet, it is only Socrates who puts the
question, "About what?" at the beginning (ἔτι πρότερον ἐξ ἀρχῆς). We must keep in mind what the goal (οὗ ἕνεκα) of this inquiry is. We are concerned with the souls of the young, or with
cultivating their souls (ψυχῆς θεραπεία) so that they become as
excellent as possible (ὅτι ἀρίστας γενέσθαι τὰς ψυχάς). This is
the height we have achieved beyond the preliminary conversation about a particular *techne*.

After Socrates has thus revealed the general problem behind
the veil of everyday talk and before the discussion itself begins,
Plato shows who this Socrates really is, first in a kind of self-
portrait, then in the reflection of others. Socrates begins by insisting that if a person claims to have knowledge, he must be
able to prove this claim by pointing either to good teachers or to
good works. Works, in the case of an educator (τεχνικὸς περὶ ψυχῆς
θεραπείαν), can only mean human beings whom he has taught
how to become excellent (ἀγαθοί). He himself had no teachers,
Socrates says; he never received (for lack of money!) any instruction from the Sophists; and he is not yet capable of becoming
accomplished in the art of education on his own. He is deferring
to Laches and Nikias. Although contradicting each other, they
obviously must be experts in matters of education. Against the
untested claims of the Athenian citizens, on the one hand, and
the claims of professional educators, on the other, Socrates stands
alone in his ironic ignorance. We surmise that he did not learn
anything because there was nothing he could learn from anybody, and that he has not yet discovered any knowledge because
his knowledge is not something ready-made as in the sense of
technical competence. His knowledge is Socratic ignorance.

This ignorance derives its special meaning from what the two men who know Socrates now say about him. Nikias describes his nature clearly and nobly: every conversation with Socrates, no matter about what, leads the partner to the point where he must give "an account of himself." In this case, too, Nikias realizes, "the conversation will be not about the boys, but about ourselves."[2] Socrates tests men. Even in what seems to be the most general discussion, he invariably states the personal question about "how one does and must live." This is the positive, "existential" aspect complementing Socratic ignorance. Laches provides another complementary aspect. Socrates has achieved the genuinely Doric, the uniquely Greek harmony of word and act. Laches has known him as a courageous man on the field of battle. We remember that he had praised Socrates, at the outset, for his steadfastness at the battle of Delion. Since courage is our topic and since the discussion will not lead to any tangible result, we must be clear about one thing. This man is not talking only—he *is* whereof he speaks. What the *logos* does not accomplish is attained through action. (This is Socratic "pragmatism.")

The conversation has now been raised to the Socratic level where it will be conducted henceforth. At this point Lysimachos drops out, just as old Kephalos does in the first book of the *Republic*.[3] Because of the necessary hierarchical differences among minds, there are those who cannot themselves take an active part in the discovery of the more profound truths; they may still participate indirectly. Lysimachos will listen and then act accordingly. His withdrawal means, however, that the conversation will not descend again to the level of the most commonplace.

The others hold forth at length on some topic or other, beginning anywhere. Socrates, however, begins "at the beginning" (ἐξ ἀρχῆς). Given the empirical fact that fathers seek *arete* for their sons, he concentrates upon the question of "principle" and asks, what is *arete*? Or, since the general concept is too broad, what is courage, i.e., the part of *arete* brought into focus by the illustration of fighting with weapons? We shall not be able to determine how it is acquired, Socrates says, until we first know "what" it is. Two things are worth noting in this move. First, there is a certain arbitrariness in the Socratic shift from *arete* to courage.[4] For the occasion is accidental; and the fact that these

II
189D–199E

fathers seriously think of military trainers as educators for their sons shows the narrow view they represent or, to put it differently, the popular confusion of a particular *techne* with the object of education in general. Actually, since *paideia* is at stake, we should not be dealing with a single *arete*, i.e., a "part" of the whole. Plato did not choose this course in order to clear the way somehow for a discussion of the special problem of courage. On the contrary, his purpose is to show that this problem is put wrongly, in a sense, because it is not stated in terms of the underlying general principle. The inconclusive ending is prefigured, as it were, in this intentionally oblique procedure.

Secondly, we note that the other question, promised for "later" —How can the young acquire *arete*, whatever it may be?—is not discussed at all, because the first question is never settled. Nevertheless, the necessary connection between these two questions is supposed to become clear, just as it does at the end of the *Protagoras* (360E) when the question of whether *arete* can be taught is said to be insoluble as long as we do not know what *arete* is. But may we really put off the urgent, practical task of education until the question has been settled in principle? We must wait a long time before Socrates has his answer. At the end of this dialogue, we see nevertheless that both men ask him to educate their sons. Thus, it is perhaps not necessary to achieve conceptual clarity about the nature of *arete* in order to ask for education. Is there a much closer connection between the first two questions? Are we perhaps in the midst of the process of acquiring *arete* while Socrates is discussing the question of the nature of courage?

The structure of the main dialogue is very simple. There are three attempts at a definition. The participants, too, are used in a simple manner. Heretofore, the two generals were on the same level. Now they are differentiated. Nikias who has "often" heard Socrates speak about these matters (194D) thinks more like Socrates; thus, he becomes Socrates' partner when the third definition opens up the problem of "knowledge." Yet, the dialogue is named after Laches, first, because there is a close connection between him and Socrates as a result of their common experience in battle, and, second, because Laches represents more clearly than Nikias the popular conception of courage.[5]

The first definition of Laches reads: "If a person holds his ground against the enemy and does not flee, then he is courageous" (εἴ τις ἐθέλοι ἐν τῇ τάξει μένων ἀμύνασθαι τοὺς πολεμίους καὶ μὴ φεύγοι, ἀνδρεῖος ἂν εἴη). This is put first, a warning model of how *not* to define a concept. The definition corresponds to the world of experience characteristic of a Laches; it is the lowest form in which this subject can be approached at all. (Lysimachos, we recall, was incapable even of this approach.) But Laches' definition is no real answer to the question; it describes a particular case of courage instead of grasping the general concept. Descending to this level, Socrates leisurely refutes the definition by showing that, even from a military point of view, it would have to be more general and, more importantly, that courage is by no means confined to the military. The field in which we encounter it is divided according to pleasure and pain, desire and fear (191E). These are the four classes of the passions that survive as a basic schema in the psychology of the Stoics. Thus, courage is assigned its own proper field, not the field of battle but the field of the soul, where it must prevail in the struggle against opposing forces. And it must be something identical in all cases.

The second definition, "Courage is perseverance of the soul" (καρτερία τῆς ψυχῆς) or "reasonable perseverance" (φρόνιμος καρτερία), as Socrates adds presently, shows that Laches has learned three things: that courage is a unity, that its proper field is the soul, and that it proves itself in successful struggle. The qualification "reasonable" is designed to distinguish this perseverance from the purely vital value of daring, or foolhardiness; in the Socratic sense, it points toward the element of knowledge as a characteristic of courage.

The definition scarcely has been formulated when the critique sets in. Socrates questions "at what" the reasonable is aiming (ἡ εἰς τί φρόνιμος), whether equally at great things and little things. This is the same question as in the *Protagoras* (318CD) where the notion of "making better" is clarified by asking: better "at what"? There follow a number of cases where a man perseveres reasonably—in money matters, as a physician, in battle, and finally even as a diver. Socrates chooses these cases to

make Laches deny in each that this is courage. Evidently Socrates
agrees with the conclusion. Yet, the two men would give quite
different reasons for their concurring judgments.[6] For Socrates
these are not cases of courage because the meaning of "reasonable" is reduced to the meaning of "prudential," or because the
concern is with "little things" and not with the "great things,"
i.e., the good. As for Laches, he does not overcome the one-
sided view according to which "manly courage" has no place in
business or at the sick bed, but functions only in war, and in
war precisely with regard to those actions where deliberation is
not possible and dash must rule. Thus, Plato assigns to the military man a meaning of "perseverance" as understood in the popular sense of a natural disposition toward bravery or foolhardiness. Although Socrates qualifies this natural capacity by the
word "reasonable" in order to raise it to the level of a "virtue,"
this improvement must be misunderstood as long as we do not
know *at what* this reasonableness is aiming. If we do not know,
then the meaning of reasonableness will be dragged down to the
level of practical, prudential calculations of profit and pleasure.
Thus, evidently, the question, "At what is the reasonable aiming?" must be answered as follows: not at what is pleasant and
profitable, i.e., what is "little," but at what is "great," i.e.,
the good.

Let us, then, inquire into courage—with courage and perseverance, says Socrates (194A). With this playful transition that
alludes to the "moral" aspect of the search for knowledge as well
as to the "cognitive" aspect of courage, we move to the third
level and here come to terms with this cognitive aspect. The
move upward is indicated by the fact that Nikias now joins the
discussion. I think I know what courage is, says Laches, but I
cannot grasp, or express, it in a concept (194B). This portrays
the image of the practical man with inadequate intellectual insight. Laches drops behind; in what follows his role is to make
sure that the superior formulation now proposed shall defend
itself against the objections advanced in the name of "sound
common sense."

II 3
194c–199E
Nikias proposes the third definition: "Courage is knowledge
of what is and what is not to be feared" (τῶν δεινῶν καὶ θαρραλέων

ἐπιστήμη). He thinks he is speaking in the spirit of Socrates, for he has learned from Socrates that "good" and "knowledge" are identical. As a matter of fact, this definition is extremely close to the Socratic view because it brings into focus what heretofore was secondary, or because, grammatically speaking, it translates the adjective (φρόνιμος) into the noun (ἐπιστήμη). The definition corresponds to the formulation ultimately adopted in the *Protagoras* (σοφία τῶν δεινῶν καὶ μὴ δεινῶν, 360D). Here we shall go beyond it, however, for it falls short of the target.[7] "Knowledge"— that is correct. But knowledge "of what"—that still is conceived too superficially.

In vain Laches attacks this formulation, for it can be refuted, or modified, not from "below" but only from "above." He senses that something is amiss; and in remarking that "there seems to be something in what Laches is saying," Socrates gives a hint that Nikias should not reject as rudely as he does (195c). Laches goes about the refutation in the wrong way, however, for what annoys him is the concept of knowledge, i.e., that which is closest to Socrates. He is citing cases of physicians, husbandmen, and artisans who "know what is and what is not to be feared" in their own fields without being courageous. It is quite delightful how Laches now uses against Nikias the very evidence by which Socrates had previously caused Laches' own downfall. But Nikias does not yield. He keeps his eye upon a kind of knowledge superior to that of an expert like, for example, the physician. He means not the knowledge of the physician who knows what is to be feared in the particular case, but a higher kind of knowledge that would decide whether health or illness, life or death is to be feared—or may in fact be "better" (ἄμεινον, 195CDE), as he surreptitiously suggests, in contrast to what is to be feared. The good—the "royal" art of the *Euthydemus* and the *Statesman*— beckons from afar. At the same time, this suggests that courage as a special *arete* is dissolving, as it were; it is merging with the general concept of "knowledge of the better."

Here, then, is the theme upon which the dialogue will end. Laches does not see these implications clearly, and this is understandable. He can only guess at who this somebody is that knows, if he be not physician or husbandman. As for Nikias, he shrouds

himself in obscurity. What he suggests is close to the image of
the "man of wisdom," the philosopher. We are left in doubt,
however, as to whether he understands what he is saying or
whether he only feels it vaguely. But when Laches says that this
"somebody that knows" must be a soothsayer and adds, somewhat sarcastically in order to emphasize the absurdity of the idea,
that Nikias must have a god in mind (εἰ μὴ εἰ θεόν τινα λέγεις αὐτὸν εἶναι, 196A), he is hitting the right target, unexpectedly and
unintentionally. This knowledge, which is coming to the fore
here in the case of a single virtue, is brought to perfection only
in God.

The attack from below launched by Laches is repelled, although
the definition itself disintegrates imperceptibly in this encounter.
There follows a refutation from above. It undoes the definition
of Nikias, but in the process also provides a new foundation.
Socrates, intending to raise Nikias' definition to a higher plane,
begins with clarification rather than refutation. He easily leads
Nikias to distinguish between boldness and courage, i.e., between a natural disposition and a spiritual form. (This is the
same distinction we find in *Protagoras* 350B, where it does not
prevail.)[8] According to this distinction, neither an animal like the
Krommyonian sow nor a child could be called courageous; courage indeed would be confined to "very few." Laches helps to
clarify the question with sarcastic remarks "from below." The
sow, then, would be "wise," if your definition of courage were
valid—thus he sounds off against the higher view. He himself
admits that he has now joined the company of the many (τὰ θηρία
ἃ πάντες ὁμολογοῦμεν ἀνδρεῖα εἶναι, 197A). Nikias confirms it:
you and the many (σὺ καὶ οἱ πολλοί, 197B), he chides Laches, do
not know the difference between being courageous (ἀνδρεῖος)
and being bold (θρασύς). Laches is quite wrong when he, after
the manner of the "many," rejects this distinction as sophistic
hairsplitting, for we know that he could use this kind of clarification himself. Plato here as elsewhere refers with mild irony
to the semantic skill of Prodikos and Damon (197D, 200A), suggesting the kind of abuse to which this skill, useful in its own
right, is exposed when it is exercised no longer as a means but
—in grotesque self-exaggeration—as an end in itself.

So far Socrates has been concerned with clarifying matters. Now, in the last part of the dialogue, he makes a serious counter-move from the perspective of a higher insight (197E). In formal terms, this is done (in contrast to the criticism by Laches) by attacking the part of the definition that is in fact weak. Knowledge here refers to what is to be feared (δεινόν) or not. Fear is concerned with the future; it is, as in the *Protagoras* (358D), the expectation of a future evil (προσδοκία μέλλοντος κακοῦ, *Laches* 198B). But what are we to do with distinctions between past, present, and future when we are dealing with *episteme*? Genuine knowledge, or science, does not involve a temporal modality. What is hinted at is the concern of knowledge with "being as such."[9]

Thus, the definition of courage, which already was moving toward the concept of a generalized "better" as a result of the criticism by Laches, now dissolves altogether. Courage is a matter of knowing every good and evil (πάντων ἀγαθῶν καὶ κα-κῶν ἐπιστήμη, 199C). This makes it clear that he who has courage has all the other virtues as well. In short, although the intent at the beginning and again just now (190C, 198A) was to define courage, what we have defined is not a single virtue but rather *arete* itself.

In formal terms, then, the definition of Nikias has been "refuted" by being absorbed into this general formula. This refutation "from above" has more than a formal meaning; it says something about the essential problem inherent in the subject itself. At the beginning, the conversation got under way with a discussion of the general matter of education and pointed toward the question of *arete* as such. But very soon, owing to the tricky interference of Socrates, a partial problem was singled out. None of the participants was attentive enough to ask, what good is the knowledge of this single virtue—instead of the whole—for the education of our sons? Now we realize that we cannot even grasp the part by itself, because it merges with the whole. Perhaps we have put the wrong question. Perhaps we can neither possess nor know courage without the other virtues, i.e., without knowing virtue itself.

In the *Protagoras*, there arise the questions whether the virtues are one, and if so, what kind of unity they have, and whether courage is a part of this unity. All efforts are directed toward proving this unity, even though the means employed are intentionally impure. In the *Republic*, we have the union of the four virtues in the soul of the individual, and, concentrically expanded, in the structure of the *polis*. If we follow the course from the *Protagoras* to the *Republic*, we see the same genuinely Platonic theme at work throughout—unity within multiplicity, the one in the many. The *Protagoras* as a whole and the *Laches* in part, but with greater depth, point toward the solution reached in the *Republic*. There is a difference in method but not in objective: the *Protagoras* achieves a preliminary result by employing an intentionally impure method; the *Laches*, using a purer method, leads the problem toward a state of *aporia*.

III
199E–201C
A brief coda completes the work. The two generals engage in a slight verbal skirmish, revealing once more the different stages of knowledge they represent. Laches remarks sarcastically that Nikias has not discovered anything either. Nikias knows or suspects, however, that something was gained despite the apparently inconclusive ending of the discussion and he invites further study of the subject (200B). For Laches the whole thing is a kind of fencing bout; Nikias catches the meaning of Socratic *aporia*. In the end, however, even Laches knows what Socrates represents. He recommends that Lysimachos and Melesias take Socrates as the educator of their sons. Thus, the closing scene unites all the participants around the educational power of the philosopher. Yet, even here we may catch a glimpse of the ambiguity inherent in Socratic *paideia*. Nikias doubts that Socrates would be willing to undertake this task of education, since Socrates often referred him to other teachers (200D). Damon is one of these others, as we know (180CD); we may recall also that Damon was mentioned repeatedly as a representative of the sophistic art of linguistic analysis (διαιρετική). We may infer that there are different stages in the educational process, with Socrates representing the highest stage not accessible to all. Socrates himself again refers to his own ignorance, and there is urged upon us the question of how a person who claims to have no knowledge can be a teacher. Indeed, inasmuch as Socrates is the

center to whom the others pay homage, the question is this: Must one not be ignorant, i.e., a Socrates in some sense or other, in order to be an educator? The last words of Socrates, however, "God willing," place the whole matter in the hands of the supreme power in whom—as suggested once before (196A)—knowledge and virtue, necessarily incomplete in the human sphere, achieve perfection.

It is sometimes said in criticism of the *Laches* that there is an alleged disproportion between the conceptual analysis, on the one hand, and, on the other, the stage setting, which is believed to occupy an excessive amount of space.[10] This kind of criticism shows how little some readers appreciate the abundance of life depicted in a Platonic dialogue. It would be quite wrong to interpret the *Laches* as nothing but an inquiry into the meaning of courage and to see the result as nothing but a definition that can be pieced together, it is thought, from the various attempts made in the course of the inquiry. On the contrary, it might be more correct to envisage the meaning of the human world created here under the aspect of *paideia*, although we must again be careful not to underestimate the conceptual achievement.[11] The educational work of Socrates begins by attracting those who are capable of sharing in his mode of life. Its formal method is to lead them to a state of *aporia*, but in such a way that, through the *aporia*, Socrates is able to make visible both the direction and the goal of the inquiry. The essence of his education consists in transforming a natural disposition into a virtue—e.g. natural boldness into courage. This, of course, is not accomplished within the restricted framework of one dialogue any more than the conceptual analysis comes to an end. The meaning of a Platonic dialogue, here and elsewhere, is to lead the way. These comments may suggest that we keep in mind these two aspects: first, the conceptual analysis of courage as part of the total process of education; and, second, the "existential" frame of the dialectical inquiry into courage, i.e., what is said at the beginning and at the end of the dialogue about the problem of education itself. This is the only way to do some measure of justice to the live, human quality of the work as a whole.

THREE

Thrasymachus

[REPUBLIC, BOOK I]

O F THE five "virtues" combined into some kind of system in the *Protagoras*, knowledge in the all-inclusive sense of *sophia* could not be the subject of an aporetic dialogue in the manner of Plato's early period. The question, What is *episteme*?, is discussed much later in the *Theaetetus*. As far as the other four virtues are concerned, the *Laches* deals with courage, the *Charmides* with temperance or *sophrosyne*, the *Euthyphro* with piety, and the *Thrasymachus* with justice. For it is practically certain, on the basis of an analysis of form and content as well as on the grounds of verbal statistics, that the first book of the *Republic* originally was a separate dialogue, written down as a whole or in part, or, at least, carefully planned and far advanced in the mind of its author as an integral part of the early group of aporetic dialogues.[1]

Perhaps there is even external proof for this view—namely, the strange little dialogue called *Clitophon*.[2] Kleitophon is a marginal figure in the first book of the *Republic*. At the very beginning (328B) Socrates meets him along with Lysias and others in the house of Polemarchos, and later (340AB) he once joins in the discussion. In the dialogue named after him he is facing Socrates all by himself. In a conversation with Lysias, Kleitophon—so Socrates has heard—took a position on the side of Thrasymachos and against Socrates. Thus, the little dialogue presupposes the first book of the *Republic*—and this applies to the very details of the discussion.[3] Yet the *Clitophon* rules out the other books of the *Republic* on this ground: the reason for Kleitophon's taking side against Socrates is that the latter is conversant only with "protreptic" and has nothing positive to teach.

The setting of the *Thrasymachus* is not strictly designed for the *Republic* as a whole, if for no other reason than that the conversation begins late in the day. If the *Republic* had been planned as a whole, the discussion probably would have begun early in the morning, as in the *Laws*.[4] The opening scene of the *Thrasymachus* is outside the city at the Piraeus—"the oldest social melting-pot of the Greek world"[5]—and a festival in honor of the Thracian goddess Bendis provides the background. Is this festival of barbarians who are barely Hellenized the right melody to accompany the struggle with Thrasymachos? "I thought the procession of our own people was fine," says Socrates, "but no more so than that of the Thracians" (327A). Is this merely part of the setting or does it say more, namely, that for this sort of thing one does not have to be an Athenian, but one must be an Athenian to do the work of Socrates, which, according to the *Apology*, is true service of the god? Socrates observes and takes part in the ritual, but he is not very much involved in the festival, as is shown by the ensuing argument with the group around Polemarchos as to whether Socrates should stay on or not. How willingly he lets himself be invited at other times and how he resists here! One reason, however, persuades him to stay: "There will be a lot of young people at the festival at night and we will talk" (328A). That is the important thing. Although we may easily forget it in the gigantic structure of the *Republic*, we will keep it in mind during the course of the first book. There, at the end, the festival of Bendis is mentioned once again, and it is quite possible that the theme "and now we shall go to the celebration" was at one time taken up explicitly. At any rate, this theme points in the direction of what is the primary concern for Socrates—conversation for the sake of *paideia*. Controversy is necessary as well, but it is not most important. This view was faintly suggested at the end of the *Protagoras*, and in the *Euthydemus* we find both forms of discourse, conversation and controversy, in constant interplay with each other.

Let us look at the participants in the dialogue, always remembering that we do not know if we are still seeing the scene

exactly as it was originally composed. Polemarchos comes up
behind Socrates, who is on his way back to the city. Socrates is
not particularly inclined to stay. But the two brothers—Plato's
brothers—Glaukon and Adeimantos, the former accompanying
Socrates, the latter with Polemarchos, bring about agreement.
"We will wait," says the one (327B). "Don't you know there
is going to be a torchlight procession?" says the other (328A).[6]
Nikeratos is in the company of Polemarchos. He reminds us of
the *Laches* (200D), where Socrates declines to educate this son
of Nikias. His presence may help to explain why Socrates is disinclined to stay.

Polemarchos—the wealthy merchant who for years has lived
in the Piraeus as a resident alien, i.e., without full rights of
Athenian citizenship—is the representative of a whole circle,
whom we meet presently at his house. His brothers, Lysias and
Euthydemos, are members of this circle. Lysias, whom we shall
see more clearly in the *Phaedrus*, is the orator, a technician and
expert. Perhaps he is even more. In the *Gorgias*, we find as the
opponents of Socrates first the rhetorician Gorgias, then Kallikles, the advocate of power, who draws the logical consequences
from the art of rhetoric as conceived by Gorgias. Perhaps there
is a similar order hidden here, with the Sophist Thrasymachos
corresponding to Kallikles. Thrasymachos, then, renowned guest
on a visit, is staying at the house of Polemarchos with his disciples—as we must assume them to be since their names follow
directly after his—Charmantides and Kleitophon. Someone else
is in the house—the old man Kephalos, set apart on one side
from the group in the middle as much as Thrasymachos is set
apart on the other side. The line that runs from Kephalos through
Polemarchos to Thrasymachos marks a progressive improvement
in the skill of argument. But this skill is inversely proportional
to the affinity of the partners with Socrates. Thus, we find again
three stages of conversation as in the *Laches*, but with this difference: in the *Laches*, these stages move toward a growing kinship
with Socrates, whereas here they mark an increasing distance
from him. This may be another reason why Socrates at the very
beginning is disinclined to accept the invitation.

I
328C–331D

Kephalos is the partner of Socrates in the first conversation.[7]
He is a man glad of his years who fulfills his duties toward the

gods and his fellow men. As compared to his grandfather who was a money-maker (χρηματιστής) and his father who let money run through his fingers, Kephalos has added a moderate amount to the wealth he inherited. Thus, his attachment to money is moderate as well. The family has inherited the money-loving spirit, however, and this spirit will break through, dangerously, in the part played by Polemarchos.

In the over-all structure of the work, Kephalos corresponds to Lysimachos in the *Laches*. Both are worthy men, but they lack any capacity for inquiry. Both drop out when the serious discussion begins. Both welcome Socrates, almost in the same words (*Republic* I 328CD; *Laches* 181C). Yet, there also is a difference. Lysimachos has only a vague notion of who Socrates is. Kephalos, however, says, "If I were not so old, I would come to see you." This is a courteous gesture, to be sure, but it clearly reveals that he knows something about Socrates. As a matter of fact, while Kephalos corresponds to Lysimachos in terms of structure, he is closer to Laches in terms of the conceptual levels in the two dialogues. For just as Laches represents a natural view about courage, so does Kephalos with respect to justice. This peculiar difference in the assignment of roles (despite the obvious similarities) is due to the different structures of the two dialogues. Since Plato in the *Thrasymachus* is employing a structure in which the three stages move progressively farther away from Socrates, he had to give greater value to the first stage than in the *Laches* where the movement is reversed.

The topic of conversation, then, is "justice" or "righteousness." Kephalos is shown garlanded for sacrifice (328c); his wealth serves him, as he says, as a means of fulfilling his debts to men and gods (331B). "Piety," in the *Protagoras* and, more clearly, in the *Euthyphro*, in the sense of fulfilling the traditional services toward the gods, is also a kind of "righteousness," i.e., an act of performing "what is due or fitting." Thus, Kephalos is the representative of a highly respectable type of "justice," although he does not use the word. It is Socrates (331c) who gives conceptual clarity to the speech of the old man.

Even on this level we can discern basic human attitudes contrasted with each other, and these will return, in more radical and dangerous form, on the level of conceptual analysis. Kephalos

himself states such a contrast: in old age, physical pleasures decline and the pleasure of conversation grows correspondingly,
indeed, in direct proportion (τοσοῦτον αὔξονται—ὅσον ἀπομαραί-
νονται). Here conversation is "talk" of any kind. But this is a
basic relation to be taken up again on a higher level where the
logoi have a philosophical meaning. Thus, according to Plato's
Seventh Letter (340B *et seq.*; cf. *Republic* I 331D), the first test
to determine if a person is genuinely striving toward philosophy
is whether he is capable of the daily renunciations necessary for
such an endeavor. In the *Phaedo*, we find the more profound statement that the soul of the philosopher must renounce all physical pleasures so as not to become infected by the body and have
its intrinsic quality impaired (83B *et seq.*). This contrast is shown
in Kephalos as a distinction due to age; it is reinforced, again
in the context of ordinary life, by the difference between Kephalos
and the other men of his age. For them the cessation of physical
pleasures is the worst aspect of being old, whereas for him, with
Sophocles invoked as a witness, the cessation of these pleasures
has a positive value. The condition achieved thereby is called
"deep peace and freedom" (πολλὴ εἰρήνη καὶ ἐλευθερία), similar
to the state of a "calm sea" (γαλήνη) attained by the philosopher
in the *Phaedo* (84A).

Now Socrates lifts the conversation to a higher level by making himself the spokesman for the many and, responding to the
plutocratic atmosphere of the house, by playing off great wealth
against character. He induces Kephalos to modify his view about
wealth, which the practical hedonists prize most highly. By this
modification, wealth as such is not rejected in radical renunciation—that was never Plato's view[8]—but rather it finds its right
place as a means for achieving what is "just." (For Aristotle,
similarly, material means, χορηγία, are a prerequisite for attaining *arete*.) Thus, the central concept of the dialogue, "justice,"
makes its first appearance as elicited by Socrates. Here, to be sure,
just and unjust, or right and wrong, are related only to punish-
ments threatening in another world and are construed in the
popular sense, i.e., only with respect to practical details.

The later conflicts with the rich yet morally loose Polemarchos and with Thrasymachos, advocate of an uncompromising

will-to-power, thus are anticipated on this preliminary level. Moreover, an important perspective has come into view. Beyond the accidents of youth and old age, what matters is the inner character (τρόπος) of man. And beyond poverty and wealth, there looms justice, to which wealth is related as a means to an end. What looms from afar is the realm of eternal forms and values.

If the *Thrasymachus* were constructed like the *Laches*, i.e., if it were moving in an ascending scale toward this truly Socratic-Platonic dimension, these matters would have been pursued. As it is, the dialogue moves in the opposite direction of an increasing distance away from Socrates.

With the second stage, the conversation between Socrates and Polemarchos, begins the conceptual analysis of the question: What is justice? In the *Laches*, the first definition was arbitrarily drawn from immediate experience and consisted in the enumeration of several cases. Similarly, the definition here reads: "Justice is to tell the truth and to return what we have borrowed" (ἀληθῆ τε λέγειν καὶ ἃ ἂν λάβῃ τις ἀποδιδόναι). Polemarchos "inherits" the definition from Kephalos—a jest related not without purpose to their world of money (330b 6), and made more significant because it is laughed at and repeated. For this world of money is now the context of the ensuing discussion; and here is the hostile power from which Socrates must wrest the concept of justice. II
331–336A II 1
331C–332B

The two stages have a peculiar structure. They are set off from each other by a change in the partners of the conversation, but they interpenetrate in the movement of thought. The first definition makes its appearance even before we have left the first stage behind; and it is Socrates who provides the definition as expressing what Kephalos meant to say. Yet he attacks this formulation immediately by pointing out that returning what we have borrowed "might sometimes be right (just) and sometimes be wrong (unjust)." Thus, justice must be an Archimedean point beyond. A humorous situation develops because the view that Socrates has just criticized is hereupon taken up by Polemarchos—despite the criticism. This is a structural shift based upon the plan that the work shall move, as we have said, in the direction of an increasing distance away from Socrates. Polemarchos seeks help from the poet Simonides who, from now on, serves as an ironic cover for the popular view, which really is Polemarchos' own view. The *Protagoras* (338E *et seq.*) shows— just in connection with a poem by Simonides—that the cause of truth is not advanced by this kind of talk about poetry. It was a different matter when the pious Kephalos (*Republic* I 331A) cited Pindar as giving poetic-mythical expression to the experience of old age at the limits of life.

Socrates had suggested that what mattered was not *that* we return what we have borrowed, but *how* we do so. Polemarchos now condescends to deal with this "how," making things worse instead of better, as it develops, for "how" means "in such a way as to benefit one's friends and harm one's enemies." This is the kind of popular morality expressed in Solon's saying about being sweet to one's friends and bitter to one's enemies. It is an attitude of mind that is overcome by the gospel of love in the Sermon on the Mount. For Socrates this is the occasion for embarking upon a hard dialectical struggle.

II 2
332c–336A
II 2a
332c–334B

The cool conceptual analysis conceals the most radical disagreement over the question of how man should live. Socrates converts the initial statement into the second definition: Justice means "to give every man his due" (τὸ προσῆκον ἑκάστῳ ἀποδιδόναι). This corresponds roughly to the second definition in the *Laches* (φρόνιμος καρτερία). It is more general, and hence formally better, than the first attempt; it is also less infected by monetary connotations. But this formulation conceals, or may conceal, the pernicious view that one must harm one's enemy. Socrates and popular opinion will always disagree on what we "owe" a man. This disagreement comes into the open when Socrates explains to his opponent that his definition is too vague. Socrates does this by citing the arts of medicine and cookery, then agriculture and cobblery, at the same time subtly teaching something about the concept of an art or conscious activity (τέχνη). In this way he elicits from Polemarchos his true meaning: Justice is "the art of benefitting one's friends and harming one's enemies as that which is their due" (332D). But in what field (ἐν τίνι πράξει) is it effective and in what direction (πρὸς τί ἔργον)? Polemarchos replies, quite foolishly, "In war," and Socrates must add "peace" as a domain with equal claim—thus permitting a first faint glimpse of life in a political community as the proper field of justice. The question, "At what" is justice aiming? is answered, "At business" (πρὸς τὰ συμβόλαια, 333A). That is not altogether wrong; according to the *Nicomachean Ethics*, for example, a part of justice is concerned with business transactions (ἐν τοῖς συναλλάγμασι, V 5 1131^a 1). It is a highly restricted meaning, however, and shows that the ordinary way of looking at these matters always is patterned after financial transactions.

There follows a verbal skirmish over the meaning of business transactions. Socrates is aiming at a more general concept, which would not have such a capitalistic connotation. He proposes "community relations" (κοινωνήματα, 333A 13 *et seq.*). Looking forward to the *Gorgias*, where Socrates refers to the "communal bond" (κοινωνία, 507E 5 *et seq.*) that holds heaven and earth together, we realize that this word may have profound meaning. For Socrates it would now be a matter of steering the course toward this higher community—the human community of the state—which rises above the specific community relations based on practical co-operation. But Polemarchos goes again in the opposite direction and repeats, "In money matters." The capitalistic spirit in him is so strong that it swallows up all other relationships—thus reintroducing explicitly the very element which was present at the beginning and from which Socrates vainly tried to turn toward the essential.

This is too much for Socrates. He resorts to the crudest sophistry as his counterweapon. Adopting the narrow formulation of his opponent, he argues as follows: if justice means to make a deposit, i.e., if it refers to a case where money is not used, then justice is useless when it is used and useful only when it is not used. Since he has now worked himself into the proper mood, he goes on in the same vein: wherever somebody is a good watchman, he is also a good thief. And if justice means to keep one's money safe, it must be a kind of thievery.

The sophistic paradox that he who is the best liar tells the highest truth is introduced in the *Hippias Minor*, where it both veils and reveals a characteristically Platonic view. The highest degree of consciousness must be equally clear about the alternatives, yes and no, confronting it; in so far as it is true "knowledge," it will, of course, never choose the opposite of the good. Some such view is applied here in the *Thrasymachus* to the case of justice, if we look below the surface. The radical formulation that justice is useless in its use and useful only when it is not used may be interpreted to suggest that, on a level where community means nothing but the field of business transactions, we do not find a superior concept such as justice in its highest form, and, consequently, that justice must be assigned to a community of a much higher order. These are some of the implications suggested by the paradoxes. In a straightforward sense, however, the paradoxes show that there are some opponents with whom Socrates, after a while, can no longer talk seriously; he can only reduce them to absurdity. Such a state of absurdity is reached when, in exploring a crucial question that affects the whole of human existence, one can think only in terms of financial interests —or in terms of harming one's enemy, a basic error that is expressed again toward the end (334B 5).

Socrates has achieved his objective. His opponent admits that he is perplexed. To put it differently, the anti-Socratic view in these matters rests on presuppositions that are muddled and confused. Despite his perplexity, however, Polemarchos surprisingly clings to the thesis that justice means to help one's friends and to harm one's enemies. This, then, is the bedrock of his position, which must be shaken because it is radically opposed to that of Socrates.

II 2b
334B–336A
The refutation occurs in two thrusts. The final move aims at revealing that the thesis of Polemarchos about justice exposes the whole question to judgments of subjective opinion. For if we substitute the objective terms "good" and "bad" for "friend" and "enemy," it may happen that we make a mistake in judgment, with the result that we injure the good and benefit the bad. This would, indeed, be a "bad view," says Polemarchos, whereas the opposite seems to be "much better." Thus, he is not altogether devoid of a capacity for making moral judgments. He is, in fact, recognizing the Socratic thesis—developed in the *Lysis*[9]—that friends must be good and enemies bad, at least ac-

cording to a subjective judgment; he also knows something about
different moral levels. He thinks he can escape the consequences,
however, by adding to the definition that a friend must be "a
man who both *seems* and *is* good." This easy connection between
appearance and reality indicates that he has little understanding
about reality.

Above all, however, the most dangerous feature of the definition is not yet eradicated. This Socrates does in a second and
most emphatic thrust. He sets out to prove that it is never right
to harm anybody, that indeed a just man cannot do harm to
anybody because this would be a logical contradiction. We know
that this move leads us to one of the most profound truths, which
will be developed and expanded in the *Gorgias*.[10] Here, however, the justification is brief and strict. Incompatibilities in the
dimension of being are interpreted as logical impossibilities.
Every being in so far as it suffers injury to its own peculiar excellence becomes less or worse. Now justice is a form of human
excellence, human *arete*. Thus, even as it would contradict the
nature of a good man[11] to say that his being good makes another
bad, so it is a contradiction to say that the just man would make
another unjust. A just man, then, by his very nature, cannot
harm anybody.

In this subtle proof, which may seem like splitting hairs, justice is fully converted into *arete* and is thus divorced from the
restricted meaning imposed upon it by Polemarchos. Moreover,
the concept of "injury" or "harm" must be understood in the
profound Socratic sense if the proof, which looks like a piece of
sophistry, is to be acknowledged as valid. For, strictly speaking,
we can harm or injure another person only if we deprive his
soul of its intrinsic excellence (οἰκεία ἀρετή), i.e., the kind of internal order that, according to the *Republic*, is the nature of justice.
Arete, then, by its own nature, can never harm anybody; it can
only produce *arete*.

Polemarchos is caught and gives up without further resistance.
At the end, Socrates observes that the saying, "We must harm
our enemies," cannot be attributed to Simonides or some other
wise man, but rather to a man of wealth and arrogance (μέγα οἰομέ-
νου δύνασθαι πλουσίου ἀνδρός)—and men of political power are

then cited. This indicates how closely a plutocratic attitude goes together with the autocratic. Abundance gives birth to *hybris*, according to an old Greek saying. This saying assumes a special significance here because Polemarchos drops out and Thrasymachos is about to begin to play his part. We move from the level of the average man, rich and unscrupulous in the means he uses, to another level. The "tyrannical man" appears, farthest removed from Socrates.

III
336B–354A
III 1
336B–338B

Thrasymachos, with the eloquent name of "Bold Fighter," is a renowned rhetorician, technician, and author of a treatise on rhythmical prose. Thus, Thrasymachos is for Plato—we do not know with how much historical justification[12]—the representative of the type of the "tyrant." In him sophistic rhetoric and a tyrannical nature are joined, because for Plato tyranny grows out of such soil. (In the *Gorgias*, Plato separates these two aspects, showing first the rhetorician, Gorgias, and then Kallikles as the spokesman for the will-to-power.) Upon his entry, Thrasymachos is depicted as being akin in spirit to Kallikles but more rude, for he bursts into the conversation like "a wild animal." In fact, if the company—or Plato's artistry—had not restrained him, he would have exploded much earlier.

The Sophist reveals himself, as usual, by his attitude, which is opposed to a philosophical discussion. It is always easier, he claims, to ask questions than to answer them (336c). He has the right answer, or rather not the right one, but an answer that is "much better" (337D), Thrasymachos says, or "very good" (338A). This reminds us of the *Protagoras* (347AB), where Hippias alludes to the fine speech he has in readiness. It is characteristic of the Sophist that Thrasymachos immediately lays down rules of how *not* to answer (336CD), and it is amusing to see how, parading four different expressions of the same kind (336D 1–2), he rejects the very concepts of advantage or interest that he will later (338c) incorporate into his own definition. Again, it is typical of the Sophist that he misunderstands Socratic irony as an intentional game of hide-and-seek (337A). Other characteristic traits are the greed and vanity that seek immediate rewards of praise and money (337D, 338c). His behavior is typical also in that "he first deluges us like a bathhouse keeper with a

long speech" and then wants to leave without giving an account
of what he has said (344D).

In contrast to Polemarchos, Thrasymachos begins by stating   III 2
his own thesis, thus suggesting the difference between the in-   338C–342E
tellectual and moral laxity in the former and the intensity of   III 2a
thought and will in himself. The famous definition, "Justice is   338C–339A
what is in the interest of the stronger party," expresses the attitude of mind that seeks to deprive justice of any reference to a
valid standard, i.e., the good—the better to use this modified
concept if one is still a member of the oppressed classes and even
more so if one is himself the oppressor. By use of an intentional
misunderstanding, Socrates compels Thrasymachos to explicate
the meaning of his statement that the "stronger party" refers to
the ruling class in the state—a succinct formulation that is probably not advanced here for the first time. This takes the concept
of justice out of the sphere of business transactions and assigns
it to the domain of the state.[13] If we said above that we have now
reached a level farthest removed from Socrates, we must make
the qualification that Socrates may be closer to his most extreme
opponent than indeed to the lukewarm men "in the middle."
The tyrannical man has more political awareness than the money-
maker: so much the worse, then, that he should abuse it!

Socrates makes his countermove. "Interest"—that is right, if   III 2b
only Thrasymachos had not just now expressly ruled against   339A–342E
bringing this concept into the definition (336D). But what about
"interest of the stronger party"? Even as we learned previously
in the discussion with Polemarchos that the words "friend" and
"enemy" do not permit a clear-cut distinction, so it is now shown
that the "interest of the stronger party" introduces a radical
sense of subjectivity. In the former case, Polemarchos tried to
escape from these subjective consequences by incorporating the
notion of "appearance" into the definition (334C), thus admitting subjectivity in a formal sense. Here Thrasymachos will put
up stronger resistance. He is a more radical and a more serious
opponent, as Plato shows in a brief interlude. For a moment he
lets Polemarchos speak for Socrates and Kleitophon for Thrasymachos; during this preliminary skirmish, Kleitophon, in fact,
tries to introduce a subjective meaning into the definition (ὃ

ἡγοῖτο ὁ κρείττων αὑτῷ συμφέρειν, 340B). But Thrasymachos the master is keener than his disciple. He rejects the subjective qualification and insists that the "stronger party" be interpreted strictly so that the "ruler," in so far as he is a ruler, can no more make a mistake than a skilled craftsman or a wise man can in his respective capacity. That interpretation seems—but only seems—to keep the subjective element out of the definition, and Thrasymachos shows off proudly and with rudeness, completely misjudging Socratic irony.

The view that the wise man or the ruler cannot make a mistake (because when he does make a mistake, he no longer is a wise man or a ruler) may well serve to reinforce subjectivistic, irresponsible tendencies, and this is precisely what Thrasymachos means—namely, that a person "who was not himself" need not assume responsibility for what he has done. Carried through consistently, however, this view leads to the Socratic-Platonic thesis that the ruler and wise man cannot make a mistake because he possesses knowledge. Thus, the Platonic Socrates might have conceded the truth of the statement by Thrasymachos that "the true ruler acts in his own interest, and that is justice," if every word is understood in the Socratic sense. Yet people like Thrasymachos deserve to be beaten with their own weapons. Let us by all means, then, define our terms precisely (τῷ ἀκριβεῖ λόγῳ, 341C, 345C). If so, it is clear that the physician *qua* physician or the ship's captain *qua* ship's captain can practice only one thing, and that is his own art or skill; and this skill can aim at one thing only, and that is the fulfillment of its own interest or purpose. Thus, no art serves the interest of those who practice it, i.e., the "stronger party"; an art always serves the interest of those for whose sake it is practiced, i.e., the "weaker party." Analogously, the art of ruling in the state can be practiced by the ruler only for the sake of the weaker. Justice, then, would be the interest of the weaker (τὸ τοῦ ἥττονος συμφέρον).

We must be careful not to record in a paragraph of Plato's ethics or political theory the view that he interpreted justice as the interest of the weaker, say, in a "social" sense. This is rather a paradoxical antithesis to a dangerously extreme thesis. It is arrived at by means of an inadequate induction and by means of verbal juggling to which Thrasymachos, with some discomfort, surrenders for the time being (342c 10, 342d 2). Plato never considered the interests of the ruled as the end, but always the interests of the whole community.[14] Yet, as against the danger of succumbing to subjective anarchy, we catch sight of ruling as an "art" or "science" (342cd) and of the true ruler, "in the strict sense," as a person who possesses the knowledge of this art.

A paradoxical thesis is dialectically defeated by a paradoxical antithesis. Thrasymachos does not feel shaken, and rightly so; for it is not a matter of clarifying a thesis, but, as Socrates will say presently, a way of life (βίου διαγωγή, 344E). And Thrasymachos now displays the life of the "unjust" man as it is and as it is generally conceived. In his countermove against the paradoxical conclusion reached by Socrates, he shows first that experience is against it. The ruler never aims at the good of the ruled and neither does the shepherd aim at the good of the flock. As another fact derived from experience, he points out that, even with regard to details and minor matters, the unjust man who is powerful and intelligent has an advantage over the just who is weak and stupid. Finally, this empirical evidence is gathered together in the image of the "tyrant," who is shown as the ideal type of the unjust man and upon whom are heaped words of high praise. With reference to the tyrant, it makes no sense to speak of crimes. Injustice is in truth a word derived from the cowardly sphere of a slave morality. Instead, the tyrant earns such fine epithets as "happy" and "blissful" (εὐδαίμονες, μακάριοι). Thus, injustice is depicted as stronger than its opposite precisely in the case of the highest type. We close again, then, on the theme that justice is the interest of the stronger party—as if there had been no refutation by Socrates.

What follows we read only in the revisions that Plato made when he incorporated this dialogue into the great work of the *Republic*.[15] Yet it must have been part of the original structure that Socrates now compels Thrasymachos, despite the resistance characteristic of the Sophist, to engage in a dialectical discussion of the subject (345B, 348B) "from the beginning" (ἐξ ἀρχῆς),[16] and that the decisive defeat is delivered in three thrusts.

To begin with, Socrates elicits from his opponent the admission that the unjust man is both good and intelligent, the "perfectly unjust man" (τελέως ἄδικος). Thrasymachos makes it clear

III 3
343A–354A
III 3a
343A–345B

III 3b
348B–354A

b1
348B–350c

that he means a tyrant, not a cutpurse. The system of values here is quite consistent, as we see when Socrates refers to a possible inconsistency that would make the refutation easier— for example, if Thrasymachos would hold that injustice is useful, but bad. Such an admission would suggest an in-between position like that represented by Alkibiades in the dialogue named after him (113D *et seq.*) or by Polos in the *Gorgias*.[17] The logical consistency of Thrasymachos does not yield to such half measures just as he himself did not yield to the compromise proposed earlier by Kleitophon. Socrates, it is evident, is up against stiff opposition; but he will prevail.

The first thrust aims at the center of the enemy's position. The essence of injustice is *pleonexia*, greed-for-more; the nature of the tyrant, according to Thrasymachos, is unlimited *pleonexia* or an unlimited will-to-power. Now Socrates establishes the following point: it belongs to the nature of knowledge that a man who knows does not compete for more (πλέον ἔχειν) with another person who has knowledge, but competes only with a person who is ignorant. This is called *pleonexia* of knowledge because it is construed in dialectical antithesis to the tyrant's greed-for-more.[18] The opposite is characteristic of ignorance. As far as justice is concerned, the argument proceeds, it is evident that one just man recognizes the equal claim of another. This is not so, however, in the case of injustice, the less so, the greater the injustice, and the least of all in the case of the unlimited *pleonexia* of the tyrant. Thus, injustice is on the side of ignorance—or of evil, since Thrasymachos earlier had acknowledged the well-known Socratic maxim that knowledge is good and ignorance is evil. Justice, however, is on the side of knowledge and the good.

b2
350D–352c

The second thrust aims at the attribute "stronger" (δυνατώ-τερον καὶ ἰσχυρότερον) which Thrasymachos had assigned to the unjust man. Why? Because it is still possible to argue that, while the just man may be better and wiser, the unjust is "stronger." Socrates suggests that he could derive the opposite conclusion from the foregoing proof, i.e., greater strength from greater knowledge. (He will pursue this idea in the conversation with Polos in the *Gorgias*.) Here he adopts a different course. Injustice in its perfect form would render the unjust incapable of action; even criminals can act together as a group only if some-how they are not completely criminal, i.e., if they are "half-bad" (ἡμιμόχθηροι). The same principle must apply to the action of an individual, since justice is a characteristic of the soul which de-termines its internal structure. (In the *Republic*, Plato will argue that justice is the element that determines the order of the "parts of the soul.")[19]

The third thrust aims at the attribute "happy" (εὐδαιμονέσ-τατον). Why? Because eudaemonia is the end of every action and the goal of human life—and here we learn what eudaemonia is if we do not know it. Every being has its own *arete*, which consists in performing its own peculiar "function" excellently. Justice is the characteristic *arete* of the soul, as was shown pre-viously (350c) when justice, knowledge, and goodness were placed on one side against injustice, ignorance, and evil on the other. Thus, when the soul is good or just (we might say, when it is just "right") it will perform its own proper function, it will live well (εὖ βιώσεται) and attain eudaemonia. These are but different ways of saying the same thing.

In sum, the struggle against the representative of the tyran-nical way of life in the *Thrasymachus* has yielded the following results: first, justice finds its place in the midst of goodness and knowledge; second, justice is a sign of strength of soul, not weakness; third, justice (not its opposite) is a means toward eudaemonia. If Socrates says that in the course of these inquiries we have lost sight of the essential question, What is justice?, we know, from the *Laches* and the *Charmides* (and, later, from the *Meno* as well), that these ironic closing lines, characteristic of the aporetic dialogues, are the concrete expression of Socratic ignorance.[20] As it is, we have come to see where justice must be situated; moreover, the claims of the opposing view have been undermined and the area into which we must push forward both in inquiry and in action has been delineated. Now we learn once more that we must ask "what" is justice, a question that opens up the dimension of "justice itself." For it would hardly be possible to put the question so sharply at the end of this in-quiry, if the dim outlines of a solution, to say the least, had not become visible as well.

b3
352D–354A

This is the only dialogue of the aporetic group to which Plato came back at a later time; he recast it as the opening chapter for the construction of his ideal state. There are, of course, many lines leading from the other aporetic dialogues to the central work of Plato, but the search for justice, after all, was the most direct route leading toward and ultimately coalescing with the highest task he set himself—political achievement.

FOUR

Charmides

SOCRATES talks about *sophrosyne*, soundness of mind, with Kritias and Charmides, who are cousins. Twenty-five years later, they will be members of the oligarchic regime of the Thirty. Despite this common fate and their close kinship, here they are depicted as different from each other. In the *Protagoras*, Alkibiades and Kritias enter the Sophists' quarters together. Alkibiades is "the beautiful," and Kritias is the son of the man with the strange name Kallaischros, the "handsome-ugly" (ὁ Καλλαίσχρου). Perhaps this is merely a play on words. Perhaps it is more. In the *Charmides*, we find this "son of Kallaischros"—thus he is addressed a few times—by the side of Charmides, whose beauty creates the exciting moment at the beginning. Charmides has a perfect endowment. His inner being seems to correspond to his outward appearance, for he has both philosophical and poetic talent. This combination must be Plato's own image; it is the stuff of which he wished men to be.[1]

Charmides is pure, unspoiled, and completely devoted to the master. Kritias is older, a person of more experience who has his own views on the matter under discussion; he also has had a course in semantics (163cd) with the Sophists, possibly with Prodikos. He is capable of detecting the tricks played by Socrates in the process of conducting a conversation, whereas Charmides is caught by them. But the older cousin lacks the other's purity: when Kritias is helpless in the face of the argument, he will not admit his helplessness in the presence of the others lest he endanger his reputation (169c). Such a trait together with the signs of rashness displayed toward his younger cousin and toward

Socrates (162D, 166C) indicate—and every Athenian reader, of course, would see in him the later tyrant—that he lacks the virtue of *sophrosyne* (soundness of mind, temperance, virtuousness, modesty, moderation, self-discipline) that is the topic of conversation.[2] Charmides possesses this quality in its natural form, and for this reason Socrates asks him to look into himself (160D) in order to discover the conceptual meaning of *sophrosyne*. Socrates is *sophrosyne* in its perfect form. Natural disposition in him is converted into *arete* through insight. This is evident from every word he speaks in the dialogue. Of the others who are present only Chairephon, the "fanatical" disciple of Socrates (μανικὸς ὤν, 153B 2), says a few words at the beginning. After saluting Socrates and leading him to his place by the side of Kritias, Chairephon speaks for the others, expressing how deeply moved they are by the beauty of Charmides when the latter makes his entrance. Chairephon represents the kind of spiritual turmoil that is not fit for a philosophical discussion. It is a preliminary stage of the mania that, in its higher forms, appears over and again from the *Ion* to the *Laws* (719C).

The setting is a palaestra, a place dedicated to the pursuit of physical strength and beauty. That is the background, then, for the spiritual struggle. Even as in the *Lysis* the scene is laid in the dressing room of a gymnasium, so it is said here that Charmides might undress for a wrestling match: Socrates proceeds to undress his inner nature (154DE). This parallelism of physical and spiritual existence—and the ideal unity of the two—enters deeply into the conversation itself.

The date is the year 432 B.C., just after the costly battle of Potidaea in which Socrates has taken part. On the day after his return from war, he goes to the customary place for meeting friends. He scarcely has reported the minimum facts about the military engagement when he turns to the question, what is the state of "philosophy" at home and the state of the youth? Henceforth, not another word is said about the war. The external affairs recede completely behind the one task that needs to be pursued at home. The reader may pause for a moment, however, for what was still known to everybody at Plato's time and what we learn from the *Apology* and the *Symposium* is that Socrates excelled in that battle at Potidaea. Thus, it is the same person who is "courageous" in battle and "temperate" at home. But are these two traits not incompatible with each other? Does not the *Protagoras* struggle precisely with this question whether courage necessarily goes together with all the other virtues? And does not the *Statesman* in the end (306B *et seq.*) reveal an antagonism between courage and *sophrosyne*? There it is the antagonism of natural dispositions in man. In the *Republic* (410D *et seq.*), this natural antagonism is shown to be overcome in the higher unity of *arete* by means of an education both musical and gymnastic. Again, at the beginning of the *Theaetetus*, we see this unity achieved in the live portrait of the dialogue's young hero, who resembles Socrates even in his physical appearance. Therefore, it is quite intentional that in the *Charmides* we are shown, in and through the person of Socrates, how *sophrosyne*, which is our topic, is joined with the seemingly opposite characteristic of courage. The conceptual inquiry would take place in a void if it were not grounded in "existence." Thus, the search into the nature of *sophrosyne* is grounded in the living reality of Socrates who is the prototype of *sophrosyne*—yet more than *sophrosyne* "only."

Socrates proves his own *sophrosyne* at once by quickly passing over his experiences and action in the battle, ignoring altogether his own contribution. Then the image of the young Charmides begins to be evoked with increasing intensity. First, he is praised by others; soon he comes in and sits down, we see, between Socrates and Kritias, thus occupying a place between the man to whom he now seems to be completely devoted and the other man whom (as everybody knew) he followed later in the opposite direction. In other words, the *sophrosyne* that the young Charmides exhibits in its incipient forms did not develop in him into the mature form, *arete*.

I
153A–159A

The preliminary conversation deals with the headache of the youth. Socrates knows a cure, but he also knows that you cannot cure the head without curing the whole body. Nor can you cure the body without the soul: this he has learned in Thrace—so the Greeks, despite Hippokrates (*Phaedrus* 270C), apparently do not know anything about it! Even as beauty of body and *so-*

phrosyne of soul correspond to each other (*Charmides* 157D,
158AB), so do health of body and soul. (The word "health"
should and must be understood in the first syllable of the word
so-phrosyne.) In the *Gorgias* (504B–D), we learn that health produces a state of order (τάξις καὶ κόσμος) in the body as justice and
sophrosyne do in the soul. The same parallelism runs through the
Charmides. The unity is even stronger, for *sophrosyne of soul* helps
to keep the body in good health as well, and it is said to be a
common mistake among men that they separate the two (157B).
Thus, psychosomatic unity is the goal of the educational work
performed by Plato's Socrates.

Socrates examines Charmides to discover whether he really
possesses *sophrosyne*. The examination is most amusing because
Socrates asks Charmides whether he does possess it or not only
after he has first praised his many excellences, putting the modesty of the young man to a severe test. Charmides passes the
test charmingly: he neither claims nor denies possession of this
virtue. Thus, after we have seen how *sophrosyne* manifests itself
in the conduct of a living person and after we have learned that
it corresponds to health in the body and is, ultimately, responsible
for such health, the groundwork is laid for the conceptual analysis. What kind of thing is *sophrosyne* (ὅ τι ἐστὶν καὶ ὁποῖον)?
It is not "knowledge" which is promised; for if Charmides par-
takes (μετέχειν, 158C 4) of *sophrosyne*, if it is present in him (ἔνεστιν,
159A 2), it must be "visible" and we must be able to form an
"opinion" (δόξα) about it. The objective, then, is to discover the
nature of the thing, but it is intimated that we may not actually
grasp this nature through knowledge.

The discussion takes place in two stages. Charmides replies
on the first stage, Kritias on the second. Strictly speaking, these
two stages are not sharply separated from each other, since the
youth, in the end, introduces a definition that belongs to his older
cousin and is later defended more effectively by Kritias. To begin with, however, Charmides proposes two definitions that correspond to his own nature. First, gropingly, as it were, he lists
various activities. This is similar to the procedure in the *Laches*,
Thrasymachus, *Euthyphro*, and *Hippias Major*. The difference here
is that, without the prodding of Socrates, Charmides himself tact-

II
159A–175D

II 1
159A–162B
II 1a
159A–160D

fully sums up the list in a general statement: *sophrosyne* is "a kind of quietness or tranquility" (ἡσυχιότης τις). After Socrates has refuted this definition, Charmides makes a second attempt: *sophrosyne* is modesty, shame, or reverence (αἰδώς). It is evident that these formulations touch only upon certain aspects of *so-phrosyne*, but not upon its essential nature; it is also evident that Plato is moving from external to internal criteria. In both cases, Socrates makes the criticism that quietness as well as modesty are qualities of neutral value whereas *sophrosyne* is said to be either something "beautiful" or something "good," depending on whether we look at it in its outward appearance or in its inner nature. *Sophrosyne*, in short, is something of value.

II 1b
160D–161B

Charmides presents his third definition. He has heard it from someone else, from Kritias, as we soon suspect. Thus, the definition goes beyond the world of this young man's own experience. It is a "riddle," as we are told repeatedly (161C 9, 162A 10, 162B 4) or a traditional formula, which may have various meanings[3] and must be clarified. The well-known formula reads, "to do one's own (business)." It is evidently meant as the opposite of the truly Athenian fault of "busy-ness" (πολυπραγμονεῖν, 161D 11).[4]

II 1c
161B–162B

Socrates proceeds to analyze the meaning of this statement by a method that seems to obscure it, employing a sophistic trick. He substitutes the words "make" and "produce" for the word "do" (ἐργάζεσθαι τε καὶ πράττειν, 162A 2). The conclusion shows what he has in mind. Socrates imagines a state in which everybody makes his own clothes, shoes, oil flask, and strigil—in short, "makes his own (things)"—and then asks whether such a state is well-ordered or temperate. (We are at once reminded of *Hippias Minor* 368c, where Hippias himself actually does make all the things just mentioned and Socrates admires this achievement with unconcealed mockery.) To Socrates' question here, it is Charmides who replies: No, that would not be a well-ordered state. The youth is not trained enough to detect the device by which Socrates has turned the meaning of the original thesis into its opposite. But the opposite throws light upon its own opposite, so that we become aware of the "political" implications. We must look forward to the *Republic* where this formula, "to do one's own," determines the structure of the state. There it will be called "justice," but justice and *sophrosyne* are often joined together and are very close to each other.[5] Moreover, in the *Timaeus* (72A), Plato uses this formulation, "to do one's own," at least with regard to a subclass of *sophrosyne*. Thus, we may be sure that he did not introduce it in the *Charmides* merely to have it refuted. Instead, it is meant to bring out the political meaning of this virtue; the fact that it is associated with Kritias points in the same direction.

II 2
162B–175D
The intervention of Kritias leads to a higher stage and is, therefore, analogous to the intervention of Nikias in the *Laches* and of Thrasymachos in the first book of the *Republic*.

II 2a
162B–164C
Kritias, then, admits to being the author of this third definition, and he cannot be subdued by a sophistic trick. He has studied semantics and sees through the transparent confusion of terms. Socrates passes somewhat cavalierly over the semantic distinctions. What word we use is less important than the matter itself to which the word refers. Indeed, it may be questioned whether Kritias is applying his own skill very aptly—especially as he is mixing it up, in typically sophistic fashion, with an interpretation of poetry.[6] And, in the end, the interpretation of the phrase "one's own" or "one's personal affairs" (τὰ οἰκεῖα) to mean what is "done beautifully and usefully" (καλῶς καὶ ὠφελίμως ποιούμενον) is quite capricious and general, although not false. The system of a body politic, both communal and individual, which Plato associates with the formula "to do one's own," does not come through in the words of this disciple of the Sophists. Instead, overleaping this stage, we ascend directly to the highest and most general level. Kritias now says that *sophrosyne* is "the doing of good actions" (τὴν τῶν ἀγαθῶν πρᾶξιν, 163E). This formulation, of course, opens the gateway to "the good" and directs us toward the central focus of Plato's thought. But the statement obviously is much too general: it is more a way of dissolving than of defining the concept.[7] Moreover, the very etymology of *so-phro-syne* suggests a reference to "mind" that is overlooked in the simple definition of "doing good actions." For can we not perform what commonly are called "good actions" without any insight into what we are doing? "Soundness of

mind," however, requires such insight, Socrates suggests. Whereupon Kritias, withdrawing all his previous statements (a move
characteristic of a disciple of the Sophists), proposes a new definition on a still higher level: *sophrosyne* is "self-knowledge."
This "Delphic saying," to which Plato's Socrates always ascribes
the highest significance, Kritias now praises in exalted language;
at the end of the sophistically embellished speech, "self-knowledge" is proclaimed once more as the goal and new definition
of *sophrosyne*.

II 2b
164c–175d

"To know oneself" (ἐπιστήμη ἑαυτοῦ)—to clarify the meaning
of this phrase is the great struggle henceforth through the remainder of the dialogue. The formulation is modified—and correctly so, if we understand "self-knowledge" in the Platonic
rather than the modern sense—to read "knowledge of itself"
(ἐπιστήμη ἑαυτῆς).[8] In the course of the discussion, moreover, it
is clarified to mean "knowledge of what a man knows and does
not know" (τὸ εἰδέναι ἅ τε οἶδεν καὶ ἃ μὴ οἶδεν, 167A) and "knowledge of itself and of the other sciences" (ἐπιστήμη ἑαυτῆς καὶ τῶν
ἄλλων ἐπιστημῶν, 166c, 168A). Again and again, Socrates turns
and tests the formula probingly. Kritias once objects, in a tone
of reproach, that Socrates has been looking at the question of
what "self-knowledge" has in common with the other sciences
and is only now considering the question of how it differs from
them (166B). This objection shows all the more clearly that
Socrates is searching for both: the *genus proximum* and the *dif-
ferentia specifica* (to use the technical terms of logic which here
have their origin). Like all other branches of knowledge, self-
knowledge must necessarily be knowledge "of something." But
it seems to differ from all of them precisely because it does not
have an object of knowledge that is different from itself. Furthermore, it seems to differ not only from other sciences (165B–
167A) but also from all other powers of the soul (167B–168A).
This seems, in fact, to give it—if there be such knowledge—a
unique status among all other relational terms in our language
(168B–E). Yet it is still questionable whether there is such
knowledge and, even if there is, we do not know whether it corresponds to the *sophrosyne* we have been seeking (169AB). The
reader is not left in doubt that hidden behind the term "self-

knowledge," there is a genuine problem worth puzzling over. Not in vain does the Delphic god bear witness to the saying, although he does not unravel the riddle (164D *et seq.*). It is more doubtful whether the saying defines *sophrosyne* itself. In fact, when at the end we turn to look back upon the dialogue as a whole, we will see that the saying encompasses a much more comprehensive domain than *sophrosyne*.

Perhaps, in this part of the dialogue, there are a few other aspects that we see sharply only in the light of Plato's later works. Is there such a thing as sight or vision (ὄψις) that is sight and vision of itself and of all other visions (167CD)? Kritias' reply is no; and Socrates leaves it at that. But it is surely not inappropriate to look forward to the "vision of the mind" in the *Symposium* (219A) and to the "eye of the soul" in the central part of the *Republic* (VII 533D), and if we do so, we may be doubtful about the reply by Kritias. Later on in the *Charmides* (168E), Socrates mentions the power of self-movement along with self-perception, and emphasizes that these relations to the self would be regarded as incredible by some people, but perhaps not by others. Some great man, he continues, would be needed to determine whether, within the universe of being, there is anything that by its very nature has the power of relating to itself. Plato would not have let Socrates struggle so suggestively if he had not been struggling with this question himself before he reached the view later expressed more explicitly in other works. In the *Phaedrus* (245C *et seq.*), he speaks of the soul as "self-moving." In the *Timaeus* (89A), he refers to the most perfect motion as that which moves itself: this is the motion of thought and of the universe. Finally, in the *Laws* (X 894C), the last in the series of ten different forms of motion is that which moves itself and everything else. At the time of the *Charmides*, to be sure, Plato was still far from developing such a system; he was on his way toward it, however, and he was certainly not so perplexed as he makes Socrates pretend to be.

Socrates only seems to have succumbed to this perplexity in which Kritias really finds himself (169C). Socrates leads the way out now, at first leaving the question open whether there is such a thing as this self-knowledge. Does this kind of knowledge

(provided that it exists) give us any concrete body of knowledge?
That does not seem to be the case; for whatever specific knowledge we have we find in the particular branches of science. This
other kind of knowledge does not even seem to be able to tell us
whether a man is a good or bad physician. Of what benefit, then,
is this knowledge (171D)? Suppose it combined factual knowledge of the particular sciences with an ability to judge whether
or not a person has such knowledge. In this case, it would indeed
be of highest benefit. Socrates now evokes the image of a ruler
who, by virtue of possessing such knowledge, would put everybody in his right place and would not permit anybody to do
anything not in his proper province. Such a ruler, in short, would
make everybody "do his own (business)." The phrase of the
previous definition crops up again and is linked with the new
definition. Here the "virtue" that we have been seeking is expanded—if only in the form of a hypothetical construction—into
the very attribute of the ruler in the state; and good actions,
well-being (καλῶς καὶ εὖ πράττειν), and eudaemonia, take us, so
it seems, on the familiar path upward to the highest level in
Plato's universe (172A).

We may surmise that in this hypothetical ascent and perspective, we are shown something that must not be given up again,
but must be clarified and perfected. Thus, we must carefully examine the objections raised by Socrates, which tend to conceal
this perspective. Are they not designed, instead, to purify the
new vision? First is the question whether *sophrosyne* merely
serves to clarify and expand what is known and practiced in the
particular sciences. This question remains unsettled; yet the
question itself suggests the possibility that *sophrosyne* must have
a meaning quite different from the knowledge that is discovered
in the particular sciences. Then there is the second objection:
granted that the order of the state such as we have just envisaged
were perfected, *sophrosyne* would indeed put the particular sciences and professions in their proper place, but it would not
create anything superior to them. We would then live according
to knowledge (ἐπιστημόνως), but in doing so, we would not
necessarily attain happiness (173D).

There follows an exchange between Kritias and Socrates to

determine the meaning and value of *episteme*. The outcome is a distinction between technical knowledge in particular fields and the knowledge of good and evil. Socrates agrees with this result so enthusiastically that we may think we have reached the heights of this involved discussion (174CD). We recall that in the *Laches*, Nikias discovers a kind of knowledge which is not the knowledge of the physician who decides matters of health and illness, but a knowledge which would enable us to decide whether it is more beneficial to live or to die. Similarly, we have come here to a kind of knowledge, or science, that is not a technical science, but is concerned with the question whether what is done in the particular sciences is "good and useful" (εὖ καὶ ὠφελίμως). Yet this "science of sciences" is of no use; hence, it cannot be *sophrosyne*. And the result is again zero. Or is it? Have we not caught a glimpse of the "knowledge of the good" that is destined to take the place of the "science of sciences"? This is to be understood not in the sense that we must discard the one in order to acquire the other, but rather in this sense: if the "science of sciences" is meant to be more than an empty duplication of the factual sciences, it must discover the meaning and purpose (*telos*) of the particular sciences and assign them their place in the system of "the good."

Let us single out another significant aspect in the to and fro of this exchange. The discussion is concerned not only with knowledge, but also with the person who knows. While prophecy is restricted to a knowledge of the future, the wise man, it is said, knows the past and present as well as the future (174A). What Socrates alludes to may be seen more clearly against the background of a significant development in the history of Greek self-consciousness.[9] In Homer it is the seer Kalchas whose knowledge extends through all three dimensions of time. Again, the aged Nestor can "look both forward and backward at once," whereas Agamemnon is foolish because he cannot "think forward and backward at once." In Hesiod, it is the Muses who proclaim "what is, was, and will be," and who have imbued Hesiod himself, at his consecration as a poet, "with a divine voice so that he may sing about things future and past as well as about the race of the eternal gods." Later, in Hippokrates' *Prognostics*, the art of prognosis enables the physician to foresee—even before the patient has said a word—"what is present, what is past, and what will be in the future." At the end of this long line of development, then, we find the man of true wisdom as Plato's Socrates makes him appear here for a moment. The rank previously held by the seer, the poet, the aged, and the diagnostician is now assigned to the person with knowledge—"if someone" were capable of surveying all three dimensions of time, past, present and future.

Behind this involved discussion which, in part, deliberately veils what is half revealed, there emerge a kind of knowledge that is superior to all other branches of knowledge and a conception of politics that is superior even to the best practical brand because both aim at the highest good. This view may be confirmed by following this line of thought from the *Laches* and the *Charmides* through the *Euthydemus* up to the *Republic*.[10]

In the *Euthydemus*, we are again seeking a kind of knowledge that, in contrast to particular possessions and skills and beyond the mere having of these, would teach us their right use and would thus assign a proper value to what are originally neutral "goods" (280D, 281D). All the particular arts and sciences are taken under review, and it is shown how each of them surrenders its results to the use of a higher art. Thus we move upward, amidst many difficulties, toward the supremacy of the "royal" or "political" art (291B)—only to find ourselves in even greater difficulties. This art in order to be productive of what is useful or good seems to require a kind of knowledge—"wisdom" and "good" were equated earlier (281E)—that has itself as the only object and whose sole purpose is to make others good so that they, in turn, can make still others good. The whole thought seems to lose its meaning and substance in this infinite regress. But the meaning is easily come by in the *Republic* (505A–C). There we behold the *Idea* of the Good as "the highest object of knowledge" and we realize that without this *Idea* all other possessions and kinds of knowledge would be useless. Not to mention those who identify the good with pleasure, we can now deal with those who identify the good with knowledge, for if we ask, "Knowledge of what?" they can only reply, "Knowledge of the good." Thus, it is "the good" that lends substance, ultimately, to both life and thought: to life, because it lends meaning to every activity and possession of man; to thought, because it puts a stop to an empty tautological circle and to an equally empty infinite regress.[11]

The *Charmides*, however, ends upon a note of *aporia*, because it can only hint at this ultimate solution. At the end of the dialogue, we are told again that we have not discovered the kind of being that the "lawgiver"—the "name-giver" of the *Cratylus*—has called *sophrosyne*. The statements that allegedly did not pass the test are summed up again: first, that there is a science of sciences (though we know that "the good" gives meaning to this seemingly empty tautology); second, that this knowledge would also be a knowledge of what a man does not know—which is impossible, because it would be "contradictory" to know in some sort of way what one does not know. "In some sort of way"—perhaps these words suggest that we must also seek further in this direction. Perhaps we should keep in mind that Socrates is the man who knows that he does not know and perhaps we should remember that, according to the *Euthydemus* (277c), in the course of a sophistic argument charged with great truth, it is shown that he who learns is a person who does not know.[12] And in the distance, perhaps there even looms, behind these seemingly harmless words, the question of the nature of non-being, a central problem in the *Sophist*. In the *Charmides*, however, Plato draws the lines of the dialogue together at this point.

CONCLUSION
175D–176D

Young Charmides again comes to the fore. We recall that he has been listening to these difficult discussions. We feel that his presence is an integral part of the dramatic structure of the work: the living embodiment of *sophrosyne* goes with the philosophical discussion of the topic. Moreover, we share his confidence in Socrates—the man who knows that he does not know—whom Charmides begs, despite the apparently inconclusive ending, that he be accepted as a pupil.

Looking back upon the dialogue as a whole, we must above all guard against an interpretation, understandable as it is, according to which the long concluding part on the subject of self-knowledge is seen as the essential message of the work.[13] In

general, it is unwise to break up the live unity of a Platonic dialogue. The outcome, never stated dogmatically, is always held in
dialectical suspension among the various parts of the whole work.
In the case of the *Charmides*, we must comprehend a double line
of tension. One tension spans the two levels on which the conversation is conducted. The Charmides level, where the youthfully beautiful and philosophically naïve kind of *sophrosyne*, characteristic of a noble disposition and an education within the strict
bounds of social conventions, is expressed in simple conceptual
terms; and the Kritias level, where the perfect kind of *sophrosyne*
characteristic of a philosophical attitude of mind is envisaged
through all the devious, dialectical detours. And both levels open
a view—though by means of ironically involved complications—
upon a social order. On the Charmides level, this order in which
everybody "makes his own (things)" is a caricature in reverse
of the true order in which everybody "does his own (business)."
On the Kritias level, we see—though in a hypothetical context
only—the wise ruler who would put everybody in society in the
right place where his special knowledge would lead to the right
action. The other line of tension runs parallel with the first. On
the Charmides level, we find calm moderation and reverential
modesty, i e., an "outward" mode of being and an "inward"
mode of being, confronting each other. Analogously, we find on
the Kritias level the two formulations, "to do one's own" and
"to know oneself," corresponding to each other, and this correspondence is intensified and generalized into the doing of the
good and the knowledge of the good.[14] Only in this rich context
of interrelationships does there become visible the nature of *sophrosyne*—and, at the same time, its absorption in a higher concept.

The polarity expressed on the Kritias level, bringing out the
twofold aspect of *arete*, the theoretical and the practical, may be
found elsewhere in Plato. The most concise formulation is a
brief statement in the *Timaeus* (72A) : "It has been well said that
doing one's own and knowing oneself are the characteristics of
the man of sound mind only." The two aspects which we distinguish on the Kritias level are combined thus into a higher
unity.[15] More contemporary with the *Charmides*, the *Alcibiades*

Major shows the same dialectical tension, although expressed less concisely. In this dialogue, more than anywhere else in Plato's works, we can clearly see the meaning of this kind of "self-knowledge." It is not what we usually think of today or what Xenophon (*Memorabilia* IV 2 24 *et seq.*) meant: knowledge of one's own subjective self. Instead, it is a matter of knowing the objective relations of order between soul and body ("man is soul") and the objective relations of order within the soul ("reason is the most divine element"). In this discussion in the *Alcibiades*, suddenly, as if in a backward glance to the *Charmides*, the phrase occurs, "If, then, *sophrosyne* be self-knowledge . . ." (131B 4). Moreover, the two formulations found in dialectical tension on the Kritias level of the *Charmides* are analyzed in their interconnection in the *Alcibiades Major* (131A). The representatives of the special sciences, the physician or the husbandman, do not know themselves, i.e., the central focus of the self, but only know the peripheral regions, i.e., what belongs to the self in a narrower or wider sense (τὰ ἑαυτοῦ, τὰ τῶν ἑαυτοῦ). The man-of-money (χρηματιστής) also lacks insight into the objective order of values; hence, as money-maker he does not "do his own (business)," but is concerned only with peripheral matters (131c). For in order "to do one's own" one must "know himself." Thus, the *Alcibiades Major* reconciles what remains an unresolved tension in the *Charmides*.

Once we have comprehended this tension of the *Charmides*, a final question is inescapable. In a dialogue dealing with *sophrosyne* we do not find any reference to the ordinary meaning of this virtue: that it consists in the mastering of one's desires and passions. If we consider that this—"which is commonly called *sophrosyne*" (*Phaedo* 68c)—is also a dominant conception in other works of Plato,[16] we must ask why he omitted it in the *Charmides*.[17] It is clear that the discussion on the Kritias level encompasses a much wider scope. What is being defined there is the "royal" art, i.e., something of which *sophrosyne* is only a part. Quite similarly, the *Laches* and the *Thrasymachus*, setting out to define courage and justice, instead come to encompass the whole range of *arete*. One cannot grasp the part without the whole—or without the other parts, i.e., without a method of division (diaeresis).

Thus, the objective of the *Charmides* was to clarify the comprehensive concept rather than the specific one. Since we have now surveyed the whole field, it would not be difficult to assign to each virtue its proper place. We gain this insight through the concepts of "self-knowledge" and "doing one's own." For to know one's self means to know the order of rank within the soul so that reason prevails over unreason. And to do one's own means to act accordingly.

FIVE

Euthyphro

THE *Euthyphro* deals with the question of "piety," ὅσιον or εὐσεβές. Piety to the Greeks did not mean, first and foremost, a private, hidden attitude of mind. It meant the objective conduct of man in relation to the gods, with man understood not as the individual, but as rooted in family and community. The *Euthyphro* is a necessary link in the chain of aporetic dialogues which deal separately with the series of virtues brought together in the *Protagoras*. For Plato these virtues were not concepts, floating in empty space, for which he would have to invent appropriate characters and situations. They come to life in Socrates, and in him only, in the form of the conscious perfection that alone deserves the name of *arete*. Thus, when Plato inquired into the meaning of piety, he had in mind the trial of Socrates on the charge of impiety. He showed the master only once in his battle at court, for this situation set definite and narrowly restricted limits. In the present dialogue, it is the moment before going to court that is chosen as the most dangerous and pregnant in meaning. And the opponent of Socrates is not Meletos; he remains in the background, for it would be impossible to conduct a philosophical discussion with him. Instead, it is Euthyphron, the seer (or the professionally pious, as it were), who represents piety just as Laches, the brave man, represents the case of courage and Charmides, the modest youth, the case of *sophrosyne*. Euthyphron expresses a kind of pseudo-piety, however, rather than a preliminary stage of the virtue in its natural manifestation as Laches and Charmides do in the other two dialogues. In fact, strictly speaking, Euthyphron is closer to Thrasymachos, the adversary of justice; hence, the dialogue moves more in the direction of refuting than purifying what the opponent considers to be the meaning of the virtue under discussion.

Plato, with sovereign freedom, combined two sets of events that were separated in time. First, there is the crime of the trial of Socrates which is evoked both at the beginning and at the end of the dialogue. But this trial is concealed ironically behind the absurdity of the case brought (an unspecified number of years back[1]) by Euthyphron against his own father on the charge of negligent homicide. The creative moment came when Plato brought these two events together to show how they reflect upon each other, and then unfolded the problem of "piety" against this double background.[2]

Plato chose for this dialogue the simplest form, a meeting of two men, as in the *Hippias Major* and the *Alcibiades Major*. All the more unusual, therefore, is the setting, outside the courthouse at the porch of the Archon King. For to Socrates, who pursues but a single task in life, a trial is a strange world and he speaks about this event, which will concern him so deeply, from a strangely remote distance. "The Athenians call it a written indictment"; the prosecutor, "I believe, is called Meletos . . . a certain Meletos." Socrates belongs, as Euthyphron intimates in the very first words of the dialogue, to another world—the gymnasium. Thus, the place where he conducts his educational work is indicated from afar, and this education itself as the most important task of his life and as a political task in the highest sense is visible behind the mocking irony with which he refers to the charge brought by the politician Meletos against him: that he corrupts the youth. "The charge against me," he says, is a written impeachment, a γραφή, not a δίκη like your suit against your father—an untranslatable sarcasm, for the word δίκη means both an "indictment" and "justice" or "right."[3]

The participants occupy different ranks. Meletos is acting as a scoundrel against the state, says Euthyphron; "he is aiming the first blow at the sacred hearth." That is a proverbial saying, yet we would have to be deaf not to hear the allusion to Socrates.[4] In the company of Meletos are the many, who are easily led astray. Euthyphron himself thinks he is different from all of them

2A–5D

and closer to Socrates with whose daimonion he compares his own power of prophecy. This is not quite without justification if we think of the intermediate region of the demonic in the *Symposium*, where soothsaying has its place. In the scale of the nine forms of life, however, which Socrates describes in the *Phaedrus* (248DE), the seer and priest occupy only the fifth level. Socrates as the philosopher and lover of beauty would occupy the highest level; Meletos would occupy either the next to lowest level as a demagogue or the lowest as a tyrant. Thus, Euthyphron would be somewhere in the middle. How far he is removed from Socrates he shows by his dogmatic rigidity and his conviction that he knows all sorts of things very well. How little we can trust his powers of prophecy we learn when he is reassuring Socrates about the outcome of his trial (3E). Measured against Socrates, the difference between the priest and the many becomes insignificant, despite the priest's arrogant insistence upon it; indeed, even his distance from Meletos becomes insignificant. For who will guarantee that the ignorance Euthyphron presently displays will not lead him, at some time, to commit the kind of crime that Meletos, again merely "from ignorance," is about to commit here?

I

5D–6E

Socrates as the ironic man wants to learn, since his partner seems "to know"; hence, the question: What sort of thing is piety and impiety? He is seeking, as he adds for the sake of clarification, but seeking in vain what is always the same as itself in all actions, both pious and impious, what is the one form they have in common (μίαν τινὰ ἰδέαν), and what is the opposite of each without admixtures and transitions.

The dialogue moves through three—or, if we like, four—definitions. Even as in the discussion about courage Laches first proposed, instead of a concept, a practical case drawn from his own world of experience, so here does Euthyphron—only to an alarmingly intensified degree. Pious is what I am doing now, is the claim which he then proceeds to expound. In other words, he does not submit his own action to a conceptual standard of piety before which he would have to justify himself; on the contrary, he sets up his own action as the highest, universal norm. The evidence he cites in support of his claim is drawn from the field of popular religion, or, more specifically, from the myth according to which Zeus himself punished his own father. Three things are connected here with each other: first, the formal mistake in the definition; second, the egocentric arrogance of a person who, in typically sophistic fashion, sets himself up as the measure of all things; third, the appeal to a pernicious myth as the basis for human action. Socrates alludes ironically to the last point by expressing his resistance to this kind of blasphemous mythology, adding that this reluctance of his must be the reason for the indictment brought against him by Meletos. Here, then, Euthyphron, who claims "to know things still more wonderful of which the many know nothing" and who "could tell things about the gods which would quite amaze you," moves over into the domain of the many and even into the camp of Meletos —his self-conscious detachment from them notwithstanding.[5] But nobody would be able to make him see this; neither can his egoism be attacked directly. Only the formal mistake can be made clear, and that is what Socrates does. The formal criticism here is more succinct and to the point than in the *Laches*. The definition lacks just what was asked for earlier (5D)—the idea or form itself (αὐτὸ τὸ εἶδος), by virtue of which all particular pious acts are made pious, the one standard (τὴν ἰδέαν) which we must look to (εἰς ἐκείνην ἀποβλέπων) and use as a model (χρώμενος αὐτῇ παραδείγματι) for judging whether any action, "yours or anyone else's," should be called pious.

It has often been asked whether we are dealing here with the "theory of *Ideas* in the strictly Platonic sense," whether with logic or with ontology, i.e., whether the word "idea" has an ontological status "already" or is "still" a logical concept only.[6] But these are distinctions that belong to the conceptual apparatus of the history of philosophy, unknown before Aristotle. He who is here using these words—similar words recur in the *Meno* (72c)[7]—had seen the "form" of virtue and had grasped the difference between the original model and the particular things patterned thereafter. And although his partner does not look into the same depths as Plato's Socrates does, these words suffice to give him a lesson in method. The critique remains strictly formal, but are not factual and formal criticism identical in the respect that anybody who has had this vision of the *Eidos* would not put up such a meaningless definition, nor would he make his own ego the measure of all things, nor would he ascribe wickedness to the gods?

The second definition shows that Euthyphron has learned his formal lesson. "Piety is what is dear to the gods" (τὸ τοῖς θεοῖς προσφιλὲς ὅσιον, 6E). This is more satisfactory from a formal point of view; it corresponds to the definition of courage, in the *Laches*, as "perseverance of the soul." Ironically, Socrates makes a great to-do about it. As understood by him, this indeed is "the answer he wanted." Piety coincides with the good or the perfect. In Euthyphron's sense, however, the new formulation is only a substitute for the old and it says nothing. It is based upon a false conception of the gods who live in discord with each other—in discord, as Euthyphron admits, over what is just and unjust, beautiful and ugly, good and evil. But if the gods disagree with each other, then what is dear to one is disliked by another, what some gods love others hate, and what is pious may also be impious. The logical contradiction expresses the contradiction inherent in the popular beliefs about the gods.

It does not disturb Euthyphron that chaos threatens at this point. He believes that the gods live in discord; he simply decrees, quite arbitrarily, that they agree with him in the conduct of his own affair (8B). He has expressed his own action in the form of a general statement as if he had learned that the standard must be a general norm, not a particular case. It is this norm which Socrates proceeds to analyze. Even though men—and, as Euthyphron thinks, the gods, too—may differ over questions of fact, i.e., over whether a particular action is just or unjust, they agree on the moral principle that wrongdoing deserves punishment. Here, then, is the first bit of solid ground amid the chaos. We may be in doubt as to what is a just or an unjust act in a given particular case, but the conviction that there is such a thing as justice and injustice cannot be shaken, nor can the necessary connection between wrongdoing and punishment. Now Euthyphron is asked to give a criterion by which we can decide whether his particular case corresponds to the general principle. In other words, one must not, as Socrates indicates, take one's own action

as the norm, but must instead measure it against a norm. Euthyphron, however, can only repeat his previous assertions. The
absurd consequence that what the gods love is also hated by the
gods remains unshaken and bars the way to an understanding of
what it means to be pious. What actually prevents this understanding is a false conception of the nature of the gods.

It seems as if the contradiction can be removed only by adding
that all the gods must agree. "All the gods"—this phrase insistently recurs on the lips of Socrates (9A–D). Euthyphron previously (8B) had conceded such agreement among the gods as
the exception applicable to his own particular case. Now, then,
compelled by Socrates to expand the definition, he states : "What   IIb
all the gods love is pious" (ὃ ἂν πάντες οἱ θεοὶ φιλῶσιν, 9E). But   9E–11E
does this really help as long as we subscribe to a false view about
the gods ? How would we determine whether they agree or not ?
And would not any agreement in one case threaten to fall apart
in another ? Or should we interpret the expression "all the gods"
to mean that there cannot be any contradiction in the nature of the
gods ? What do we know about the nature of the gods ? These
questions are not posed directly. Instead, the definition is attacked, as at the earlier stage, from a formal point of view only.
What is pious, or holy, is loved because it is pious; it is not
pious, or holy, because it is loved. Thus, our definition—whether
in its simple or in its expanded form—has not disclosed the
essence (οὐσία) of the thing, but only a certain quality (πάθος τι)
belonging to this essence (11A). In other words, the definition
is logically defective.[8] It will not do to appeal to a remote authority as the basis for the human attitude of piety, especially since
the dialogue has shown what sort of unholy state of mind prevails in the region where someone like Euthyphron dares speak
of the gods as a person who knows their nature.

Since Euthyphron does not know how to go on or since, as   III
Socrates remarks ironically, he keeps a superior silence, Socrates   11E–14C
himself proposes the third definition, in which piety does not
disappear in the unknown, but reappears as a human attitude.
First, it is said in general that "whatever is pious is just," even
as in the *Protagoras* (331A *et seq.*) the pious and the just are
shown to be the same or very similar. That was not so strange

a view for a man in the Greek world as it is for us.[9] For both
modes of conduct—piety and justice—have their place in society
or in the state. We practice justice, as is said in the popular formulation of the *Thrasymachus*, when we render to each his due.
This kind of conduct as it applies to the sacred sphere was the
point of departure in the present dialogue, and the idea of justice
came up again in the critical discussion of the second definition.
Now we define the meaning of piety within the larger area of
what is just by distinguishing, as in a logical exercise, between
the more general and the more specific concept. Thus, we get
the first definition that is formally correct: "Piety is that part
of justice which attends to the care of the gods" (τὸ περὶ τὴν τῶν
θεῶν θεραπείαν, 12E) or, in a modified form, that part which attends "to the service of the gods" (ἡ τοῖς θεοῖς ὑπηρετική, 13D).
It was quite customary, and inoffensive, to speak of the "care"
of the gods, and Plato himself does so elsewhere (*Alcibiades
Major* 122A; *Republic* 427B; *Laws* 930E). Why, then, here the
subtle distinction?[10] Socrates shows Euthyphron that "care"
means to improve someone, or to make someone better. We can
improve horses, dogs, and cattle. (Perhaps the reader will add:
human beings, too, can be improved, and this is the essential
task.) Gods cannot be made better, however, as both men agree
without asking for or giving a justification. Yet, is it not self-
evident that gods cannot be made better for the simple reason
that they are "good"?

If I put myself at someone's service, I work for his purpose.
What, then, is the work of the gods that I help to promote in
serving them? We note that we are close to a profound insight.
Later (15A) Socrates will express this truth—which has a new
and deeper meaning for Plato—quite simply and in a Homeric
spirit, as it were: "All that is good for us the gods have given
us." This must be read in the context of replacing "care" by
"service." Much later, in the *Republic*, we shall be initiated into
the radiating power of the highest good. In the *Timaeus*, we shall
see the demiurge at work. Because he is "good" he can only
create what is perfect and well ordered. Finally, in the *Laws*
(716c), we shall learn that God is the "measure of all things"
for man—and the word "measure" must be read in its full Greek

meaning. It connotes not only an outward spatial limitation, but an inner structure and order as well. From the beginning of the present dialogue we have been alarmed by—and Socrates has opposed—the lack of order and measure among the gods as they are conceived by Euthyphron. Now we begin (although as yet vaguely) to see behind the Socratic question, "What is the work of the gods?" a kind of order in which man, resembling God according to human powers (*Theaetetus* 176c), becomes a servant of divine action. Yet, when this very question about what the gods do is asked, Euthyphron gives up. He says that they do "many and beautiful things" (13E 12); "it is a big task to grasp all these things accurately" (14A 11). We know that he would have to entertain an entirely different conception of the deity in order to be capable of a reply in the Socratic sense. And when there is no reply to the question by Socrates, "What, then, is the chief thing among the many and beautiful things that the gods do?" we may surmise that Plato's Socrates would have replied: "the good." We also know that this good for him occupies the highest place and that in the presence of Euthyphron it cannot be discussed without being misunderstood and desecrated.[11]

At this high point of the dialogue where, in the words of Socrates, his partner comes "very close" (14c), the movement goes down again and, in a strange curve, turns back to the beginning. The loose talk by which Euthyphron tries to define the meaning of "service" reveals the kind of unholy piety that seeks reassurance for one's mundane welfare through prayer and sacrifice. This attitude is summed up in the last definition proposed by Socrates: Piety, then, would be "a knowledge of what to ask of and what to give to the gods" (ἐπιστήμη ἄρα αἰτήσεως καὶ δόσεως θεοῖς ὁσιότης, 14D). This is not really a new definition, but as the components of a mathematical equation may be transformed, so the previous definition about serving the gods is transformed from a Socratic to a Euthyphronic version—and hereby exposed to absurdity. "Knowledge"—that is still something genuinely Socratic. But if we stop to think what *episteme* meant to Socrates, we are all the more alarmed at what happens to this lofty meaning here. It is reduced to the low level on which the relationship between man and god is a kind of business transaction (ἐμπορικὴ

IV
14c–15c

τέχνη), and on which we are doing the gods a favor by observing religious rituals, so that, indeed, piety is again "what is dear to the gods." Thus, we have come back to the earlier definition, except that the wording (κεχαρισμένον instead of προσφιλές) expresses still more clearly the base attitude of mind behind it.

This circle is the basic movement in the conversation between the two partners, and this is called to our attention by means of a special decorative touch. Between the second and third definitions, there is a playful interlude (11b–d). The *logos*, Euthyphron complains, refuses to stay put where we have brought it to a standstill. This, it seems, is the fault of Socrates, who has inherited the skill of his ancestor Daidalos. It was said in praise of the sculptures of Daidalos that they did not remain fixed where they were, but were always on the move; so is it with the *logoi* in Socrates' hands. This is an amusing metaphor for the ceaseless labor of examining himself and others as performed by Socrates. But he makes it quite clear that, for him, this endless movement of the *logos* is not an end in itself. "I would give anything in the world to have the *logoi* stay put and fixed on the spot." That is the difference from the sophistic movement for its own sake; that is the outlook upon eternal being. At the end of the dialogue (15b), Socrates comes back once more to this jest, which is deeply serious: You are much more artful than I and Daidalos, for you contrive not only that the *logoi* move, but that they move in a circle.

What, then, is the meaning of this circular movement? We may look at other dialogues to which the *Euthyphro* is related. The *Laches* and the *Charmides* first present courage and moderation, respectively, as natural dispositions and then carry these concepts to a point where they merge with the comprehensive concept of *arete* as such. The *Thrasymachus* moves in the opposite direction; the enemy of justice is attacked and his position is annihilated. The *Euthyphro* steers a middle course, as it were. The professional seer does not have piety as the general has courage or the youth has *sophrosyne*, but neither is he the open enemy of piety as the tyrannical Sophist is the avowed enemy of justice. In the case of Euthyphron, the opposite is hidden behind the appearance of his alleged piety, but this opposite remains hidden. Thus, it is possible neither to progress from the appearance to the depth nor to attack the avowed attitude of mind openly. The symbol of the circle suggests that, in such a situation, it is impossible to catch sight of what is essential. If we are to see the essential, a radical break out of the circle must be made (as later in the *Meno*). As long as we have not made this break, we remain on the same level as the "unjust" man depicted in the *Republic* (II 361E *et seq.*) who is using his unending accumulation of wealth in order to offer splendid sacrifices and gifts to the gods so that he may be more "beloved" by them than the just man who is poor. Only after making the break do we know that no man's character remains hidden from the gods and that the good man is "beloved" and the bad man "hated" by them (*Republic* X 612E). Toward the end of his life, Plato will reinforce this theme emphatically. The moderate (σώφρων) and the just man are dear to God, for they are like him. Only the good man may offer prayers and gifts. From a person whose soul is unclean neither a good man nor a god will accept a gift. Thus, for the unholy man the great efforts expended on observing religious rituals are meaningless and in vain. For the pious they are most appropriate (*Laws* IV 716c *et seq.*).

At the very end of the *Euthyphro*, Plato refers once more to the two indictments mentioned at the beginning, the case of Euthyphron against his father and the case of Meletos against Socrates.[12] This does more than bring the work as a whole to an aesthetic completion. "You knew what piety is; otherwise you would not have brought this charge against your father. . . . And here I wanted to show Meletos that I had been instructed by Euthyphron in the knowledge about the divine so that I would no longer act, at random, from ignorance, but become a better person in what remains of my life." We cannot miss the profound irony in these last words of Socrates or the irony displayed by Plato in juxtaposing the two indictments. "To lead a better life" —this is the note upon which Socrates concludes the conversation. Thus there emerges, behind the search for a definition, the human agent whose life must be based upon reverence toward the deity. And at the end of the inconclusive chain of definitions, there looms the moral command and the existential commitment of the self.

v
15D–16A

Lysis

PRELUDE
203A–206E

SOCRATES is going "from the Academy straight to the Lyceum," i.e., from gymnasium to gymnasium. This is impressed upon us twice. And he is following "the outside road which is close under the walls." This means he avoids both the route through the city where he might be detained and the longer detour across country where the trees have nothing to say to him (*Phaedrus* 230D). We can easily imagine what he is looking for in the gymnasium. Yet, he is diverted or lets himself be diverted: he is called into a palaestra or "wrestling school." Someone (a certain Mikkos) is even "teaching" there; after Socrates has entered, however, no further word is heard about this "Mr. Small."

To begin with, we witness, at the entrance to the palaestra, the exchange with the two young aristocrats Ktesippos and Hippothales. Each has his own favorite boy inside. For the former it is his nephew Menexenos, for the latter it is Lysis. From Ktesippos we learn about the extravagant fashion in which the fop Hippothales is spoiling, not educating, his beloved Lysis. Ktesippos, of a more sober spirit, will handle Menexenos differently—a first hint at differences in rank among the participants. As a matter of fact, these differences are soon shown more directly; for, whereas Menexenos simply sits down by the side of Socrates and Ktesippos, Hippothales hides behind the group of spectators so that he can observe Lysis secretly (207B). This corresponds to the artificial manner in which Hippothales plans to draw Lysis into a conversation with Socrates, instead of simply calling him (206CD). Thus, it is anything but chance that, in the

Phaedo (59ʙ), both Ktesippos and Menexenos are mentioned
specifically among those who are present at the death of Socrates.
And Menexenos—what sense does it make to think of a name-
sake?—listens, in the dialogue named after him, while Socrates
delivers his encomium upon Athens. Lysis and Hippothales, however, do not appear again in any other work of Plato.

After Socrates has joined the two young men outside the palaestra, Ktesippos turns his comic vexation at Hippothales into
a comic indictment. Socrates, it is understood, is to be the judge;
he expressly claims to be an expert in matters of love (204ʙᴄ).
Then he takes up the judicial role: "Show yourself" (ἐπίδειξαι,
204ᴇ)! "How must one behave toward a beloved friend" (205ᴀ)?
The criterion for judging is clear. It is the state of mind (διάνοια),
not this or that particular action, that determines the value of
the relationship. Hippothales is shown that his way of flattering
the boy and of paying homage to him and his family—in the
manner of Pindaresque poetry, which is really out of date—
merely serves to make himself ridiculous and the young boy
proud and arrogant. Hippothales, in short, is shown to be harming himself in this kind of pursuit. Socrates confines himself to
this appeal to self-interest, and this indeed is enough to make
Hippothales beg for advice on what to say and how to act in
order to win the love of his friend (206ᴄ). Thus, it is not only
Ktesippos who calls upon Socrates to be the judge of Hippothales;
the latter himself puts his case into the hands of Socrates. Moreover, a principal objective pursued in the dialogue has come to
life: the relationship of love and education.

The dialogue itself takes place inside the palaestra, or, more
specifically, in the dressing room. The ensuing dialectical "wrestling match" and the intellectual "undressing" correspond to
this concrete setting. We catch a glimpse of Plato's concept of
the symmetry of physical and spiritual form.[1] Socrates will talk
first with Lysis and then with Menexenos; but before these talks
begin, Plato shows the two boys sitting together for a moment
until Menexenos is called away, not to return until later. This
is more than stage management. The two boys are sitting by
the side of Socrates, who asks them what they are quarreling
about. It turns out that although they may disagree on many

MAIN
DIALOGUE
206ᴇ–222ᴅ
PREPARATION
206ᴇ–207ᴅ

things, they agree on one thing—that they are "friends." Even
as Charmides first is shown as embodying *sophrosyne* in its natural form before the philosophical discussion about the nature of
sophrosyne begins, so the two boys here are shown as friends in
the natural, ordinary sense of the word before friendship (*philia*)
becomes the subject of philosophical discussion. In the *Charmides*,
it was enough to have one person because *sophrosyne* is a characteristic of the individual. Friendship, however, involves two persons; hence, we need both Lysis and Menexenos. We see in the
Lysis a rich scene of "friendships" arranged in peculiar stages:
the natural stage is shown in the friendship between the two
boys; a higher stage (on which the dangers inherent in the relationship are seen to be increasing) is depicted in various shades
through the love of Hippothales for Lysis and Ktesippos for
Menexenos; finally, the highest stage of love is shown in the
service of *paideia* as displayed by Socrates in his relationship to
the two boys and to Ktesippos and Hippothales as well.

ɪ
207ᴅ–210ᴇ   The conversation with Lysis is adapted to the naïve understanding of the boy. "To do what one likes or wills" (the frequently recurring theme) seems to represent the supreme form
of human happiness. Socrates takes for granted that it applies
to Lysis, for the formula expresses a natural desire in man. At
its greatest intensity—and here the danger inherent in this natural view is revealed—it is also the principle invoked (in the
Gorgias) by Kallikles, the man of violence. Lysis must admit
that precisely those who love him and wish him to be happy for-
bid him to do all sorts of things; in short, they do not permit
him "to do as he likes"—not because he is young, but because
he is ignorant. If this ignorance were removed, everything might
be permitted, for presumably he would then know what he should
"will," whether in the family or in the life of the city. Reading
and writing are the first steps in this learning process; political
action is the final goal; and the criterion for action is knowledge.

This analysis, complete in itself, is linked with the phenomenon
of *philia*. At first, the fact that the young boy is not permitted to
do as he pleases seems to be incompatible with the love his parents have for him (207ᴇ). In the end, however, it is clear that
these restrictions are precisely an expression of parental love

(210c *et seq.*). Thus, love and education—ultimately, *paideia* toward a political life—are revealed in their dialectical interaction. He who truly loves educates. For this reason, Socrates' brief conversation with Lysis can now be used as a model to show the right way of treating young boys in contrast to the wrong way of spoiling them, which is the way of Hippothales. In revealing the relationship between love and knowledge, love and education, this section provides the indispensable foundation for the conceptual structure of the dialogue as a whole.[2]

The conversation with Menexenos (who returns at the right moment) has a different tone. It is eristic.[3] Plato assigns to Menexenos—both Socrates and Lysis call him a "sharp debater" (ἐριστικός)—a higher degree of consciousness and intellectual flexibility than to Lysis.

The eristic aspects derive from the ambiguities inherent in the crucial term *philos*. It may be used both in a passive sense and in an active sense. It also may be used both as a noun (to be somebody's friend) and as an adjective (to be dear to someone, or to be loved by someone). One purpose of this analysis is, obviously, to bring out these verbal ambiguities. Moreover, in addition to warning against these linguistic dangers, the analysis serves also to clarify substantial problems that are concealed by the ambiguities of language.

The initial question is whether love is mutual or one-sided. If we follow Menexenos, who is convinced that it is mutual, we run into an antinomy. (1) If only one person loves the other, then both are "friends" and "dear" to each other. (2) If they do not love each other mutually, then neither is a "friend" or "dear" to the other. The two statements are complementary in substance, but they are a formal contradiction that seems to refute the view of Menexenos from which they are derived. If we take, as Socrates does, the case of one-sided love, then it follows, both from the active and from the passive use of the word, that it is impossible that one be hated by, or be the enemy of, one's beloved or that one be dear, or friend, to a person who is hated, i.e., one's enemy. In summing up, Socrates concludes that neither lovers nor beloved, nor both together, can be friends or dear to each other. How do we find our way out of this confused tangle?

For Menexenos it is self-evident that friendship must be mutual. This is the point of view of the naïve, uncritical friendship represented by the two boys. Socrates, however, cites some evidence from experience which shows that love may be one-sided. Love of material things is a less important matter than the one-sided love of parents toward their immature children; most important is the case (facetiously mentioned in passing) of the "love of wisdom which wisdom does not return." We must recall the live point of departure for this whole discussion. Socrates proclaimed with great emphasis that, from his youth on, he had pursued nothing more passionately than his aim to acquire and possess friends and that he was quite amazed that the two boys had come by this possession so quickly and easily. Evidently, we must see their preliminary, natural form of friendship in contrast and ironic tension to the highest form as envisaged by Socrates. He almost says that the friendship he is seeking is something very difficult to acquire, but that it must achieve the same kind of reciprocity realized so easily (all too easily) in the early stage of youthful friendships. In the first eristic antinomy where both statements point toward recognizing this reciprocity, this early stage is used as a model for the perfect type of friendship pursued but perhaps never achieved, even by Socrates. Through the paradoxes resulting from the assumption that friendship may be one-sided, we learn that such one-sidedness (as we find it frequently in life) has a tendency to break down or to become a reciprocal relationship. Finally, the brief, ironic reference to the "lovers of wisdom whom wisdom does not love in return" points to the possibility of true philo-sophy, i.e., love of *sophia* that is returned by *sophia*. Thus, the dialectical dissection of the concept of *philia* not only leads to an awareness of linguistic ambiguities, which we cannot overlook without risk; it also provides an insight into differences of value inherent in the concept and therefore suggests an upward movement from the lower forms of love to Socratic love—a love perhaps never completely achieved even by Socrates himself.

III
213D–222D   The conversation with Lysis was a simple inquiry into the connection between *philia* and *paideia*; the conversation with Menexenos, an eristic exercise revealing different levels of value

in the domain of *philia*. Now the conversation with both of them continues in a highly dialectical zigzag.

III 1
213D–215C

Socrates cites a statement by poets such as Homer and some natural philosophers according to which "like associates with like." The statement is to be qualified not to mean that the bad associate with the bad.[4] But this is only an apparent restriction since the bad are not really "equal," i.e., balanced, within themselves and still less vis-à-vis others: they are without equilibrium. Thus, the statement ascribed to the poets and natural philosophers is a hint (αἰνίττονται) that good associates with good, so that being a "friend" and being "good" are practically synonymous.

III 1a
213E–214E

As soon as the statement has risen to such paradoxical heights, it is overthrown. "And yet . . ." says Socrates, turning the discussion in a different direction. Friendship rests on a need; but the like can neither improve nor harm the like; the good sufficient (ἱκανός) unto himself needs nothing. Thus, the good cannot be friend to the good, nor the like to the like.

III 1b
214E–215C

On the other hand, the poet Hesiod also teaches us that like must be the enemy of the like, whereas those who are unlike need each other. This thesis, too, finds support in natural philosophy and in ordinary experience, where the case of the ignorant person who loves the man with knowledge (τὸν μὴ εἰδότα ἀγαπᾶν τὸν εἰδότα καὶ φιλεῖν, 215D) has special significance.

III 2
215C–216B

III 2a
215C–216A

But this thesis, too, is quickly overthrown by an "eristic" argument, as Socrates himself admits, according to which the enemy would have to be the friend of the friendly and *vice versa*. Thus, neither is like a friend or dear to the like nor are opposites dear to each other. It appears as if both theses have been discarded, but this only seems to be the case; in truth, these distinctions serve as a system of co-ordinates, as it were, drawn through reality to clarify a complex structure.

III 2b
216A–216B

Menexenos and Lysis—Socrates and Lysis as well—meet as like with like. They are like each other; otherwise, they would not come together. A pseudo-likeness is ruled out. If they were both "bad," there would be between them no friendship or, at best, only the kind of friendship as among wolves. In other words, what they have in common is a desire for the good. In the language of myth, a god makes them be friends (214A) as, on the higher level of the myth in the *Phaedrus*, the love of two human beings is due to their common attendance in the cortege of the god. In speaking about the good, however, we must not forget that perfect goodness is beyond the power of man. If human beings were capable of such goodness, there would not be the need that attracts Lysis to Socrates and Socrates—in a more mysterious and puzzling way—to Lysis. Thus, we have come to the second thesis. In addition to being alike, Socrates and Lysis are also quite unlike each other. The one knows; the other is ignorant. Yet this contrast, again, is valid only in a peculiar and ironic involvement; for if it were absolute, so that one were completely ignorant and the other had perfect knowledge, friendship would again be impossible.[5]

III 3
216B–221D

III 3a
216B–220B

The reality of life is not as rigid, it appears, as the two theses between which it moves, and their refutation is not as radical as it seemed to be. The goal of love, to be sure, is the good—or the beautiful, for, in the words of the proverb, "what is beautiful is loved." The person who loves, however, is "in between, neither good nor bad" (220D 6). Thus, the condition between knowledge and ignorance is the locus of friendship as it is the place of philosophy in the speech by Diotima (*Symposium* 204AB). Moreover, friendship and philosophy are inseparable as they are embodied by Socrates and Lysis. Lysis loves Socrates. Socrates loves truth. Love tends upward.

We must add something else. That which is "neither good nor bad" loves what is good "because of the presence of evil," that is, when evil is present in what is neither good nor bad but has not taken complete possession of it.[6] This is stated again as a provocative paradox; yet the meaning behind it is also made quite explicit. He who is neither wise nor foolish loves wisdom— i.e., is a *philo-sophos*—and he does so because he feels the presence of ignorance. Objectively speaking, Lysis, not overcome by stupidity but hovering between being wise and foolish, desires wisdom because he does not have it; subjectively speaking, he loves Socrates. The same relationship is repeated on a higher level. Socrates himself is not a wise man but a lover of wisdom, because he lacks perfect wisdom which, according to the *Sym-*

posium (203 *et seq.*) and the *Phaedrus* (246D), is a prerogative
of the gods.

A final addition must be made in order to see "love" (φίλον)
in the fullness of its manifold relations. Love as such is nothing.
A "reason" (διά τι) is as necessary a part of it as a goal or object
(ἕνεκά του) is.[7] Thus, love is "intentional"; and, we must add,
love is for the sake of the good and the beloved (ἕνεκα τοῦ ἀγαθοῦ
καὶ φίλου).

Here the dialogue rises to its highest level. For as soon as we
catch sight of this goal, we realize that there is a hierarchical series
of goals leading upward to the "first object of love" (πρῶτον
φίλον) which is not loved for the sake of anything else and of which
all other objects of love are but "copies" or mere words as compared with reality. In this supreme love all other loves and af-
fections (φιλίαι) of man terminate (τελευτῶσιν, 220B 3). Thus the
highest goal of love becomes visible.[8]

The pointed thesis that what is "neither good nor bad, the
in between, because of the (presence of) evil, is the friend of the
good for the sake of goodness and love" (219AB) has done its
work, because it enabled us to perceive the "highest love" which
is at the same time "the good."[9] Live dialectics, however, does
not tolerate any dogmatic thesis. Thus, this thesis is now rejected
from the very perspective of the highest insight to which it gave
access. What is "truly loved" is loved not for the sake of anything else, but for its own sake. Nevertheless, in the case of a
particular act of desire or love, it is still legitimate to recognize
that the act aims at an ultimate goal superior to the immediate
object of desire. Only in the case of the highest and most perfect
love, there is no longer this distinction between the good that
we desire and the good for the sake of which we desire it. Thus,
the knowledge of the "first love" cancels (ἀπήλλακται, 220B)
the notion of a final cause; it does so because this final cause coincides with the highest object of desire.

Meanwhile, the tearing down of the rigid thesis continues:
now we also reject the notion that there must be "something
bad" as the "reason," or the efficient cause (διά τι), for the desire of the good. This notion makes sense in the world of human
experience. But when we perceive and love the highest object,

III 3b
220B–221D

the *Eidos*, "for its own sake," if only from afar, then it is obvious that the good cannot depend on evil. Otherwise, the good would no longer exist when evil is overcome. The absolute nature of the good, therefore, cancels the need for evil as an efficient cause for the good.[10]

Thus, if we now learn that the great definition of "love" (φίλον) that moved upward to the vision of the "first love" seems to be nothing but mere chatter (ὕθλος), because both the final cause and the efficient cause have been thrown out, this is intended to make us see the absolute nature of "the beloved and the good." What looks like a refutation is a clarification. The difference between the mixed states characteristic of ordinary human life, for which the original statement is valid, and the realm of absolute essences for which it is not valid could not be shown more effectively than in this dialectic.

III 4
221D–222D
III 4a
221D–222B

The ceaseless dialectic comes to a rest once more in the last definitive statement of the dialogue. Efficient and final cause are given new meanings; the former as desire (ἐπιθυμία), the latter as the congenial or the akin (οἰκεῖον); for desire derives from a need (ἐνδεές), and there is a relationship between a person in need and the object of his need such that they are complementary or reciprocally congenial. We must note, in particular, that this concept of the congenial has both a personal and an objective side in the kind of interpenetration that seemed to us elsewhere[11] to be the special characteristic of the nature of the Platonic *Eros*. First, there is the personal side. Love is based upon a kinship of the "soul," and he who loves truly must, because of this kinship, find his love returned. This, we may note, throws a new light on the problem discussed in the first conversation with Menexenos. It is also worth noting how differently the participants react to these conclusions. When the notion of congeniality is applied to the love between human beings, Menexenos assents, whereas Lysis remains silent. This shows the difference in their experiences. But when Socrates goes on to talk about the true love and the reciprocity of true love, both boys are reluctant to give their assent, whereas Hippothales blushes in delight. The reader knowing Hippothales, however, will look around and recognize, not far off, who is "the true and not only the counterfeit lover."[12]

Next, there is the objective side of this concept of the congenial. Earlier we learned that the goal of love was the good and the beautiful. Now we find, instead, that we must necessarily love that which is congenial by nature. Thus, the question arises whether the good is not the "congenial," and the reciprocal relationship between the soul and the *Agathon* is felt: the soul in need of the good, but at the same time congenial and akin to it.

That this interpretation is not too farfetched becomes clear when we look at the end of the dialogue where the last thesis, that love intends the "congenial," is dialectically dissected and refuted in a manner characteristic of the *Lysis* as a whole. The "congenial" is first identified with the like or the similar (ὅμοιον), and we are back at the first "refutation" of the third conversation: that like is friend of the like. Next, the congenial is interpreted as a relative term. For good people it means the good is congenial, whereas for bad people, the bad is congenial. This brings us back to the other thesis, also refuted previously, according to which the bad can be friend to the bad. There remains only the third possibility of equating the "congenial" with "the good."[13] From this it follows that only the good can be friend to the good. But this, too, we "refuted"—or, rather, "we thought we had refuted."[14]

III 4b
222B–222D

Thus, all these theses are refuted; yet all of them also have a degree of validity. The first, to be sure, is inherently ambiguous and is recognized as such when converted into the second. If we move upward to the third thesis, however, we are shown once more the kinship and mutual interdependence of Socrates and Lysis, of the soul and the good.

CONCLUSION
222E–223B

The place this dialogue occupies in the body of Plato's works is evaluated differently according to two major tendencies. On the one hand, interpreters have seen its intimate connection with other dialogues on the theme of love, and the *Lysis* is said to be either a worthy dialectical counterpart to the others or simply a satellite to the *Symposium* not deserving any special consideration.[15] On the other hand, looking at the total structure of the philosophical work, observers have been impressed by its kinship with the aporetic dialogues, and especially by its close affinity with the *Charmides*.[16] This correspondence with the aporetic dialogues is made explicit in the very last words, ". . . and we have not been able to discover what is a friend." In accepting this second aspect, there is danger that we may lose sight of the kinship of the *Lysis* with the *Symposium*. Actually, the two types of perspective belong together.[17] The *Lysis* shows the philosophical *Eros* on the level of Plato's early works.

That *Eros* is behind *philia*—"When friendship grows passionate," it is said in the *Laws* (837A), "we call it love"—is clear from the very beginning of the *Lysis*.[18] The first scene communicates the atmosphere of Athenian παιδικὸς ἔρως. We meet the two beautiful boys who have such unlike friends: Hippothales who makes himself quite ridiculous, and Ktesippos who is sarcastically critical of Hippothales and more sensible from a social point of view. Opposed to both, there is Socrates as the "genuine lover" (γνήσιος ἐραστής) because he imparts to the boys a lesson in loving education. If somebody says that this is "merely dramatic setting" which has nothing to do with the "intellectual content" of the dialogue, he cuts straight through the living reality of the whole. For it is not the case that the erotic atmosphere is confined only to the frame of the dialogue. In the discussion whether friendship is mutual or not, we learn at the beginning that the lover is sometimes not loved in return by the object of his love (οἷόν που ἐνίοτε δοκοῦσι καὶ οἱ ἐρασταὶ πάσχειν πρὸς τὰ παιδικά, 212B). And at the very end, Socrates shows that the "true lover" must necessarily be loved in return by the "object of his love" (ἀναγκαῖον ἄρα τῷ γνησίῳ ἐραστῇ καὶ μὴ προσποιήτῳ φιλεῖσθαι ὑπὸ τῶν παιδικῶν, 222A). This is a climax of the dialogue, especially when we read the general formula in the light of the participants present. The terms "friendship" and "love" are interchangeable throughout; e.g., Socrates says at the beginning that he is pursuing the objective of acquiring friends with passionate love (πρὸς τὴν τῶν φίλων κτῆσιν πάνυ ἐρωτικῶς ἔχω, 211E), and, toward the end, he lists "love, friendship, and desire" (ὅ τε ἔρως καὶ ἡ φιλία καὶ ἡ ἐπιθυμία, 221E) as closely akin and overlapping concepts.

In the movement of ideas, too, there is a close connection with the *Symposium*. In the third conversation of the *Lysis*, friendship is said to be a striving of like toward like (see III 1 above), then, antithetically, a striving of unlike toward unlike (III 2);

and this desire in each case is attributed to nature (in the one case with an explicit reference to "those who speak and write about nature and the universe," 214B). At the end of this part (III 4a), friendship is related to what is congenial or akin. In all these respects we are reminded of the *Symposium*, where Eryximachos, the natural scientist, interprets the relationship of love in terms of like and unlike (186B *et seq.*) and Agathon interprets it in terms of like and like (195B), and where the concept of the congenial or akin is rendered in mythical language by Aristophanes (193CD). A significant part of the great movement characteristic of the *Symposium* is the fact that Socrates takes this last notion over; that is, he does not reject it, as is sometimes said, but instead he elevates it to the level of "the good" (205E). In the *Symposium*, a work of Plato's maturity, all these levels are clearly set off from each other. But the same movement from the congenial to "the good" is present in the *Lysis*—only in the latent, aporetic form of an early dialogue.

Moreover, after the two theses about friendship as a relationship between like or unlike are discarded, the *Lysis* shows how that which is "neither good nor bad" loves the good and how, for this reason, neither those who have perfect wisdom ("whether they be gods or men") nor those who are perfect fools love wisdom, but only those who are in between. Similarly, in the *Symposium*, Diotima leaves the one-sided views of Eryximachos and Agathon behind, and the same formulation of "neither-nor" found in the *Lysis* is incorporated, almost verbatim, in her speech (*Lysis* 218A; *Symposium* 204A). In Diotima's speech, however, it is no longer expressed as a thought; for, with the poetic-mythical power characteristic of the later work, this dimension between good and bad, wise and foolish, is converted into the demonic intermediary region where Eros, the lover of wisdom, is ruler, "joining the universe together with itself."[19]

Thus, if the *Lysis* is an initial move upward toward what is "most beloved," the good and the beautiful, then the *Symposium* will render *Eros*, the ascent, and the highest realm itself in the concrete images of myth. In the *Symposium*, the necessary correlation between love for a beautiful human being and love for the *Eidos* will be pursued far more deeply than in the *Lysis* where it is shown in a live context without reaching full consciousness. The *Symposium*, then, repeats at the height of maturity the intellectual themes of the *Lysis*. The latter, in turn, presents the *Eros* of the *Symposium* as a live power, within a context of problems in which a delightful abundance of life is combined with a dissolving dialectical method in the peculiar—and, at times, irritating—way characteristic of Plato's early works. This means that the "great demon" belongs from the very beginning to the dimensions of the universe that Plato explored throughout his life. For him there was no philosophy without friendship or love. This is shown by the place the *Lysis* occupies as an integral part of the group of dialogues that includes the *Laches*, the *Charmides*, the *Thrasymachus*, and the *Euthyphro*.

SEVEN

Hippias Major

IT IS still a matter of dispute whether this dialogue is a genuine work of Plato. Opinions pro and con are about equally divided.[1] At any rate, it is a work of great vitality. As to its chronology, there has been no argument strong enough to prove that, appearances to the contrary, it belongs to Plato's late period or even to a period after Plato's death. According to the verbal statistics of Hans von Arnim, the *Hippias Major* would fall somewhere between the *Symposium* and the *Phaedo*; yet in its structure it belongs not with those mature works, but with the group of aporetic dialogues. Thus, it might be a latecomer or a study from the workshop. Or perhaps future investigations into its language may show that it belongs where we have put it according to its structure.

Socrates meets Hippias. As in the *Euthyphro* and the *Alcibiades Major*, no other person intervenes in the conversation. Only a certain Somebody speaks again and again through Socrates— sharply, and rudely critical, at times, not only of Hippias but also (it seems) of Socrates. Philosopher and Sophist differ radically and in concrete detail with regard to every trait.[2] The Sophist is "beautiful," according to the first words of the dialogue; he is well dressed and shod (291A). His remark, "A man wearing clothes and shoes that are becoming will appear more beautiful, though he be ridiculous" (294A), is meant to strike at Socrates who is barefoot, but presently it turns against the speaker himself. Hippias "has no time," time rarely to come to Athens even; for he is very busy playing big politics (281A *et seq.*). Moreover, he makes big money in his practice as a

1
281A–286C

105

Sophist (281B, 282B *et seq.*, 284B, 300D); yet he regards the
rigorous dialectics of Socrates as "fiddle-faddle," without any
value as compared with the art of rhetoric, which triumphs in
public life; like the mythical Palamedes, he has a comprehensive
knowledge (285BC); and, in contrast to the kind of inexorable
examination as practiced by Socrates, he would like to withdraw
into prepared speeches (286AB, 304AB) or into solitary medita-
tion (295A, 297E).

These are features characteristic of the Sophists. As a class,
moreover, the Sophists are cited by Socrates at the very beginning (282B) in contrast to the sages of old who did not take
money and did not deliver polished speeches and of whom it is
said, against historical evidence, that most of them did not care
about public affairs (281C). This, too, is said in ironic contrast
to the "busy-ness" of Hippias and his like who, in addition to
everything else they do, also pursue political projects. Compared with such "progress" (281D), the attitude of these wise
men of old, who concentrated on one thing and who nevertheless
were much better "statesmen" in Plato's sense of the word, must
seem to have little value indeed.[3]

The political mission of the Sophist, then, is the first thing
depicted in this ironic portrait. The second is his educational
work. Moving about from place to place, he gives lectures—
about what? His subjects include everything, from astronomy
and geometry to mythical prehistory (285D). How remote these
activities are from Socrates we can see from the lecture Hippias
is about to deliver in Athens (286A *et seq.*). Playing the mythical
role of Nestor to whom Neoptolemos comes for advice, the
Sophist launches into a series of exhortations designed to urge
his young listeners on to doing beautiful works.[4] The dialectical
examination by Socrates provides the critique from within—a
formal critique, because this kind of polished speech cannot perform any educational work, and a substantial critique, for it will
be shown that Hippias does not know anything about the nature
of the beautiful, and, hence, can know nothing about doing "beautiful works."

In fact, even in this prelude, Socrates is ironically critical of
the educational work of the Sophist. He cites the case of the

Spartans who do not pay Hippias any money and do not entrust their sons to him. That, Socrates asserts, seems to be incompatible with their highly prized *eunomia*. By the way they treat Hippias, their strict observance of the law is—in jest—shown up as a prejudice. "I agree," says Hippias (285в), "for since you seem to be speaking in my favor I must not oppose you"—which shows that agreement was induced by flattery. The truth is that the "newfangled" methods of education are disavowed by contrast with a system based on traditional loyalties and a closed organic unity. Compared with the ideal state, this system takes second place. Here it is cited—with obvious irony—as evidence against other political communities, especially Athens, that open their gates to the educational experiments of the Sophists. (Plato would not have lived in Sparta and Socrates died as the teacher of Athens.)

The topic of the dialogue will be beauty, but, as is the rule with Plato, we have learned something in advance from the prelude about the problems to be examined later when the strict analysis begins. "Hippias, the beautiful" was the first phrase of the dialogue. We must add that the prelude ends with an outline of the lecture soon to be delivered by the Sophist. This lecture deals with "beautiful endeavors" (καλὰ ἐπιτηδεύματα, 286ΑΒ) and sets up "many and beautiful rules" (ὑποτιθέμενος πάμπολλα νόμιμα καὶ πάγκαλα). The scale of love outlined by Diotima (*Symposium* 210Α *et seq.*) begins with the beauty of the body and ascends to "what is beautiful in endeavors and laws" (τὸ ἐν τοῖς ἐπιτηδεύμασι καὶ τοῖς νόμοις καλόν), moving upward to still higher stages until it has reached the last. Do we not find a hint of this ascent in this passage of the *Hippias Major*, even if only as a shadow play or in the form almost of caricature?

The area of the beautiful is shown from afar, but the distorted form in which it is depicted makes the question regarding the true nature of beauty all the more urgent. Socrates puts the question as if a certain Somebody—and this Somebody will be heard through Socrates as the playful, ironic voice of the dialogue— had questioned him. "What is the beautiful?" or, as he repeats more precisely, "What is the beautiful itself?" By this is meant the beautiful, as Socrates explains, by virtue of which all beauti-

II
286c–293c
II 1
286c–287E

ful things are beautiful, the being of beauty itself as distinct from a particular case. The Sophist, disregarding this clarification, makes three replies, all of which seem to be equally foolish: (1) A beautiful girl is something beautiful (287E). (2) Gold is beautiful (289E). (3) The most beautiful thing for a man is to reach old age rich, healthy, and honored by his countrymen, and these objects of desire are expanded upon still further (291D). It is obvious that Hippias, instead of defining the nature of the thing, wrongly equates the beautiful with what he likes. In formal terms, this mistake is expressed in the logical defects of the definitions. But when we examine these defects critically and submit—cautiously, to be sure—to the guidance of Socrates, we find a way that leads beyond them.

II 2
287E–293C
II 2a
287E–289D

The first reply refers to somebody or something that may be judged beautiful or not, depending upon our standards of comparison. In his critique[5] Socrates makes his point so clearly that Hippias cannot miss it. We are inquiring into what is always beautiful, into "the beautiful as such, through which all other things become beautiful—if this form (εἶδος) is added" (289D). We cannot fail to see what the term *Eidos* is aiming at; yet, as in the *Euthyphro*, it is not in the spirit of Plato to distinguish between the "logical concept" and the "theory of *Ideas*" and to speculate whether Plato is "still" using the term in the former sense and has "not yet" progressed to the latter.[6]

II 2b
289D–291C

The second reply is not merely a variation upon the first. (It is this *only* in the sense that, for a person as avaricious as Hippias, "gold" is always beautiful.) In the critique of Hippias' first reply, Socrates mentioned the "form" that must be "added" or present. Similarly, in the *Phaedo* (100D), he will speak of the "presence or the association of the beautiful as such—or whatever name we may give to this relationship" (προσγενομένη).[7] Hippias, twice repeating this formula of being "added" or "joined to," mistakes it, in his avarice, for monetary "in-come."[8] Moreover, the reference to "form" he has missed so completely that his reply, "gold," designates a material substance, i.e., the very opposite of form. The critique of the certain Somebody citing the gold and ivory statue of Athena by Pheidias points out that it is not the material substance that makes this a beautiful and great work of art, and that a particular object is beautiful by virtue of what is "appropriate" or "fitting" (πρέπει) to it (290D). This avoids the mistake of confusing beauty with some material substance in which it is expressed, but places us in danger of becoming lost in subjective categories. Nevertheless, if only in a negative sense, the absolute nature of the object of our research is indicated. It must be of such a kind that it will never appear to anybody as its opposite (291D). Moreover, the notion of what is "appropriate," "suitable," or "fitting" points in the direction that Socrates himself later will pursue. We must, of course, depart from the crude and obvious manner of the Sophist, as Socrates here conveys ironically by suggesting that a discussion of such lowly things as the "appropriateness" of pot, porridge, or ladle is most "inappropriate" when measured against the beautiful ornaments and the fame of his opponent.

The third reply by Hippias is a definition of broader scope and it is reached on a higher level. He tries to raise the ordinary aspirations of social existence to the level of the beautiful itself, beginning with wealth and ending with a description of splendid burial in the family crypt. Again, the critical Somebody intervenes. Even as a way of life, there is something higher and more beautiful: the heroic life of the sons of the gods and the existence of the gods themselves (292E *et seq.*). Above all, however, as he points out, the reply by Hippias overlooks the beautiful itself, the beauty that must "enter" or be "added" to and be present in particular things so that they may become beautiful—in short, beauty that is always the same and the same for all (292C–E). Thus, according to this certain Somebody, the third definition seems to be of the same kind as the previous two if not more ridiculous.

Yet, the three replies by Hippias also differ from each other, and their significance lies precisely in what distinguishes them from each other. From the beauty of a girl to a beautiful life: is not this transition the same as that, depicted in the prelude, stretching from Hippias, the beautiful, to beautiful strivings and endeavors? And do we not again catch sight of Diotima's way of love, more clearly recognizable now because the certain Somebody speaking through Socrates has pointed toward the *Eidos*

II 2c
291D–293c

of beauty and because this beauty beginning with a stone ascends
to the level of the god (292D 2) and because, above ordinary
civic life, there is a heroic life and, still higher, divine existence
(293A 1)? The direction toward the central area of Plato's
thought is unmistakable.

III
293D–303D

On the third and highest level of the dialogue, it is no longer
Hippias, but the certain Somebody who sets out to define beauty.
But these "definitions," since they invariably correlate the beautiful with another concept, are intelligible only if we keep in
mind what we have learned on the second level of the dialogue.

III 1
293D–294E

This is immediately apparent in the case of the first definition,
taken over from the previous discussion, which equates the beautiful with what is appropriate, becoming, or fitting (τὸ πρέπον).
We are also informed again about the methodological point at
stake: what we are looking for must be such that its presence
will make particular things beautiful. The analysis shows—and
this is, at the same time, the basis for the criticism of this first
definition—that it is the reality, not the appearance, of beauty
that must be produced. Now the notion of what is fitting (πρέπον)
may refer to both; since Hippias cannot distinguish between the
two and since, as a practitioner of the art of dissembling, he puts
the highest value on appearance, this definition fails. Yet, actually, it does clarify the meaning of beauty. For the Greek word
πρέπειν and its derivatives (εὐπρεπής, πρεπώδης) refer to an order
of things and to a harmonious structure in all fields, whether
visible or invisible. Thus, the correlation between what is beautiful and what is fitting is quite familiar to Plato (*Alcibiades
Major* 135B) as well as to Aristotle (*Topics* IV 102^a 6, V 135^a
13).[9] From this it follows that the definition is not cited here
merely to be refuted. On the contrary, the notion of the πρέπον
need not be rejected; it must be clarified so that the possibility
of referring to the mere appearance of beauty is eliminated. By
contrast the character of the *Eidos* as real being emerges all the
more sharply.

III 2
295A–297D

The second definition identifies the beautiful with the "useful" (χρήσιμον) or, in a variation, with the "advantageous"
(ὠφέλιμον).[10] First, what does this variation mean? Useful for
something, we are told, means capable or having the power

(δυνατόν) of producing some effect. Here lurks a danger, as is shown presently when the Sophist appropriates the phrase. To have power in the political world, he says, is most beautiful, indeed. We recall that the political theme has been present from the beginning in the caricature of the busy diplomat. Socrates never loses sight of this political theme. Moreover, through the delight expressed by the Sophist, we begin to see the basic problem of the *Gorgias* taking shape in the distance. In the *Gorgias*, the crucial issue will be put into the radical phrase that power to do evil is not a capacity, or strength, but a weakness. Here, however, the matter is stated more simply. To be capable, or useful, may also be a capacity or usefulness to produce evil. But that which may be used to produce evil cannot possibly be the beautiful. Thus, the beautiful must be useful for producing good; i.e., it must be "advantageous."

As soon as this formulation is adopted, it is overthrown; for the impression should be avoided that this is in any sense a final definition. Yet, the criticism of this definition is as instructive as the road leading toward its adoption. Now we distinguish between cause and effect (γιγνόμενον). Can the beautiful be the cause of the good or the good be an offspring of the beautiful? Since cause and effect—father and son—are necessarily different, the beautiful seems to be different from the good. This conclusion, however, as Socrates points out emphatically (297cD), is unacceptable. Thus, unity of the beautiful and the good, or at least the closest possible link between them, is impressed upon us.

The good as offspring (ἔκγονον) of the beautiful—so it stands for a moment here. We cannot help but anticipate the core of the *Republic* (VI 506D *et seq.*) and the beginning of the myth of creation in the *Timaeus* (29D *et seq.*) : the *Republic*, where Socrates evokes the image of highest perfection, the good, only to leave it at a distance as something inexpressible, while we learn something about the offspring (ἔκγονος) of the good, i.e., the sun, in our world of becoming; the *Timaeus*, where the mythical demiurge who is perfectly good can only create what is most beautiful. What we find in this passage of the *Hippias*, then, is an anticipation (some will say "a reminiscence"[11]) of the realm of transcendence in the *Republic* and the *Timaeus*. Perhaps we are expected to guess that we would come a little closer to the right answer if we said that the beautiful must be the offspring of the good (or the perfect) instead of the good's being the offspring of the beautiful, assuming that any distinction be made between the two. And perhaps we may even see emerging in the distance the *Philebus*, where "the power of the good" (which we are seeking) "takes refuge in the nature of the beautiful" (64E).

At the same time, the sophism that father and son are necessarily different needs to be removed. Cause and effect do differ, indeed; but since all beautiful things are made beautiful "by virtue of beauty," or all tall things made tall "by virtue of tallness" (294B), cause and effect are also similar. (This is a dialectical relationship that is pursued most systematically in the *Parmenides*.) Accordingly, the beautiful, although it cannot be the cause of *the* good, may be the cause of *a* good, not in the realm of being but in the world of becoming, as the frequently repeated expression "becoming" (297AB) brings out clearly. On the other hand, beauty in the realm of being is related to the good in the world of becoming as prototype to copy, and the beautiful and the good approach each other to the point of identity. Yet, beauty in the realm of being also differs from the good in the world of becoming as the prototype differs from its copy. Thus, the form of beauty (and goodness) as cause is different from, and opposed to, everything that is related to it as effect.[12]

In this sense, we carry away from the second definition, in its variations and its refutation, a clear impression of what is the beautiful. Again, as in the first and second stages of the discussion, we are directed toward the wide domain of beauty, beginning with the beauty of the "body" and ending with beautiful "works" and "laws" (τὰ ἐπιτηδεύματα καὶ τοὺς νόμους, 295D 5). Here the anticipation of Diotima's ladder of love is even more evident. The political meaning—in our time we would think of it last— enters directly into the discussion; the impact of the political is reinforced by the fact that Hippias interprets it, falsely and dangerously, in terms of power politics (296A). Viewed as a whole, however, the beautiful—first identified with the fitting (πρέπον) and then with the advantageous (ὠφέλιμον)—belongs to the sphere of the good from which it must not be separated. What binds these related terms together is the typically Greek concept of measure and symmetry (μετριότης καὶ συμμετρία), which plays such an important role in the *Philebus* (64E *et seq.*) in determining the nature of the beautiful and the good.

The third and last Socratic definition reads as follows. Beauty   III 3
is what gives pleasure through the eye and the ear. This desig-   297E–303D
nates another important domain of the beautiful; beautiful "works" and "laws" would not fit into it or, as is suggested (298D), they could be made to fit only with some violence.[13] Yet they, too, are beautiful and pre-eminently so; we are reminded again of Diotima's stages upward. There is also a downward order of rank, for pleasures are here called beautiful. Now as against the pleasures of sight and hearing, there are others, derived from the senses of taste and touch, to which we do not apply the predicate "beautiful." Thus, there appears a deeper stratum of pleasures not reaching up to the region of the beautiful. From afar we can see the complex of problems analyzed in the *Philebus*, where the pleasures of sight and hearing are cited as pure pleasures and the pleasures of smell as less pure, or "less divine" (51A *et seq.*). In the *Hippias*, there arises the question of whether these distinctions and rankings rest merely on subjective prejudice, but there is no answer. It is only made clear that the opinion of the many can never take the place of an objective norm. Viewed as a whole, this third definition serves to reveal a new aspect of the beautiful, i.e., that it is capable of exciting pleasure, and to remind us again of distinctions in rank. Yet it has still another meaning, as we shall see.

The definition will not do because it selects one admittedly important but fragmentary piece from a unified concept (which it is supposed to bring into view). In formal terms, this is shown when it adds up the two sensory criteria, "by sight and by hearing"; for the result is that it would not apply then to a single object grasped by only one of them and not by both. Aristotle, therefore, in the *Topics*, cites this case as an illustration of a faulty definition.[14] Plato adds an extensive criticism that analyzes, partly in strict terms and partly in sophistic procedure, the concepts of "both" (ἀμφότερα), "one or the other" (ἕτερον), and "each of both" (ἑκάτερον), and ends by refuting the definition (303D).

The positive aspect of this critique evidently is this: the two kinds of pleasures must have something in common that distinguishes them from all other pleasures and that we must look toward (εἰς ὃ ἀποβλέποντες) if we wish to call them (but not the others) beautiful. This is not unlike the *Euthyphro* (6E), where we are told to look toward the idea of piety (εἰς ἐκείνην ἀποβλέπων) in order to know whether a particular act may be called pious. It is this "common" element (κοινόν), then, that makes the two kinds of pleasures beautiful (300A). The two sensory criteria, just because they are two, therefore require that there be a kind of being that is common to both (τῇ οὐσίᾳ τῇ ἐπ' ἀμφότερα ἑπομένῃ, 302c). In other words, they serve only as fragmentary or secondary characteristics; they do not give us the essence, which would become visible only beyond them and possibly through them.

IV
303D–304E

With this view the dialogue breaks off, turning back upon itself, as it were, in a bold move. What, then, asks the certain Somebody at the end, is the beautiful that these two kinds of pleasures have in common (τὸ καλὸν τὸ ἐπ' ἀμφοτέραις ταῖς ἡδοναῖς, 303E)? The answer is: the least harmful and the best pleasures — which means that the beautiful is revealed as "advantageous pleasure." Thus, we have come back to the second definition on the Socratic level that was criticized previously. The circle perhaps suggests—it is expressed more clearly and more consciously in the *Euthyphro*—that this way of defining things must miss its mark, especially when we are dealing with a Sophist who thinks he knows and possesses beauty. At the same time, however, what is advantageous and what is pleasant are brought into closest possible connection, and beauty finds its place close to both of them, not to one or the other only.[15]

At the very end, the two men face each other once more. On the one side, we have the Sophist, for whom the whole discussion is nothing but trifling talk. Earlier (301B) he had reproached Socrates, charging that he and his like could not grasp, with their dialectics, the totality of things (τὰ ὅλα τῶν πραγμάτων), the great and continuous material objects of being (μεγάλα καὶ διανεκῆ σώματα τῆς οὐσίας), that instead their *logoi* (arguments) were chopping up every bit of being.[16] This judgment, both arrogant and unintelligent, confuses being with material substance; yet, as a critique of sophistic hairsplitting, it might even be justified to a certain extent—if it did not come from Hippias, the Sophist. As for him, he finally withdraws into one dimension of "the beautiful": to prevail in the political struggle and thus to preserve himself, his possessions, and his kin. The anti-Platonic form of life of the ordinary politician (alluded to previously) reappears here, with the ultimate prospect of the "tyrannical man" as shown most clearly in the *Gorgias*.

On the other side, we have the certain Somebody speaking through Socrates and revealing himself gradually as Socrates' own self. Thus, at the end of the *Hippias Major*, the self emerges in its "existence" even as, in the other aporetic dialogues in search of a definition, in the *Protagoras*, in the *Laches*, and above all in the *Euthyphro*, the existential dimension finally breaks through the series of conceptual constructions and raises them to their true meaning.

"The whole work is filled with abundant hilarity," Schleiermacher said about the *Hippias Major*.[17] Yet, one must listen carefully to what the certain Somebody is saying. To be ignorant about beauty is a condition in which life has no advantage over death, for without a knowledge of "what is beautiful," we cannot pass judgment on the beauty—i.e., *the rightness*—of any statement or action. Thus, what is at stake is not only an "aesthetic" problem. This is also a moral and political problem, and, ultimately, it is a matter of existence. When Hippias throws into the discussion a reference to proceedings in a court of law or public assembly, Socrates takes this reference up with vigor (304B–D). Athenian readers must have been reminded how Socrates, during the trial of the generals in charge of the battle at Arginousai in 406, took a stand against the raging mass of Athenians—and after the year 399 B.C., they would be reminded first of all of Socrates' own trial. So deep is the seriousness of the matter after all the "hilarity." Sophist and philosopher divide in their attitude toward the majesty of the beautiful and the good. To find the path leading to this region is the genuine task of philosophical existence, fraught with danger to one's own life.

The *Lysis* asks: What is love? The *Hippias Major* asks: What is beauty? Both dialogues as works of Plato's early period end in *aporia*. But even as in the *Charmides* (167E 8) it is said (quite casually, and hence all the more convincingly with regard to their intrinsic connection) that "beauty" is the object of *Eros*, so the *Symposium* combines the two lines of thought still separated in the *Lysis* and the *Hippias* by showing that love is the love of the beautiful.[18]

PART II

A Group of Smaller Early Dialogues

Philosopher – Sophist – Poet

EIGHT

Hipparchus

F EW scholars nowadays consider this brief dialogue genuine.[1] Avoiding, to begin with, any discussion of whether it is or not, we may simply refer to Schleiermacher who, "after long and extensive reflections," decided to strike the *Hipparchus* off the list of genuine works of Plato while observing that "the intention which an intelligent reader might read into it is Platonic enough." This is perhaps sufficient reason to view the various themes of thought and form in this dialogue in their relationship to kindred themes in other writings of Plato.

The dialogue takes place between Socrates and a person who remains anonymous. Usually we find this device only in the frame of a Platonic dialogue. Yet the anonymous partner of the *Hipparchus* is not without character.[2] At the very beginning (225AB), he dresses his speech with such fancy ornaments that we realize he is a pupil of the rhetoricians. Socrates teases him about this (225c 6). The young man (225D *et seq.*) replies quite vehemently and "haphazardly as if someone had done him an injustice" (225B 10). But his sharp reply is not accidental or inconsequential; on the contrary, his reproach that Socrates is "deceiving" him (228A 9) is profoundly significant both for the problems and for the artistic form of this minor work.

Socrates opens the dialogue with the genuinely Socratic question: What is . . . ? The little word γάρ—"what then really"— suggests that there was some previous discussion, within the indeterminate circle of this Somebody, about profit seeking or, perhaps, about profit-seeking persons. (This kind of discussion, evidently critical and controversial, probably happened then as now quite frequently.) Next we hear the probing voice of Socrates.[3]

The structure of the dialogue is simple. The discussion deals dialectically, and it seems without a result, with a certain concept. In the middle, however, there is a digression, apparently lacking any connection with the remainder of the dialogue. We get a portrait of the beneficent rule of Hipparchos, the son of Peisistratos. The similarity to the *Alcibiades Major* is obvious, for there in the middle section we find the portrait of an ideal Persian empire which also seems to be unconnected with the rest of the dialogue. In both cases, interpreters have gone astray because they took these ironically iridescent portraits with deadly seriousness, and because, instead of inquiring into the meaning of these sections within the total structure of the dialogues, they thought they were dealing with samples of sophistic erudition.[4]

The concept to be discussed is the "love of gain or profit" (τὸ φιλοκερδές). Whether the *Hipparchus* belongs to the group of early dialogues of Plato or whether it is a work originating within the Platonic circle and especially if it is a later imitation, we gain a better understanding of it when we take a brief survey of the concept of the profit-seeker or the money-lover (φιλοχρήματος, φιλοκερδής). The profit motive inherent in the Greek people as in any other is recognized as dangerous even in early times. Hesiod—the earliest moral voice, speaking out because of his brother's avarice—warns against "evil gain." Solon, another didactic poet, censures the citizens who "following the call of money would destroy the city by their folly" and "are rich because they obey unjust works." The concept of the money-lover conveys, from early times, a sense of excess or of acquisition by evil means. Aristotle frequently alludes to the logical and semantic peculiarity, which also plays a part in this dialogue: in a literal sense, "all human beings love money and love honor" (ἐπεὶ φιλοῦσι γε πάντες ὡς εἰπεῖν); yet, in ordinary usage, these expressions tacitly imply excess.[5] The "lover of money" is often put side by side with the "lover of honor" for the purpose of comparison or contrast.[6]

In Plato's order of rank, the "lover of wisdom" is added as

superior to the other two types who, as in the *Phaedo* (68c, 82c),
are grouped together—and devaluated—as "lovers of the body"
(φιλοσώματοι).[7] In the *Republic*, this order is depicted still more
clearly in the hierarchy of the parts of the soul, the social classes,
and the forms of government. The decline of governments, as
shown in Books VIII and IX, is due to the fact that reason—
or, in more human terms, the lover of wisdom—cannot stay in
power. Thus, disintegration sets in. In a timocracy, the courageous part of the soul prevails, or the love of victory and honor
(φιλονικίαι καὶ φιλοτιμίαι, 548c *et seq.*); still lower, in an oligar-
chy, the appetitive part of the soul prevails, or the love of
money and acquisition (φιλοχρηματισταὶ καὶ φιλοχρήματοι, 551A).
At the end of the *Republic*, when Socrates draws up the balance
sheet of happiness, he assigns to each part of the soul the kind
of "pleasure" peculiar to it. The lowest part, aiming at "profit,"
loves money and gain (φιλοχρήματον καὶ φιλοκερδές), the next
highest loves victory and honor, and the highest loves wisdom
(580D *et seq.*). Each type of man appreciates only the pleasure
peculiar to himself. Hence, the lover of profit thinks the pleasures
of honor and wisdom are worthless; the lover of honor thinks
the pleasures of profit are base and those of learning "smoke
and bubbles." Only the philosopher knows that the lower pleasures are indispensable for other people, but that he can do without
them. After this rapid survey, we may come back to the *Hipparchus*.

In daily life we constantly come up against "love of gain or
profit." As Socrates begins to inquire into the meaning of this
phrase, however, we encounter difficulties that are not overcome.
Socrates asks first, and with emphasis, "What is the true nature
of love of gain?" and only then—as if the second question re-
sulted from the answer we give to the first—"Who are the
lovers of gain or profit?" The young man ignores the first question, emphatically as it is put, and immediately shifts to the personal aspect of the problem. "Nobody loves profit" is the result
of the first section (225A–226D); "everybody loves profit" is the
result of the second section (226D–227c). What, then, is at stake?
Is this merely an exercise in dialectical logic-chopping, or something quite different? We can answer this question only by care-

ful examination of the respective paths leading to these antithetical results.

The proof that no one loves gain or profit begins with a definition of the "lover of gain"; he is a person who thinks it is worth making a profit from what is not worth anything (οἳ ἂν κερδαίνειν ἀξιῶσιν ἀπὸ τῶν μηδενὸς ἀξίων). This common view is inherently contradictory, as Socrates presently shows, and his first question points to the central problem involved. Does such a person act as somebody who knows? Or is he ignorant and, hence, foolish? Socrates refers here as elsewhere to the distinction between a radical "knowledge" and a radical "foolishness," the latter quite compatible with purposeful action in the practical field. His partner, however, takes knowledge and foolishness only in the particular and practical sense. Socrates does not clarify this distinction, but makes use of it ironically as a ferment for the ensuing discussion. The difference is stated still more clearly in the reply of the young man describing the seekers of profit as scoundrels who succumb to their passion, but know very well what they are doing.[8] He does not realize how he is joining together what, according to Socrates, is incompatible. Socrates tries to show this by citing the case of the husbandman and other specialists who, in their respective fields, know that they cannot gain profit from what is inappropriate. That moral and political action cannot be compared with the secure knowledge had in these technical professions would be an objection to which Socrates would reply as usual: moral and political action must be in a bad way as long as it does not attain the certainty of professional knowledge.

Whereas the first section proceeds inductively, the second employs a deductive method. The two methods, in fact, are intentionally combined. In the second section, Socrates looks still more rigorously at the concept "profit loving." It contains the elements of love and of profit. "Profit" is the opposite of "loss" or "deprivation" (ζημία).[9] The former is called "good," the latter, "bad." The necessary relationship between love and the good, between hate and evil, becomes apparent. This, evidently, is the point. In the paradoxical result that everybody loves gain or profit, the phrase, "loving gain or profit," apparently is deprived of its precise meaning; in truth, the concept of gain is lifted beyond its ordinary sense. This makes it clear that the goal of the first two demonstrations is not dialectical dissection for its own sake. On the contrary, concepts that are crucial to Socratic-Platonic thinking are developed by means of this dialectics. In the first move, the concept of knowledge is introduced, in the second, the notion of the good. The second demonstration, in particular, with the emphasis upon "love" and its proper object, incorporates some of the problems treated in the *Lysis* and in the *Symposium*.[10]

Despite the dialectical devices employed by Socrates, his part- III
ner is quite right in clinging to the ordinary concept and meaning 227c–228a
of "profit-seeker." And he does so, since Socrates repeats his last argument by distinguishing between bad profit, which is harmful to people, and good profit. He is on the right track; for, in the *Gorgias* (499c *et seq.*), the view about the primacy of pleasure in life—profit seeking, according to the *Republic*, is a form of pleasure, the lowest form—is refuted when Socrates compels Kallikles to distinguish between good and bad pleasure. Granting this distinction, it is easy to show that the object of desire is not pleasure as such, but the good. Here in the *Hipparchus*, however, Socrates pushes his partner out of the position he has taken by referring to what was conceded previously, to wit, that gain is opposed to loss as good is to evil. That is the radical opposite to the ordinary view. The partners charge each other with deception—Socrates, one must suppose, in jest, but the other in earnest. In this exchange, the two forms of thought and life separating the two men collide. Does this not mean that the ordinary view is without danger only if it is complemented by the higher and more radical view of Socrates, or that, for ordinary people like ourselves, the latter is understandable only if we look upon it as rising above the ordinary view?

We pass, for the moment, over the middle section (from which IV
the dialogue derives its name) and look instead at the ending 229e–231c
where, seemingly on the same level as before, the same problem is dragged back and forth. The basic proposition that "all men desire the good" is recapitulated at the outset. We do well not to let this slip from our minds as easily as it slips from the conversation of the two partners. For now Socrates concedes that

there is a difference between good and bad profit, but he clings all the more insistently to the concept of gain or profit itself. What, then, do good and bad profit have in common *qua* profit? This question is posed with reference to good and bad foods and to human beings who are good and evil. These too, despite their differences, have something in common *qua* foods or *qua* human beings. What, then, is common to both (ταὐτὸν ἐν ἀμφοτέροις)? This is a question with strong accent upon the ontological implications.[11] Profit, it is shown, is a return that exceeds one's investment or expenditure. Thus, not every kind of return is profit. Profit is something good; and we are back at the result of the second section. The good has come into view again, all the more emphatically and confusingly (231c 5) because now it seems as if it is the good that is the common element in both good and bad profit, or that the good is what makes for profit in general. In truth, however, the good eliminates bad profit as an inappropriate way of speaking from the domain of "profit" and proves, through the victorious cunning of Socrates, to be that which constitutes true profit.

v
231c–232c The confusion of the pupil is increased, not removed, in the last encounter. For now the concept of smaller expenditure is examined in connection with the exchange of silver for gold and it turns out that, in this case, gain or profit is not measured in purely quantitative terms, but depends upon the higher value of the return as compared with what is expended. Value, however, is useful; and what is useful—here, as elsewhere in Plato, both on the surface and in a deeper sense—is good. Thus, again and for the last time, we have reached the view that profit is good. In the indirect methods of proof employed in these early dialogues, it could not be shown more clearly that the perplexity cannot be removed without the *Agathon*.

The partner is referred to the future (232B), when his doubts may be resolved; the reader also may need to think more about these problems. At the end of the dialogue, the darkness in which we are left is ironically reinforced once more. We learn that the good desire the good. Previously, the partner asserted that the bad love gain or profit. These two statements now are added together blindly, and Socrates ironically puts the responsibility for the outcome upon the other (κατὰ τὸν σὸν λόγον, 232c 4). The summing up reads (as at the end of the second section) that everybody loves gain or profit. In truth, however, this is the last opportunity to grasp the distinction that goes to the heart of the matter. In the first statement, i.e., that the good desire the good, the concept of the *Agathon* is used in the absolute sense: it is the *Idea* of the Good that is the goal of the "will" (βούλεσθαι) which, in contrast to "inclination," can aim only at a good. This distinction is alluded to mysteriously in the *Hippias Minor* (see p. 138 below) and is spelled out more clearly in the *Gorgias* (467B *et seq.*). The second statement, i.e., that the bad love gain, instead of being added to the first, however, should be overthrown by it. For subject and predicate do not fit. The bad do not "love"; and the object (gain) has different meanings, depending upon whether gain is seen as something that the bad person desires or as something that is "loved," i.e., something good. But the opportunity for making these distinctions is missed—so Socrates (or the author) decides—and the ending goes back to the beginning. The dialogue closes banteringly with a eulogy of the "lover of profit" instead of the *Agathon*.

So far we have passed over the central section of the dialogue consisting of the story of Hipparchos, the good prince and educator of his people. But is this history or, say, legend? Or is it not capricious play with historical or legendary realities? This prince whose will it is to educate his people so that his subjects may become as excellent as possible—does he not resemble Socrates himself, or Plato's philosopher-king? He is wise and he has acquired his wisdom as one does acquire it, according to Socrates, partly by "learning" it and partly by "discovering" it.[12] Yet, the *way* he goes about educating his subjects (first the people in the city by means of the poets, Homer, Anakreon, and Simonides, then the people in the country by setting up hermae with moral inscriptions[13]) looks much more like a caricature of Plato's conception of an educator. Again, the question of whether this is a caricature or whether it is an image pointing toward Plato's educator-king is not put correctly. The portrait is thoroughly ironic, but it is drawn with the kind of positive irony that permits the truth to shine through the distortion.

MIDDLE SECTION 228B–229D

The simple content of the Hipparchian instruction is this: one is "to be mindful of the just" and "not to deceive a friend." These, at least, are the teachings that Socrates selects from "the many and beautiful inscriptions on the hermae." Why just these? Because they have a special bearing upon the theme of the dialogue, the definition of the "profit-seeker," who satisfies his desires by means that are not "just" and, if necessary, by means of cheating his friends. Let us look at the *Thrasymachus* where "justice" is the topic of discussion. The initial level beyond which the discussion moves is the love of money, vividly shown in the house of Kephalos and especially in Polemarchos (ἀγαπᾶν τὰ χρήματα, χρηματιστής, *Republic* I 330BC). In his talk with Polemarchos, Socrates is bent upon wresting the concept of justice from this sphere of money-making into which the other keeps trying to drag it. In the *Hipparchus*, by contrast, the concept of profit seeking occupies the foreground, and the fanciful central section is designed to make us see, faintly yet clearly, the concept of justice and the education leading up to it.

Looking more closely, we see some other things as well. One is "not to deceive a friend"—but what about an enemy? Does not this formulation lead to the popular and dubious view that justice means helping one's friends and harming one's enemies, the very view which Socrates is at pains to refute in the *Thrasymachus*? The educational methods of Hipparchos are becoming more and more dubious. He enters into competition with the wise sayings of the god at Delphi. His people are to admire his own sayings more than "Know thyself," which Plato's Socrates, while constantly seeking to give it new meaning, never discarded. Thus, it appears that the prince does not act from true "love of wisdom." His motivation is "love of honor," as it is said in the *Protagoras* (343C) in connection with the similar competition between Simonides and the Delphic god. At the end of the narrative section of the *Hipparchus*, moreover, we learn what must become of the citizens under such a ruler. Educational jealousy may even lead to tyrannicide. The educational mistake of the ruler finally turns against himself. This, indeed, is a lesson fitting with the stern pronouncement in the *Gorgias* (515E *et seq.*) that if the people first obey and then overthrow the ruler, he is a bad educator and himself to blame for his fate. Thus, as suggested earlier, we may discern the outlines of the scale of values that will prevail in the *Republic*: the lover of honor and ambition is superior to the lover of money, but the lover of wisdom is superior to both.

It is the task of the philosopher to unfold all the higher possibilities inherent in the concept of love of gain or profit, "as, indeed, this concept lends itself to being converted, by means of Plato's dialectics, into the higher and genuinely ethical notion of the love of the Good."[14] The device employed by Socrates is "deception." And it is a delightful moment in the dialogue when both partners bring this charge against each other. Deception must have a special meaning for the author. He uses it as the means for making the transition to the central section of the dialogue where the injunction against deceiving a friend occupies a prominent place. After the narrative inserted in this section has come to an end and the conversation is resumed, the partner repeats the charge against Socrates: "You are deceiving me, I don't know how." Indeed, he does not know, for this is the most peculiar deception in the world, the knowing deception of the educator. (This subject is treated in the *Hippias Minor*.) Thus, the theme of deception is not only a literary device by means of which the author succeeds in linking the central, narrative section with the remainder of the dialogue. It is also a theme of special philosophical significance. It is the *aporia* of Plato's early period, a consciously and intentionally induced perplexity, here disguised by a provocative and misleading label.

Schleiermacher rejected the *Hipparchus* as a genuinely Platonic work because, among other reasons, this dialogue "did not link up with any other work of the master." We have shown that there are quite a number of themes, in both form and content, which link this ingenious little work with others that are indubitably Platonic.[15] Of course, we cannot deprive anybody of his subjective doubts.[16] Yet, one thing should not be in doubt: that this dialogue belongs to the period around the year 400 B.C., and not to the time of Speusippos or Aristotle. This is as certain as it is that a vase by Douris cannot be from the time of Meidias or an engraving by Schongauer from the period of Dürer's maturity. There are no grounds for assuming, as a general possibility, that a late imitator was at work in this dialogue as long as we cannot find, in the language, in the philosophical terms and problems, or in the artistic form, the slightest indication pointing toward a later time of composition. At about 400 B.C., the dialogue is a natural product; at about 330, it would be an incomprehensible anachronism.[17] If the work was written as early as the simplicity of structure and the undeveloped character of ideas indicate, it is difficult to think of any author but Plato, with whose other writings we find connections everywhere. Is it not the most probable hypothesis, then, that in the *Hipparchus* we possess one of Plato's earliest dialogues ?[18]

NINE

Ion

SOCRATES meets the victorious rhapsode, Ion of Ephesos. We witness in Ion a strange mixture—probably typical of the time—between the ancient artistic tradition of reciting Homeric poems and a newfangled pseudo-knowledge of talking about the meaning of Homer.[1] In this respect, Ion does not differ from the Sophists who, as shown in the *Protagoras* and the *Hippias Minor*, engage in moral interpretations of a poem by Simonides or deliver an ornate lecture on Homer. Ion, too, misses the irony behind the admiration expressed by Socrates for the rhapsode's outward appearance and achievements; Socrates is wishing him a victory at the Panathenaia at the very moment Ion is about to suffer a defeat.

Socrates begins the conversation itself by sketching a portrait of the rhapsode as he ought to be. The rhapsode is an "interpreter" (ἑρμηνεύς) of the poet; he must be conversant with many good poets, and especially with Homer; he must understand the thought (τὴν διάνοιαν) of the poet, not merely his words. Even the nature of a rhapsode—though far below that of a poet— has its own intrinsic laws, and we observe how little Ion lives up to them as he proceeds to boast about "the many and beautiful thoughts" (διανοίας) he has about Homer. Instead of the one meaning that Socrates has in mind, Ion like a Sophist always plays with several possibilities. (In *Protagoras* 347AB, Hippias, we recall, had "still another fine speech" up his sleeve.) The thought of Homer is less important to Ion than his own thoughts about Homer. Moreover, he neglects to notice that he does not satisfy a basic requirement set up by Socrates. Ion knows something about Homer only, but nothing about the "many other poets." This is the very point by which Socrates will catch him.

Socrates teases the vain rhapsode into giving a display of his skill—only to be cruel enough to postpone this performance until later and now to assail Ion with questions.[2] Ion is to tell "just this": whether his knowledge extends also to poets other than Homer. This question contains the seeds for the critique of the type of rhapsode Ion represents. He admits that his knowledge applies to Homer only. In making this admission, Ion characterizes his skill as something that, in the sense of Socrates, does not belong to an activity practiced by virtue of knowledge (τέχνη or ἐπιστήμη). For each branch of knowledge aims at a "whole" (ὅλον), and the "whole" here is the total field of poetry (532c). Homer speaks about the same world as Hesiod and the other poets (531c, 532B). Either we grasp the subject as a whole—or not at all. Here, even at the start, we find the grotesquely exaggerated emphasis upon technical knowledge illustrated by the prophet who knows better than the rhapsode what Homer and Hesiod have to say about prophecy. This theme will dominate the scene in ironic play at the end of the dialogue.[3]

When Ion tries to retreat to the position that, of all the poets, only Homer is worth anything and that he, as a rhapsodic interpreter of Homer, is therefore preoccupied with the core of the subject, Socrates points out to him that he could justify these claims only by knowing precisely what he is rejecting and why. This is made clear to him when Socrates cites the case of the expert in numbers and that of the physician. These are used often by Plato as examples of experts who are invariably able to judge whether others in their respective fields have knowledge or not. Thus, the result in the end is: "You are not able to speak of Homer with art or knowledge" (τέχνη καὶ ἐπιστήμη, 532c).

Plato might have been satisfied with this negative verdict passed upon the existence of the rhapsode if he had been interested in Ion as an individual only. But why did he choose Ion? It was not simply because, as Goethe thought, "Ion, famous, admired, crowned and well-paid, was to be exposed in all his nakedness."[4] Plato always sees the individual, even Gorgias or Alkibiades, as the representative of a profession, an age, or a way of life. But why should he attack a profession that, at his time, had already lost its dignity, its representatives having become notorious for their stupidity (Xenophon, *Symposium 3 6*; *Memorabilia* IV 2 10)? The attack upon the rhapsodes and their claims to educate the people was, at best, a secondary intention of the dialogue.[5]

After the negative result, Socrates continues the examination —being a "simple man," speaking "only the truth,"[6] not possessing the "knowledge" of his partner—and again shows Ion something about the field of human arts (ὅλη τέχνη) where we find, in each particular case, a knowledge of the whole. When he mentions the wooden horse[7] among the objects to be judged in sculpture and Ion himself among the rhapsodes who, in turn, are subject to a general judgment, this reinforces, with charming playfulness, the profound insight that "knowledge" is always concerned with a "whole." Shortly afterwards, his partner repeats the confession that he is aware of understanding Homer only. Whereas Socrates previously criticized this vague consciousness in negative terms, he now proceeds to interpret it in a positive sense by placing the existence of the rhapsode in the wide domain of those who act from divine inspiration.

This domain Socrates describes in two complementary speeches that are, in every sense, the center of this little dialogue. The simile of the magnet imparting its power to a chain of iron rings depicts the effect of the Muse upon the poet, transmitted by the poet, in turn, to the rhapsode and eventually to the audience. Thus, the rhapsode is assigned a place in the larger context of an "enthusiastic" way of life (*533D et seq.*). But we must not overlook the fact that this placement is withdrawn presently (534B 8). Ion, as he himself claimed at the beginning (530D 3), can say many beautiful things about Homer. The poet, however, acting "according to divine fate" (θείᾳ μοίρᾳ), can say only one thing. We sense the satire and the ambivalence. The rhapsode does indeed belong in the domain of those who are inspired, but only upon the condition that he is a true rhapsode and not, at the same time, a sophistic, golden-tongued orator. We recall that this ambivalence in Ion's nature was conveyed to us at the very beginning of the dialogue.

II

532D–535A

Thus, the portrait of the rhapsode has led us to the figure of the poet. We soon suspect that the former was introduced so that we might come to see the latter. The poet's existence is conjured up in ecstatic words. The poets "gather their melodies from honeyed fountains out of the gardens and dells of the Muses where, like bees, they wing their way. For the poet is a light and winged and holy thing; and there is no invention in him until he has been inspired and is out of his mind, and reason is no longer in him. As long as he clings to a state of reasonableness, he is powerless to be a poet or to utter oracles" (534B). This is strange language for Socrates, especially when we think of the beginning of the *Phaedo* (60E *et seq.*). Yet, granting the element of playfulness, we realize that Plato is also serious here. For in the *Phaedrus* we find that divine mania is celebrated when the soul of the poet is praised as "tender and untrodden like a sanctuary" (ἁπαλὴν καὶ ἄβατον ψυχήν, 245A 2) and we read the famous words that he who comes to the doors of poetry without being possessed by the Muses is turned away. In the *Phaedrus*, too, we see that this mania is bestowed through a "divine gift or fate" (θείᾳ δόσει, 244A 8; θείᾳ μοίρᾳ, 244C 3) and, analogous to the prophets and augurs in the *Phaedrus* (244B *et seq.*), we find the prophets and oracle singers in the *Ion* (534D) as being of a kindred art. In both dialogues, the speeches of Socrates are filled with poetic echoes; in the *Ion*, he specifically refers to what "the poets themselves tell us" as the basis for this expression of poetic ecstacy.[8]

This "enthusiastic" kind of existence is of highest significance because "the god himself" speaks (λέγων, φθέγγεται, 534D) "through" (διά) the poet, oracle singer, or prophet. Thus, it is through this mode of ecstasy that the divine is experienced in an immediate act of uplift, not accessible by means of an act of will, but bestowed as a gift from above. In this way, the poets become interpreters (ἑρμηνεύς, 534E *et seq.*) of the divine to men, and "through them" (διὰ τούτων, 536A) the god draws the souls of men wherever he will. In addition to the ecstatic speech in the *Phaedrus*, we must think also of Diotima's speech in the *Symposium* (202E *et seq.*). According to her, all community and exchange (διάλεκτος) between gods and men take place through the demonic realm in which prophecy, priesthood, and magic dwell. It is this demonic realm-in-between that is shown (though not yet named) here in the *Ion*.

Again, the author of the *Ion* is concerned not only with praising the divine madness, but also with delimiting its sphere. Precisely because the poet does not create by conscious art (οὐ τέχνη), he can create in one field only, in dithyrambs or choral songs, in epic or in iambic verses. Thus, in contrast to the enthusiastic and hence irresponsible way of poetic creation, there is the kind of conscious knowledge that must—as shown at the beginning (532c)—extend over a "whole." This requirement distinguishes the thinker from the poet. Is it a mistake to think that the same criterion emerges at the end of the *Symposium*, where Socrates compels Agathon and Aristophanes to admit that he who is a poet of tragedies by conscious art (τέχνη) must also be a poet of comedies?[9] This thesis of the *Symposium* bridges and supersedes the division revealed in the *Ion*, and we catch sight of a mode of creative activity that unites both artist and thinker. The *Ion*, however, is concerned with showing their difference; and what is peculiarly confusing in its method is that, after poetic existence is celebrated in enthusiastic and poetic language, the limits of this existence then are drawn by means of a precise conceptual analysis. Irony fuses these two aspects of the work. Plato could see poet and philosopher together and distinguish them from each other precisely because he was both within himself.

Once we see that, behind the professional "possession by the Muses," as it were, there is the dimension of genuine enthusiasm, we cannot help but think of the passage in the *Apology* (22a *et seq.*) where Socrates reports on his experiment of examining his fellow citizens. He went also to the poets, he says, in order to learn what they were doing. And he came to the conclusion that they were acting not from knowledge, but from natural talent and divine inspiration (φύσει τινὶ καὶ ἐνθουσιάζοντες), just like the prophets and augurs. Yet, caught in self-deception, they thought they were wise in other things as well. In the *Ion*, Plato presents one such examination—but in a peculiarly indirect manner, by making us see the poet through the rhapsode. The two of them are linked in the same magnetic chain. Thus, the levels of human existence are extended downward. We avoid the difficult dilemma either of dealing with an insignificant poet (in which case poetry would not have come into its own) or of dealing with a great figure (in which case our attention would be fixed upon one specific poet instead of on the subject of poetry).[10] In the *Apology* there is an attack upon the excessive claims made by the poets; in the *Ion*, the attack is upon the excessive claims made by the interpreters of poets. Both works make us see the poet from the perspective of the "seeker after truth"—except that in the *Ion*, there is a greater emphasis upon the positive aspects of poetic existence.[11]

In the *Apology*, Socrates shames the poets because their claims exceed their true nature. In the *Ion*, Plato chose the derivative figure of the rhapsode who is but an "interpreter of the interpreter" (535A 9).[12] Owing to this difference, we need an ironic refutation to make us feel the distance between the poet who is truly possessed and his counterfeit caricature. This happens in the concluding section.

III
535B–542B
The refutation is based upon the thesis that every "science" or "art" deals with its own specific subject matter and with no other. And now we witness how the claim of the art of the rhapsode to be the proper judge of Homer is rejected, step by step, in favor of the arts of medicine, fishing, prophecy, and navigation. At first glance, it might seem as if Goethe were right in his comment: "In reply to the silly question by Socrates, Who understands Homer better when he describes the driving of a chariot, the charioteer or the rhapsode?, Ion could have boldly asserted, Obviously, the rhapsode." But Plato does not need the "incredible stupidity" of an opponent to make Socrates appear clever. On the contrary, the issue here concerns the nature of the poet (for whom the rhapsode is a stand-in) at a time when the poet still claimed to be the teacher of his nation and the philosopher is challenging this claim. And the point is to warn against the danger inherent in the nature of the poet who claims—and is expected—to produce effects that go beyond his true powers and responsibilities. Perhaps Euripides is the best example for this kind of poet; but the common practice, long before the Stoics,

of making Homer the inventor and guide in all spheres of life also shows the misunderstanding and the need for drawing limits.

The rhapsode did not wish to rest his case on the grounds of divine madness. That he has little actual claim to it he reveals himself by intimating that, during the ecstasy of his deliveries, he still can keep his eye on the "box office" (535E). The sphere in which he claims to have competence as a man of knowledge is restricted more and more as Socrates proceeds. Instead of resolutely renouncing any such claim and falling back upon his artistry, however, Ion grasps foolishly for the last straw in fear of being entirely dispossessed. It happens to be the art of generalship. He clings to this desperately until Socrates charges him with having the nature of Proteus. This Protean nature, something formless, is an essential characteristic of the "doxosophic" way of life (*Euthyphro* 15D; *Euthydemus* 288B; *Sophist* 223C, 226A). In the end, Socrates gives Ion the choice of whether he prefers to be called an "expert" or "divinely inspired." Whereupon Ion, to the amusement of the reader, chooses divine inspiration instead of expertness. Moreover, when Socrates at the end confirms once more that Ion is "divinely inspired and not an expert" (θεῖος καὶ μὴ τεχνικός), we know how well the negative judgment—and how little the affirmative—fits Ion's case. As long as there is talk of the "divine," however, and of "inspiration," the poetic mode of existence remains in sight from afar. Indeed, "praiser of Homer" ('Ομήρου ἐπαινέτης) are the last words of the dialogue.

The problems raised in the *Ion* may be seen more clearly from the perspective of the last part of the *Meno*. In the *Meno*, political art (as it is generally called) is said to be based upon "right opinion," not knowledge. This puts political art on the same plane with those ways of life and professions that are bestowed upon men "by divine fate" only (θείᾳ μοίρᾳ). Among such men who are full of the god (ἐνθουσιῶντες) are oracle singers, prophets, and "poetic" (i.e., creative) men of all kinds (χρησμῳδοὶ καὶ θεομάντεις, 99C; χρησμῳδοὺς καὶ μάντεις καὶ τοὺς ποιητικοὺς ἅπαντας, 99D). Similarly, in the enthusiastic speech by Socrates in the *Ion*, "oracle singers and divine prophets" (τοῖς χρησμῳδοῖς καὶ τοῖς μάντεσι τοῖς θείοις, 534CD) are associated with the poets; and from the very beginning of the dialogue, Socrates again and again strikes the same theme that prophetic existence goes with poetic existence—both set in ironic contrast to that of the rhapsode (531B, 534B 7, 538E 7, 539D).[13] In the *Meno*, the contrast between an "enthusiastic" way of life and the Socratic-Platonic conception of knowledge is worked out clearly. The *Ion* moves in the same direction, but everything remains quite undeveloped.

Nevertheless, we may say that the *Ion* takes the first steps toward working out the distinction between the man of knowledge and the poet as expressing different modes of existence. We are also shown, by the way, the vague intermediate and derivative form of the rhapsode and interpreter, who is quite justified in his existence as long as he performs what is proper to his own profession. Yet, we come to see all the more sharply the outlines of the two prototypes that are clarified and delimited in the *Ion*. Why did Plato deal with this problem at such an early stage and why was it still so much on his mind when he wrote the *Meno* and the *Phaedrus* and, even later, the *Laws* (IV 719B *et seq.*) ? Evidently this was because he felt within himself both Socrates and "Homer, Hesiod, and Archilochos." That "ancient quarrel between philosophy and poetry" to which he refers in the *Republic* (X 607B) cut through the center of his own existence, and he was compelled to create order between those two powers—knowledge and enthusiasm—now converging, now diverging within himself. The primary intention of this dialogue is not to depict satirically the clash between Socrates and a vain artist. Instead, Plato has grasped the Herakleitean tension in his own nature as a thinker and has given it form as a poet.[14]

Ultimately, of course, this is a personal problem not for Plato alone, even though in him it reaches its heights. Xenophanes, Parmenides, Empedokles, Herakleitos—and Nietzsche—also are poet-philosophers. Homer and Hesiod are the ancestors of both Greek poetry and Greek thought. The same tension extends even to the threshold of Socratic existence. On the last morning of his life, Socrates first speaks (*Phaedo* 60c *et seq.*) about his attempts at poetry and about the meaning of the voice that he, philosopher par excellence, has often heard in a dream: "Practice the art of the Muses."

TEN

Hippias Minor

HIPPIAS has just finished his lecture "on Homer," i.e., not on the ancient, great *vates* and perpetuator of a heroic race of men, but on that best-loved, moral picture book. In contrast to the rhapsode Ion, who talks about Homer but only as a side line, Hippias represents a purer type. Since he knows how to talk about other poets as well, he is safe against the critique that he arbitrarily selects from the "whole" field. On the other hand, one cannot discover a trace of mania in him, even facetiously, and therefore there is no hint at a higher existence—that of the poet—behind his own. Instead, as the resourceful Sophist alone he faces the philosopher.

Socrates does not think highly of Hippias' kind of interpretation of the poet, "since it is impossible to ask Homer what he thought of when he composed his verses" (365CD). In the *Protagoras* (347E), Socrates protests in similar words against the practice of invoking a poet as witness and of arguing about what he really meant. The difference (so characteristic of the *Protagoras*) between sophistic speechmaking and Socratic conversation may be heard here (*Hippias Minor* 364B, 369B *et seq.*, 373A), though by no means with the intensity of the *Protagoras*. Once we are accustomed to recognizing the significance in Plato's choice of places, it is no accident either that the lecture by Hippias took place "inside"[1] whereas the examination by Socrates now takes place somewhere in the open (364B). But even as Socrates, in the *Protagoras*, displays his virtuosity in appropriating the technique of his opponent, so he takes his position here on the sophistic level by asking, "Who is 'better' or deserves a

137

higher rank among the Homeric heroes, Achilles or Odysseus?"
—and he will continue to move with expert skill on this level.
Yet, he does not open the conversation himself. The initiative
is taken by a certain Eudikos, a follower of Hippias who takes
part in the conversation only at the beginning and again at a
crucial point in the dialogue. Why he is present at all becomes
clear at the end. For the time being, it seems merely that Socrates
needed a push from somebody else.

I
364B–371E
I 1
364B–365D

Achilles is the best (or bravest), Odysseus the wiliest—this
is the Sophist's thesis. Socrates, taking the lead immediately,
converts the second attribute, which is appropriate for the poet
but not for the thinker, into a clear conceptual term. Odysseus is
"deceptive" or "false" or "capable of deception and falsehood"
(ψευδής). Achilles, then, as his opposite, is "truthful" and
"straightforward" (ἀληθής, ἁπλοῦς). Let us not fail to notice that,
in addition to these two heroes, Hippias also mentions Nestor
as the "wisest" and that Socrates repeats this judgment (364E).
Nestor does not enter into the subsequent discussion. But is it
not true that, hidden behind all the ensuing display of cleverness,
there is "wisdom"—if only we could lay hold of it?

I 2
365D–369A

To move forward the discussion must, for the moment, leave
Homer (to whom Socrates, however, returns later—369E). Now
we move into the Socratic sphere itself; for, instead of a sophistic
lecture, we find the method of question and answer, and, instead
of a discussion about Homer, we have an inquiry into the subject
matter. To begin with, we learn that the false man is "capable"
(δυνατός) and "prudent" (φρόνιμος) in the field in which he practices his deception. More specifically, he is capable of deceiving
"whom he will and wherein he will." Then Socrates shows, by
citing the case of mathematics—in which Hippias, Jack-of-all-
trades, also claims competence—that the expert in this specific
field can make both true and false statements and can do so better
than the ignorant man can. In this way, the capacity to speak
both truth and falsehood is located in one person—a position
which, though somewhat extreme, is still correct. The next move,
however, though apparently quite harmless, leads the Sophist
astray, and the reader as well if he is not careful. For now we are
told that the true man and the false man are one and the same.

As Hippias is unable to gainsay him, Socrates now returns to the interpretation of Homer, where he displays, or exceeds, the virtuosity of the Sophist. Odysseus, he argues, is both true and false at the same time, and so is Achilles. The latter's craftiness is proved by reference to the ninth canto of the *Iliad*—Socrates shows a knowledge of Homer as great as his sophistic cleverness —so that the difference between the two characters, Achilles and Odysseus, disappears entirely. Here Hippias, threatened in the field of his own competence, firmly and justifiably challenges this blurring of the lines. But just when he thinks that the difference between the two is due to the fact that Odysseus deceives intentionally or voluntarily, whereas Achilles does so only when the situation compels him to or when he has changed his mind, Socrates intervenes with this paradox: Odysseus, then, acts as a person who knows, Achilles as someone who does not; hence, Odysseus is superior to or "better" (371E) than Achilles. In the beginning (363B), and in accordance with popular opinion, Achilles was the "better" man (ἀμείνων) or the "braver" man, in the more narrow sense. Thus, we have completely reversed ourselves. What, then, is the meaning of this game that Socrates plays with Hippias?

The paradoxical identification of the deceptive and the truthful person makes good sense; and Socrates himself shows most clearly what this means, because he knows how to deceive better than all the Sophists. Yet, the paradox that Achilles is "similar" to Odysseus, or, in the exaggerated version, that Odysseus is "better" than Achilles, no longer makes any sense. The fact that the Sophist can only protest against it, but not refute it, is designed to call our attention to the hidden flaw in this whole discussion. For the two men mean quite different things by the word "false" or "deceptive" (ψευδής). Hippias means a false person who derives pleasure or advantage from his deception. Socrates means a person who deceives in a specific situation but can just as well tell the truth, and who, as a man of knowledge, will use the one or the other as a means to achieve his end, "the good." Thus, in reminding us that this ambiguity in the meaning of "deception" must be removed, Plato performs an educational task of benefit, if not to the vain Sophist, then perhaps to

Eudikos who is listening and certainly to anybody who reads with attention.

The reader must immediately go to work at the point where Socrates lifts the discussion from the plane of commenting upon Homer to the level of a conceptual analysis (365B). He asks whether deception is a "lack of capacity," i.e., a weakness, or a strength. The Sophist decides emphatically in favor of strength. If we go along with him, we must at once add (in the spirit of the *Hippias Major*, which seems to look back upon this passage of the *Minor*[2]): yes, but this strength is by no means something "beautiful." We would be more correct in calling deception a weakness, and Socrates throws some light upon this aspect by his comparison with sickness. In Plato's sense, it would be best to say that deception or falsehood as understood by Hippias and by the many is, indeed, a defect, weakness, or sickness, and that only the kind of deception practiced by Socrates is a power—in fact, the same power, which is all the more effective in its opposite manifestation.

Presently the concept of willing, repeated three or four times, carries us further. The person who is capable, or has power, can do "what he wills when he wills." Later, the *Meno* (78B) shows that "no one wills evil." Moreover, the *Gorgias* (466D *et seq.*) clarifies the distinction between genuine willing and arbitrary inclination (βούλομαι–δοκεῖ μοι). A true act of the will always aims at the good; arbitrary action is not—as Polos and the many believe it is—a power, but a lack of power. All this is implicit here in the *Hippias*, as in a puzzle. And if the solution is that we can "will" only the good, then we may reply, in retrospect, to the first question of Socrates in this way: what is commonly called "deception" is indeed a lack of power—a lack of power for the good. Only Socratic deception "willing" the good is power.

This solution is all the more evident from the final result of this section. To identify the "truthful" and the "false" is more than a sophistic trick, and the paradox reveals something essential, namely, that the man who can both deceive and speak the truth may be the wise man. For he will speak falsely only when he "will"—i.e., when in doing so he is aiming at the good.

He who deceives voluntarily, Socrates concluded at the end
of the first part of the dialogue, is better than someone who deceives involuntarily. True, for the Socratic-Platonic conception
of a voluntary act is closely connected with that of the good.
"Voluntarily" we move only toward the good and avoid evil
(*Protagoras* 358A *et seq.*; *Republic* 412E *et seq.*; *Laws* 731C, 860D
et seq.). If someone does wrong, apparently on his own will,
this is a mistake, a sickness of the soul, so that, in truth, he has
acted "involuntarily." Thus, throughout this discussion, the Socratic paradox can be understood only if we take it not to mean
lying, but to mean deception practiced by a man who is both
knowing and good. Hippias, however, in order to refute Socrates,
transforms this paradoxical, though correct, statement into the
thesis that, in this case, he who voluntarily does wrong must be
better than someone who does wrong involuntarily. In other
words, Hippias has not yet understood that "deception" in the
sense of Socrates cannot possibly be a case of "wrongdoing."
In clearing up this misunderstanding, we can clarify once more
the true meaning of the Socratic statement.

Against the view that voluntary wrongdoing is better than
involuntary, Hippias cites both public opinion (δοκεῖ) and the
authority of the laws. Plato, who will discuss the difference between voluntary and involuntary wrongdoing in a section of the
Laws (860E *et seq.*), might have permitted Socrates to agree
with the Sophist and might have proceeded, as he does in the
Laws, to clarify the meaning of voluntary action. But such agreement would have obscured the difference in the basic attitudes
of the two men. Instead, Plato gives Socrates the assignment of
carrying the paradox to an extreme, of adopting as his own view
what Hippias has shown to be an absurd consequence, and of
making it prevail in this contest. If the first part of the dialogue
dealt with a statement that, although paradoxical, was meaningful and needed only to be interpreted correctly, the second part
deals with a statement that is pernicious from Plato's own point
of view and would require a proper refutation. This is lacking
here just as a correct interpretation was lacking in the first part.

The reader is most strongly challenged to unravel this tangled
skein when Socrates, at the very beginning and again at the end

II
371E–376C

II 1
371E–373C

of this discussion, admits his wavering uncertainty about the whole matter (πλανῶμαι περὶ ταῦτα, 372D, 376c) and proclaims in praise of his ignorance that he is always ready to learn and change his mind (372c). And soon after, at the only place in the dialogue where Eudikos joins the discussion once more, Socrates replies—when he is reproached by Hippias that he is causing troublesome or malicious confusion (ἀεὶ ταράττει ἐν τοῖς λόγοις καὶ ἔοικεν ὥσπερ κακουργοῦντι, 373B)—by playing ironically with the concept of voluntary action, which is the topic of discussion: he is causing trouble not voluntarily, he points out, but involuntarily. The rogue, however, does throw Hippias into confusion most intentionally. (If we agree with Hippias that this is wickedness, however, we cannot say it is intentional; for, indeed, according to the basic principle of Socrates, it could not be.)

This episode is an anticipation, rather than an echo, of the much more severe conflict between Socrates and the Sophists depicted in the *Protagoras*, where another person (Kallias) also intervenes at a crucial point (348c).

II 2
373c–375D To prove the absurd statement about voluntary wrongdoing, Socrates cites a long series of examples. (According to Aristotle, *Metaphysics* XIII 4 1078b 28, Socrates discovered induction, and Aristotle subjects this particular inductive inference of the *Hippias Minor* to a criticism in *Metaphysics* V 29 1025a 6–13.) Each example shows that the man who voluntarily commits a wrong is superior to someone who does wrong involuntarily. For the man who knows is in command of both excellence and failure of performance in his field and, even though there is no mention here, as there is in the *Ion*, of the "whole," the cases cited invariably lead to the conclusion that the expert knows the whole of his particular field of knowledge.

Socrates moves upward from physical to spiritual activities. The soul of an archer is better if he deliberately misses the mark than if he misses the mark against his will. The soul of the physician is better when he does harm to the body voluntarily (ἑκοῦσα κακὰ ἐργαζομένη). That an archer might deliberately miss the target is quite conceivable; in the case of the physician, however, it is quite evident that it would contradict his nature to inflict real harm upon the patient. For the activity of the physician

aims essentially at health (*Euthyphro* 13D; *Euthydemus* 291E),
and the pain inflicted upon the patient during the healing process
is a means toward health (*Gorgias* 467C). Now Socrates ascends
beyond the series of spiritual activities to the soul itself, to "our
own soul." This move, or leap, from the mediate to the essential—to "existence"—is somewhat obscured by the long series
of preparatory steps. In truth, we are confronted suddenly with
the decisive question of how we should live. At this point, when
it looks as if, on the basis of the long list of examples, our soul
were better if it did wrong voluntarily instead of involuntarily,
Hippias ceases to follow; he can utter only a few words of protest. Thus, the reader must take his place and ask whether a
soul is ever permitted to do wrong and whether it would ever
do so voluntarily.[3]

Socrates helps us to take another step forward by driving
Hippias into still greater confusion. Justice, he proclaims, is a
"power" (δύναμις) or a "knowledge" (ἐπιστήμη) or both. Hence,
more justice means more power, more knowledge, or both. This
puts us on the right track for recognizing that a soul true to its
own nature is "just," i.e., endowed with power and knowledge,
and cannot go wrong in the opposite direction. But now we come
up against the unrefuted conclusion of the previous discussion,
according to which the expert in his own special field can always
do both the good and the bad. Thus, the inference is turned
around and it is argued that the stronger and better soul must
be capable of doing wrong voluntarily—as if wrongdoing were
a kind of specialty, like arithmetic or archery, and as if we had
not just now reached the point where we could almost see justice
as a knowledge (and a power) of the soul. How close we came
to this solution may be seen from the supplementary remark that
the just and right soul "when it does wrong" must do so voluntarily, and from the concluding remark immediately following:
he who voluntarily does wrong and acts disgracefully and unjustly—"if there be such a man"—can be no other than the good
man.[4] With this statement, the discussion itself comes to an emphatic end. Only a brief postscript follows. Perhaps we have come
close enough to realize that the just soul, acting in accordance
with its own nature, cannot do wrong, and that nobody acting

II 3
375D–376C

in accordance with his own nature would voluntarily do wrong.

The Sophist cannot agree nor can he refute. The last words of Socrates stress his own "wavering." But we may take a last look at the dialogue as a whole. The statement in the first part that he who knows the truth best can also deceive best is correct, though dangerously overdrawn. It corresponds to the paradoxical statement in the *Thrasymachus* (*Republic* I 334A) that "the best watchman is also the best thief" and to the deeply serious statement in the *Phaedrus* (262A) according to which he who wants to deceive without being deceived himself must know the "truth."[5] The statement, however, that he who does wrong voluntarily is better than someone who does so involuntarily is wrong and indeed criminal according to common usage and valid legal principles; according to Socrates, the statement is meaningless, because it is self-contradictory. By recognizing that these two statements are opposites—though the second is derived from the first—we can use the absurdity of the second in order to see the true meaning of the first: malicious deception is ruled out. Thus, the question arises, what distinguishes the two kinds of deception, that practiced by Socrates from that intended by Hippias? The answer would have to invoke "the good" as the goal, as indeed "the good man" is the phrase that concludes the discussion itself (376B 6). To dispose of the second statement would require that we clarify the nature of "injustice" and the nature of "voluntary" and "involuntary" action—in short, that we gain insight into the nature of the soul. The essential problems posed in the *Protagoras*, the *Gorgias*, and the *Republic* lie just below the surface of the *Hippias*.

The dialogue contains still other matters in an undeveloped form. Why is the concept of "deception" made the focus of discussion? Philosopher and Sophist confront each other in the *Hippias Major* and in the *Protagoras*. There beauty and *arete* are the subjects of discussion. In the *Hippias Minor*, however, what is at stake is the basic sophistic attitude itself—deception, or the *pseudos*—on one hand, and on the other, the Socratic existence aiming at the realm of true being, the good or the *Agathon*, never mentioned explicitly but repeatedly sighted from afar. It would provide the solution to all the puzzles—if we but had it. Socrates,

however, who is seen here "deceiving" his opponent apparently
in the manner of a Sophist, is the living witness to the fact that
he who knows the truth can deceive better than he who does not,
and he who deceives as Socrates does "voluntarily" is better
than he who does so involuntarily—better not only in the sense
of displaying a greater virtuosity, but also in the sense of more
closely approximating the *Agathon*. Thus, this dialogue is the
purest portrait of the Socratic mode of existence depicted so often
(along with the most diverse problems) not only in the early
dialogues, but even in the maturest works of Plato: the portrait
of Socrates as the sovereign master of all the sophistic techniques
with the view toward the good, or as the deceptive educator
with his mind fixed upon the right goal. Seen from this perspective, the presence of Eudikos may perhaps be regarded as necessary. Since a true deception of this kind requires that somebody
be instructed by it and since the Sophist cannot be taught, someone else must be present. (It is risky to indulge in fantasies, but
is it not possible that Plato, fond as he was of playing a serious
game with significant proper names, also meant to convey to us
a hint at the good and the just by choosing the name *Eu-dikos*?)

At a much later period, the *Phaedrus* will confront the sophistic
art of rhetoric with a genuine art concerned with "what is the
true nature of each existing thing" (262B 7). Only he who knows
the truth can safely take those imperceptible steps in an argument that will safely produce deception in the other person. In
contrast to sophistic rhetoric, therefore, which is devoid of any
principles and makes a practice of "(mis)guiding souls," there
emerges the image of another art of speech that conveys both
truth and falsehood safely because it knows "true being." The
antithetical forces in the *Hippias Minor* grow apart in the *Phaedrus* into two basic modes of verbal expression—and forms of
life. Above all, the question of the nature of the Sophist occupies
a central place in the dialogue named after him. The existence
of the philosopher, the real target of the *Sophist*, is treated mar-
ginally, as it were, and comes to the fore only now and then, as
if by chance. Since the Sophist deals with all sorts of subjects in
his public debates, it is obvious that he has no claim to knowledge
(*Sophist* 235A). This thesis of the *Sophist* will be reminiscent of

the *Hippias*, where Socrates ironically runs through the list testifying to the alleged omniscience of this particular Sophist (*Hippias* 366c *et seq.*), thereby suggesting that Hippias actually does not have any serious knowledge of all the sciences and arts named. Moreover, as the concept of deception is the central theme in the *Hippias Minor*, so the *Sophist*, in its central philosophical sections, is entirely concerned with an analysis of this concept and with a demonstration of how *pseudos*—deception or falsehood—is possible. In the *Hippias*, the philosopher can practice *pseudos* better than the Sophist; but, we shall add, he will practice it only with a view toward the good, truth, and being. The late work leaves the Sophist in the realm of deception and in the darkness of nonbeing, whereas the philosopher as dialectician has knowledge of both being and nonbeing, i.e., equal command over truth and *pseudos*. Thus, a richer and deeper insight into the nature of being also creates a deeper knowledge of the possibility of *pseudos*, whereas in the *Hippias Minor* the realm of being emerges only in the distance behind perplexities and paradoxes and the *pseudos* is presented as if we knew all about it. Nevertheless, the early dialogue carries a faint suggestion of what will be developed in the *Sophist*.

Let us be frank to learn from the admission that without the explicit testimony of Aristotle, probably few critics would consider the *Hippias Minor* a genuine Platonic work.[6] Theodor Gomperz called it "the first dialogue" composed by Plato.[7] Let us say instead that it is one of the first, for the *Hipparchus* could be just as early or still earlier. As Wilamowitz pointed out, after 399 B.C., no member of the Socratic circle could afford to depict Socrates—though the disguise be ever so transparent—as representing immorality. So the *Hippias Minor* must be earlier than 399, perhaps by several years.[8]

ELEVEN

Theages

DEMODOKOS, accompanied by his son Theages, approaches Socrates in the market place in Athens to ask for advice about the son's education. Demodokos begins with a stilted, solemn address.[1] Then he recites some of his experiences as a husbandman, together with what alarms him at the moment: the passionate desire of his son to "acquire knowledge." Socrates, replying at first with friendly compliance, at once becomes very serious because he is asked for advice on education. To give such advice is something sacred, to educate is something divine, he says, and the name Theages is significant.[2] Then he turns to the boy himself, inquiring what it is that he really wants and leading Theages to the point where he asks Socrates to be his teacher. "If you are willing to be with me, that would be enough; I would not seek another" (127A). Socrates mentions other teachers who are available, but gives his consent as the boy insists. The decision, however, is not in his own hands, Socrates declares, but with the "demonic."[3] "God willing," Theages will make rapid progress (130E).

The basic structure of the *Charmides* and the *Laches* is here modified in a peculiar way. As in the *Charmides*, we find three participants, except that in the *Charmides* the older cousin Kritias is present instead of the father. There is an even closer affinity with the *Laches*, despite the greater number of persons in that dialogue. The *Laches* presents two fathers who seek instruction for their sons and have been advised by friends that Socrates would be the best person to consult. The ensuing conversation makes it clear, in the end, that Socrates would also be the best

teacher. "If Socrates were willing to take care of the boys,"
Nikias says (200c), using almost the same words as Theages,
"we would not look for anybody else." And Socrates agrees,
provided that "God be willing" (201c). Thus, there remains an
uncertainty about the assignment, and this is intentional; not
without reason did Nikias just say that Socrates was not willing
to undertake his son's education, but was always recommending
someone else as a teacher when this subject was mentioned
(200d).

What remains unspoken in the background and is only suggested by alluding to the will of the god is shown in the scene
of the *Theaetetus* where Socrates holds forth on his skill as a midwife (150b *et seq.*). There the same Aristeides who in the *Laches*
is taken to Socrates is mentioned as someone with whom the
teaching of Socrates was of no avail. And Socrates goes on to
say that he often recommends Prodikos and other teachers to
those who seek instruction with him. The *Theaetetus* reveals what
is still concealed in the *Laches*: it is the "demonic" that determines whether the association is possible or not. To come back
to the *Theages*, we may add that the two boys, Aristeides and
Thoukydides, who in the *Laches* are recommended to the care of
Socrates, are here cited by the master (in the speech at the end)
as strange cases that show how little his own will can guarantee
the success of his teaching. Thus, the *Theages* is evidently conceived in terms of the basic structure of the *Laches*. Moreover,
it carries the action of the *Laches* further with respect to an important matter of substance—the fate of the two boys who appear
there. This, as the *Theaetetus* shows, is no accident. For that
human fate is bound up with the essential subject of the *Theages*,
the problem of the "demonic" and its significance for the educational work of Socrates. This subject—directly revealed in the
scene of the *Theaetetus* where the art of midwifery comes to self-
expression and only hinted at in the *Laches*—Plato developed in
a separate dialogue, provided we accept the *Theages* as one of
his own works.

In the *Laches*, the question of the boys' education is confined
to the frame of the dialogue, whereas the core of the work appears
to be something quite different—the clarification of the concept

of courage. There is no such problem of definition for its own sake in the *Theages*. Here the emphasis is put on what is, or seems to be, marginal in the *Laches*. Yet, without some kind of examination in the manner of the *elenchos*, however brief, no contact is possible between Socrates and a disciple. Here where the only question is education and where we are shown a young boy eager to learn and seeking instruction, the subject of the cross-examination is not the formal clarification of a concept. Instead, the question is put in personal terms: What do you wish to become? At the beginning of the *Protagoras*, Socrates conducts a similar examination in personal terms of the young Hippokrates who is eager to study with Protagoras, just as Demodokos here is thinking of sending his son to a Sophist. In both cases, it is quite amusing that Socrates is consulted for this purpose. And in both cases, the conversation reveals that the young boy wants to acquire "knowledge" but cannot state the object to which this "knowledge" applies. In the *Protagoras*, this theme is one part of the great dialogue and it is set in ironic counterpoint to the main conversation. In the *Theages*, the corresponding part is placed in the center of the dialogue. It does not break off in a confession of ignorance as in the *Protagoras*. Instead, the discussion leads up to the central question of the whole work—education and the limits imposed on it by the demonic. Thus, Plato here not only gave a special turn to the peripheral theme of the *Laches* but also connected this theme with the preliminary conversation in the *Protagoras* and developed both in the same direction, i.e., toward the demonic—provided, of course, that the *Theages* is one of Plato's own works.

A final comment may be suggested on the subject of affinities. It long has been recognized that the *Theages* is closely related to the *Alcibiades Major*, though this affinity usually is interpreted as an imitation.[4] The two young men are depicted as being very similar, except that Theages is younger and Alkibiades is more sharply delineated. Both have learned the usual things: reading, writing, zither-playing, and wrestling (*Theages* 122E; *Alcibiades* 106E). Both want "to rule," "to be a tyrant"—or, preferably, "to be God," as Theages puts it quite naïvely. This is not an imitation, or exaggeration, of the *Alcibiades*. On the contrary, what is here expressed motivated the minds of most young Athenian aristocrats. The name for this particular type when grown up is Kallikles. Moreover, the claim exactly fits the case of Theages as we know it from the *Republic* (496BC), which says that only sickliness prevented Theages from deserting philosophy in favor of party politics.[5] In both the *Alcibiades* and the *Theages*, Socrates challenges the young man to state over whom he wants to rule, although the *Alcibiades* goes beyond in this respect by developing a hierarchy in types of ruling. In both dialogues, Socrates is shown as the true teacher and is asked to be the youth's educator. In each case, the pupil expresses his confidence by saying, "If you will." In each case, Socrates demurs, "God willing."

Along with these similarities, however, we find differences between the two dialogues. Each has its own center of gravity, and we must acknowledge, in each case, the mysterious law of individual creation rather than mechanical imitation by the hands of some stranger. In the *Theages*, the *elenchos* is very brief. Three types of rulers are distinguished: first (125E), the tyrant, which is what Theages really wants to be; next (126A), the legitimate statesman like Themistokles, Kimon, or Perikles (yet we know from the *Gorgias* what Socrates thinks about these men whom Theages takes as models); and finally (125B), in the peculiar paradox of the poet's language, "the tyrant who is made wise through association with the wise."[6] Anybody who has ever listened to Socrates will note that the words "tyrant" and "wise," strictly understood, contradict each other. They are compatible only in the following alternative: either wisdom sinks to the level of practical prudence or the art of ruling is raised to the level where it really joins wisdom—i.e., where the philosopher-king is sighted in the far distance. All these things, however, and their connection with education are only hinted at in the *Theages* playfully. In the *Alcibiades*, the *elenchos* occupies a dominant place. The theme of "politics and education" is central. On the other hand, the demonic, though deeply embedded in the structure of the *Alcibiades*, is mentioned only at the beginning and then as something that is already overcome. In the *Theages*, the demonic carries an entirely different weight and emerges at the end as the goal. The whole dialogue moves toward this goal, so that a comparison with the *Alcibiades* shows again what was Plato's peculiar intention—provided the *Theages* is one of his own works.

The nature of Socratic education—that is the central theme of the *Theages* in a peculiar turn because, in the other dialogues, it provides or seems to provide only the background against which a special problem is treated dialectically. To set off Socrates as educator requires, as elsewhere in Plato, a confrontation with other educators and noneducators. First, there are the politicians. Socrates recommends them as teachers because Theages "wishes to acquire knowledge in political affairs." Theages, however, cites Socrates against himself by recalling the latter's words that the sons of these men are no better than the sons of cobblers. This, in youthfully blunt terms, refers us to the kind of demonstration we find, in different ways, in the *Protagoras*, the *Alcibiades*, the *Gorgias*, and the *Meno*.[7] The brief hint in the *Theages* is enough to show the distance between true education and complete failure of education. After the politicians have been rejected, Socrates next recommends the Sophists. He uses almost the same words as in the *Apology* (19E) to describe such men as Gorgias, Prodikos, and Hippias. (In the *Theages*, Polos takes the place of Hippias.) These people come to the city from abroad and attract young men so that the latter will pay money to seek their company instead of the company of their own fellow citizens, available to them for nothing (127E *et seq.*). The same words are used because the author has in mind the same picture, evoked by the same contrast. Socrates is not an educator in the sense in which all others, except himself, think of education. How much he would like, he comments ironically, to command such fine wisdom![8]

Socratic *paideia* emerges against the background of these contrasts. It is an education through love—and this is shown with special emphasis in the *Theages* precisely because this dialogue does not deal with any other problem. "I do not know anything about this fine knowledge of the Sophists; I only have a small body of knowledge: the nature of love (τὰ ἐρωτικά)," as Socrates says (128B) in words reminiscent of the *Lysis* (204BC) and of the *Symposium* (177D). Theages himself feels the effect of this instruction through love; it draws him to Socrates, who would send him to other teachers. The effect is also heard at the end in the report of one of the youths, as cited by Socrates. "I have never learned anything from you as you know yourself." (These words recur almost exactly in *Theaetetus* 150D, with the positive supplement: they do not learn anything from me, but discover and produce many beautiful things in themselves.[9] And this corresponds to Socrates' insistence in the *Apology*—19D *et seq.*— that he has never taught anybody.) "Yet," so the youth's report continues, "I have made progress every time I was together with you . . . and I have advanced most rapidly and profoundly when I sat close beside you and touched you."[10] Nowhere in Plato do we find this education through love, education through immediate presence, expressed more powerfully than in this passage. Nor can there be—with Socrates—a silent sitting side by side. Conversation, after all, is an indispensable part of the Socratic presence. Nevertheless, we cannot object if others scent magic powers and hence consider these matters un-Platonic. As for ourselves, we see no magic, or at least not the kind of magic that Faust would "like to remove from his path." We see only the magic of the great man and educator. Moreover, we believe that questions of this kind cannot be decided by means of philological criticism only, but that they require a certain breadth of human experience.[11]

As Socratic education through love differs from sophistic instruction without love, so Socrates' demon which removes the educational work from human will and planning is most sharply opposed to the Sophists' practice of peddling their knowledge to all and sundry. This theme is latent in the *Laches*, as we observed earlier. Suffice it to say here that the strange affairs and stories in which the daimonion—or, rather, the "demonic"— manifests itself merely prepare the way for showing what is really at stake, namely, what effect this inner voice of warning has upon Socratic education. These stories need not be recounted here. Having read them once more the reader should ask himself seriously whether the reproach that Socrates is boastful is not derived from a very modern conception of "modesty," and, in particular, whether these stories are so incredible as they are held to be in our time.[12]

Socrates, it is said, knew by looking at the young Charmides that he would fail in his race at the Olympic games. Socrates told "the beautiful Sannion" in advance that his participation in the campaign of the general Thrasyllos (410/409 B.C.) would mean a great danger to him; in fact, Socrates rightly expressed the most serious doubts about the issue of this campaign in Asia Minor. Should Socrates really have had fewer misgivings about the outcome of the Sicilian expedition than so many others who, according to Thucydides, "felt this danger much more at the moment of departure than when they had voted for the expedition in the Assembly" or those to whom, according to Aristophanes, the Adonis-cry of the women was an evil omen for the departing expedition? Again, one may not even need Socratic powers of premonition to detect something threatening when one's table companions plot a murder. No one can dispute that this story is possible, told as it is in a highly individual style. It gains in credibility when we observe that a certain Nikias, the victim of this murderous assault, is called the son of Heroskamandros and that this rare name, perhaps not accidentally, turns up on several of the inscriptions found at Alopeke, the birthplace of Socrates.[13] Regardless of what one may think of this reading, one thing is certain, because the author makes Socrates say so himself: these stories are not told to gratify boastfulness or pleasure in the miraculous. They are designed to illustrate the power of the demonic in Socrates "since this power means everything to those who become my companions" (129E). Socrates shows what this means in the case of the young Aristeides and the young Thoukydides whom Plato had in mind when he was writing the *Laches* and even later when he wrote the *Theaetetus*.[14]

Anybody who today tries to find—however tentatively—a place for this strange dialogue, the *Theages*, in the total body of Plato's works must expect to be charged with being uncritical. The date of the small work has been pushed forward as far as the late Hellenistic period! But before one talks about a "private oracle" with which Socrates seems to be endowed here in entirely un-Platonic fashion, one should recall what is found at the

end of the *Phaedrus* and at the beginning of the *Theaetetus*. In
the *Phaedrus*, Socrates passes a "prophetic word" (μαντεύομαι)
as he calls it himself upon the young Isokrates. In the *Theaetetus*,
Eukleides of Megara who has just brought home the severely
wounded hero of the dialogue now remarks looking back that
he often has remembered with astonishment how "clairvoyantly
or prophetically" (μαντικῶς) Socrates had spoken of so many
things, as he also did shortly before his own death when he
talked about the promise of the young Theaitetos. "Prophetic
in many things"—does not the *Theages* provide impressive evidence for this? Why, then, is it so surprising—and thought to
be un-Platonic—if, in the *Theages*, this prophetic vision into the
future is included in the general concept of the "demonic"? Is
not all this one unitary power at work in the same great soul?

Even so, opinion may still differ over this dialogue as a work
of Plato's own hands.[15] The science of classical philology is far
from possessing the safe techniques by which, say, art criticism
can distinguish among original works, works of disciples, and
works from the workshop with finishing touches by the master.
Yet, in all strictness, we may say something—against the critics
—about the date of composition. The style in the most general
sense (i.e., structure, language, and conceptual content) points
to the conclusion that this dialogue was written around the year
400 B.C., and not at the time of Xenokrates[16] or some indefinite
later period.[17] (Would anyone try to date the tombstone of He-
geso in the age of Lysippos or at the time of the altar of Perga-
mon?) The action of the dialogue takes place in the year 410/
409; Archelaos of Macedonia (124D) has been reigning "for a
few years" (i.e., since 413). The Athenian expedition against
Ephesos (410/409) is still undecided, but Socrates does not expect any good to come from it (129D). Is it not most probable,
then, that the dialogue was written at a time when these events
and the reactions they produced were still alive in the minds of
the author and his readers?

PART III

Self-portrait and Disguises
of the Philosopher

TWELVE

Apology

SOON AFTER the death of Socrates, it became customary to write fictitious speeches in his defense, or speeches for and against him. The last and longest of these was composed by Libanios more than seven hundred years later. How Socrates appeared in court and what he actually said there continues to agitate men's minds, and we are reluctant to admit that we know nothing about it. Nothing at all, really? Nobody, to be sure, would claim today that Plato's *Apology* reproduces, in its essentials, the actual speech delivered by Socrates.[1] Would a man of the fifth century—above all, a man who was committed, more than any other Greek, to the principle of oral conversation and who, in Plato, proclaims repeatedly that he is incapable of making long speeches—would and could such a man have delivered a polished speech in the style, we may say, of the early fourth century? Perhaps the fragmentary and conversational nature of Xenophon's *Apology* resembles, at least remotely, the proceedings at the trial as heard by an objective witness—if there could have been such a witness. Yet, we may doubt whether Xenophon was capable of what he had the best intention to do: namely, to write down what Socrates "actually" (τῷ ὄντι) had said in court.[2]

But did Socrates really say nothing, or very little, in the stormy confusion of the session at court? Does Kallikles, the tyrannical man in Plato's *Gorgias*, give us a correct picture of what happened when he predicts, "When they hale you off to court, Socrates, you will be in a daze and have nothing to say" (*Gorgias* 486AB)? Socrates does not object to this prediction, but even seems to confirm it at the end. "I shall have nothing to say in

157

court" (521E). Again, speaking to Kallikles, he says, "When you stand trial before the judges in the lower world, you will open your mouth and be dizzy as I shall be before an earthly tribunal" (526E *et seq.*). Can we really believe that Socrates submitted to the indictment without saying a word? And if he did, would not such silence be open to different interpretations?[3] Let us not forget that Socrates, even in the early dialogues of Plato, refers to himself in almost the same words. "Things went dark before my eyes and I felt dizzy" (*Protagoras* 339E). "I feel dizzy because the discussion leads nowhere" (*Lysis* 216C). Can we fail to hear the irony in these words?

In the second century A.D., the orator Maximus of Tyre composed a speech (*Orations* III), "Whether Socrates was right in not defending himself." The speech was directed against those who were "still" attacking Socrates. Does Maximus mean that Socrates made no defense or as good as none on his own behalf? Or does he mean that Socrates did not deliver a speech of defense in the ordinary sense of the word? At times he seems to suggest that Socrates kept silent throughout. But even if the orator meant to say this, he would still contradict sharply the modern view that "Socrates was a failure in court" (Heinrich Gomperz). For, as Maximus makes perfectly clear, if Socrates had delivered a speech in his own defense, this would have meant "to turn his back and to retreat from the blows; thus it would have been an act of cowardice disguised behind a fine façade." What Socrates actually did, according to Maximus, was the opposite. "He stood his ground; he caught the blow; and he proved himself a hero" (III 8 *et seq.*). In those stormy proceedings at court, Socrates may have said very little that resembles the sustained speech characteristic of the early fourth century; at times, he may even have "felt dizzy." But not even Plato would have had the power —assuming he would have wished to do so—of converting the vanquished into a victor and making him then, throughout a long lifetime, the center of his own work. Socrates did not fail before the court of Athens any more than Jesus failed before the Sanhedrin or before Pilate. Were it otherwise, world history would have taken a different course.

The title of Plato's *Apology* is rather an obstacle to grasping the essential meaning behind this "apology." We need but compare Xenophon's *Apology* to see a defense in the ordinary sense. Xenophon sets out to show that the separate charges brought against Socrates are false. Though we come to see something of the nature of the speaker, especially at the beginning where it is said that the entire life of Socrates was a preparation for his speech of defense, this background is marginal and not very deep. How could it be otherwise, since this Socrates as depicted by Xenophon seems to be interested primarily in proving that he is no different from anybody else, that he participated in public sacrifices and celebrations, that others, too, have heard "voices" like himself, and that not only in his case, but in the case of others as well, experts have more power than parents? Xenophon's document is "apologetic" in still another sense. It aims at clearing Socrates of the charge that the proud, defiant tone of his speech was senseless; and Xenophon thinks he can do this by asserting that Socrates wished to die (§§1, 5 *et seq.*).

Plato's basic intention, on the contrary, was decidedly not apologetic—even if the literary controversy over the memory of the executed man as conducted by literary politicians like Polykrates and Lysias should have provided him with an impetus for his own work.[4] Plato's objective is not to make Socrates vanish, as it were, among others who are like him, but to show how Socrates differed from other men (*Apology* 35a 1) and why. For the *Apology*, as any other writing of Plato, provides us with a view of the existence of the philosopher.[5] Even as this existence is a "challenge," so is the defense an attack—a moment in the everlasting struggle between the individual and the mass of mankind, between *arete* and vulgarity, between philosophy and sophistry. In this respect, it is an educational document. "It will be to your advantage to listen" (30c 4). "I am pleading not on my own behalf, but on yours" (30d 7). This time, however, the occasion is not merely a significant moment or a typical encounter. It is the ultimate decision itself. What happens in the *Crito* reaffirms this decision. What happens in the *Phaedo* is the last and most sublime confirmation and, going beyond this, a disclosure of the conceptual and mythical horizons. In the *Apology*, it is the philosophical existence as such that is at stake. For this reason, the work of the philosopher must be shown once more as he conceived it, for here the decision is made about his triumph or failure.

The "outline" is easily seen and may be presupposed.[6] In accordance with the course of the trial, the work is divided into three speeches. The first speech, the actual speech of defense, deals initially (18E–24B) with the popular charges as depicted in the *Clouds* by Aristophanes and then with the official indictment as such (24B–34B). Each part is expanded beyond its immediate purpose. We inquire into the inner structure.

First Speech

17A–18E   The opening criticizes ironically this type of peroration in court. Socrates admits that he is carried away by the speeches of his accusers as he is, in the *Protagoras*, by the oratorical display of the Sophist and, in the *Menexenus*, by the eulogies for the dead in battle. Even as he says in the *Menexenus* (235C 3) that he "barely collected himself on the fourth or fifth day" (ἀναμιμνή-σκομαι ἐμαυτοῦ), so he says here that he "almost forgot himself" (ἐμαυτοῦ ἐπελαθόμην, *Apology* 17A 3), so powerful were their arguments (πιθανῶς ἔλεγον, 17A 3; ὑπὸ τοῦ λέγοντος ἀναπειθόμενοι, *Menexenus* 235B 7). This is the pathological effect of rhetoric (πεπόνθατε, *Apology* 17A 1) against which, speaking seriously, Socrates is of course more immune than the others. His defense against this power derives from the one word "truth." Here truth emerges with the kind of simplicity characteristic of that which is simply taken for granted, just as—in a much lighter and gayer context—truth overcomes the beautiful speeches of the others at the turning point of the *Symposium*: "They did not care whether what they said was false" (198E 2). "But I will speak the truth as I always do" (199A 7). So it sounds in this social setting. Here in the context of the serious struggle at court, the same contrast has a sharper edge: "These men have lied; but from me you will hear the truth" (*Apology* 17B 7).

It is no accident that the accusers lied. Speeches in court, like silver-tongued oratory in general, have no necessary relation to the truth. They aim at persuasion, not at truth; but that which does not aim at the truth falls prey to the *pseudos*. Now Socrates, too, is compelled by law to make a speech in court. Therefore, he will do something that is contrary to usage: he will speak to his judges as he is wont to speak in the market place (17c 7 *et seq.*). This will mean a difference not only in the style of oratory. Again contrary to usage, Socrates will speak the truth. This he proclaims, with raised intensity and bitter sarcasm, to be the "virtue of any speaker" as such (18A 5). Even so, this type of oratory, though transformed in its own nature, is not appropriate to the nature of Socrates. Hence, there is a continuous struggle against it in the *Apology*.

These charges against me have been drummed into you for so long that I will not be able to dispose of them "in a short time" (19A, 24A). . . . . In the *Gorgias* (455A), it is said to be a basic law of rhetoric that the orator cannot really teach anything "in the short time" at his disposal, and, therefore, must resort to dishonest tactics of persuasion. At the same time, a consequence of the proceedings at court is that one cannot examine—and refute (ἐλέγχειν)—one's opponent in the Socratic manner since there is no one to answer (18D). The opponent, to begin with, consists of a mass of listeners who respond only by making inarticulate noises. Hence, there is the repeated and emphatic request (17D 1, 20E 4, 21A 5, 27B 1, 30c 2), "Quiet please!" (This is not uncommon in Xenophon and in other pleadings in court.) Whenever the law permits him to do so, Socrates does replace the type of speech imposed upon him and exercises instead his own kind of cross-examination proving, by keen questions, how ignorant Meletos is (24c 4 *et seq.*). During this part of the trial especially, he must ask the judges to be quiet while he proceeds according to his familiar method of examining by question and answer. Thus, he succeeds in disposing of one accuser in a manner not otherwise customary in court; yet the hostile crowd remains. Only if the law would permit him to converse (διειλέγμεθα, 37A 7) with his judges for many days instead of one, he might perhaps succeed in convincing them, as Socrates puts it ironically (37AB). The idea behind this is that if Socrates had the right and the time to deal with each of his accusers and the five hundred judges in the same manner as with Meletos . . . . But we see at once that this idea is absurd, and Socrates goes to

I
18E–24B
I 1
18E–20C

his death by virtue of this absurdity. The formal treatment itself, therefore, suggests something of the deep antagonism and deadly clash enacted here.

The paradox that the enemy of formal speech must use such a speech in his own defense conceals a still more profound paradox. Socrates charged with impiety—this is the worst kind of confusion. For this reason, he deals first with the charges going back to Aristophanes (18B *et seq.*) in order to distinguish himself, in a backward thrust, from the professional teachers of wisdom, stargazers, and seducers of the young for whom he was mistaken on the stage. Socrates does not take money. The brief sketch of a conversation (charged with deep ironic implications) which he claims to have had with Kallias, the wealthy friend of the Sophists, shows two things: how much Socrates pleads the cause of education and how much he differs from the professional educators who advertise their own product. The conversation with the fathers in the *Laches,* and with young Hippokrates in the *Protagoras,* provides similar ironic comments on the same subject. The struggle against mistaken identity continues; Socrates proves to Meletos himself that the accuser cannot distinguish him from Anaxagoras (26D). Thus, the outcome is that the charge of impiety rests on a mistake of identity—in short, on ignorance. The whole work narrows down more and more to this conclusion.

^{I 2}
20c–24b

Even before the formal charge is stated, the character of the speaker begins to reveal itself. Socrates has acquired a bad reputation because he has a "kind of wisdom" (σοφία τις, 20D 7), consisting in his art of examining men and derived, ultimately, from the command of the god at Delphi. We grasp the contradiction between the words of Apollo according to which Socrates is the wisest among men and his own conviction that he is ignorant, or, to put it differently, the paradox (probed in its true depth) of the man who knows that he does not know. This paradox is the source for his lifelong mission of examining others (21B–23B) and of experiencing this task as a service to the god (θεοῦ λατρεία, 23c 1). With this confession, the genuine piety of Socrates is set, in powerful tension, against the senseless charge of impiety, and we can see what "piety" and "impiety" mean to him. Piety is not a feeling or an inner disposition (this would be alien to the age), nor is it (and this would be quite in the spirit of the age) the fulfilling of one's civic duties toward the deities of the state. For Socrates, piety refers to his mission based on the conviction that he and others are ignorant. This piety, therefore, is "a kind of wisdom" in the Socratic sense, with a touch of something like "courage." "I realized with distress and alarm that I was making myself hated. *Nevertheless*, I felt compelled to serve the cause of the god" (21E). It will appear that the unity of the "virtues"—the separate virtues unified in the one virtue— which is the basic problem in Plato's dialogues from the *Protagoras* to the *Republic*, is also of crucial significance in the *Apology*.

Thus, we are prepared for the official indictment itself (24B 7).[7] As in the case of a false statement in other dialogues, so the accusation here is followed by an examination—and refutation— of Meletos, which we mentioned above for its formal significance. A few additional features must be noted. The whole population of Athens are educators, the judges, the audience, the councilors, the members of the Assembly, all of them are educators—with the exception of Socrates. This is not only an absurd exaggeration, but more. It expresses, on the one hand, the sophistic relativism as in the *Protagoras* (327E) according to which everybody is a teacher of *arete*—thus destroying the possibility of any genuine education. On the other hand, it drives home to us, in an ironic counterthrust, that Socratic education is unique, indeed, and different from what the general population calls education. The sharpest rejoinder will be made in the *Gorgias* (515C *et seq.*) where it is said in a striking paradox: even the greatest statesmen of Athens have ruined the state; Socrates is the only political man.

II
24B–34B
II 1
24B–28A

The indictment conceals another absurdity. Socrates asks whether Meletos means that he is corrupting the youth intentionally or unintentionally. Meletos, again expressing the popular view, replies without hesitation—intentionally. This provides Socrates with an opportunity to show how absurd it would be for someone intentionally to run the risk of being harmed by those whom he has badly educated. The argument sounds sophistic—more so than that by which Xenophon (*Apology* §19 *et seq.*) repudiates the same charge—but only because it is backed up by the profound and paradoxical thesis, previously touched upon in the *Protagoras* (345CD), that voluntary wrongdoing is impossible. The reasoning here reminds us of the *Gorgias* (519C): the Sophists have no reason to complain about the ingratitude of their disciples because they should have taught them justice and evidently failed to do so. In the *Apology*, we must add as an affirmative supplement what is said later (33C *et seq.*) The loyalty of the disciples of Socrates proves that the charge against him is baseless.

26B–28A   Finally, there is the defense against the charge that Socrates does not honor the gods of the state according to custom, or that he does not believe in their existence (νομίζειν θεούς, νομίζειν εἶναι θεούς)[8] and is introducing new demonic beings. Socrates, rightly criticizing the vagueness in the wording of this part of the indictment (εἰπὲ ἔτι σαφέστερον, 26B 9), compels his accuser Meletos to make the point more precise. (At times, one might think Socrates is driving him into another exaggeration.)[9] The crime, then, of which Socrates is accused is out-and-out atheism and the dissemination of unbelief through his teachings. The trial of Anaxagoras, a generation earlier, is mentioned as a precedent. Socrates objects to being mistaken for this famous philosopher of nature. The mistake shows, indeed, how little his accusers know about Socrates and, incidentally, about Anaxagoras as well. Then he shows that it is contradictory to allege that someone denies the existence of the gods and to assert, at the same time, that he believes in the existence of demons that must be either gods or their descendants. This is stated sharply. It is less attuned to eliciting a sympathetic response among the judges than the corresponding passage in Xenophon (§11) where Socrates appeals to his record of participating in official religious ceremonies.[10] There are hints in Plato's *Apology* that will be developed in the *Symposium*: first, of a biographical nature, when Alkibiades relates the event as remarkable as it is simple that Socrates remained lost in thought for a whole day and night until "he went away after praying to the sun" (220CD); second, of a philosophical-mythical nature, when Diotima assigns the demonic to the region "in between" the human world and the divine (202D *et seq.*). We seem to hear an anticipation of this when, a little later in the *Apology* (31CD), Socrates calls his inner voice something "divine and demonic."

Now it is shown, however, that the defense against the official indictment is not the main thing. Even as he did in the first part, when responding to the popular charges repeated in the *Clouds*, so Socrates now again proceeds to reveal his own existence and to bear witness to it. "Piety" is the over-all concept, and the speech ends with the strong affirmation: I revere the gods more than any of my accusers do (35D). Thus, by "reverence of the gods" Socrates means something very different from what his accusers mean. It is piety together with, or indissolubly linked with, justice, courage, and wisdom. The unity of the virtues is visible throughout, even if it is not stated as an explicit theme. At the same time, since *arete* has a "political" meaning as well, the remainder of the *Apology* shows the paradoxical relationship between Socrates and his own *polis*.

To have followed a line of action that, ultimately, puts him in danger of death—this popular criticism does not mean anything to Socrates. What matters is not the consequence of our actions, but whether we act justly or unjustly, whether we do good or evil. Otherwise, the popular complaint might be brought also against "the demigods who died at Troy, the son of Thetis and all the others." Here the "just" act is linked with "courage" manifested in one's resistance to the threat of death. The manliness of the philosopher finds its prototype in the life of the hero. *Amor fati* in the case of Achilles and in the case of Socrates is cast from the same mold.[11] There is even more behind this mythical analogy. Previously Socrates had refuted the charge of impiety by showing—quite eristically, as we saw—that in honoring the descendants of the gods he could not be a despiser of the gods. Now do not the words about Achilles convey a sense of true piety: reverence for the gods and the heroes of our land, or acknowledgment of the mythical tradition as a personal commitment? This adherence to tradition, however, becomes true piety only in so far as it is combined with justice and courage.

The necessary connection among the various virtues comes through even more clearly in the next section. "Just as the com-

II 2
28A–34B

28B–28D

28D–30C

manding officers assigned me my post in battle which I held at
the risk of life, so the god has appointed me to conduct my life
as a lover of wisdom, i.e., to examine myself and others. If I
now deserted my post, through fear of death or any other danger,
then the charge that I do not believe in the gods would indeed
be justified. For then I would disobey the oracle and be afraid
of death thinking that I am wise when I am not." The loyalty
of Socrates serving as a hoplite in the Athenian forces seems to
be inconsistent with his struggle against the authorities of the
state. Yet, both derive from the same *arete*. Piety, courage, and
wisdom—these are the traditional names of the virtues that here
converge upon the same point. To fear death is cowardice. It is
ignorance as well, for it means to act as if we knew that death is
the worst of all evils. To run away from death would be an act
of disloyalty to the oracle or, in other words, to the divine mission.
"To be called by the god"—this calling means a definite mode
of knowledge and action, and a definite attitude toward death.
The seal of a divine calling, in turn, lifts this kind of knowledge
and this courage beyond the sphere of the accidental and merely
human. They are not something *had* (along with other things);
instead, they determine one's existence.

30c–31c   "You cannot harm me; for the better man cannot be harmed
by the worse. You can put me to death or banish me or deprive
me of my civic rights. But these are no evils as compared with
the wrong committed by those who would put an innocent man
to death." These words anticipate the profound problem treated
in the *Thrasymachus* and, with greater intensity, in the *Gorgias*:
to do wrong is worse than to suffer wrongdoing. He who does
wrong harms himself, i.e., his own "soul." He who acts justly
and is a good man will be well off; he will be eudaemonic, "of
good genius"—or happy. So speaks the man who knows what
"justice" is. He knows also that "the god appointed me as
gadfly to this city as if it were a noble, but sluggish steed.[12]
Thus I stir you up ceaselessly by settling upon every one of you.
That I was really sent to you as a gift from the god is shown by
my poverty—a consequence of caring for you only and of neglecting my own affairs." Here justice combines with piety. The
gadfly is a concrete image for the *elenchos*, the delivery of the

kind of "knowledge" that is unique to Socrates. Plato's *Apology* is meant to be such a gadfly to the reader.

"Strangely enough, in pursuing this work upon individuals, I 31c–32a have completely avoided any public appearance." Is this a lack of daring (οὐ τολμῶ, 31c 6)? By no means, for "anybody fighting for justice must do so" (32a 1). Thus, again, courage and justice. . . . "The divine voice has urged me to take this kind of action." Thus, again, piety. . . . Can this detachment from the affairs of the state reveal a lack of civic spirit? On the contrary, *arete* is directly related to the community. Here are the roots for the paradox of the *Gorgias*, where Socrates is shown as the only political man.

"My endeavor was always to do nothing unjust or impious— 32a–32e under the regime of the Thirty, despite imminent danger of death, as much as at the trial of the commanders at the battle of Arginousai where I also was on the side of the law, despite personal danger, and opposed to carrying through the illegal decision of the masses out of fear of imprisonment or death." Here, too, justice, piety, and courage are linked, indissolubly, in one act and attitude. Here, too, self-detachment from the state saves the dignity of Athens.

These references to political affairs show, on the one hand, 32e–34b that Socrates was right in keeping his distance and, on the other, that he acted in a public spirit. "I have never permitted anybody to transgress the limits of justice, least of all those who are maliciously called my pupils. In truth, I have never been anybody's teacher." Along with the theme of justice, the conception of Socratic education emerges here once more as something altogether different from what is ordinarily called "teaching." Why, then, are his pupils so attached to Socrates? They are amused by his method of cross-examination—a reply that conceals rather than explains the truth. The task of examining others is again attributed to a command of the god, thus combining knowledge, action, and piety. On these grounds, there cannot be any corruption. "It is clear that I did not corrupt my pupils: they and, above all, their parents and brothers will testify that I speak the truth." The names of the most important members of the Socratic circle, including Plato's own, are cited here—less for historical reasons than as a moral power—before Socrates declines to follow the customary course of using friends and relatives as a means for arousing the sympathy of his judges.

34B–35D   Xenophon, a loyal though average disciple, tries hard, as we saw, to show that Socrates was no different from other people. In sharpest contrast to this portrait, Alkibiades will show the master, in the *Symposium* (221C), as somebody "resembling no one among men." In the similar words of the *Apology*: "It is a fact that Socrates is different from the common run of mankind."[13] For him who has the reputation of wisdom or courage or any other virtue, it would be shameful to act as the majority of people do. It would be cowardice. It would also be a breach of justice, which the judges have sworn to uphold. Thus, if someone were to entreat them to be sympathetic despite their oath, he would violate and they would violate the duty they owe toward the gods (οὐδέτεροι ἂν εὐσεβοῖεν, 35C). With this plea, the whole speech concludes by reassuring them again that Socrates, contrary to the indictment, reveres the gods more than any of his accusers do. His reverence, to be sure—as we have now seen more than once—has only the name in common with what is ordinarily called "piety."

Second Speech

35E–38B   In Xenophon's *Apology* (§23), Socrates, following custom, declines to propose a penalty for himself and forbids his friends to do so, for that would mean an admission of guilt. Plato describes the factual situation differently. Socrates finally does give an estimate of himself and his friends are present to corroborate it, though only with regard to a marginal matter.[14] Surely, this must be correct; else, how could we explain that Plato mentions himself as one of the friends? The most important matter, however, is that the plea is shifted from a legal to an existential context. Penalty (or reward) must be "appropriate" (ἀξία, ἄξιος, 36B 5, 36D 3) to the deed. Thus, we see once more the difference in the two forms of life shown in the *Gorgias* and elaborated in the *Republic* (cf. *Republic* II 365D with *Apology* 36B). On the one side stands the life of the professional politician, primarily concerned with self-preservation (σῴζεσθαι) and, on the other, the

life of the philosopher, a warning, searching critic fulfilling his
duty toward the whole community by being "of greatest benefit
to each individual." How he addresses and corrects the individual
is shown in the sketch of a conversation most reminiscent of the
Alcibiades Major (127E *et seq.*) : One must not care for the peripheral things of life, one's belongings, until one has learned to
care for what really matters—one's own self.[15] Thus, Socrates
proposes for himself something "good" as appropriate to the
service he has rendered—free maintenance at the sacred hearth of
the state as is due its benefactor.

"He who deserves a reward must not propose something bad
for himself, i.e., a penalty. I must not wrong anybody, least of
all myself." (This is a peculiar variation upon the basic theme
of the *Gorgias*.) Having just demanded the highest reward for
himself, Socrates considers various possible penalties, imprisonment as well as banishment, only to reject them as subterfuges
which would serve no point. Then, once more, the voice of temptation is heard: "Leave the city and quietly spend the rest of
your life somewhere else." And now it is made quite clear what
is at stake for Socrates in these proceedings and in his own self-
estimate. He knows death awaits him. If he were to evade it, he
would thereby renounce his mission and its fulfillment. This,
then, is at stake: the reaffirmation of his own existence.

That is why this existence is shown once more in contrast to
the pseudo-political life. That is why Socrates demands that the
highest honor of the state be conferred on him. That is why the
various other penalties are rejected; they would merely serve to
evade death. And that is why it is impossible for him to disappear
quietly. Once more, this existence—thus confirmed—is presented
to the audience as a command of the god and the supreme fulfillment of life (μέγιστον ἀγαθόν) in victoriously overcoming the
temptation of life itself.

Does not the plea for a fine of one mina (or, upon the urging
of his friends, of thirty minae) contradict what we have just
said? The rigid conception of Socrates that we find in Xenophon
must have thought so. According to this conception, the action
of Socrates was consistent only if he refused to propose any
penalty. Plato, it seems to us, knew better.[16] Socrates proposes

a ridiculously small fine; he would have suggested more if he could afford it, for then he would not "suffer any harm" (οὐδὲν γὰρ ἂν ἐβλάβην). He raises the amount upon the urging of his friends. In doing so he yields to the *nomos* and shows, precisely through this act of compliance, that he is interested not in making the great gesture, but in avoiding what will do harm.

Third Speech

Xenophon, too, makes Socrates address the judges once more after sentence of death has been pronounced. This agreement with Plato would seem to prove more than can be proved by general reasons adduced to show that this last speech cannot be historically true because it is impossible.[17] It must, of course, remain uncertain how many of the judges stayed to listen to the condemned man and how much, or how little, of what he said resembled a well-constructed "speech." According to Xenophon, Socrates defends himself again (I have done nothing deserving death); he accuses the others (the false witnesses and the judges are impious and unjust); and he consoles himself (Palamedes is better off than Odysseus). Plato knows how to say something more essential.

38c–39d   If the first speech presented the existence of the philosopher and the second speech confirmed this existence in the face of death, the third speech anticipates the voice of posterity condemning the judges on two grounds: "By putting to death this man who is as ignorant as he is profoundly knowing you commit an act of supreme injustice—and a meaningless act, besides, for he is an old man who would soon die anyway." A prophecy follows shortly afterward (39c): "You wanted to get rid of an annoying critic, but in doing so you will only get more and harsher critics. For a man like myself cannot be got rid of by putting him to death, but only by changing one's own way of life." Socrates lives on beyond his death—lives, especially, in the works of Plato—precisely because he was true to himself unto death.[18] For this reason, he asserts once more after the death penalty has been imposed: "I stand by what has happened because I willed it. I chose courage instead of cowardice." Upon this choice rests the power of Socrates throughout the ages.[19]

From those who condemned him Socrates turns to those who
acquitted him. His words, now no longer embroiled in argumentation, convey the purest revelation of the significance of his life
and death. "What is the meaning of this sentence? Since the
prophetic voice, the sign of the god, did not once oppose me
during my defense, it follows that what happened to me must
be something good. And I cannot expect anything but good from
death that is either a dreamless sleep or a reunion with the heroes
of old." There are the judges in the lower world; there are the
poets and bards of the heroic age; there are the heroes celebrated
in myths. Socrates will stand his ground before them and in their
midst. In their circle, he will continue his conversations and his
examination of men's lives—as one of them, though unique in
his own way. Come what may, the life he has led and its end are
reaffirmed, once more, as being good. Or, as it is said in more
general terms: "A good man cannot suffer any harm. Therefore,
it must be best for me to die." This death is good. Hence, death
is good—provided he who dies is a good man.

Thus, once more, one's own fate and, ultimately, death as fate
are put into man's own hands. If we interpret the word "good"—
a dominant theme in these final words—in the rich meaning of
Plato's thought, we begin to realize what goal emerges here at
the end of the whole work. We may approach it through a passage similar in its wording at the end of the *Republic* (X 613AB):
"Whatever happens to the just man must be for his ultimate
good in this life and after death. For the gods will not neglect a
man who strives to become as like a god as it is humanly possible."
These words are spoken by Socrates. His partner concurs: "Yes,
it goes without saying they cannot neglect him who is like one
of them" (ὑπὸ τοῦ ὁμοίου). Here the reference back to the actual
wording (*Apology* 41D)—and that means to the situation of the
Apology—is just as evident as the fact that what is said in the
Apology is both clarified and deepened in the *Republic*, where the
highest good has emerged as the central focus of the whole work.

Another look into the future stands with a final request: "Do
unto my sons as I have done unto you—in case they should become as you are." Thus, Socrates is challenging, in an extreme
paradox, those who condemned him to death—and us ourselves

—to follow in his steps. "But now it is time to go, I to die and you to live; which is the better prospect is not known to anyone but God." We must respond not only to the dignity expressed in these last words. We must also realize what they say about Socrates and how they illuminate his "being unto death." Even as he does not evade death, so he does not try to gain by death what he did not possess in life. He does not strive, like an early Christian, for the martyr's crown; nor, like Peregrinus the Cynic, for the acclaim bestowed upon a despiser of life; nor, like a Gnostic, for release from the unnatural chains of the flesh; nor for nirvana, like a Buddhist monk. He does not die like a Stoic or an Epicurean to whom man is a part of nature and death a natural process known to man. For Socrates, death is the last yet decisive confirmation of life. Thus, his final words set him apart from all the dogmatists within and outside the Socratic circle. Even when he said that death was something good, this was not a dogma. He dies Socratically—truly human in the spirit of genuine piety. This piety is shown once more as identical with his ignorance and it reveals this ignorance once more as akin to the deepest knowledge.

THIRTEEN

Crito

THIS brief dialogue seems, at first, to stand apart in Plato's work as does the moment in the life of Socrates that it depicts. Tradition has it that the "associates" of Socrates secretly planned his escape from prison; according to another traditional version —its value is not certain—we find the Socratic Aischines in place of Plato's Kriton.[1] Why did Plato choose this futile attempt as a topic for a work of his own? It was not to preserve the historical record. This would be alien to his nature, especially as it appears that he changed the record arbitrarily. Nor did he do so to achieve a special effect—say, to justify the friends of Socrates or possibly even Socrates himself.[2] For how could he hope to justify the friends, against the opinion of the many, in a dialogue designed to show that this very opinion is worthless? And before whom should he justify Socrates when everybody else would have reason to justify himself before Socrates? Instead, Plato seized the moment when, at the very last, the temptation of life itself threatened to destroy the work of Socrates—a temptation without "sound and fury," to be sure, so that there is no sign of an actual struggle. Thus, perhaps this is not even a temptation, but simply a moment of decision. The fact that the philosopher dies voluntarily, as a logical consequence of the way he has lived, needed to be confirmed even after the *Apology*. Otherwise, the objection that death was forced on him by external compulsion could not be refuted. Hence, it must be shown clearly that Socrates' death was an act of free choice.

Unique as this work seems to be, it is related to other dialogues, even if we disregard its natural affinities with the *Apology* and the *Phaedo*. In the preliminary conversation of the *Protagoras*, it is the young Hippokrates—here it is Kriton—who comes to Socrates "at the break of dawn" while Socrates is still resting on his couch. In either case, the visitor has an urgent request to make and Socrates leads him to acknowledge the general principle behind it. (The difference between the two dialogues is significant as well; for example, in the *Crito* Socrates reveals his inner calm, to the astonishment of his friend, by quietly sleeping on.)[3] Yet, this is still a very general kind of agreement. The affinity with other works is shown more strikingly when we realize that the *Crito* is their exact counterpart. In the *Thrasymachus*, the *Euthyphro*, and the *Hippias Major*, Socrates always asks a "What is . . .?" question, and the immediate answer of his partner always seeks to define the thing in question in terms of his own personal life or inclination, whereupon Socrates begins with his refutation. In the *Crito*, however, Kriton's plan and what he urges Socrates to do are judged according to an unshakable, absolute standard. It is true that, in either case, the partner aims at dragging the absolute principle down to the level of his own subjective will. But whereas in the other dialogues just mentioned, Socrates merely shows that this will not do and lets the conversation end on a note of *aporia*, in the *Crito* he pulls the subjective will of the other up to the absolute standard to which he himself subscribes.

I
44B–46B
Clear as the decision was for Socrates, the structure of the work is just as simple. In the first section, Kriton gives his reasons for urging Socrates to escape. For Kriton, the situation is a multiple misfortune (οὐ μία συμφορά). First, it means the loss of a friend; then it means, in particular, facing up to what the many will say, namely, that Kriton was not willing to make any sacrifice for his friend. At the end he returns even more explicitly to this concern about what others will think. It is not only a matter of concern for Kriton and the associates. Kriton appeals to what people will say also in order to influence the decision of Socrates. In between, "among other things," as it were, the action of Socrates and his friends is judged—or, at least, seems to be—in terms of certain objective principles. First, there is an appeal to what is "just": by abandoning himself

Socrates is doing the same thing as his enemies, and by deserting his sons he is neglecting what he owes them. Second, there is an appeal to "bravery": even the trial itself might have been avoided by displaying a little more manly courage, and people will say the same thing later about the present crisis. Kriton is piling up, and mixing up, different reasons,[4] but the idea of what others will say obviously carries the greatest weight with him. He is closest to the spirit of Socrates in his appeal to justice and in the following statement (45D): "You must choose what a good and brave man would choose, especially since you claim to have pursued manly virtue all your life." But this argument, too, loses its force—if only because it is buried among all the others.

Yet, we must not overlook one aspect. Modern interpreters who find the role of Kriton "by no means enviable," or see in him "the enemy in the friend," judge invariably by remembering how Socrates himself responds to these appeals. They forget that —without him—most of us would be inclined to listen to good reasons such as these as the basis for our own action. I once heard a professor of philosophy argue that Socrates should have followed Kriton's advice. This was an honest attitude and not as outrageous as it may seem.

When Socrates begins his reply, the *logos* is invoked, at once, in opposition to "opinion." The nature of the *logos* requires that it be valid independent of the circumstances; else, it would degenerate into mere "talk." The method of the *logos* is joint inquiry. Its first triumph is the defeat of *communis opinio*. The "tyrannical opinions of the many" are overruled by "the one person who has knowledge" (εἷς ἐπαΐων), especially if this person knows something about justice and injustice. The tyrannical power of the many "who have the power to kill us" is overruled by the principle that the important thing is not to live, but "to live well" (εὖ ζῆν) and that means justly. Thus, in contrast to the many divergent and hence suspect "points of view" (σκέμματα, 48c 4), the inquiry converges upon the crucial question: Is the action we are considering just or unjust?

The second move of the Socratic *logos* is to expand upon this norm. We have agreed often before that wrongdoing is never good or beautiful (honorable), but always ugly and harmful to

II
46ʙ–54ᴄ
II 1
46ʙ–48ᴇ

II 2
48ᴇ–49ᴇ

the agent himself. This thesis is not developed here, yet its justification was at least alluded to (47E) : as bad nourishment ruins
the body, so injustice harms the soul, which is the most precious
possession of the person who acts justly or unjustly.[5] For a demonstration of this thesis we must go to the *Thrasymachus* or the
Gorgias. It is not that Plato would cite one of his dialogues.
Socrates is simply referring to previous discussions where Kriton,
too, evidently was present. From the conclusions reached in those
discussions it follows that it is never right to repay (ἀντἀδικεῖν)
one wrong by another. Socrates realizes that, for all time to
come, he shares this conviction with but a few others and that
he is in radical opposition to the many who, without reason,
easily put people to death and then, just as easily, would bring
them back to life if they could (48c). It follows, without further
proof, that we must act as we are obliged to act according to
justice.

II 3   On the third level, the escape proposed by Kriton is judged
49E–54c   according to this norm. Kriton, too, had previously argued in
favor of this escape by invoking, among other reasons, the name
of justice. How, then, can we determine in this concrete situation
what is just? Justice, according to Plato's Socrates, has its foundations in the state and in its decrees or laws. Thus, if Socrates
escaped, he would violate the sacred laws of the state. This is
shown in the last section where the laws themselves challenge
Socrates to justify himself. Justice is shown in its concrete embodiment in the laws of the state—again, not in general terms
but (in spite of everything) in the specific laws of the city of
Athens. That these laws here speak for themselves is not a rhetorical formality, not a "prosopopoeia." On the contrary, what
is heard here expresses something sublime and sacred, with an
objective life of its own. It is the ideal Athens—better than Crete
and Sparta despite their eunomy (52E) or good legal order—
that speaks here.[6] By making this Athens speak for itself, Socrates puts the blame for his death upon the individuals admin-
istering the law, and acquits the state and the laws themselves
(54c).

Socrates had shown before that wrongdoing harms the wrongdoer, that it is never right to repay one wrong by another, and

that it is wrong to break a contract. Now the laws prove to him, by talking through him, that if he escaped he would break an agreement that he had tacitly acknowledged all his life. The laws, then, compel him by question and answer to "agree" with them. The same word (ὁμολογία, ὁμολογεῖν) is used to express the legal commitment and the dialectical necessity.[7] Thus, Socrates submits his action to judgment by a universal norm both in the legal and in the dialectical sense.

Yet, the fatefulness of his decision still needs to be made explicit. Socrates—so the laws now show him—would destroy his life work if he yielded to the temptation to escape. In words he has dedicated his whole life to *arete*, justice, the state, and the law. Now he must confirm his teaching through action. If he should escape, he would not refute his judges, but prove them right. Moreover, he who has always advocated order and discipline would have to live in communities where disorder and lack of discipline prevail. He would have to adapt himself to evil men and associate with them—which, according to Plato's last work, the *Laws* (V 728B), is the worst kind of punishment for wrongdoing. Thus, he would destroy, in one stroke, what he has always talked about and taught. His life heretofore moving in the sphere of the *logos* would be nothing but idle talk.

At the very end, the speech of the laws probes, for a moment, still more deeply. Socrates must be able to justify himself also before the rulers "in Hades." If he violates the laws on earth, "our brothers, the laws in Hades, will not receive you kindly." The laws of Athens are related not alone to the laws in any other well-ordered state; all these laws are related to the laws in the world beyond. Earthly norms—in a view similar to that of Herakleitos—cannot be divorced from eternal laws. Thus, the decision of Socrates is not only a fulfillment of his own law; it is also a confrontation with eternal law. This brings Plato's work back to its beginning. Kriton found Socrates asleep and, fortunately, did not awaken him, for Socrates was dreaming of how a beautiful woman dressed in white robes promised him that he would "come to the fertile land of Phthia on the third day" (44AB). In Homer, it is Achilles who so speaks of his homeland. We are reminded that Socrates is returning home—to his eternal home.[8]

That this is more than an emotional appeal is shown at the conclusion of the dialogue. In this home the rule of law prevails supreme and firm forever.[9]

The "philosophical" meaning of this dialogue often has been misunderstood.[10] Such misunderstanding is possible only when philosophy no longer understands itself because the philosopher —to cite Kierkegaard—has forgotten that he exists.

A final word about a slight yet unmistakable affinity with the *Gorgias* may be added. Kriton mentions being afraid of the many, who have the power to kill us (44D). In the *Gorgias* (486AB), Kallikles makes this threat of the many explicit. They will inflict any act of violence, even death. In neither case is Socrates moved by fear, but against dire warnings, he defends the thesis that wrongdoing must be avoided at all cost. In both cases, this truth is based upon the recognition that wrongdoing harms one's own soul. Again, at the end of both dialogues, we hear a myth—in the *Crito*, invoking the eternal laws of the beyond, and in the *Gorgias*, depicting the judges in the lower world who dispense justice in accordance with these eternal laws. Thus far can we detect similar features in the quite dissimilar structures of the two dialogues.

FOURTEEN

Euthydemus

THE CONVERSATION between Socrates and Kriton, at the beginning and at the end, provides the framework for the main dialogue. At the most crucial point (290E), this conversation actually breaks into the dialogue itself. What this frame means for an understanding of the work as a whole can be assessed only at the end.

FRAME
271A–272D
304B–307C

Socrates is the narrator. The story of the main dialogue comes to us as filtered through his ironic screen; and just as at the crucial moment the listening Kriton doubts the truth of the story, so we have reason to believe that this irony is at work from the very beginning, as, for example, when Socrates says (272E) that he was sitting in the Lyceum "by divine providence" and when he appeals to his "familiar, demonic sign" (τὸ εἰωθὸς σημεῖον τὸ δαιμόνιον) which prevented him from getting up.[1] As so often in Plato, play and seriousness are intimately linked. For the dialogue deals with the difference between genuine education and clowning, between truth and deception, between being and appearing. It is indeed a comedy, but beyond that something quite different as well.[2]

272D–275C

As in the *Lysis*, the action takes place in the dressing room of a wrestling school. Just as the two boys there, Menexenos and Lysis, come and sit down beside Socrates, so does Kleinias here when he sees Socrates (*Lysis* 207B; *Euthydemus* 273B). The power emanating from Socrates cannot be shown more simply and forcefully. They sit together on a bench with the others who take part in the conversation, again as in the *Lysis* and in the *Charmides*. Another link with the *Lysis* is that in addition to the boy about

179

whose education Socrates is concerned, there is a flattering ad-
mirer—Hippothales in the *Lysis*, here Ktesippos—who represents the false mode of loving. In fact, Ktesippos also was present
in the *Lysis*. The two dialogues even agree on such a detail as
the following: after a hard mental effort, Socrates, as experienced
an educator as he is kindly, will let the boy "rest up" (βουλόμενος
ἀναπαῦσαι, *Euthydemus* 277D; *Lysis* 213D).[3] It will appear that
the *Euthydemus* also has much in common with the *Charmides*
in the development of thought until both dialogues ultimately
end in *aporia*.

The basic theme of the *Lysis* and the *Charmides* provides only
one thread of the fabric of the *Euthydemus*. Intertwined with it
goes another. Kleinias, we learn, is a cousin of Alkibiades. Athenian youth, the noblest substance the world has seen, rises before
our eyes. At the same time, there arises—as always—the danger
here expressed by Socrates: someone may come and turn the
mind of Kleinias in another direction and ruin him (275B). This
threat comes to life in the eristic debaters Euthydemos and Dionysodoros, and in the dangerously false instruction with which
they overwhelm Kleinias. Thus, the latter is placed between the
false educators and the true one just as the young Hippokrates,
in the *Protagoras*, stands between the sophistic chief and Socrates.
In both dialogues, the conflict between the two opposing principles of education takes place in an exchange between sophistic
and Socratic sections; of these, the Socratic sections are connected with each other and lead, in an essentially unified movement, toward a definite—though ultimately hidden—goal. In
the *Protagoras* as in the *Euthydemus*, the Sophist or the two
Sophists walk up and down in the covered arcade followed by
their disciples. In each dialogue, Socrates brings his protégé
together with the dangerous adversary and elicits the claim
that his opponent is teaching the "political art" or (what is
ultimately the same) *arete*, whereupon Socrates, in the *Protagoras* (319B), declares this art to be unteachable and, in the
Euthydemus (274E), at least expresses grave doubt as to whether
it can be taught.

In both dialogues, the struggle ultimately is waged over the
boy's soul. In the *Protagoras*, however, Hippokrates is not men-

tioned again after the beginning. Thus, this personal concern is not made explicit—as it is in the *Euthydemus*. The *Euthydemus*, in the rich counterpoint characteristic of its construction, combines the *Lysis–Charmides* theme with the *Protagoras* theme. The latter provides the struggle of conflicting principles of education; the former takes care that the Socratic principle is shown not only in conflict with what is false (as in the *Protagoras*) but also in the actual work of education as applied to the boy in search of such education.[4]

Finally, we must add what lends a special edge, ludicrousness, and danger to the struggle in the *Euthydemus*. The form of speech, whether a set lecture or a conversation, is of utmost importance in the *Protagoras*. The condition Socrates lays down for his own continued presence is that the partner agree to a conversation conducted in the form of question and answer (338D). Here, however, the same condition is laid down by Euthydemos (275BC). This formal correspondence is most important. For the sophistry of the two fencing masters is not the beguiling art practiced by Protagoras; on the contrary, it is a kind of eristics that no longer can be distinguished from Socratic dialectics by its external form—not even by the fact, say, that Socrates avoids conscious fallacies, since, as we know, he frequently does just the opposite. It can be distinguished only by a difference in mental attitude and orientation. In Socrates there rules the conscious will to educate or (what is the same thing seen from another angle) obedience to the *logos* even when the educator thinks he must resort to dialectical tricks. The eristic fencers wish only to display their brilliance and earn their fee.[5]

This polarity of will hidden behind the same external method is revealed most strikingly when Socrates and Dionysodoros get into a controversy over the game of question and answer (287B–D). Socrates has just proved to his eristic opponents, by using their own arguments, that they undo themselves if they deny (in the familiar sophistic manner) the validity of the principle of contradiction and the possibility of error. The Sophist tries to evade the issue, maintaining that Socrates is not sticking to the last argument but is falling back upon an earlier one—as if the time factor made any difference to a valid argument. To get on,

Socrates poses a searching question; but Dionysodoros, instead
of answering, replies: *You* answer! Thus, one demand confronts
another. It becomes clear, however, that only one speaker has
the right to make a demand as soon as Socrates asks for the
logos (κατὰ τίνα λόγον, 287c 9) to which Dionysodoros would
appeal to justify his demand. Then it appears that the Sophist is
guided by caprice only. "You have come to us," says Socrates,
"as a great wise man in both thought and speech who knows
when to answer and when not to answer." In the systematic
question by Socrates, however, the *logos* itself emerges as the
power guiding the genuine Socratic inquiry. There are similar
violent subterfuges elsewhere (297B *et seq.*) by which the eristic
fencing masters, driven into a corner, try to cover up and Socrates
makes it quite clear that he sees through their tricks. For the
"outsider," however, as for someone like Kriton in the frame of
the dialogue, it was difficult to distinguish the sophistic type of
eristics—which in the "logic" of the Megarians and Cynics found
its way into the Socratic schools—from the dialectics of Plato's
Socrates. This confusion could make men skeptical about the
value of philosophical education in general (306D *et seq.*). It was
the threat of this confusion and the need, therefore, of drawing
clear lines of demarcation against the hostile power, including
the one within himself, that forced Plato to write the *Euthydemus*.

We must bring the individuals of the dialogue into a still more
definite view. (The symbolic meaning of the spatial world of the
dialogue has been discussed elsewhere.)[6] The dangerous Sophists
appear as a couple. This fact has special significance, as we may
learn at the beginning from Kriton's mistake of thinking he has
seen only one. The author lets him make this mistake so that the
correction—it was not one but two—will attract all the more
attention. It is necessary that they be two because like jugglers
they play into each other's hands, whereas the true teacher is one
as truth itself is one. The two Sophists have traveled far and
wide. They are homeless (271c)—in this respect Sophists always
differ from Socrates who is rooted in his own city—and Ktesippos
alludes to their homelessness with contempt (288AB). They are
called "all-wise" (πάσσοφοι), as Plato is fond of calling Sophists
elsewhere. The verdict rendered by the prefix "all" is shown

most clearly in the tenth book of the *Republic* (598CD), where it is said that when someone pretends to be a Jack-of-all-trades, such "all-around knowledge" reflects the belief of a person devoid of judgment who has let himself be deceived. In the case of the Sophists here, the activities in which they are engaged are mounted amusingly. Even as their mastery of boxing and fencing achieves its "perfection" (*Euthydemus* 272A 5) in their battles at court and in their instruction for such legal battles, so they also teach *arete* as a fencing game which they have added to their program—just recently!

The main dialogue is composed with great structural clarity: three eristic sections are separated by two Socratic sections.[7] In the eristic sections, the opponents of the two fencing masters are Kleinias, Ktesippos, and Socrates respectively, following the changing level on which the conversation is conducted. The Socratic sections are almost entirely given over to the master and Kleinias; here one individual is shown the right path by the one true educator. In the eristic sections, as we shall see, the ball is thrown back and forth among all who wish to catch it.

The two Socratic sections form a coherent demonstration beginning with man's striving for happiness and ending with the goal of the "royal" or political art toward which the boy is to advance. As this royal art comes into view, however, the narration breaks off and the dialogue moves back to the conversation between Socrates and Kriton, which ends in *aporia*. In contrast to this firm movement, the sophistic sections consist of a loose series of eristic acrobatics. Such a lack of systematic method is meant again to be characteristic of the Sophists. "But this does not exclude the possibility that, in this artistic imitation of eristic techniques, Plato does not also permit us to glimpse a certain order behind the apparent disorder and caprice."[8] As a matter of fact, there is a kind of orderly sequence—not strictly carried through, but clearly recognizable—both in the formal means of deception and in the content of the eristic sections. While the Socratic conversation ascending in a straight line and approaching very important insights culminates in *aporia*, the Sophists, who at least touch upon some serious topics in the beginning and pose logical knots not easily untangled, end up by being simply silly. If we read the work in the light of these suggestions, which only spell out sharply what other critics have said as well, we gain a certain understanding of it. Yet, the true richness of the work with all its ironic tensions and countertensions is revealed only if we go beyond this level of interpretation.

The young boy is to "become virtuous"; he is to "acquire philosophy and *arete*" (275A)—as yet an undivided unity of what will be distinguished later (in Aristotle) as theoretical and practical knowledge. At once the problem arises whether "arete can be taught," or, in other words, whether education is possible. We sense that Socrates here would not simply affirm this proposition; we know, from the *Protagoras*, the ironic complex of problems associated with this question and we remember how the same question there occupies the same place in the economy of structure (*Protagoras* 319B). What we previously have called the *Protagoras* theme of the *Euthydemus* comes to the fore here at the beginning of the discussion. For the time being, Socrates limits the scope of the problem by simply asking the Sophists: "Implant in the young boy the conviction that he should learn something." But we have seen already that the success of this enterprise depends upon a basic condition that has not been established.

First Eristic Section

1
275c–277c

Two questions are put to the boy: whether those who learn are wise or ignorant and whether they learn what they know or what they do not know. All the terms here are ambiguous, at least in Greek. Wise or learned (σοφός) and ignorant or stupid (ἀμαθής) are used both with regard to a natural disposition and with regard to the possession or lack of acquired knowledge. To learn or understand (μανθάνειν) is used both with regard to acquiring knowledge and with regard to applying the acquired knowledge. In addition, there is the ambiguity inherent in the word γράμματα, referring both to "letters" and "the written work." Thus, Kleinias is refuted in each case. The ignorant or stupid learn, but not the wise. (Ignorant and wise are used in the sense of "possession.") The wise learn, but not the ignorant or stupid. (Stupid and wise are used in a dispositional sense.)

We learn what we know, not what we don't know. (Learning is used in the sense of "understanding.") We learn what we don't know, not what we know. (Learning is used in the sense of "acquiring knowledge.")

Soon (277D *et seq.*) Socrates kindly explains to the perplexed youth that we must practice the art of Prodikos—the semantic doctrine so often and somewhat ironically alluded to by Plato's Socrates—or that we must simply pay close attention to the ambiguities of words, and that the masters are "not yet" serious (278C). It is not enough to see in these eristic antinomies nothing more than fencing thrusts that disable the opponent. They undermine, first with regard to the subject, then with regard to the object, the possibility of knowledge and learning as such and thus they defeat, in a peculiar reversal, the fencing masters themselves, as Socrates will show them later in connection with other instances of their counterfeit art (287A, E).

Even so, the meaning of these statements is hardly exhausted. Neither the wise . . . nor the ignorant—if we put this disjunction together, do we not suddenly perceive a hidden meaning? Does this not sound like Diotima, in the *Symposium* (203E *et seq.*), explaining that those who practice philosophy are neither wise nor ignorant, but somewhere in between wisdom and folly? Even if we reject the *Symposium* as a source for understanding the earlier dialogue, we cannot disregard the *Lysis* (218AB) where we find, almost verbatim, the same line of argument. Those who are wise do not seek wisdom nor do those whose ignorance is such that they are stupid and devoid of reason, but only those seek wisdom who do not as yet think they know what they do not know.

Neither what we know . . . nor what we don't know—the disjunction put together yields the "eristic thesis" cited by Menon, a pupil of Gorgias, against Socrates (*Meno* 80D *et seq.*), according to which we cannot seek one or the other. In short, we cannot inquire or learn at all. This view which "would make us lazy and which is sweet music in the ears of the indolent" is rejected by Socrates. He defends a thesis which "will make us active and inquiring men"; according to this, all learning is recollection of what the soul knew in a previous existence. The geometrical

demonstration in the *Meno,* which is so well known, culminates
in the conclusion that the slave boy did not have knowledge, yet
"these opinions were somehow in him." Thus, "a person who
is ignorant may have true opinions on a subject which he does
not know" (*Meno* 85c). The *Lysis,* then, and still more clearly
the *Meno* show that we have not read an artificial meaning into
the antinomies of the *Euthydemus.*

Let there be no misunderstanding. Plato puts fallacies into
the arguments of the two fencing masters, and the reader is supposed to catch, and possibly remove, these fallacies. They make
us conscious of what an eristic method is in contradistinction to
the Socratic. But there seems to be a secret irony as well in so
far as, in the presence of Socrates, these fallacies not only turn
against their own masters, but reveal new meaning in a depth
that is quite inaccessible to the speakers themselves. Whether
we are here still interpreting the text or reading something into
it can be decided only when we look back upon the work as a
whole.[9]

First Socratic Section

II
277D–282D

Coming to the rescue of Kleinias who is caught up in the en-
tanglements of the eristic wrestlers, Socrates first offers him
kindly counsel about the guile of the Sophists. Then he begins
his questioning designed as a conversation "leading toward"
philosophy. He starts out with a statement that is self-understood: "All men desire to be well off or happy." (The Greek
phrase εὖ πράττειν puts a special emphasis upon one's own activity.) First, the various goods are listed, both external and
internal, which produce well-being. They ascend upward to "wisdom." Then "good fortune" (εὐτυχία) is introduced, apparently
a completely external good, for the term generally means a
"lucky hit" or "fortunate accident"; yet, in the course of the
subsequent discussion ranging over various fields, it is shown
that "good fortune" depends upon knowledge.[10] We observe how
Plato is at pains to divest human "happiness" of any "ac-cident"
and to ground it in an act of choice. In the end, the various "goods"
that previously were said to contribute to well-being lose their
own distinct value. What matters is not the possession of a good,

but the right use; right use, in turn, depends upon knowledge (ἐπιστήμη) interpreted, in typically Socratic fashion, by analogy with knowledge in various technical disciplines; hence, happiness or well-being, the goal of human life, depends upon one's own knowledge. Since it is knowledge and wisdom (φρόνησις καὶ σοφία) that alone convert possessions into "goods," it follows that everything must be done to acquire such knowledge. Since happiness is reduced to knowledge, the latter is shown to be the only thing of value.

Toward the end (282B), the theme of love enters into this simple, straightforward discussion. It is not a cause of dishonor or reproach if anybody shall, for the sake of wisdom, "serve or minister to the lover or any other person." We hear, in the very words, an anticipation of Pausanias and Alkibiades in the *Symposium* (184BC, 219E).[11] Finally, at the end of this section, we return to the great problem posed at the very beginning and still to be clarified, namely, "whether virtue can be taught."[12] Kleinias answers yes. And Socrates is delighted because he need not discuss this matter. Plato wants to say that this question, "How is education possible?"—previously discussed in the *Protagoras* and again to be discussed in the *Meno*—here remains in the background. When we observe how Socrates, in contrast to the Sophists, approaches the teaching of Kleinias, the question is settled with regard to this concrete case. In lovingly leading the way to knowledge, Socrates is the living proof that virtue can be taught. This means, however, that as the question is ordinarily stated and understood, it would more properly call for the answer no.

Second Eristic Section

In the first eristic section, the Sophists disposed of the possibility of knowledge both with regard to the person seeking it and with regard to the object of knowledge. In the first Socratic section, Socrates showed that knowledge is the ruling power in human affairs. The Sophists, of course, did not know what they were doing. Now as Socrates again surrenders the conversation to them, we come to the second eristic section. Here, in a series of arguments, the Sophists will deny the possibility of error and

III
282D–288D

deception (hence, of truth as well) and finally declare that contradiction is impossible. The various theses are all the more absurd the more "deception" and "contradiction" there is in the dialogue. But these capricious theses, which Plato develops in a series of artfully constructed verbal battles, are needed to reveal the depth of the skeptical and subversive sophistic looming behind the two eristic debaters.

III 1
282D–283E

III 2
283E–286B

Ktesippos is drawn into the controversy in defense of his beloved Kleinias by means of an amusing skirmish beginning with an analysis of the concepts "becoming" and "not-being" and proceeding, in three rounds, to prove sophistically that deception, or lying, is impossible. In the first round, he asserts that a person who deceives "says what is not" (οὐ τὰ ὄντα λέγει, 284B); in the second, he asserts that such a person speaks of things in a certain manner, but not as they are" (ἀλλὰ τὰ ὄντα μὲν τρόπον τινὰ λέγει, οὐ μέντοι ὥς γε ἔχει, 284C). This formulation, evidently, points to a solution of the antinomies in Plato's sense as is suggested in the *Cratylus* (385B; cf. 429D), more fully discussed in the metaphors of the lump of wax and the aviary in the *Theaetetus* (191C *et seq.*, 197C *et seq.*), and eventually brought to a conclusion in the *Sophist*. Here, however, Plato does not go on to clarify the nature of *pseudos*.[13] On the contrary, the suggestions implicit in the *Euthydemus* are covered up by eristic machinations; and it is amusing to see how Ktesippos, in the third round, conducts the controversy no longer by referring to the topic itself, but entirely in the style of his opponents, thus proving that their method can be learned quickly (303E). He is, however, not yet sufficiently practiced in it and must make one "concession" after another. At last, he is silenced by the eristic proof that there cannot be any contradiction at all.

III 3
286B–287B

At this point when Ktesippos has nothing further to say, Socrates himself confronts his opponents. "There is no contradiction" (ἀντιλέγειν) —this is the sophistic thesis that Socrates attributes "to Protagoras and others before him" and that, as we know, was an important part of the logic of the Cynics. Here it serves to abolish the general principle of contradiction which could not be dealt with in the particular instances. These arguments, Socrates objects, are nothing new to me. Ultimately, they coincide with the earlier thesis according to which "there is no such thing as falsehood." Unlike Ktesippos he does not go into a discussion about being and not-being. Instead, he compels his opponents to admit that their thesis in overthrowing the others collapses by itself.[14] This argument is analogous to that in the *Theaetetus* (170A *et seq.*) where the view of Protagoras according to which truth is strictly relative to the individual is shown to be self-defeating because it deprives the person who holds it of any superiority over anyone else. Here in the *Euthydemus* Socrates argues: "If you deny falsehood, then you also deny unreason and the possibility of wrong action. In doing so you have repudiated your claim to teach *arete*." Thus, eristics refutes itself through Socrates. When the Sophists try to cover up once more by an amusingly silly thrust (they prove that Socrates has committed an error), he strikes back with their own weapon, in fact, with their own antilogical formulation: If I have not erred, you cannot refute me. If I have erred, you cannot refute me either, since you do not admit the possibility of error.

III 4
287B–288D

Thus, what was anticipated in the first eristic section is now completed. Eristic thinking has refuted itself, or, as Socrates ironically explains to the vexed Ktesippos, the two Sophists have not yet been in earnest—as if they ever could be! The first Socratic section concluded on the note that *sophia* is the ruling power in life. These two concluding notes, then, are exactly opposed to each other.

Second Socratic Section

The second conversation conducted by Socrates resumes where the first one left off, with the demand that one must "pursue philosophy."[15] We must look back upon the second eristic section in order to appreciate how this simple thesis here resumed is filled with content. "Saying what is" (whatever that may be) has come to the fore; error and hence truth, too, have received their due; eristics has emerged as the very opposite of "philosophy" and has collapsed as far as any careful observer is concerned. Now we learn, on the basis of the previous arguments, that the new kind of knowledge must aim at our true advantage and must, therefore, go beyond the mere possession of things

IV
288D–293A

to a determination of their right use. Production and making the right use of what is produced must coincide in that knowledge.

The various arts are examined, and it is shown, in every case, that they know only how to produce but not how to use what they make. We begin with the crafts; then a blow is struck against "speechmaking" in the style of Lysias;[16] finally, we ascend to those regions where we find what we are looking for. Geometry, astronomy, and arithmetic are cited and, above them, using their results, dialectics. We sight the system of sciences developed in the *Republic*.[17] Along another line, the political art rises over and above mere strategy. Dialectics and politics go together—as they do later in the larger dimensions of the *Sophist* and the *Statesman*—and await their unification to be found in the image of the philosophical ruler.

Here the discussion breaks off—or rather, it spills over, with profound significance, into the ensuing frame conversation between Socrates and Kriton (the transition is intentionally vague) where the "royal" art emerges into view.[18] This suggests evidently how the union between dialectics and politics is to be envisaged. The question arises concerning what this political art does. It must do "good." This "good," however—as the first Socratic section had shown—is wisdom or knowledge, which alone gives value to all other goods. Is wisdom or knowledge, then, the good that is realized through the royal art? Yet, since this knowledge is now viewed no longer in relation to other goods, but in relation to its meaning for one's own happiness, it turns out that knowledge only produces knowledge and so on *ad infinitum*, i.e., apparently, into nothingness. Thus, what previously seemed to be the highest level is now again merely a stage beyond which there is something higher.[19] There is no knowledge without an object of knowledge. If we should say that knowledge serves to make men "happy," this well-being of some men again would mean that they make others "happy"; hence, we would have the same infinite regress. We end on the same note of *aporia* where we found ourselves, after much more labor, in the *Charmides*.[20] There we came up against a "science of sciences" which is empty as long as "good" and "evil" do not appear as objects of this knowledge. When they do appear, the "science of sciences" dissolves or is transformed into a knowledge of the good. Thus here, too, the knowledge of the good beckons from afar, still an empty concept until the *Idea* of the Good shows the way out of the *aporia* and checks the detour into nothingness. This is where the *Lysis-Charmides* line of the *Euthydemus* terminates. It is anything but an accident that it should reappear in the central portion of the *Republic* (505ʙ) where the *Agathon* comes into sight.

Third Eristic Section

The three eristic sections enclose the two Socratic ones. This is part of Plato's irony—the same irony that, in the symbolic space of the dialogue, assigns to Socrates his place between the two Sophists, not opposite them, and the same irony that lets the Socratic conversation fade out on a note of *aporia*. Eristics is dead; the royal art has taken its place; yet this has happened so inconspicuously that the dead art does not know how dead it is, but continues to function as a ghost. Now once more we encounter a genuine Platonic irony. In the sophisms of this last eristic section, which seem more and more devoid of content, there are some that have a hidden meaning—beyond the comprehension of their protagonists—and carry the constructive message of the dialogue forward.

"Would you rather," asks Euthydemos at the opening of this last section, "that I teach you this knowledge about which you are in doubt, or shall I prove to you that you already have it?" We hear echoes of the antinomies of the first eristic section. Socrates prefers that the Sophist prove the second alternative; and so he does. He proves that Socrates knows something: indeed, knows everything, has always known it, and will always know it. Socrates tries several times to bring the conversation back to a concrete context, but in vain. For the reader, however, these marginal comments, disagreeable to the Sophists, are most significant—especially so when they ask Socrates whether he knows what he knows "by means of something" (i.e., through some instrument, ἐπίστασαί τῳ) and he replies, "Yes, through the instrument of my soul" (295ʙ). The reply irritates the questioner precisely because it opens up a new dimension, later to be

v
293ᴀ–304ʙ

explored in detail in the *Theaetetus* (184c *et seq.*). We perceive with our soul by means of our sense organs (διὰ τούτων οἷον ὀρ-γάνων), but we think by means of the soul alone. Thus, one reply by Socrates turns the discussion, for a moment, in a direction that is most undesirable to the eristic minds. Yet Plato, in the peculiarly ironic transparency we observed in these eristic conflicts from the beginning, has the Sophists go on spinning their own thread involuntarily and unknowingly.

"If you know one thing, you know all things." This was a startling statement heard earlier (294A). Does it not have a meaning for Plato's Socrates quite different from what Dionys-odoros intends—if we think of the *"Idea* of the Good," which confers both the power of knowing to the thinker and the reality of being to the objects of cognizance (*Republic* 508E) ? Later in the *Euthydemus* (296c *et seq.*), the same thought continues: You knew all things, as a child, at birth, at generation, before you were born, and before heaven and earth existed. You will always know and know all things—if I so will. . . . Apart from the ab-surdity and the megalomania of these last words, do we not catch in this passage an entirely different meaning if we think of the soul, just come into view, that knows the one thing? We may also think of the *Meno* (85D *et seq.*) where the demonstration of the Pythagorean theorem leads to the conclusion: the boy has always had this knowledge; hence, he did not acquire it in this life. His soul knew these things before he was born. Thus, if the reality of things (ἡ ἀλήθεια τῶν ὄντων) has always been in the soul, the soul must be immortal.

Dionysodoros, of course, does not "mean" this, but these im-plications—or, at least, most of them—are contained in his words. Doubt of this, if there be any, is removed by the last sophistic argument, which always has been singled out from the series of logical juggleries as an undeniable reference to what is called Plato's "theory of forms" (300E *et seq.*). Dionysodoros asks whether beautiful things are something other than the beautiful itself. Socrates says that they are indeed something other, and adds that beauty is present in (πάρεστιν) each beautiful thing. The Sophist promptly misunderstands "being present in" in a grotesquely physical sense. Then, however, without noticing it, he raises a serious question. How can one thing become another by virtue of the fact that the other is present in it? Those who understood must have sensed a genuine problem. How the "presence" of beauty in a beautiful thing or, conversely, how the "participation" of a beautiful thing in beauty itself is possible— this is the kind of problem developed in the *Parmenides*, and we know from Aristotle that the problem was widely discussed. It was touched upon in the *Hippias Major*,[21] and nobody has had any doubt that this is the problem aimed at here in the *Euthydemus*.

If, as it is customary,[22] we interpret this section as a polemic against Antisthenes we move, rightly or wrongly, beyond the sphere of the dialogue itself before it has been understood in its own terms. Interpreted within its own context, the problem that the Sophist opens up is more serious than he suspects. Socrates finds himself in an extreme dilemma, and we are at the point of decision. What is the *Eidos* and its relation to the things in this world? But what would be the purpose of raising this problem if it were completely isolated? It makes sense only if it is seen as the outermost limit of the train of thought underneath the actual conversation. The royal art, whose object of knowledge remained hidden in *aporia* at the close of the second Socratic section, receives unexpectedly—here in the third sophistic section—its proper reference: to *psyche* and *Eidos*.

By making Socrates the narrator, Plato is able to suffuse the whole work with those iridescent ironies we have discussed elsewhere.[23] But Socrates is not simply the narrator, as in the *Lysis* and in the *Charmides*. Kriton also talks with Socrates, and Kriton and the people whom he reflects in life are significant for an understanding of the work as a whole: they represent the class of people who make it necessary to set off sharply Socratic dialectics from sophistic eristics. Kriton is one of the benevolent capitalists (304c) as we know them, say, from the *Thrasymachus*. His son Kritoboulos has reached an age when the father thinks he must give him an education, as do the two fathers at the beginning of the *Laches*; again, as in the *Laches*, Socrates is the right man to consult in this matter. In the presence of Socrates, Kriton agrees that it is madness to do everything for one's sons and yet neglect their education. He correctly infers from Socrates'

FRAME
271A–272D
304B–307C

pointed irony that there is nothing to be learned from the two eristic debaters. But he does not notice—as Nikias does in the *Laches*—that Socrates himself would be the right educator. In fact, in view of the people who claim to be educators, Kriton doubts whether he should entrust his son to any of them.[24] This doubt is reinforced by a certain Somebody (left nameless), one of those powerful professional orators at court, who after listening to the debate concluded, so Kriton reports, that "philosophy" was worth nothing.

Commentators are always curious to discover the name of this Somebody. Most of them have decided that it is Isokrates, while others have opted for Antisthenes or Antiphon or yet another name.[25] Even if Plato had a particular person in mind and not a type, however, this kind of interpretation tends to overlook the more important question, what function has this Somebody in the dialogue itself? He declares flatly that all "philosophy" is worthless, while Kriton does not know where to find the right philosophy. The Somebody, therefore, represents the many, who do not know how to distinguish between eristics and dialectics and who scorn Socrates because Euthydemos is so contemptible. The influence of this type of person and others like him—for example, Anytos in the *Meno*[26]—is responsible for the confusion of which Socrates is a victim. The *Euthydemus* is meant to clear up this confusion. For this reason, these practitioners of politics must be repudiated in the end. Plato, conscious as always of the principle of order, does not simply destroy them, but assigns them their proper rank. These influential men of politics are "intermediates"; they fall between philosophy and politics. Hence, they occupy third place after the pure types of the philosopher and the political man, although they claim to be first. This ranking recalls once more the royal art—the acme of the conversation between Socrates and Kleinias.

The confusion of which Socrates was a victim—this thought comes to us at the end. Yet it is a theme that can be heard much earlier in the dialogue. Right at the beginning of his report when Socrates is introducing Kleinias, it is emphasized twice that the latter is a youth (νέος, 275B 2) and that there is danger of his being corrupted (διαφθείρη, 275B 4). Plato could not let Socrates speak these words without thinking of the indictment that charged Socrates with the "corruption of the young." Socrates defends himself against this charge in the *Apology* (25AB); and in the *Euthyphro* (2C 4, 3A 1), this charge is the first thing he reports about the indictment, whereupon Euthyphron inquires as to the nature of this "corruption" (3A 9). But there is more. Why did Plato in the *Euthydemus* choose Kriton as the partner of Socrates and why does he allude, at the very beginning (271B) and again at the very end (306D), to Kritoboulos, Kriton's son, who has just reached the age when education is especially needed? Kriton belonged to the same demos as Socrates; he was his contemporary; he stood up for Socrates and wanted to help him escape from prison. This would be enough to explain why Xenophon, in the *Memorabilia* and the *Oikonomikos*, chose Kriton and his son as partners of Socrates. In Plato the choice means more. In the *Apology* (33DE), Kriton is the first in the list of friends mentioned by Socrates and he is among those who would guarantee the fine that would set Socrates free (38B). In each case Kritoboulos is mentioned along with his father. In the *Phaedo* Socrates directs his last request to Kriton, and the dialogue *Crito* is unforgettable —whether Plato already had written it at this time or was still planning it. In reading the frame conversation of the *Euthydemus*, one must remember the ultimate fate of Socrates; one must not completely forget it either in the midst of the eristic fencing bouts that occupy the central sections of the dialogue.

FIFTEEN

Cratylus

THE DRAMATIC features of this dialogue look as if they were treated rather superficially. Socrates is drawn into a controversy over the nature of language; and the dialogue is constructed in such a way that the first and longer part is an exchange between Socrates and Hermogenes only, while in the shorter, concluding section, Socrates and Kratylos are the only partners. This peculiarly thin frame, Plato makes us realize, is due to the nature of Kratylos. He is the kind of person who joins the argument by proposing a blunt thesis, but does not explain himself "so that one cannot tell whether his obscurity is intended or not" (427D). He withdraws into silence evidently copied after the "obscurity" of his master Herakleitos, but concealing ignorance rather than profound knowledge. Underneath this very simple dramatic structure, the *Cratylus* has a rich inner movement.

The debate, to begin with, has nothing to do with the problem of the "origin of language," as we know it from Epicurus and the Stoics, or from Herder and Humboldt. It deals with the problem of the "correctness of names"; i.e., with the relationship between words and things, or with the appropriateness of the basic tools employed in speech and discourse.[1] The debate proceeds along the well-beaten track in which these matters used to be pushed, back and forth, in the period of the Sophists: to wit, whether the correctness of names is based on *physis*—i.e., the nature and essence of things—or on usage and custom, agreement and convention (συνθήκη καὶ ὁμολογία, νόμος καὶ ἔθος).[2] If one chose the former alternative, strange paradoxes ensued; if the latter, there basically was no such thing as the "correctness" of names, and the way was open for a completely arbitrary use of this most important tool. This acute danger explains why the debate is conducted with such lively intensity. One has the distinct impression that thesis and antithesis and their respective arguments were fixed, and that the two opponents "take a stand." Kratylos maintains that the correctness of names is based on *physis*. Moreover, he asserts boldly that this correctness is the same for Greeks and for barbarians, which means that the differences in the structure of natural languages are covered up by decree instead of being treated as a problem. Indeed, he goes so far—or is this merely a malicious exaggeration on the part of his opponent?—as to claim that even proper names belong essentially to the person named. Hermogenes, on the other hand, defends the view that there is no correctness of names except by "agreement and convention," from which it follows ultimately that any name may be given to anything.[3] This view of Hermogenes, then, seems at first to be more dangerous (hence, Socrates makes his first move in this direction) because it implies that one cannot trust words at all, that one can do anything with them since a person's relation to words is that "of master to slave" (384D 5). The view of Kratylos, however, is just as dangerous in its consequences, for one can put too much confidence in words, and "etymo-logy" may become a weapon that is used as threateningly and arbitrarily as the other view according to which words are not rooted in things.

Kratylos, as we know, is a Herakleitean; but for him the secret harmony between words and things, which the great Herakleitos himself felt intuitively, has become a purely rational exercise by which the mind tries to gain easy access to the nature of things. While for Herakleitos, language expressed the "harmony of opposites" that is nature itself or, more correctly, the *logos* of nature, the superficial Herakleiteanism in Plato's time tried to justify, by means of etymologies, the doctrine of the flux of all things.[4] It does not matter whether this portrait corresponds to the historical Kratylos. What matters is that we recognize the impulse to etymologize (an impulse deeply seated in the Greek temperament, and in Plato's as well), which is carried here to the point of a rigid theory, and this theory, for the sake of perspective, is attributed to this late Herakleitean thinker.[5]

Hermogenes belongs in the sphere of the Sophists because of his brother Kallias (391BC). Moreover, the view advanced by him is dangerously compatible with the enthronement of the detached self, which Protagoras expressed in the notorious statement that man is the measure of all things (385E *et seq.*). Perhaps the well-informed reader suspected even more when he encountered the name of Hermogenes—if the ancient report is true that the latter was a follower of Parmenides.[6] As a matter of fact, it is a decisive characteristic of the philosophical poem by Parmenides that naming is opposed to true being and is an act of human caprice: "Hence, everything is (merely) a name which mortals have posited in the hope that it be true" (frag. 8 vss. 38 *et seq.*). Were we to think also of the Eleatic philosopher when we hear the name of Hermogenes, we might say that the antithesis of Herakleitos *versus* Parmenides, which is so significant for the course of the dialogue, is represented by the participants themselves. Indeed, the work achieves its delightful perfection when we realize that as the Herakleitean is confronted with the doctrine of eternal being, so the doctrine of eternal flux is held up to the Parmenidean. However that may be, Plato's irony presented this antithesis in such sharp contrast primarily in order to show that these two fellows, apparently so different from each other, both wore caps of the same color. When properly developed, both views, it will appear, come to the same point where— along with Protagoras and Euthydemos, Antisthenes and the Megarians, i.e., as far as Plato is concerned, along with the whole Sophist front both outside and within the Socratic circle— the possibility of error is put into question, and hence, at the same time, the possibility of truth.[7]

PREPARATION
383A–384E

The discussants cannot agree; they cannot even conduct a conversation; they simply confront each other with opposing theses. A conversation develops only when Hermogenes submits the dispute to Socrates. When Socrates tries to hide by appealing to the authority of Prodikos, who would be able to supply a ready-made solution for their difficult subject, this, of course, is Socratic irony employed in teaching. The Sophists have their "knowledge" ready-made. In Socrates the conviction that knowledge in these matters is very difficult or that one may not ever discover the final truth combines with a willingness to embark upon a joint inquiry (384c).

The entire first conversation (385A–427D), then, is conducted between Socrates and Hermogenes. The first part of this conversation reaches the point where Hermogenes is refuted and where the thesis of Kratylos is apparently vindicated. The second part restricts the thesis of Kratylos. There follows the second conversation, where Socrates talks with Kratylos himself (427D– 440E). It completes the refutation of Kratylos and leads upward to a view of the central core of Socratic-Platonic thought. This is the simple, outward structure of the dialogue.[8]

The first move made by Socrates aims straight at the point of greatest danger and serves to provide a secure foundation. There is a difference between "true" and "false"; there is speech that is true and speech that is false. True speech "says that which is as it is"; false speech says "as it is not." On this the two men agree; and we are reminded of the *Euthydemus* where the same subject is debated in a sophistic context and where the expression "to say that which is as it is" is purposely ignored (*Cratylus* 385B; *Euthydemus* 285E). A sophistic rejection of this expression would be much more appropriate in terms of the consequences inherent in the view held by Hermogenes. But Plato did not make Hermogenes a consistent thinker. Thus, Hermogenes does not realize that the Socratic distinction between true and false has practically destroyed his own position already. He even agrees with Socrates that true and false may be ascribed to parts of speech, i.e., to words or names (ὀνόματα), although it would have been easy and proper for him to put up some resistance here.[9] Yet, when Socrates repeats to him his own view in the form of a question, Hermogenes restates it emphatically without realizing that his thesis has been undermined by acknowledging the distinction between true and false.

Socrates makes a second move. He combines the view that the correctness of names is a subjective, or relative, matter with the statement by Protagoras that man is the measure of all things. Thus, the uncertainty about names is transferred to the realm of being, and the danger inherent in what seems to be such a harmless thesis becomes clear—still clearer when presently, in

I
385A–427D

I 1
385A–390E
I 1a
385A–385E

I 1b
385E–386D

addition to Protagoras, Euthydemos appears with his eristic formula that "all things equally belong to all men at the same moment and always." (The name of Euthydemos suggests that dialogue, with its flood of eristic arguments.) Socrates, however, already has added another distinction between "good" and "evil," or, what is the same, as he says, between "wise" and "foolish," to the original pair of opposites (true and false). Again he secures ready acceptance from his partner. Since there is a difference, a radical difference, among those who judge in these terms, this refutes the view that all judgments are of equal value and disposes of the danger inherent in the thesis advanced by Hermogenes.

i lc
386D–390E

After we have eliminated these dangerous aspects, the following results appear to a mind with a clear view (δῆλον). Things (πράγματα) have their proper nature (οὐσία) in themselves, not relative to us, and they cannot be dragged to and fro arbitrarily as Protagoras imagines. Similarly, actions (πράξεις), as modes of being, have their own proper nature and do not happen according to our pleasure. Socratic "pragmatism" is opposed to arbitrary practice. Craftsmen and physicians prove through their actions that arbitrary dealings with their respective objects, or tools, would not do justice to the nature of their work. Thus, only by heeding the nature of one's work does one "advance and succeed in it" (πλέον τι ἡμῖν ἔσται). The criterion in the context of technical disciplines is that the product be right. The act of naming (ὀνομάζειν) is now envisaged after this familiar Socratic model of doing expert work. In naming, too, there must be a method that goes beyond caprice and corresponds to the nature of naming, the nature of the object named and of the word as the instrument of naming. This is the only way to advance and succeed in this field. Thus, "words" are envisaged as "instruments" after the model of tools in the crafts. We perform specific operations with an awl and a weaver's shuttle. With words we teach one another (διδάσκομεν, διδασκαλικὸν ὄργανον) and we discriminate among things according to their proper nature (διακρίνομεν ὡς ἔχει, διακριτικὸν τῆς οὐσίας).

If we pursue this analogy, we may distinguish between a craftsman who knows how to use tools correctly and another craftsman who is an expert in making tools. Thus, we may envisage a "law-giver" or a "wordmaker" (νομοθέτης, ὀνοματουργός)[10]—whether he be called usage or law (νόμος)—who has created the instrument of words; he would be "the rarest of all artisans among men" (389A 2). This shows that regardless of how he may be envisaged or whether he can be conceived at all, he cannot be Hermogenes or anybody else who might come forth with such a claim, and this removes the danger from the initial view of Hermogenes. The *nomos* begins to lose the arbitrary aspect orig-inally suggested by its connection with "convention" and "agree-ment." We now hear, instead, the venerable law of an ancient tradition. Sophistic *nomos* becomes Platonic *nomos*; as such, it belongs to the sphere of *logos* and *nous*. Thus, *nomos* here appears also in a peculiar conjunction with *physis*, and we begin to realize that the customary contrast between *nomos* and *physis* does not penetrate to the depth of the real problem.[11]

The case of the craftsman who is an expert in making tools to be used by other experts serves to clarify the method of word-making. This expert toolmaker looks only toward that which in its essence is such that it is proper for weaving (ὃ πέφυκει κερκίζειν); i.e., he looks not toward a material model, but toward the form (εἶδος) that is always present even if the particular instrument breaks, toward the "shuttle-itself" (αὐτὸ ὃ ἔστι κερκίς) that is the ideal model for the particular shuttles serving their own and different purposes. And what we see here—the permanent form (εἶδος, 389B 3; ἰδέα, 389E 3), the specific purpose served by the particular instrument (389B 8), the material out of which it is made (ἐξ οὗ, 389C 5), and the process whereby the expert makes the instrument according to the form out of the proper material and for a specific purpose—we may see also in the case of words or names. Here, too, we must envisage a "lawgiver" looking toward the "name-itself" (αὐτὸ ἐκεῖνο ὃ ἔστιν ὄνομα) and impress-ing upon the material of sounds and syllables the name appropriate to each thing according to its own nature (τὸ ἑκάστῳ φύσει πεφυκὸς ὄνομα).

In contrast to the view held by Hermogenes, names now are securely anchored because the form and its copies are seen as prototypes of their existence. The differences of words in different languages, far from proving that the process of naming is purely arbitrary, show only that these differences are necessary owing to the different materials used in the process. The name-in-itself: this is one of the most profound suggestions in Plato's "philosophy of language." We must look forward to the simile of the cave in the *Republic* where the prisoners enchained inside the cave hear echoing from the walls all sorts of sounds, which they associate with the shadowy images passing by (515B). Far superior to this "echo language" (we must assume) is the real language of those who move behind the backs of the prisoners, far and high above them—inconceivably superior in clarity and objective reference. Decades later, the demiurge in the *Timaeus* corresponds to the lawgiver of the *Cratylus* in Plato's thought.[12] In the *Timaeus* we are told a myth concerning the world of becoming about which we can have no certain knowledge, but the myth is designed to refer appearances to that realm of being toward which all true knowledge is directed.

There remains a last step. Even as the maker of tools passes them on to other experts for their use and judgment, so the wordmaker passes his work on to him who "knows how to ask questions and how to answer," i.e., to the dialectician. We are reminded of the passage in the *Euthydemus* where the highest knowledge was sought and was to be found when making ($\pi o\iota\epsilon\tilde{\iota}v$) and use ($\chi\rho\tilde{\eta}\sigma\theta\alpha\iota$) would coincide. There we were close to a decision when it became clear that the geometer, astronomer, and mathematician pass their findings on to the dialectician who knows how to use them (290c). Here in the *Cratylus*, the helpful analogy drawn from the crafts has led to a point where the "correctness" of language is shown by the fact that the dialectician can do something with it, or, more precisely, by the fact that Socrates is using language at this moment correctly in the manner of an expert craftsman.

At the end of this discussion, then, we sight the dialectician just as we saw the eristic Sophist in the beginning. Ultimately, it was a struggle between them that was here fought through. Language has been rescued from sophistic abuse and has been secured as the proper instrument of the philosopher who knows how to use it seriously and objectively. It finds its real foundations

where the *Eidos* comes into view—as yet by way of analogy
and in the distance. At the end, Socrates says the conclusion
corresponds to the view of Kratylos, which he declares to be
"right" (390D 9). This ironic identification reveals that an
empty and dangerous thesis such as that held by Kratylos is
given substance and meaning only through Socrates (in a personal sense) or through the concept of "form" (in an objective
sense). In other words, it is Socrates who makes the *Eidos* visible
in the *physis*.[13]

The result of the discussion—more precisely, of the foreground
discussion—was that there is correctness in names. This seemed
to confirm the view held by Kratylos, according to which we can
grasp the nature of things through words. Here lies the other
danger; hence, dialectics must make a countermove. "A certain   I 2
correctness" is in names, to be sure (391A, 397A). If we think   390E–427D
we can directly exploit this result for a knowledge of things,
however, we are going to be disappointed. This is shown in the
second part of this first conversation, where Socrates now pours
out a veritable flood of etymological interpretations in order to
reduce to absurdity the premature and presumptive claim that
we reach the nature of things through words.

Socrates himself warns repeatedly against the strange power   I 2a
that is at work in him. We must use it today, he says, only to   390E–421D
purify ourselves tomorrow as after a bad dream (396E). He refers to it, with ironic playfulness, as the Muse or the inspiration
of Euthyphron with whom he had been since early morning.[14]
Whether the historical Euthyphron used etymologies we do not
know, though we may assume that etymological tricks would
have served to buttress his bad theology. It was certainly Plato's
intention to make us think of the dialogue *Euthyphro*—as, previously, of the *Euthydemus*—and to recall the contrast between
the figure of the professional expert who claims to have knowledge about things divine, and the philosopher both knowing and
ignorant who restricts himself to what is human, not from skepticism, but from reverence.

Thus, Socrates here is opposed to the belief that we have
knowledge of the gods through the etymology of their names.
He affirms as his own guide in these matters that "we do not

know anything about the gods, neither about themselves nor about the names which they give themselves."[15] This sounds distinctly like the famous statement that Protagoras made about the gods, but only so that the following words may make the opposition to any disintegrative skepticism all the more clear: "For it is evident that they call themselves by their right names." In our knowing ignorance we can only content ourselves reverently with pious usage that leaves to the gods "how and whence they wish themselves to be named." At best we can know only the opinions that the name-givers among men have had about the gods (400D–401A).

That is the theological contrast between Socrates and Euthyphron, and now we can see why the Euthyphron theme keeps coming back. The gods and their names—here the ambiguity inherent in the practice of etymology shows itself most pointedly. Etymology does not yield knowledge about the nature of things; it yields only opinions, or, at best, insights of wise old men mixed indiscriminately with errors which are easily combined with a good deal of dubious materialistic physiology.[16] Thus, it is not in vain that, at the end of the long series of etymologies of divine names—amidst the urgent pleas by Socrates that, by the gods, let us be done with the gods (407D 6)—we find the interpretations of Hermes and Pan as representatives of speech. The function of Hermes is, on the one hand, to interpret and to be a messenger, and on the other, to deceive, defraud, and bargain. Does this not mean that words can be both intermediaries that disclose the nature of things and veils that deceptively conceal them? Still more significant is the symbol of Pan—divine and true above, deceptive and beastly below, and both aspects indissolubly joined together in one creature. Does not this playful allegory reveal the hybrid nature of the *logos*, especially the etymological *logos*?

The actual inquiry into the correctness of names begins by mentioning Protagoras as the teacher, thus putting itself into the right company even though Hermogenes brushes the "Truth" of Protagoras aside casually (391C). Socrates then suggests that we can learn from Homer what he has to say about language; yet we know since the *Protagoras* that an exegesis of poetry does not yield knowledge. Here in the *Cratylus*, nevertheless, the air is presently filled not only with discussions about the language of the gods, but with dangerous etymologies. From the arabesque pattern emerges a substantial result: there is a constancy of natural kinds, a constancy of species (γένος), designated by a common name, that contradicts the arbitrary employment of words. I cannot call the foal of a horse a lion, nor the just man unjust (393B et seq.).[17] Here is an area where the structure of language mirrors the structure of facts.

Making a fresh start (ἀρξώμεθα, 397A 4), the inquiry then leaves the poets and proceeds, in a sort of systematic succession, to expound the nature of things and, above all, the nature of immutable things (τὰ ἀεὶ ὄντα καὶ πεφυκότα, 397B 7), through the etymological meaning of words. A system emerges of interpretations based on the Herakleitean doctrine of flux. To be sure, when this doctrine is first introduced, Socrates remarks that we are quite ignorant about it (401E), or, perhaps more precisely, about its practical application to etymologies. So the reader is warned, just as he previously was warned (399A 4–5) when Socrates reminded himself to "go easy" in his ostensible enthusiasm as an etymologist. Soon, however, the stream of etymologies sweeps everything up in a relentless current. Socrates himself finds that the interpretations run away with him (410E), somewhat as the sophistic tricks did in the *Euthydemus*. And here, too, signs of warning are scattered throughout in plenty.[18] It seems as if Plato meant to convey to his readers that once we have set out in this one-sided way, there is no stopping anywhere. Not only is the air ever-flowing; virtue, knowledge, and justice also are caught up in the flow of things. In Greek we need add but one letter to "being" (ὄν) in order to make it into something "moving" (ἰόν). "Truth" without adding or deleting a single letter is "hammered together" out of two words—"divine whirl" (ἄλη θεία)—whereupon the stream of etymo-logies comes to an end.[19] It has been shown that, contrary to Kratylos, the correctness of words which we must indeed presuppose cannot be grasped in this manner. Moreover, when we turn from words to things, the whole doctrine of flux, as Socrates says, is a kind of dizziness whirling about in the heads of "sages" who mistakenly transfer it to the world of things (411BC).

In spite of all this, there are traces of a science of linguistics.

"Etymo-logy" in the proper sense is limited by an element of the capricious (395E), and "sound changes" particularly for the sake of euphony (εὐστομία, 404D, 414CD) are vaguely apprehended. True, an excessive use is made of this means of transforming words—so that Voltaire's satirical comment about the science of linguistics in which vowels mean nothing and consonants little seems justified. Socrates himself points out that this transforming procedure is easily followed, and he demands that changing letters be practiced with moderation and according to probability (414E). We are dealing with matters that are rather uncertain. Again, going back to older forms of language is at least recognized as a principle of method, even though old forms of writing and speech are confused (410c). The "barbaric" elements in one's own language, i.e., elements that no longer can be explained, restrict interpretations still further; at the same time, there are the first rudiments of a comparative linguistics (410A) in that several languages are put side by side. Above all, a symbolic imitation of sounds is envisaged as the principle active in the basic words of a language (426A *et seq.*)—and there is nothing better even today, despite the great development of linguistics as a science.[20]

Plato's interpretations and discoveries differ, nevertheless, from a scientific linguistics in our time because, ultimately, Plato is not altogether serious about them. Sometimes he is quite explicit in this respect. There is, says Socrates (406BC), a serious and a facetious explanation of the names of gods like Dionysos and Aphrodite. We leave the serious explanation to others. What Plato intends to convey is that the connection between words and things must neither be broken nor be so unbreakable that we think we have the nature of things in the words. It is the things that count. Plato shows the most important things through his etymologies, but he also shows that we must deal with gods, with the soul, and with justice in ways quite different from the interpretation of words. A "demonic wisdom" has seized him, Socrates says ironically. For Plato, the demonic is the intermediate realm between man and god, between knowledge and ignorance.[21] Thus, in the midst of these etymologies, there emerges not infrequently a suggestion which, though it does not reveal the nature of things, at least leads in this direction. In general, this is so because the "Herakleitean" doctrine of flux runs dead, and hence calls for something to resist and limit it. Yet, Plato would not have set up this mass of false etymologies—nor the fallacies in the *Euthydemus*—if he had not thought that they also were instructive with regard to particular points.

There is, for instance, the word "right" or "just," δίκαιον (412c *et seq.*). In its etymology, it seems to be derived from the swiftest or subtlest (power) that passes through (δια–ιόν) everything and by comparison with which other moving things appear at rest. Now the wisest men disagree as to what this power is: some say it is fire; others say the sun; Anaxagoras says it is "mind." As for himself, Socrates concludes, he is "in greater perplexity about the nature of justice than when he began to inquire" into these matters. These expressions do indeed refer to the way in which earlier and more recent philosophers of nature rendered spiritual qualities in terms of material substances, a material mode of expression from which even Anaxagoras could not free his "mind" (*Phaedo* 97D *et seq.*). The perplexity of Socrates, however (*Cratylus* 413c 8), points ironically to the fact that the "nature of justice" can be grasped only through a radical change in perspective, away from what is material and endlessly moving.[22]

Even in the case of the names of gods, there is reason to listen carefully in the whirl of etymologies.[23] The usual interpretation of Hades as the "unseen" (ἀιδές), which is alluded to in other works of Plato, is here rejected (though recalled) in favor of another interpretation linking it with knowledge (τὰ καλὰ εἰδέναι, 404B). Hades is the perfect teacher of wisdom (τέλεος σοφιστής, 403E) and the great benefactor to those who live in the world below; he holds men by the strongest bonds—the striving for virtue (δήσας τῇ περὶ ἀρετὴν ἐπιθυμίᾳ, 404A)—and he reveals his philosophical nature by the fact that he will not have anything to do with men until their souls are purified of the body and its evils and desires. Even to the men on earth he bestows much good (403E 5), a knowledge (as Jaspers would say) of the "boundary situation" that is an integral part of human existence. Beyond the mythical and etymological game that is being played, do we not catch sight of the world of the *Phaedo*: the soul purified of the body, the philosophical pursuit completed in death, death and knowledge? This impression seems to be reinforced when Hades wise and knowing is joined by his consort Persephone-Pherephatta, whose name is interpreted as "seizing that which is in motion" (ἐπαφὴ τοῦ φερομένου, 404D). Does this not suggest a knowledge of the *Eidos* in the midst of the world of changing things?

I 2b
421D–427D
In short, hints for those already instructed by Plato, "hooks" for those who still need his guidance—that is what these etymologies mean. In the interchange between nonsense and profundity they make it clear that words strive for or have a tendency toward things.[24] Again and again we are directed toward the things, i.e., the realm of being. If language, to begin with, seemed to find its right place in the class of imitative gestures, by which we also make things clear to each other (δηλοῦν ἀλλήλοις τὰ πράγματα, 422E), we soon learn that it has a status of its own. For while it is the function of the arts of music and drawing to reproduce the voice, shape, and color of things, it is the function of language to deal with the nature (οὐσία) of things.

Toward the end of this part of the conversation, Plato makes some suggestions designed to clarify the structure of being by means of the structure of language. He takes the system of sound formations as developed in the teachings of an expert in the rhythmic arts, a man like Damon.[25] Syllables are seen as parts of words, sounds or letters as parts of syllables; sounds, in turn, are classified as vowels, semivowels, and consonants, then further subdivided into natural groups of a lower order. Then, because of the parallelism between signs and things designated, the question is posed how to discover a similar division in the system of things (διαίρεσις, 424B 7; διελώμεθα, 424D 1; διελομένους, 425D 1). Only an intensive study could show whether the world of things also is composed of such primitive elements to which everything can be reduced[26] and of such higher "forms" (εἴδη) as the system of sounds and letters. If things are so composed, it would be our task to discover how the two systems correspond to each other. This correspondence would be the last step.[27] It presupposes that there is an ordered structure in the two domains. The whole dialogue shows that this task of co-ordinating elements of language with elements in things, and with higher forms, cannot ultimately be achieved but can only be envisaged as a possibility and a demand. At this point (425B), Socrates makes it clear that he is not equal to the task, which means either that it is not to be carried out for the moment or that, ultimately, it may be unattainable. Yet, there is not even a suggestion here that Plato renounced his quest for a system of forms of being. He never did. In the *Gorgias*, a distinction is made between the genuine arts and the arts of flattery, and in the *Republic* (Book VI), modes of knowledge and of being are divided and ordered in proportional relations. In fact, as we know, the quest for a many-faceted schema of division in which each thing has its place—and a definite place—in a series grows with the development of Plato's thought until it reaches the degree of intensity that appears in the diaeretic dialogues of the late period. It is no accident that, as in the *Cratylus*, the system of letters (together with the system of sounds) is still a symbol for an ordering of the forms of being in the *Philebus* (18B *et seq.*) and in the *Sophist* (252E *et seq.*).[28]

We have shown something of the inner movement of the dialogue beneath the surface. The first part of the conversation with Hermogenes, beginning as it did with the distinctions between true and false, good and evil, culminates—after an initial glimpse of the *Eidos*—in the dialectician; the second part of this conversation, after first establishing the constancy of natural species, eventually leads to the demand that a system of division be developed for all kinds of being—a demand obviously addressed to the dialectician (to whom else?).

So far the conversation has been between Socrates and Hermogenes. The view of Kratylos that the "correctness" of names is based on "nature" came into the discussion by way of Hermogenes. At the end of the first part, this view—in response to the ironic guidance of Socrates—prevailed over that held by Hermogenes, only to be so whittled down in the second part of this conversation as to be just as discredited, in its radical form, as the original view defended by Hermogenes.

Why, then, does Plato continue the dialogue (instead of ending it here) with a conversation between Socrates and Kratylos? The latter declares himself quite satisfied with the result (428BC).

II
427D–440E

In spite of this—or precisely because of this—Socrates continues to express his distrust of the results of their inquiry. The
hardest step and, at the same time, the most necessary to avoid
self-deception, he says, is this : to develop a sense of detachment,
or, in practical terms, to retrace one's steps in the inquiry and
(as Homer puts it) to "look both forward and backward." The
meaning of Socratic-Platonic dialectics is shown to be deeply
rooted in the nature of man.

After the conversation is resumed, it appears that Kratylos
has not noticed how deeply his own thesis that "all names are
correctly given" has been shaken. In other words, it is not enough
to refute this thesis by an implicit critique, i.e., by raising it to
a higher level; it must be shown expressly in its dangerous implications and then be overthrown.

II 1
428E–435D

The "correctness" of a name consists in showing the thing as
it is. This is the way Socrates formulates the result of the foregoing discussion, and Kratylos agrees. But at once there is disagreement. For Socrates this correctness holds only in a very
limited sense, as we saw previously and as is now emphasized
by analogy with good and bad laws. Kratylos, however, asserts
that words or names which are not "correct" are not words at
all, but empty noise (φθέγξασθαι, ψοφεῖν, 429E 9, 430A 4). He
says this in order to reinforce, by means of this paradox, his
original thesis that all names are correct (429B). Here lies danger, for if all names are correctly given, it is impossible to speak
falsely. We are back at the statement, then, and the reasons for
it, that we know from the fallacies in the *Euthydemus*: to say
what one says is to say what there is; what there is not cannot
be said. Here too, then, a thesis reveals its dangerous implications before the eyes of Socrates. Even as the view of Hermogenes denying that there is a correctness in names, if carried to its
logical conclusion, would undermine the possibility of naming
anything correctly (i.e., the possibility of truth), so the view of
Kratylos denying that names can be given incorrectly would destroy the possibility of error (i.e., again, the possibility of truth).
The logical consequence of the two opposing views leads in the
first case to the sophistic thesis of Protagoras that every opinion
is valid for its author and in the second case to the sophistic

thesis of Euthydemos that all statements are true. Even as at
the beginning of the dialogue (386D) one sees that these two
sophistic principles are closely akin to each other, so it is now
most delightful to behold how the two views that fought each
other so bitterly, and seemed to be so radically opposed to each
other, combine in the sight of Socrates to yield the same principle
—or lack of principle—whose overthrow seems to have been
the mission of Socrates.

So it is clear why Plato had to add a Kratylos section to the
part given to Hermogenes. The course taken by the new conversation aims first at undercutting the dangerous exaggeration
in the view advanced by Kratylos. Socrates is not sidetracked by
the terminological distinctions—speaking, sounding, making
noise (429E et seq.)—into which Kratylos would like to retreat,
nor by a restatement of the radical thesis into which Kratylos
relapses occasionally (431E, 433C). Instead, he compels Kratylos to make clear to himself the difference between a name
and the thing named, and to envisage the act of naming as "des-
ignation" (δήλωμα) or "imitation" analogous to the image (εἰκών)
of a thing in drawing and painting. This analogy makes error
possible—if picture and sign are not applied to the object whose
picture and sign they actually are. (A major problem in the
Euthydemus here finds its preliminary solution, to be elaborated
later in the similes of the lump of wax and the aviary in the
Theaetetus.) Moreover, if both nouns (ὀνόματα) and verbs
(ῥήματα) may be used wrongly, then the same is true for the
sentences (λόγοι) composed of them. This is a first approxima-
tion of the treatment of error as it later is clarified in the Sophist.[29]

This discussion about the nature of linguistic signs, however,
not only eliminates the dangerous consequences of the Kratylos
thesis; it also restricts the validity of the thesis itself. A picture
is never identical with what it depicts, else there would be a
duplication of things in the world. A picture is always different
from what it depicts (ἐνδέουσιν αἱ εἰκόνες τὰ αὐτὰ ἔχειν ἐκείνοις ὧν
εἰκόνες εἰσίν, 432D). Consequently, it follows that if the nature
of words is to "designate" (δήλωμα) or "imitate," they may
achieve different degrees of approximating the thing named,
then, but never complete identity. If identity were achieved, the

word would cease to designate and would become the thing itself. Thus, it follows from an analysis of the function of linguistic signs that while there is an element of natural affinity with things, there must always be an element of difference as well. There are arbitrary elements as may be shown in the concrete cases where, in a dialect, an *s* is replaced by an *r* without change in meaning, or where an *l*-glide occurs in a word signifying something hard. Now in order to rescue his own view about the natural connection between words and things, Kratylos must appeal to the view of his opponent, i.e., to the view that these are matters of custom (ἔθος) or convention (συνθήκη). In a final summing up (435A–C), Socrates, with the agreement of Kratylos, pulls together the two views that had opposed each other so radically. They cannot be so incompatible if their epistemological consequences are the same.

II 2
435D–440D

The dialogue would end here if the philosophy of language were its last word. But we have seen throughout that, beneath this discussion on the surface, there is a constant concern with the nature of things. What words teach us about things and how we can have knowledge of things: this is the primary problem to which we are now directed again after the characteristic features of language have been fixed as being due partly to nature and partly to convention.

Socrates inquires about the effect or power (δύναμις) of words, and Kratylos replies that he who knows words also knows the things designated by them. This statement follows from his original thesis and cannot possibly be maintained after this thesis has been impaired so severely. Since Kratylos does not notice this and withdraws, despite the doubts expressed by Socrates, into the assertion (long since refuted) that the creator of names invented them with full knowledge (εἰδώς) because otherwise they would not be names at all (436BC; cf. 429B), it is clear that Plato must be pursuing a still different objective. He wants to examine the most important consequence of the Kratylos thesis (the consequence that a knowledge of words is a knowledge of things) independently of the thesis itself, because it contains the dangerous implication that one might think a knowledge of things is all too easy. Thus, at the end of the whole work, Plato directs our view once more to what is most important: the realm of being and the possibilities of knowing it.

Socrates is very doubtful about the complete knowledge of things that Kratylos attributes to the creator of names. Nor is Socrates impressed by the new argument that all words show a great consistency of structure (σύμφωνα, κατὰ ταὐτὸν καὶ ἐπὶ ταὐτόν), i.e., a consistency derived from the doctrine of eternal flux; for with the irony characteristic of him, he has just treated all interpretations according to the same doctrine. Thus, it is easy for him to shift the point of departure (ἀρχή)—the importance of this is stressed—and to proceed upon an etymological interpretation of words according to the opposite view of eternal rest. Moreover, amusingly enough, etymologies are offered not only for words like knowledge and memory, firm and credible, but also for words like ignorance and lack of restraint, so that we may see again how little is accomplished by this new series of derivations. The Herakleitean—that is the joke of the matter—is defeated by a system of etymologies in the Eleatic manner. But the reader discovers how he can work his way through these opposing methods and perhaps suspects, if he keeps his mind fixed on the things, that Herakleitos and Parmenides are called upon not to defeat each other, but to help build Plato's own world by means of their dialectical—or Herakleitean—tension.[30]

The statement that a knowledge of things is derived from a knowledge of words, or, expressed differently, that the creator of names, especially the first creator, gave names knowingly, is open to a still more fundamental criticism. It is this criticism that leads to the ultimate depths plumbed in the *Cratylus*. How did the first creator of words have knowledge of things if such knowledge comes through words only? Or, to return to our own case at hand, since words seem to make contradictory statements about things—i.e., since words may be interpreted in a Herakleitean and in a Parmenidean sense—a decision as to which is correct cannot be made by appealing to words again. Rather, "it is obvious that we must seek another standard beyond words that would make clear to us without words which of the two is right," i.e., that would show us "the truth (or reality) of things" (τὴν ἀλήθειαν τῶν ὄντων, 438D).

There are, then, two modes of knowing, one above the other: knowing things through words and knowing things by themselves. The second mode, no sooner mentioned than concealed again, "is greater than what would be proper for you and me to determine." It is left ambiguous whether this mode refers to a kind of knowledge that would dispense with the interpretation of words or knowledge that would dispense with language itself.[31] The former alternative is, strictly speaking, the result of the previous arguments; the latter is suggested now and then by the wording. Perhaps this iridescent ambiguity is intentional. The path of knowledge in the *Seventh Letter* begins with "word" (ὄνομα) and "sentence" (λόγος), only to reach with the "image" (εἴδωλον) a stage of knowledge that goes beyond verbal expression. Then it ascends upward to *episteme* in which verbal and visual means are combined, and culminates in what no longer can be said in words. We may leave open the question of how much of this system Plato perceived when he wrote the *Cratylus*. He did perceive a hierarchy—something beyond the word, something that is no longer expressible in words.

There remains a final point (439B *et seq.*). In contrast to the doctrine of incessant flux, Socrates cites "what I often dream about" (439C 7): there is something beautiful and good in itself, an eternal being that does not change its form (ἰδέα, 439E 5), a genuine mode of knowledge, an object of true knowledge (440B). If there were nothing but incessant change, it could not be known as such by anybody. Moreover, there would be no knowledge since this would have to change at every moment. Indeed, there would be no way of saying anything about the state of flux (439D) because language "de-fines," i.e., stabilizes and delimits things. A world of perpetual flux would be a rheumatic world, like a sick man with a running nose, as it is said at the very end (440CD), and the people who hold such views are themselves afflicted with rheum and catarrh. One cannot help being reminded of the amusing story that Kratylos ultimately did not speak at all, but only wagged his finger. Aristotle records it in his *Metaphysics* (IV 5 1010ᵃ 12) at a place where he is discussing in detail the problem that here comes into view. The story may have been current in the Platonic circle at the time when Plato wrote this

dialogue. It does not fit here because the Kratylos of the dialogue
is a young man confronting a mature Socrates.

Socrates takes leave of his companions. They are going to the   440E
country. He remains in Athens. Landscape and trees, as he explains in the *Phaedrus,* do not have anything to teach him, only
people in the city do. He bids Kratylos to carry on boldly with
his studies, and the young man returns the advice—to Socrates
of all people!—intimating that he thinks he himself has already
found something solid in the doctrine of eternal flux.

The reader, however, looks back once again upon the work as
a whole. The two sets of etymologies—as amusing as they are
wearying—were of some use after all, it appears at the end,
even though we must not put too much confidence in the method
itself. They have raised the two worlds of being and becoming
into consciousness, and have assigned them to an intellectual inquiry that now must begin beyond all etymologizing. Furthermore, the fact that at the end of the *Cratylus,* the *Eidos* appears
as the object of knowledge—or the "theory of forms," as it is
commonly called—has hardly escaped anybody's attention.[32] In
truth, however, this is only the last time that this subterranean
stream, which we have followed throughout, emerges above the
surface. We recall how, at the end of the conversation with Hermogenes, a system of division was set up as the task for the
dialectician and how, at the very beginning of the dialogue, the
simple distinctions between true and false, good and evil were
firmly established. From this beginning to the emergence of
goodness and beauty as such runs the extended tension that must
be recognized underneath the surface of jest and seriousness regarding the "philosophy of language."[33] To this deeper layer
of thought there also belongs, for example, the interpretation of
Hades as the great knower and dispenser of wisdom. The dimension of "existence," the reality of life and death, finds its place
in the structure of knowledge and the *Eidos.* Even as the dialogue
moves between two levels constantly interacting with one another, so it moves back and forth in opposite directions. Fighting,
on the one side, against hostile forces it leads us, on the other,
deeply into a world that is genuinely Platonic.

SIXTEEN

Menexenus

THIS is Plato's most confusing work and, among his numerous portraits of Socrates, it is the most paradoxical. Socrates, the enemy of polished speeches and political affairs, delivers a public oration before the people of Athens at the memorial celebration of their dead. Moreover, this oration is delivered in the year 386 B.C., i.e., half a generation after his own death. The long speech itself is framed by a brief dialogue in which Socrates explains to Menexenos, who is listening somewhat skeptically, that he has learned the speech from Aspasia. It is quite understandable that commentators have for a long time been reluctant to consider this work authentic; it is less understandable that they have berated the work instead of trying to explain it.[1]

Those who have treated the work seriously tend to oversimplify its confusing aspects.[2] They claim that it is a satire aimed against patriotic oratory or against Athens or both. Others have argued that Plato wanted in all seriousness to prove that he could write a public oration as well—or as badly—as anybody else, and they think that he downgraded his own product by the dialogue introducing it. The fact that the work is the only one among Plato's writings which carries an exact date is used to read into it political intentions that Plato is supposed to have pursued at the time: to influence Athenian politics or to reconcile himself with his native city. The reference to Aspasia, finally, is interpreted as a literary allusion, ultimately not altogether comprehensible, to the lost *Aspasia* dialogue by Aischines[3]—which means that we renounce any attempt at interpreting the work by itself.

Before we can take seriously any such interpretation as to specific intentions, we must settle a fundamental question. In terms of Plato's spiritual biography, the *Menexenus* is a document testifying to the tense relationship between him and his native city. Athens is one of the basic facts of his life. He was a Greek and an Athenian who still knew in his old age that a human being belongs to his family and that both family and goods belong to the state (*Laws* 923A). As an Athenian aristocrat, he was especially marked for service in the state; yet, at the same time, he grew up with a hatred of *this* state, and the course of political events reinforced his antipathy toward it. As a disciple of Socrates, he inherited two convictions. On the one hand, he believed that it is of the nature of the philosopher to be rooted in his homeland—as it is of the nature of the Sophist, a peddler of intellectual merchandise, to be rootless—and he was committed unconditionally (as shown in the *Crito*) not to an abstract "idea of the state," but to the concrete community of Athens. On the other hand, he also inherited a hostility against this very Athens that had condemned to death the man who was "most just." He had learned through bitter experience that he could not take part in the political affairs of this state (*Letter VII* 326AB; *Republic* IX 592A) and he has set out to seek the true state, which is not of this world. Yet, he continues to live in Athens; in Athens he founds his Academy as the nucleus of a new state. And "in Athens" is more than a spatial term. It is a fact of living reality, despite Plato's withdrawal from public affairs.

This *odi et amo* must be the clue to an understanding of the *Menexenus*. It would be a miracle if the dialogue were free from unresolved tensions with which Plato came to terms only gradually in the course of his life and work.[4] There remains in him the destructive gesture of the judge who, in the *Gorgias*, condemns all the famous statesmen of Athens, and who condemns democracy in the *Republic*. Yet, the repressed love for Athens returns in old age. In the *Timaeus* and in the *Critias*, Plato creates the ideal image of an original Athens, and in the *Laws* he shows, in a more historical setting, the Athens of the Persian Wars as a model state in which—far from an unbridled "freedom"—

reverence is the supreme sovereign and the citizens are subject to the bondage of the laws.[5]

234A–236D

Menexenos[6] is just coming "from the market place; in fact, from the Council." Socrates infers that the young man must have had enough of "education and philosophy" and now wants to "govern," despite his youth. Govern or rule—the same aim is proclaimed by Alkibiades and Theages in the dialogues named after them. They are persuaded, in due course, though with some difficulty, that they need nothing more urgently than education, that, in short, before they are ready to "govern" they must first "be governed." Here, by contrast, Menexenos submits the decision as to whether and when he should enter government to the advice of Socrates. At the end of the dialogue, he thanks Socrates for the "political speech" just delivered and hopes to hear more like them in the future. Thus, the relationship between *paideia* and political action is set down from the beginning. Socrates appears as the educator on behalf of the state and, therefore, his oration—in spite of everything—must be meant as a means toward achieving education.

The strangest means, to be sure, are employed. Where in the body of Plato's works do we find anything comparable to the very odd structure of this work as a whole? The *Menexenus* can be understood only if we see it, in the unfolding of Plato's thought, as an anticipation of the *Phaedrus*. Perhaps it is no accident that there is a parallel in the opening words: "Dear Phaidros, whence come you and where are you going? From Lysias, Socrates, the son of Kephalos." / "Whence come you, Menexenos—from the market place? Yes, from the market place, Socrates, in fact, from the Council." In the dialogue named after him, Phaidros first recites a love speech by Lysias which the latter had composed at his leisure (ἐν πολλῷ χρόνῳ κατὰ σχολήν, *Phaedrus* 228A). Socrates displays a mock enthusiasm (ἐκπλαγῆναι, 234D) and Phaidros replies with a slight reproach (οὕτω δὴ δοκεῖ παίζειν). Socrates feels that he can match the speech with something that is at least just as good (ἔχειν εἰπεῖν, 235C). He has filled himself like a vessel from some stream or other, without knowing how or from whom he has heard what he is about to say. Thus, he delivers a speech in competition with Lysias—and only as a third installment, "sweet water after salt," he adds a speech truly his own. In the *Menexenus*, the solemn funeral orations which the professional rhetorician keeps on hand "for a long time" (ἐκ πολλοῦ χρόνου, 234c) correspond to the speech of Lysias. Socrates cites them with mock enthusiasm (ἐξέστηκα κηλούμενος, 235A); to this Menexenos replies that Socrates always is making fun of the rhetoricians (ἀεὶ σὺ προσπαίζεις τοὺς ῥήτορας). Then, suddenly, Socrates himself is ready to deliver such a speech (οἵῳ τ' εἶναι εἰπεῖν, 235E), only it is not his own, but Aspasia's. He recites the speech and, in the end, promises more fine political speeches coming from the same source. This puts the speech in its proper place. It corresponds to the second speech in the *Phaedrus*;[7] not fundamentally different from others of its kind, it is merely better. Thus, in announcing more beautiful "political speeches" in the future, Socrates—as the *Phaedrus* shows—is pointing toward something on an entirely different level. The beginning of the *Menexenus*, which we must connect with the end, makes us think of an education toward political *arete*.[8]

The reference to the *Phaedrus* also throws some light on the figure of Aspasia. Why this strange concoction—Socrates, in the year 386, receiving instruction in rhetoric from the widow of Perikles? The *Phaedrus* helps to clarify this situation. Aspasia takes the place of the "Somebody" whom Plato's Socrates splits off from himself ironically, in the *Phaedrus* and elsewhere, in order to hide behind him.[9] This "Somebody" is here called Aspasia in order to establish a connection—in a fantastic kind of playfulness—between the most famous funeral speech, that of Perikles, and Socrates' fiction. Aspasia inspired both. So that we may see quite clearly what this lesson in rhetoric means, Socrates adds that in addition to being instructed by Aspasia, he also has had lessons with Konnos, the music master on the zither. This is analogous to the situation in the *Euthydemus* where Socrates goes to school with the eristic fencers. Old man Socrates learning to play the zither—this grotesque scene did, in fact, occur in current comedy.[10] The comic element is quite pronounced in the *Euthydemus*, and this picture here—Aspasia side by side with Konnos—is comedy as well. Plato's Socrates can play with the art of rhetoric as expertly as with eristics; he can even achieve effects that leave the rhetoricians themselves behind. For Socrates can use their means, inappropriate though they be ultimately, to lead us toward what is essential.

249D–249E   The final exchange serves to dispel the reality of the teacher Aspasia. Menexenos himself does not quite believe in her. Thus, we shall read the public oration quite differently depending on whether we attribute it to Aspasia or to Socrates. We also shall expect something different from the "political speeches" that Socrates promises for the future. We shall expect them to be something other than this public oration, i.e., something more Socratic in the true sense.

Now as to the oration itself, we see that it corresponds, both in organization and execution, to the customary *epitaphia* and *encomia*.[11]

236D–237C   Praise of "noble birth" (εὐγένεια) comes first. The Athenians are proud of their indigenous heritage. Mother Earth has borne and nourished them and will take them back again into her bosom. The praise of hereditary aristocracy becomes praise of the Great Mother.

"Noble birth," as we know from many dialogues, is both a blessing and a danger. In the *Lysis* (205B *et seq.*), praising one's ancestors turns into a dubious game; in the *Alcibiades Major* (104AB, 123DE), noble birth, in addition to being a source of "greatness and beauty," is also a danger to the young man. The endowments must be earned and transformed by *arete*. In the *Euthydemus* (279A *et seq.*), it is shown that health, beauty, noble birth, and all the other things called "goods" of life are not, properly speaking, "goods" at all without "good fortune" (εὐτυχία), without proper use, i.e., without "wisdom" (σοφία). This is how Plato—aristocrat that he was—looks back upon the old aristocracy at a time when membership in a noble family conferred privileges only but no longer responsibilities. In the *Theaetetus* (174E), the philosopher taking a broad view asserts that it is ridiculous to praise a person because he has seven rich ancestors or because he can trace his family tree through twenty-five steps back to Herakles. The *Republic*, however, founds a new aristocracy. As told in the myth (III 414B *et seq.*), all citizens in this state are brothers because they are descendants of the same Mother Earth. But their respective rank in the state as a whole depends upon the degree to which they are composed of gold, silver, iron, or copper.

We do not need Socrates—we can learn the same thing from the rhetoricians themselves[12]—to take offense at the statement that "they were good because they sprang from good fathers" (*Menexenus* 237A 6). We only need think of the dialogues just mentioned to realize how dangerous it is to be enchanted by praise of one's own noble birth and aristocratic heritage. But if we listen to this praise through the voice of Socrates, we may hear the moral demand implicit in the doctrine of noble birth and in the myth of the Earth Mother. Moreover, we may observe that Plato's Socrates expresses this mythical genealogy with greater seriousness than anybody else.

The first praise of the land is that it is "dear to the gods" (θεοφιλής), as proved by the fact that the gods contended over it. The second praise is that there are no savage beasts in it, but that it brought forth man who is superior to all other creatures in intelligence and who alone reveres justice and the gods. The proof for this is that the land like a true mother provided nourishment for her offspring—grain and oil. Then the great Mother Earth gave to her children the gods to rule over them and teach them the crafts and the use of arms. 237C–238B

The phrase "dear to the gods" has a new meaning for Plato. "He who lives justly and honorably is dear to the gods" (*Alcibiades* 134D). "The just, god-fearing, and truly good man is dear to the gods" (*Philebus* 39E). The phrase does not connote here, as it does in ordinary language, a welcome distinction with which one can rest content; instead, it serves as a seal put upon a degree of human perfection that is a genuine possibility, but the possession of which is always in doubt. "The moderate is dear to the god, for he is like him," as we read in the *Laws* (IV 716D); "the undisciplined and the unjust are unlike, and incompatible with, the god." Yet, the naïve anthropomorphism according to which, in this funeral oration, the concept of being "dear to the gods" is combined with a "quarrel among the gods" (ἔρις καὶ κρίσις) is condemned by the severe critique in the *Euthyphro* (7D *et seq.*) and, on a still more radical level, in the *Republic*

where we find a critique of the traditional myths about the gods
in general. He who makes the gods quarrel among each other
cannot avoid a contradiction in the concept "dear to the gods."[13]

Thus, though the notions of popular mythology are tacitly
destroyed by Socrates as he plays the role of public orator, the
inner contradiction nonetheless suggests, in a germlike state,
the future myth of an original Athens. The gods, as we read in
the *Critias* (109BC), have acquired their respective lands not
"through strife," but "through the lot of the law." Attica belongs
to Hephaistos and to Athena as "joint property." The traditional
myth of a quarrel between these two gods is transformed into
the opposite: they have a "common nature" because they are
descended from the same divine father and because "love of the
arts" and "love of knowledge" is common to both. The gods as
teachers—this aspect of the *Menexenus*, then, is also deepened.
The *Agathon* as origin and goal is seen vaguely behind a veil of
myth. Only when the gods are again prototypes in the true sense
will the other glories of the land—the autochthony of its in-
habitants and the fruitfulness of its soil (110E *et seq.*)—be a
blessing instead of a danger.[14]

238B–239A   The praise of origin and education is followed by a praise of
government, closely linked with the previous eulogies. The government of Athens, "speaking generally," has existed unaltered
since ancient times. Though the form of government may have
received various names, it has always been "an aristocracy based
upon the consent of the mass of the population." It is a fortunate
blending of elements that occur elsewhere only in separation.
The monarchic element is represented by the "king" even though
that is now an elective office. The true authority is in the hands
of the people. The offices are in the hands of the best or, more
correctly, "of those who seem to be the best." Descent from the
same mother (ἰσογονία) guarantees equality before the law (ἰσονομία) without excluding the government of the best.[15]

The description in this passage is in a state of tension between
a yes and a no. The blessedly mixed government described here
is still considered in the *Laws* (IV 712c *et seq.*) to be the highest
form of government in the actual world as realized in Sparta and
Crete. Royalty or aristocracy, depending on whether there is

one ruler or several, is the name in the *Republic* (IV 445D) for the perfect form of government—a government in which the unity guaranteed by the common descent from the same mother is compatible with the superiority of the best. In the *Menexenus*, then, Socrates is already aiming at these ideal images characteristic of Plato's maturity and old age. But this "ideal" is not realized—in Athens. Anybody who keeps his critical faculties knows how governments in Athens have changed constantly. He knows that the "king" does not really mean much and that his "election" depends upon drawing lots. Nor do we fail to hear that whenever Socrates refers to the election of the best, the emphasis shifts to the domain of *doxa*, opinion and appearance (τοῖς δόξασιν ἀρίστοις εἶναι, *Menexenus* 238D 5; ὁ δόξας σοφὸς ἢ ἀγαθὸς εἶναι, 238D 8; ἀρετῆς δόξῃ καὶ φρονήσεως, 239A 4). Thus, the *Menexenus* reveals a peculiar tension. There is, on the one hand, the critique of democracy. We find an expanded version of this critique in the *Republic*: democracy as a "department store" for all possible forms of government (παντοπώλιον πολιτειῶν, VIII 557D), not as a happily balanced constitution; democracy as a regime not of the best, but of those who know best how to please the people; and democracy as a system in which equality, bestowed—alike—upon the like and the unlike (558C 5), is not an equality before the law that acknowledges the superiority of *arete* and *phronesis*. On the other hand, the *Menexenus* also contains the seeds of Plato's wish for an ideal state.

As Socrates turns to praising the great deeds of Athens— quickly passing over the mythical past, but dwelling in detail upon the Persian Wars—he sums up once more the nature of the Athenian constitution. The Athenians have grown up in complete freedom (ἐν πάσῃ ἐλευθερίᾳ τεθραμμένοι, 239A). To this—in addition to their birth—they owe their greatness. They were convinced, moreover, that one must fight for freedom whether in a war of Greeks against Greeks or in the Greek struggle against the Persians. The repeated mention of "enslavement" (239D *et seq.*) refers to the expansion of the Persian empire and the threat posed to all the Greeks. This threat was resisted, ultimately, by the Athenians, who thereby saved Greece from such enslavement. Thus, the war of liberation against the Per-

239A–246A

sians, in a strange concatenation, apparently becomes the model for the altogether different wars fought among the Greeks themselves.

Should we say, then, that the wars fought by the Athenians against other Greeks were democratic wars of liberation, as the campaign against the Persians was indeed a war of liberation? When Plato was writing the *Menexenus*, was he not yet aware of the critique of democracy that he would expound later in the *Republic*? There, in Book VIII, it is excessive freedom which is the misfortune of a democratic government; and in the *Laws* (III 698A *et seq.*) it is said expressly, as if to contradict the popular thesis of the *Menexenus*, that it was not complete freedom from any kind of authority (παντελὴς καὶ ἀπὸ πασῶν ἀρχῶν ἐλευθερία) which brought victory to the Athenians. On the contrary, reverence ruled and the people were servants of the laws (*Laws* III 698B, 699C). This produced "friendship" (φιλία) within and power without. Only later were the people introduced to "complete freedom" (ἐπὶ πᾶσαν ἐλευθερίαν), to the detriment of the state as a whole.

It goes without saying that Plato did not have to wait for old age to assess the value of this "complete freedom" so highly acclaimed in Athens. In the *Gorgias*, rhetoric is hailed, by the rhetorician himself, as the highest good and "cause of freedom" (425D). What Kallikles is aiming at, through the use of rhetoric, is called "government, tyranny, and ruling." At the same time, it is "luxury, freedom, and lack of restraint" opposed to what is called "justice and discipline," i.e., *arete* and *paideia*. This is the concept of freedom against which Socrates prevails in the *Gorgias* by arguing that discipline is better than lack of it, that order is better than disorder, and that "geometrical equality," i.e., proportion, which gives everybody not the same, but rather his due, keeps heaven and earth together (507E *et seq.*). The "freedom" rejected here is the license to do as I please—or to "rule" (as I please), as the young people say. Thus, the reference to the proud heritage of freedom in the speech of Socrates must be qualified by the genuinely Socratic reservation expressed in the first words of this dialogue, where Socrates asks why Menexenos had gone to the Council and whether it was to embark upon a career of "governing." Now since growing up in "complete freedom" seems to be the prerequisite for all the great deeds cited by Socrates, the following conclusion appears inescapable. If these deeds were really good and great, then they did not spring from "complete freedom." If, however, there was such freedom, then we must re-examine the prevailing judgment about the great deeds. The history of Athens' glory is subject to this ambiguity.

Even though Socrates, as is but proper, leaves the greatness of the victories in the Persian Wars untouched, the question arises how they were won. Marathon shows that numerical superiority in men and materials can be overcome by *arete* (*Menexenus* 240D). *Arete* when invoked in a speech by Socrates has a very special meaning; we suspect that there is an incompatibility between *arete* and "complete freedom." A principle must be found to oppose this kind of unlimited freedom, as we learn in the *Laws* (in a literal allusion to the *Menexenus*[16]) and as we learn here in the ensuing section which deals with the civil wars among the Greek states down to the fall of Athens. They were caused by jealousy and envy (ζῆλος καὶ φθόνος), and Athens succumbed not so much to external force as to internal dissension. That the Athenians in those days "did not lay hands on each other out of malice or enmity, but because of misfortune" (δυστυχία, 244AB) may sound credible to Aspasia or to anybody else who wants to believe it. As spoken by Socrates, however, the words remind us of the *Euthydemus* (278E *et seq.*), where it is shown that there is no "good fortune" (εὐτυχία) without "wisdom." We may then apply this statement to the "misfortune" of Athens and remember the pernicious thesis of the many as repeated by Adeimantos in the *Republic* (II 364B), according to which "the gods bestow misfortune and unhappy life upon many men who are good and good fortune upon those who are bad." According to Socrates, therefore, neither was the civil war an undeserved misfortune nor was the delivery from it an undeserved good fortune. If the state in those days did not completely collapse as a result of the civil wars, it owes its survival to the spirit of "friendship" still fostered by the common mother (*Menexenus* 244A).

Thus, we see what was lacking at the time of the Hellenic

Wars and what still prevailed—as the *Laws* shows explicitly—at the time of the Persian Wars. It was friendship. How those wars between the Greek states are viewed in contrast to the Persian Wars is shown by a remark in the *Menexenus* (242D) which is later repeated verbatim in the *Republic* (V 470c *et seq.*): Against people of a common race, one must fight only until victory is gained; one must not destroy the "community" (τὸ κοινόν) of Hellas. Against the barbarians, however, a war of extermination is justified. Thus, the principle of "community," originally based upon membership in the same *polis*, is expanded as a call to the whole nation—which came to grief because it did not heed this call.

The lack of community continues its destructive work in the wars of the fourth century until the Peace of Antalkidas. The hostility against the Persians persists as well; it is due to the natural "hatred of barbarians" (μισοβάρβαρον, *Menexenus* 245c 7), which, even in the *Republic* (470c), is still considered an indispensable complement to Hellenic solidarity. So much the worse, then, is the ironic condemnation implied when the speaker, at the close of this section, without batting an eyelash, also celebrates the dead for having helped—"to liberate the Persian king" and to deprive the Spartans of their naval supremacy.[17]

246A–247C From praise of the dead, the speaker turns to the living. They are exhorted not to desert the ranks of their ancestors. This plea, with Socrates as the speaker, is subject to the same reservation as was the encomium of Athens. The following words: "Whenever I meet one of you I will exhort and urge you that you resolve to become as excellent as possible," remind us of the *Apology* (30A) and, as spoken by Socrates, they have a special meaning that we cannot fail to hear.[18] Next, the forefathers speak through Socrates as the laws of Athens do in the *Crito*. Just as Socrates there does not withdraw into a state built in the clouds, but meets the challenge of his own Athens, so here—all tacit and explicit critiques to the contrary notwithstanding—the principle is upheld that the young should listen to the voice of their fathers, especially if Socrates is their spokesman. He could, indeed, say of himself with more right than the nameless dead: "Though I might have lived without honor (μὴ καλῶς), I preferred to die

with honor (καλῶς).'' The appeal to *arete* without which all possessions are of no advantage and without which "even knowledge
becomes base cunning, and not wisdom"—this appeal, too, has
a new and richer meaning through Socrates. Again, the exhor-
tation to become better than one's ancestors, and not to base
one's own merit upon their achievements, contains a twofold
truth if we have learned from the foregoing what these ancestors—lacked.

Finally, the appeal to the parents urging them not to mourn too   247c–248d
much and to bear their sorrows bravely is justified as follows[19]:
"To make one's happiness depend upon oneself, at least as far as
possible, and not to cling in suspense to others and make one's
own life be subject to the vicissitudes of their fortunes—this is
the best equipment for life. He who lives according to this principle is of a healthy mind, brave and wise" (247e *et seq.*). Un-
controlled outbursts of grief as among the Homeric heroes, we
read in the *Republic* (387e), are incompatible with an education
designed to promote courage. In the *Laws* (800d), it is pro-
hibited to play passionate music conducive to arousing tears at
sacrifices and funeral rites. Thus, the *Menexenus* also shows us
the goal of Socratic education: a man who is as self-sufficient as
possible. For it is Plato's Socrates who is speaking here and who
is saying (many years after his own death—who knows how
much is meant to apply to himself?) in the name of the dead that
"our life has the noblest end and deserves more to be glorified
than lamented," and that it is better to care for the survivors
than to lament the dead (248cd).

At the end, the speaker adds a few words in his own name: 248d–249c
we will provide for the old and care (ἐπιμελησομένων) for the
young "wherever one of us meets one of them." Other speakers
may say similar things in speeches at funerals, but we know the
special significance of a "meeting" with Socrates and his special
way of "caring." Then the speaker turns our attention once more
to the city itself, remembering how it educates and cares for its
orphans and how it celebrates public, gymnastic festivals in honor
of the dead. Here it seems as if Plato accepts the tradition without reservation. The funeral oration of Perikles concludes similarly with an assurance that the state will provide for its orphaned

sons. At the same time, nevertheless, the state on whose behalf Socrates is speaking here sounds, in its care for the young, like an anticipation of the *Republic* and the *Laws*. It is no accident that the *Laws* (947E) decrees, for the highest officers of the state, memorial celebrations which consist of the same kind of gymnastic competitions mentioned here in the *Menexenus*.[20] It is the sacredness of Athens that—in spite of everything—asserts itself again at the conclusion of the eulogy.

The iridescent and reflecting quality of the *Menexenus* is not caught easily. The sharpest contrasts seem to vanish behind the uniform structure of an encomium, and its open praise as well as its hidden censure seem to be again qualified (ironically) by the reservation that Socrates has about formal speechmaking. It is difficult to grasp this fluid quality of the work, and this difficulty accounts for the divergent interpretations in which usually a single aspect of the dialogue is thought to contain the meaning of the whole work. Yet, the most divergent views seem to agree on one thing—that the *Menexenus* is not a philosophical work.[21] Now, surely, this is correct only if we set up specific requirements of a conceptual or systematic nature in order to define the meaning of philosophy. The more a philosopher remembers, however, that in doing philosophy he exists as a person, the easier it will be to see the philosophical content even in this work.

We must read the *Menexenus* as a contribution to the effort that finds an increasingly radical expression in other works of Plato, from the *Thrasymachus* to the *Gorgias* and to the *Republic*. To the extent that Plato's ideal state grew beyond the sphere of historical reality, he was compelled to think more and more seriously about the natural—i.e., political, historical, and human —roots of his own existence, precisely for the sake of the future. This is why Plato's Socrates cuts through the historical tradition, ironically and for the sake of reform, and breaks this tradition down critically by using it in his own way. He preserves what is worth preserving and thus achieves a more genuine identification with this historical (and, rightly understood, eternal) heritage of Athens. Whether the *Menexenus* has any philosophical content may be decided within this perspective.

PART IV

"The *Logos* Takes a Stand"

SEVENTEEN

Alcibiades Major

THE *ALCIBIADES* is the strangest case in the Platonic corpus. *"Candidissimus Platonis nostri liber, qui Alcibiades inscribitur, Alcibiade ipso venustior et omni carior auro"*—so wrote Marsiglio Ficino enthusiastically. Schleiermacher was the first to regard it, with strong antipathy, as un-Platonic. He thought "there were a few very beautiful and genuinely Platonic passages" in the work "floating sparsely scattered in a mass of inferior material." Platonic scholarship has largely followed his lead.[1]

In antiquity, however, there was no doubt about Plato's authorship. In fact, during a period of some nine hundred years this work was singled out for special honors. According to Iamblichos, the *Alcibiades* contains all of Plato's wisdom "like a seed." It is "the entrance gate to the works of Plato," in the words of Olympiodoros, whose commentary we have in addition to the more comprehensive commentary by Proklos. There are at least traces of other interpretations in the Neoplatonic tradition.[2] When Plutarch wrote his biography of Alkibiades, he used this dialogue, even in its actual wording, as the basis for the description of his hero's youth.[3] A satire of Persius (IV) begins with a critical speech by Socrates addressed to young Alkibiades, "Deinomache's son," the aspiring politician, and culminates in the principle, "Know thyself."[4] Polybios is deeply indebted to the *Alcibiades* for that great scene of his *History*: his first conversation with the young Scipio.[5] In his dialogue *Eroticus*, Aristotle adapted—with echoes of the actual wording—the striking image in the *Alcibiades* about the eye looking into the eye of another.[6] Several scenes in Xenophon's *Memorabilia*, and the *Alcibiades* by the Socratic Aischines, are modeled after Plato's dialogue.[7] If the reverse order of composition were true, then the author of the dialogue must have been the first to provide philosophical depth to the themes touched upon by Xenophon and Aischines.

The first meeting between Socrates and the young Alkibiades that is dramatized in this dialogue must be placed around the year 433 B.C., shortly before both of them participated in the battle at Potidaea. The portrait of Sparta that Socrates develops in the "royal speech"—Sparta at the height of its political and financial power—is an anachronism at this early time. All the more probable, therefore, is the assumption that the dialogue was composed before the collapse of Sparta at Leuktra (i.e., before 371), a dating adopted by Eduard Meyer.[8]

PRELIMINARY
CONVERSATION
103A–106C

Socrates meets an Athenian youth and forces upon him a Socratic inquiry. While the dialogue corresponds, in this general situation, to others like the *Charmides* or the *Lysis*, there are no secondary figures in the *Alcibiades* nor is there any setting full of charm or symbolic meaning. Instead, we find something very different from the other dialogues. In them we have a handsome and talented youth who bears a celebrated name as if by accident. Young Charmides, for example, does not suggest to us the "tyrant" he became in later years. In the *Alcibiades*, however, the historical person himself comes to life in his character and fate, and "this characteristic portrait here, as in actual history, weighs more than would the presence of a dozen other people" (K. F. Hermann).[9] The economy with which this dialogue concentrates upon the two protagonists is also its unique strength. The *Charmides*, the *Lysis*, and, say, the *Euthydemus* show a young man with admirers swarming all around him, and Socrates must first prove himself as the true lover in competition with others. In this case, however, all the other lovers have run away. Socrates alone remains. Hence, a silent struggle ensues which is puzzling. Alkibiades is amazed—as we are—at the "strangeness" of this man (ἀτοπώτερος αὖ φαίνῃ, 106A 2).

The encounter itself is fraught with a tension unequaled in Plato. In the case of Charmides, Lysis, Theaitetos, and others,

Socrates meets the young men for the first time just when they are ready for him. There is scarcely a hint that previously there may have been obstacles to their meeting, or that the newly formed bond may later be in danger. The situation here is altogether different. Socrates long has been in love with Alkibiades and never has lost sight of him. Yet this erotic attachment has met, quite paradoxically, with a "demonic resistance" that up to now has sealed the lips of Socrates. We share the experience of the unique moment when this resistance is overcome and Socrates pours forth the first words, long repressed, in addressing Alkibiades. "The god," we soon learn (105E), "did not permit me to talk to you, lest our conversation be futile. Now, however, he has sent me to you; for now you can listen.[10]

At the end of the dialogue, the puzzle of the beginning is cleared up somewhat, yet we leave on a note of new tension. If the *Laches* and the *Charmides* close with the suggestion that the work of love and teaching must be continued, we find here, in addition to the same suggestion, Socrates' concern that Alkibiades may be ruined by becoming a "lover of the people" (132A), as well as the prediction, expressed in Socrates' last words (135E), that the state may win out over him and over Alkibiades also. This prediction connects, in an ironic paradox, the political career of Alkibiades and the death of Socrates. Thus, the dialogue begins with a tension between past and present; it ends with a tension between present and future.

The course of the conversation moves between these two tensions. In this movement, too, there is at least one thing that distinguishes this human portrait from all others in Plato. If we recall the conversation of Socrates with some other youth, say, Charmides, or his struggle with the Sophists and politicians in the *Gorgias*, we find that the dialectic takes its own course whether it leads to the impasse of *aporia* or to the refutation of the opponent. What about the partner himself? At the end Charmides is still more fond of Socrates or Kallikles is more subdued than at the beginning. But they have not changed in any way, neither Charmides (because he did not feel any resistance to begin with) nor Kallikles (because he is incapable of changing). In the *Alcibiades*, however, we meet for once a human being who is deeply

threatened within, at the most dangerous time of his life, and
we witness for once how this human being undergoes an inner
change, in the context of a Platonic work.[11] At the beginning,
Alkibiades is both irritated because Socrates is "annoying" him
(ἐνοχλεῖς με, 104D) and curious to know just what Socrates wants
—a mixture of defiant rejection and willing attention. In the ensuing discussion, he vacillates between pride and dejection, until,
at the end, his pride seems for the moment completely broken.
"Then, my friend, a slavish state is to be avoided?" "Certainly,
Socrates." "And are you now conscious of your own state, as
befits a noble character?" "I think I am only too conscious of
my own state." With this, defiant rejection is transformed into
its opposite. "Our relationship," as Alkibiades says himself, "has
changed. It cannot be otherwise: from now on I shall attend
upon you and you will let yourself be attended by me." Socrates
confirms the inward change: "O noble friend! My love, then,
will be like that of the stork. It has hatched out a new love in
you and will, in turn, be nourished by this love."

This change, without parallel in Plato's works, is closely related to the progress of the dialogue. Socrates begins by showing
Alkibiades the unlimited scope of his pride and ambition. Then
comes the critical examination. In the first part, the master tries
to convince the youth that the latter does not know anything
and to show him, at the same time, what is the true aim of political
action.

I
106c–118b

First step: Alkibiades insists that he knows better than the
Athenians what is useful for them. But arrogant as he was only
a moment before, Alkibiades cannot say, as he finally admits, what
he means by the "better": the word is stressed again and again
by Socrates. Incidentally, in the course of this discussion, Alkibiades, quite unawares, receives a first lesson in "dialectics"
(108c 6). Gymnastics is composed of boxing and wrestling
(107E, 108c). The art of music consists of singing, rhythmic
dancing, and playing on the zither or the flute (106E, 108c).
The method of "division" shows through—a favorite method
of the Academy.

ı 1
106c–109a

I 2
109a–113c

Second step: In place of the word "better," Alkibiades eventually proposes the word "just," suggesting immediately—in

the true manner of an aspiring politician—that there is a difference between what one says and what one means (109c 1–3). Thus, when it is shown later that he does not know what just and unjust mean, this is more than merely a conceptual failure. The Socratic equation between ignorance and wrongdoing is hereby made evident. Socrates shows Alkibiades that he is ignorant; rather, he shows that Alkibiades ignores his ignorance. This is naïvely confirmed by Alkibiades himself. He never has learned anything about right or wrong from any teacher; he has always known, even as a boy in competition with other boys, that he "was in the right," and indeed now he is quite sure that he was right in having no doubts (110a *et seq.*). What dramatic irony this conveys inasmuch as he is now, for the first time, confronting the only true teacher, the only true doubter and "ignorant" man, who is explaining to the aspiring politician the "madness" of his project.

The third step is the proof that good, beautiful, and useful are one and the same. Hence, we cannot use any discrepancy among these concepts to defend the kind of uncertainty about the nature of justice that has just come out in Alkibiades. The young man formulates his own experience as follows: in politics, it is a matter not of just or unjust, but of useful and harmful practices. Great injustice—this Alkibiades does not bother with trifling matters!—often has proved useful to the wrongdoer. It is quite admirable how Socrates, after a few dialectical moves, throws the concept of "courage" into the discussion (115b) because now the disciple must remember his own special "virtue." When one's own honor is at stake, the distinction between good and useful is no longer valid. This means, then, that the distinction cannot hold in the case of justice either; and with this the pride of the young man begins to collapse (116e). His perplexity is due to the fact that he does not know, but thinks that he does. In showing him this, Socrates sums the case up in a sharp judgment, applicable beyond the scope of the dialogue to historical reality: "You throw yourself into politics before you are properly educated."

The need "to care for oneself" (ἐπιμέλεια ἑαυτοῦ)—this is shown in the central section of the work, particularly in the "royal

I 3
113c–118b

II
118b–124b

speech," by Socrates as he evokes with ironically iridescent images the princely education in Sparta and Persia. Here Socrates is trying to keep the disciple from falling beneath himself. At the very beginning (105c), Socrates had pointed out that Alkibiades did not think anybody worth anything except Cyrus and Xerxes. Now when Alkibiades thinks he can easily dispose of his competitors, Socrates shows him—"high-minded man" that he is—that he must measure himself not against any political hack in the market place, but only against the kings of Sparta and Persia.[12]

The "royal speech" is the core of the dialogue. For purposes of comparison, we may recall that in the *Protagoras* (342c *et seq.*), Socrates invents a secret philosophy of the Spartans, and that in the *Charmides* (156c *et seq.*), he plays with the notion of a special art of healing which King Zalmoxis is supposed to have taught the savage Thracians. The "royal speech" of the *Alcibiades* goes far beyond these analogies. Amidst all the playful fancy, we discern the first outlines of a state dedicated to education; for instance, the heir to the Persian throne, in the third seven-year period, is educated by four royal tutors in the four Socratic virtues, whereas in Athens the care of the young is left to the most useless slaves, "unless a lover takes an interest in you."

III
124B–135E

In the third part, the concept of "caring for oneself" is interpreted, on the highest level, as self-knowledge. Throughout this part, Alkibiades replies submissively. His former mood erupts only once when he expresses, as in the beginning, his confusion and humiliation in the face of another as yet unresolved *aporia* (127D). This contrast between the first and the third parts is no accident, nor does it signify a weakening of creative power. It shows that the pupil's pride is broken and that he has come to see his own emptiness before the superior strength of his master. Thus, humiliation and submission belong to the inner development of the dialogue which leads from the strong resistance displayed by Alkibiades at the beginning to his surrender at the end. At the same time, an attitude of listening and replying, quietly and objectively, is a necessary prerequisite for developing—as Socrates now does—the complex of problems dealing with the structure of the state and with self-knowledge.

These are the two divergent directions pursued in the last part of the dialogue. The first movement explores the nature of political action up to the point where we see, as yet in unresolved opposition, the centripetal principle of "friendship" or "community" and the centrifugal principle of "doing one's own." This contradiction is resolved—if we think beyond this discussion—when we realize that it is the task of the true statesman to reconcile these two principles, in thought as well as in action, in a "harmony of opposites." III 1
124B–127D

The second movement defines "caring for oneself" in terms of "self-knowledge" and interprets the "self" as "soul" which is superior to the body and, even more so, to the external possessions associated with the body. Yet, again, these two problems—the state and knowledge—only seem to be independent of each other. In truth, the two converge upon the same point in so far as the divergence of political aims (as yet unsettled) can be settled only through knowledge and in so far as the kind of self-knowledge intended here does not isolate the individual, but leads him to his true task: the state. III 2
127D–135E

A few hints point toward ultimate depths. While discussing the meaning of the Delphic inscription, "Know thyself," Socrates asks (129AB): How can we discover the "self-itself," i.e., the self in its real nature? Once stated, the question seems to disappear from sight. But after we have learned that man, in the true sense, is "soul," Socrates returns (130D) to the question, what, then, is the "self-itself"? We have found no answer. The discussion, as we should see, has pointed toward the sphere of true being without attaining it.[13]

How self-knowledge is possible is shown through an image that has lasted through the ages and alone would put the seal of authenticity upon this dialogue.[14] Even as one eye sees itself reflected in another and, especially, in the pupil of the other, so the soul sees itself reflected in another soul and, especially, in that region of the soul where its noblest and divine powers dwell— the region of knowledge. He who looks into this region sees "what is divine."[15] "God and knowledge" are once more brought together as inseparable.[16] A loving community of those who seek the truth, aiming at the highest knowledge of true being and approximating, ultimately, divine perfection—these aspects of

Plato's thought are here outlined as in a preliminary sketch.

We may note a peculiar similarity in structure between this dialogue and the *Hipparchus*, which we have claimed—let us hope with some reason—is one of Plato's earliest works. In the center of each dialogue, we find a long speech by Socrates. This speech has been misinterpreted, in each case, as an un-Platonic exposition of historical or ethnological learning, because the commentators failed to see the supercilious play with these historical realities and the ironic self-reflections upon them. The *Hipparchus* depicts the fanciful educational practices of the son of Peisistratos. We see how he educates the Athenian people in "justice," with zeal, but using un-Socratic methods, i.e., by means of poetry and didactic epigrams. We see how he enters into competition with the Delphic injunction, "Know thyself"; and, finally, how —regardless of his educational efforts—he falls victim to the conspirators who are acting from motives very similar to his own. The *Alcibiades* depicts a fanciful world of wealth and education as they are said to be combined not only at the Spartan court, but especially at the Persian court, and shows that an Athenian aristocrat could not even think of competing. In the *Hipparchus*, we find a world that does rise above the level of "love of gain or profit"—the theme of the dialogue—but is still an inadequate world, calling for true education. The historical reality as described in the *Alcibiades* (a reality as in the *Lettres Persanes* and not as in scientific ethnography) rises above the existence of the ambitious youth. Moreover, the situation depicted with playful irony generates by itself the demand that Socrates attributes to the queen of Persia: "It is impossible to imagine what this man (Alkibiades) could rely upon in his project, except careful training and wisdom. For these are the only things which are worth anything among the Greeks."

Thus, while the two dialogues reveal an unmistakable similarity in structure, the *Alcibiades* clearly shows a greater maturity. The first section of the *Hipparchus* analyzes the concept of "love of gain" without result; after the speech of Socrates in the central section, the conversation continues without coming to any conclusion and returns, ultimately, to its point of departure. In the *Alcibiades*, however, the first and third sections of the dialogue are sharply set off from each other. In the first part, Socrates humbles the proud youth, breaks down his opinions which are both false and dangerous, and begins to make it clear that the true aim of political activity is justice. In the third part, Socrates brings the humbled youth affectionately to his own side and guides him so that he can see the fundamental problem of the state and gain a first insight into the structure of man. The central section of the *Hipparchus* reveals a level, rising above the rest of the conversation, toward and even beyond which the latter would have to be raised. The "royal speech" in the *Alcibiades* also reveals a level that rises above the lack of education represented by the young man. At the same time, however, the concepts of "careful training" and "wisdom" provide a transition to the third part in which the true objective of the dialogue comes through. It is Socratic-Platonic education.

These comments may serve as a first attempt at placing the dialogue in the total body of Plato's works. Beyond this, however, we have been particularly concerned to show how, in spite of many similarities, the *Alcibiades* differs from other works of the early period. This difference consists, above all, in the portrait of human existence charged with extreme tension. Among the minor dialogues of Plato, there is none in which such a moment—deeply saturated with what precedes and with what follows—is depicted with such irresistible power. Should we infer from this that someone else surpassed Plato? Or is it not rather Plato himself who is here surpassing his own previous achievements?

Let us look in more detail at the place of the *Alcibiades* in the total body of Plato's works. We recall that this dialogue resembles the early aporetic dialogues in that it depicts a meeting between Socrates and a young man, followed by a Socratic cross-examination. This resemblance is evident both at the beginning and at the end. In the *Charmides*, the *Lysis*, and the *Alcibiades*, we first are shown, in a very similar manner even though with different nuances, the noble birth and the beauty of the young man. The conversation itself begins, in each case, with the partner and his characteristics: the *sophrosyne* of Charmides, the friendship between Menexenos and Lysis, the plan of Alkibiades to present himself to the people of Athens. And the conclusion in each of the three dialogues points to the newly formed bond that unites master and pupil. Yet, as the conversation moves into the subject matter itself, the *Alcibiades* differs from the other dialogues, which are concerned with the search for a definition and result in *aporia*. In the *Alcibiades*, to be sure, we also find many aporetic moments, but the great movement of the dialogue is of an entirely different kind. The Socratic-Platonic principle of the state and *paideia* prevails against the hostile forces of tyranny here manifesting themselves in Alkibiades—as it prevails, on a much larger scale and in a more severe struggle, against the tyrannical danger in the *Gorgias*.

The *Gorgias* and the *Alcibiades* are related, to begin with, in their points of departure. Alkibiades wants to appear in public to "advise" the Athenians and to "persuade" the people in the Assembly. Gorgias, when asked about the nature of rhetoric, puts first its power to "persuade" judges and members of the Assembly (*Gorgias* 452E), or, as Socrates defines it, the power to "produce persuasion" (πειθοῦς δημιουργός, 453A). Both dialogues then describe the area in which this persuasion is practiced as "the just and the unjust," thus focusing upon the ultimate objective. Thereafter, to be sure, the *Gorgias* takes its own course in analyzing the nature of rhetoric; yet, parallels with the *Alcibiades* become visible again on the second level, i.e., in the conversation between Socrates and Polos. For Polos wants to divorce rhetoric from any relationship with justice. He recognizes as the basis for action only such concepts as useful and harmful, not just or unjust. Socrates thereupon refutes him by showing that, in the dimension of depth intended by Socrates, there is no difference between ugly and evil and that injustice cannot be useful. This corresponds in the *Alcibiades* (see I 3 above) to the thesis that in the political sphere, it is a matter not of justice or injustice, but of usefulness and harm. Socrates refutes this thesis of Alkibiades, in a very similar fashion, by showing that the good and the beautiful are identical; hence, the just and the useful must be identical as well.

The third conversation in the *Gorgias*, between Socrates and Kallikles, again has a great deal in common with the *Alcibiades*.

"You have begun to occupy yourself with public affairs," Socrates says (515A) in addressing Kallikles, just as he does in the case of Alkibiades (105AB). "But before doing so," as we read in both dialogues (*Alcibiades* 109D; *Gorgias* 514B), "must we not first ask whether we understand the art which we wish to practice and see from whom we have learned it?" In the *Gorgias*, there follows the devastating criticism of Perikles and the other statesmen of Athens who failed to educate the people; in the *Alcibiades*, later on, we find a similar, though more concealed, criticism of Perikles (see II above). In the end, the two dialogues converge surprisingly upon the same point. The *Gorgias* ends, in a wide sweep and after evoking a myth of the world beyond, by drawing up a balance sheet with respect to the fortunes of the just man and the unjust; the *Alcibiades*, briefly but sharply, puts happiness on the side of *arete*, misfortune on the side of tyranny. The *Gorgias* closes with the words (527CD): "First we must practice *arete* in order to achieve the highest good and the best way of life. Then we can turn to politics; for it is shameful to act in our ignorance as if we were persons of importance." Similarly, we read in the *Alcibiades* (135B): "You must acquire *arete* and not strive for tyranny. But before we possess *arete*, it is better to be commanded and governed by the superior."

We need but fix our attention upon the beginnings and the ends of the two dialogues to see that the *Gorgias* presupposes the problems raised in the *Alcibiades*. These problems are treated with larger scope in the *Gorgias*, where they are expanded into such specific inquiries as the nature of sophistic rhetoric and the meaning of deliberate amoralism and are represented by different individuals. In the earlier work, the same problems are still compressed, as it were, in the one person and character of Alkibiades. Thus, to sum up, we find that our dialogue is related, in its human movement, to the group of aporetic dialogues—though it has grown beyond them in its dramatic tension. The conceptual problems that are interwoven with this human movement, however, are clearly recognizable as an anticipation of the *Gorgias*.

Next, we must deal with the relationship between the *Alcibiades* and the *Republic*. We find that the conflict between the basic forces at work in the state—the centripetal force of "friendship" or "concord" (φιλία, ὁμόνοια) and the centrifugal force of "doing one's own"—remains unresolved in the *Alcibiades*, whereas in the *Republic* the structure of the state is based upon the reconciliation of these two opposing forces. The concept of justice quickly becomes a major concern in the first part of the *Alcibiades*. What Socrates discovers in his pupil—and seeks to overcome—is that the latter does not know what just and unjust mean. This ignorance is present both in thought and in action. The *Republic* begins, similarly, with an inquiry into the nature of justice and with the refutation of the tyrannical ideal, which is unmistakably rooted here in Alkibiades and against which Socrates struggles (*Alcibiades* 105A *et seq.*, 134C). In the concluding part of the *Alcibiades*, moreover, we find that the analysis of what it means "to care for oneself" leads first to an unresolved *aporia* about the structure of the state and then to the individual whose own structure—body and soul, the ruling and the obeying parts of the soul—is disclosed in the act of self-knowledge. No results are reached as far as the nature of the state is concerned; the findings about human nature are but preliminary; and the sphere of "being-itself" (αὐτὸ τὸ αὐτό, 129B, 130D) is only sighted from afar.

All these matters recur in the *Republic*—only on the largest scale, with unequaled depth, and in firmest conjunction with each other. Justice becomes the cornerstone of the *polis*. The *aporia* about the structure of the state is resolved by founding it upon the harmony of seemingly opposite forces, centripetal and centrifugal. The individual struggles upward from his existence in the cave to a view of the *Idea*. The respective structures of state and the individual are no longer set side by side; instead, they are correlated with each other in a concentric conjunction that, more than anything else, defines the essential nature of the *Republic*. The *Alcibiades*, then, must be seen also as an anticipation of Plato's chief work. It represents a transitional movement that leads from the aporetic dialogues in search of a definition to the foundation of Plato's thought in the *Gorgias* and to the final development of this thought in the *Republic*.

A word may be said about the significance of *Eros* in this dialogue. To understand fully the speech of Alkibiades in the *Symposium*, we must look to the dialogue *Alcibiades* as its background and we must be aware constantly, in each dialogue, both of the extraordinary greatness and of the catastrophe of the historical Alkibiades.

That Plato while writing the *Symposium* had the earlier dialogue clearly in mind is shown by the first words Alkibiades addresses to Socrates. In the *Symposium* he says: "You always lie in wait for me"; in the *Alcibiades*: "You annoy me always." (In Greek there is an even greater similarity in the sound of the words: ἐλλοχεῖν, *Symposium* 213B 9; ἐνοχλεῖν, *Alcibiades* 104D 3.) The "strange nature of this man who does not belong anywhere" is used by Alkibiades as a characteristic of Socrates in both dialogues (ἀτοπώτερος, *Alcibiades* 106A; ἀτοπία, *Symposium* 215A). And here is the immediate effect of this "strange nature." In the *Alcibiades*, Socrates compels the young man to confess that he feels ashamed (109A), and this confession is repeated later (127D). In the *Symposium*, Alkibiades when drunk confesses —and, surely, nothing could better characterize the nature of this extraordinary man than his confession—that Socrates is the only person who makes him feel ashamed (216B).

The leading theme in the central section of the *Alcibiades* is "to care for oneself," which Socrates sets up against the premature political aspirations of the youth. In the *Symposium*, Alkibiades reveals that before Socrates—and before no one else, of course—he must admit that he has neglected himself (216A) while attending to the political affairs of Athens. Moreover, in the conversation the two had during their night together, the disciple said to the master: "Nothing is more important to me than to become as excellent as possible; and there is no greater helper than you" (218D). With this statement, the speech of Alkibiades in the *Symposium* reaches the same goal toward which the dialogue *Alcibiades* is moving. At the end both of the speech and of the dialogue, it is Socrates who is wooed, and the beloved has become the wooing lover.

The simple, great theme of love that dominates the *Alcibiades* from beginning to end becomes the second most powerful theme in the *Symposium*. There the undercurrents of tragedy are still stronger than in the earlier work; for in the eulogy of Socrates, Alkibiades himself admits that he has long since deserted Socrates for professional politics.

EIGHTEEN

Gorgias

IN THE *Gorgias*, Plato returns to the *Thrasymachus*, raising both form and content of the earlier work to a new creative level. The theme in both dialogues is the problem of justice and the struggle against its opponents. In each dialogue, Socrates has three such opponents, and they are progressively farther removed from him. Thus, both dialogues move through three stages with the intensity of the struggle progressively increasing.

Let us at once note the differences. In the *Thrasymachus*, we find, on the first level, old Kephalos, a simple, unphilosophical man representing justice as a natural disposition. Gorgias, however, formally corresponding to Kephalos, bears the stamp of *adikia* even though he is not consistent enough to admit that he belongs to the sphere of the lawless. Thus, the two dialogues differ in their points of departure from which the movement of the whole proceeds to the finale of ruthless exposure. Another difference is connected with this. In the *Thrasymachus*, the problem of justice is presented naked, as it were, in the form of a search for a definition, and this search, in the nature of the early dialogues, must end on a note of *aporia*. Thrasymachos, the sophistic orator, is the extreme spokesman on behalf of injustice. Yet, his profession—his name, "Keen Fighter," would make everybody think of it—is not brought into the dialogue explicitly, so that the connection between sophistic and *adikia* remains obscure. It is precisely this connection that is brought into full consciousness in the *Gorgias*; for here the figure of the famous orator—Gorgias himself—represents sophistic rhetoric, and the figure of Kallikles represents the kind of immoralism consistent with it. Just as Kallikles, at the beginning, admits to being a follower of Gorgias, so the principles he represents are founded upon sophistic rhetoric. The struggle of Socrates is directed not only against these principles, but against the cultural system itself that is shown to be the breeding ground of this immoralism and must be overthrown intellectually.[1]

In contrast to the two other great antisophistic dialogues, the *Protagoras* and the *Euthydemus*, the *Gorgias* is presented not as a report, but in direct dramatic form. This accounts for the absence of almost all background and symbolism in the spatial setting. The persons of the drama confront each other, directly expressing themselves and their objective differences. The situation at the beginning is similar to the *Hippias Minor*. A famous visitor from abroad has just delivered a polished speech and is still surrounded by a circle of admirers, whom Plato later brings back into the conversation now and then.[2] Gorgias is staying with Kallikles, as Protagoras is staying with Kallias. Socrates, coming from the market place, first meets Kallikles, the host, entering his house. The very first words are spoken by the man who will prove to be the most formidable opponent in the last part of the dialogue; he does not, like Anytos in the *Meno*, burst into the conversation with uncanny abruptness. Thus, the connection between Kallikles and Gorgias, between immoralism and oratory, is made visible concretely from the outset, as indeed the structure of the whole work is founded upon it.

"War and battle"—it is no accident that these very first words convey the theme of the dialogue. "War and battle," says the proverb playfully quoted by Kallikles, "war and battle should be missed"—as you have just missed the lecture by Gorgias. "In other words, we are arriving late for a feast," Socrates replies in the same tone. Peculiar, dramatic irony: what happened before was really play, the serious struggle is about to come.

PRELIMINARY CONVERSATION 447A–449A

It is introduced by a brief squabble between the pupils Chairephon and Polos. The genuinely Socratic question, "What, then, is it (τί ἔστιν, 447c) that this famous man professes and teaches?" immediately touches the heart of the matter. But the callow Chairephon, whom Socrates is using as a kind of advance guard against the enemy, knows as much about the Socratic art of asking questions as Polos, the pupil of Gorgias, knows about the art of his master. Instead of defining the art of rhetoric, Polos, the aspiring orator, delivers a short panegyric upon the subject, ending with a tribute to Gorgias (448c). The conversation lags. Chairephon does not know what to ask next, just as a beginning teacher is thrown off his track when the pupil's reply does not correspond to his preconceived plan. Socrates himself then takes the initiative and draws Gorgias into the discussion. The main dialogue begins. One must be Socrates to conduct a Socratic dialogue.

Let us first note a structural similarity to the beginning of the *Protagoras*.[3] Even as Socrates there tests the young Hippokrates by asking "who" is this revered Protagoras of yours, so here, too, he has Chairephon ask, "who" is Gorgias? In each case, examples drawn from medicine and the arts of sculpture and painting make it clear that the reply should aim, to begin with, at the nature of the profession to be analyzed critically. The initial comments made by Protagoras in praise of himself and his art (*Protagoras* 318A *et seq.*) correspond to the short eulogy of rhetoric, and of Gorgias as its master, that is delivered here by Polos. In both dialogues, the question about the nature of the art is taken over into the main body of the dialogue; in other words, it is discussed by Socrates with the two great Sophists themselves. For, in each case, the assault aims at the sophistic world itself—envisaged in the *Protagoras* more as a system of education, while here in the *Gorgias* more as the sphere of oratorical and political action. In the *Protagoras*, the discussion subsequently shifts to the question, what is the nature of *arete*? In the *Gorgias*, however, the nature of sophistic oratory remains the primary subject matter.

Once we see these structural similarities between the two dialogues, we also may hear, in the preliminary conversation of the *Gorgias*, echoes that are only meant to reach us as if from afar. Above all, there is the difference between speechmaking and dialogue. Gorgias has just delivered a "great" speech. Kallikles, in addressing Socrates, states the hope that his master will soon give another splendid performance. Socrates, however, immediately pins him down to a "conversation." The speech can wait

until later. ("... Until later," indeed, when the claims of oratory
have been defeated, just as in the *Ion*—530D—Socrates puts off
the oration by the rhapsode "until later.") Gorgias can hold his
own in a conversation as well. In his case, however, this does
not mean that he is moving closer to the Socratic principle of
discussion. His conversation is rather another form of rhetorical
display, or, in short, a caricature of Socratic dialectics. Here we
find echoes of the conflicts that, in the *Protagoras*, are fought
through to a point where the conversation threatens to collapse.
We are especially reminded of the earlier great dialogue with
its characteristic tensions when we hear Gorgias announcing the
same program as Protagoras. He boasts of being able to give
speeches of unparalleled length as well as answers of unsurpassed
brevity (*Gorgias* 449BC; *Protagoras* 329B, 334E). These are for
the Sophists the two extremes of the same total know-how.

When Polos is asked to define the nature of his master's art
and his own, he answers—despite the examples which should
serve as guides—that it is "the finest of all arts" (448C). Neither
Gorgias nor his pupil sees what is wrong with this definition
which, as so frequently, conceals a more serious defect behind
the logical flaw; namely, that orators care much less for the
subject matter itself than for the formal splendor of their speech
and its reflection upon them personally. Thus, Socrates must explain the difference between *describing* an art (ποία τις τέχνη)
and *defining* its nature (τίς τέχνη). This is a distinction already
formulated in the *Hippias Major* and in the *Euthyphro*, there (*Euthyphro* 11A) even with terminological precision (πάθος—οὐσία),
as later in Aristotle.

Socrates turns to Gorgias as the professional representative   I
of the art of rhetoric and asks him what is the object of the knowl-   449A—461B
edge and education on which he prides himself (περὶ τί τῶν ὄν-   I 1
των τυγχάνει οὖσα; *Gorgias* 449D). Gorgias may still think that   449A—454B
the question of his fame is of primary concern and, if Socrates
had not expressly ruled against it, he might have replied with a
panegyric on his art, as Polos did on a smaller scale and as Protagoras does in the dialogue named after him. Gorgias does not
suspect that, in submitting to questions by Socrates, he has Socrates' own law imposed upon him, and that sophistic rhetoric

now must justify its claims before the bar of philosophy. Gorgias defines the object of his art as "speech" (περὶ λόγους). This is very general and much too broad, again revealing in Gorgias both a lack of logical precision and an exaggerated conception of himself. Socrates helps to clarify matters. He shows that oratory teaches not only how to speak, but how to think and speak (φρονεῖν καὶ λέγειν). Thus he prevents the word from being nothing more than empty sound. Next, he helps—by the method of division—to delimit the field in two aspects. First, he eliminates those arts in which speaking is a relatively minor aspect as compared with doing. But even in those cases where speech is paramount, oratory must be assigned a more definite place as compared with other arts (including mathematics) by clarifying the question, "about what" (περὶ τί)? Gorgias, as if to recapture in strength what his art is losing in scope, defines its subject as "the greatest and the most beautiful" (451D), lapsing back into the error of Polos and, like Polos, betraying both a lack of logical discipline and an abundance of vanity. Yet, this seemingly empty phrase of Gorgias prepares the way for what follows in a peculiarly dramatic irony. For after Socrates has criticized the flaw in the last reply, what now emerges (in a move more wordy than is necessary) is that oratory deals with "persuasion" and, more specifically, with persuasion in public assemblies (ὅστις ἂν πολιτικὸς σύλλογος γίγνηται). The political life comes into view as the characteristic field of rhetoric, and the significance of oratory is heightened inasmuch as it is said to be the source of one's own freedom and of power over others (452DE). We see the main theme of the dialogue emerging briefly. In the concise restatement by Socrates, rhetoric is "productive of persuasion" (πειθοῦς δημιουργός, 453A).[4] Yet, again, this is too broad. And, again, the question is, persuasion "in what"? Gorgias finally defines the subject matter of oratory as right and wrong, or just and unjust (περὶ τούτων ἅ ἐστι δίκαιά τε καὶ ἄδικα, 454B). This makes the claim of rhetoric explicit: it is the highest claim in the Socratic sense. It is much higher than someone like Gorgias realizes, for it is a claim to be made legitimately only by an art altogether different from his own.

12
454B–455D   Against this claim, Socrates must continue his work of setting logical limits. Together with Gorgias—and, again, by division

—he distinguishes between knowledge and belief. Belief may be true or false, but there cannot be false knowledge. It follows that persuasion, or conviction, as practiced by the rhetorician produces belief, or acceptance on faith. It does not produce the certainty of knowledge, if only because it is impossible to teach so large a number of people the truth about matters of such importance in so short a time (455A). Thus, the field of oratory is limited in two respects: first, in scope, for it does not deal with areas of life in which experts are competent; second, in depth, for in the area that remains, the just and unjust, rhetoric can make no claim to knowledge. What, then, is left to it?

Yet, at this point when rhetoric seems to have lost so much of its ground and power, the reality of life asserts itself unshaken by dialectics however ingenious—the reality of political and historical life as represented by such names as Themistokles and Perikles, who wrought great things by the power of speech. Goaded on by Socrates, Gorgias once more unfolds the nature of oratory, developing the power (δύναμις, 455D 7, 456A 8, 456C 6, 457A 5) which this art has in the life of the individual and the state, superior to all specialized branches of knowledge such as medicine and the crafts. Along with such power, to be sure, goes the danger of abuse. Gorgias, speaking on behalf of rhetoric but otherwise subscribing to an ordinary code of morality, feels compelled to warn against the possibility of abusing such power. He ascribes the responsibility for such abuse not to rhetoric, but to the individual abusing it, not to the master, but to the pupil.

13
455D–457C

The contradiction inherent in this view as seen from the perspective of the *logos*, and the danger inherent in it as seen from the perspective of life, are now shown by Socrates. This is his crucial move against the view of Gorgias. As if to heighten the significance of what follows, Socrates first agrees with Gorgias that they are interested only in the matter itself and that personal feelings must not enter into the discussion. Gorgias assents, a little stiffly, and needs some reassurance from the others in the circle to continue with a conversation that is now heading toward his defeat.

14
457C–461B

From what Gorgias has said about his art, Socrates infers, in a somewhat pointed formulation, that an ignorant person (i.e., the orator) is more convincing than the expert before an ignorant audience (ὁ οὐκ εἰδὼς ἄρα τοῦ εἰδότος ἐν οὐκ εἰδόσι πιθανώτερος ἔσται, 459Β). The dubious character of rhetoric cannot be expressed more sharply than in this formulation, to which Gorgias assents, though with some discomfort (τοῦτο ἐνταῦθά γε συμβαίνει). Previously we had learned that the proper subject matter of oratory was "the just and the unjust." Is it the case, then, that the ignorance of the rhetorician—or the fact that he does not even need to know anything—applies to right and wrong, beautiful and ugly, or, in short, to the realities that regulate life? It would be consistent to say that oratory has no factual knowledge in these areas either. Gorgias, who combines the power of the new art with a traditional morality, however, does not go this far. Instead, he asserts—again goaded by Socrates—that it is necessary to have knowledge in the field of justice and injustice. A person trained in oratory (ῥητορικός) *knows* what is just. Thus, he is just, must act justly, and cannot do wrong. Here Socrates shows that Gorgias is caught in a contradiction, for how are these two views compatible with each other: the view that the person trained in oratory cannot do wrong, and the other view according to which not oratory, but the individual abusing it must be blamed?

We might raise some objections to this alleged contradiction. We might cite—with Thrasymachos in the *Republic* (I 340D *et seq.*)—the "orator in the strict sense of the word" (τὸν τῷ ἀκριβεῖ λόγῳ ῥητορικόν) and say that the claim of not being able to do wrong applies to him only, whereas the orator in the general sense—who, strictly speaking, would not then be an "orator"—would be capable of doing wrong. Yet, we would have to ask ourselves again, seriously, on what grounds rhetoric claims to have a knowledge of right and wrong since it disclaims such knowledge in all other fields. It would turn out that rhetoric never can justify this claim. This kind of analysis would lead to a distinction between oratory as represented by Gorgias and the true kind of rhetoric, which—paradoxically—comes into view at the end of the dialogue and is identical with philosophy. That this polarity is inherent in the contradiction here demonstrated by Socrates becomes evident once again, at a more advanced stage of the dialogue (*Gorgias* 508c), when Socrates, looking back to the previous discussion, states: "The orator in the strict sense must be just and understand what is right and wrong." The accent is on "strict." It is clear that to resolve the contradiction in this first part of the dialogue, Plato would have had to embark here upon a positive course. But the opponent's position has not yet been developed adequately and, hence, is not yet adequately criticized. Socrates breaks off: "By the dog, it would take a long discussion, Gorgias, to make sufficiently clear to ourselves how these matters really stand."[5] Polos, the pupil of Gorgias, intervenes at this point, and the self-portrait of rhetoric becomes more radical. The dialogue enters upon its second stage.

The portrait of oratory presented by Gorgias was inconsistent in this respect: rhetoric was said to be concerned with appearances only in everything except matters of right and wrong, where a knowledge of the true nature is required. This inconsistency was due to an adherence to traditional commitments, which interfered with a pure statement of the view both in life and in thought. Polos, who is a younger man and does not feel bound by the traditional ties of the older generation (461c 7), now proposes a more radical formulation. By giving up the claim that oratory needs knowledge of right and wrong, Polos puts the emphasis all the more strongly upon the moral problem at stake in the discussion. Thus, when Socrates hails the entrance of Polos on the scene as a welcome move by which youth comes to the aid of an older generation that is faltering, this welcome wavers —as all true irony does—between a yes and a no.

II
461B–481B

Again, the difference between Socratic and sophistic form enters into the discussion. Polos intervenes at this stage of the conversation, in a precipitate, anacoluthic statement.[6] (He had similarly attracted attention by delivering a brief speech at the beginning of the dialogue itself.) Socrates makes it a condition that Polos submit to the form of dialogue. In this Polos plays the role of the questioner probably because, like Thrasymachos in the *Republic* (I 336c), he thinks it is easier to ask questions than to answer them. An amusing game develops because he does not know how to ask questions in a logical manner and because Socrates guides the questioning, thus putting the questions to himself by way of Polos.[7] The young man shows clearly that he does not understand the basic principle of a Socratic conversation—logical progression of the argument (τὸ ἑξῆς περαίνεσθαι τὸν λόγον, 454c). For, though he is now the questioner, he makes the same mistake as he did in the preliminary conversation and as Gorgias did later (448E, 451D). And the mistake, again, reveals both a logical and a moral flaw. By asking repeatedly and at the wrong moments whether oratory is not "something beautiful" (462c, 463D), Polos reveals the fact that he cannot distinguish between description (ποῖον) and definition (τί). He also reveals his own vanity; he is more concerned with becoming famous than with gaining insight. As the Sophist lightly adopts the Socratic form of conversation, which is a noble instrument only in the hands of the master and which the Sophist does not know how to use, so Socrates replies by usurping on his own part the sophistic form of delivering a long speech. He justifies this exception explicitly on the grounds that his partner is incapable of conducting a philosophical conversation (465E). It is particularly amusing that the decisive and destructive critique by which rhetoric and sophistic are included in the system of pseudo-arts is delivered by Socrates in this rhetorical-sophistic manner.

The formal conflict runs through the whole conversation as a mild but continuing skirmish. Socrates criticizes a long speech by Polos as violating their agreement (471D); yet, immediately afterwards, he replies with a long speech of his own. Even some of the questions asked by Polos, it seems, are intended as rhetorical assertions, not as searching questions in the Socratic sense. This is pointed out to Polos, whereupon he tries to give his questions a different character (466A–c). Instead of offering proof, Polos resorts to ridicule and threats (473DE) or he appeals to the judgment of others in the company or of people in general. As Socrates puts it in a jest, Polos wants to bring matters to a vote—an ironic reference to Socrates' own ineptitude in parliamentary procedures and to the fact that such methods are unsuitable in the pursuit of true knowledge (473E, 475E et seq.).

One other significant detail of the formal structure should be mentioned. At the point where Polos no longer knows how to help himself in the use of the Socratic method, Gorgias intervenes once more (463D). The conversation continues, for a while, between him and Socrates. Then follows the great speech in which Socrates assigns oratory, at least on a preliminary basis, its proper place—which, if proved true, would defeat it. That Gorgias is drawn anew into the discussion is not only a device to show, all the more insistently, how helpless Polos is. It is also a structural symbol indicating that the level of the first conversation here penetrates the second stage. Thus, for Plato, the two stages of the dialogue are not as distinct from each other as a schematic outline might lead us to believe.[8] The question, What is the nature of oratory?, is deeply rooted in the question of its effect and its relationship to justice.

This question, then, is posed anew. It finds a surprising— though still preliminary—answer in the speech of Socrates where oratory is defined as an art of flattery, or a pseudo-art. This definition emerges within a system of the arts constructed by the method of division, a system distinguishing between those arts that, although counterfeit, claim to benefit body and soul, and those arts that really do benefit body and soul (464B–465D).[9] Thus, oratory appears as a counterfeit of a branch of the true art of politics (πολιτικῆς μορίου εἴδωλον, 463D). This means that it is unreal and fragmentary, and that the serious matters of genuine value—true government, legislation, and jurisprudence— are opposed to it. This is what rhetoric becomes, in the judgment of Socrates, when it is deprived of all necessary connections with "justice." The opponent, however, is not impressed by this critique; after all, it is only asserted, not proved. Thus, it stands here only as a preliminary answer to the question raised on the first level of the dialogue. Also, the principle according to which the system of arts and pseudo-arts is constructed will be developed more clearly in the dialectical struggle conducted on the third level, i.e., the distinction between the good and pleasure (βέλτιστον–ἥδιστον, 464D).

There are two things the opponent regards as indubitably certain: the power of oratory and the fact that it is conducive to happiness. These two theses must be attacked. Their overthrow is the real task of the second level of the dialogue. Since the

II 1
461B–466A

II 2
466A–481B

form of speech was not convincing enough, the refutation must now proceed by means of a dialectical examination.

Let us first note, however, the structural similarity between this second level of the *Gorgias* and the third level of the *Thrasymachus*. There the view that injustice is superior was overthrown in three moves: first, by proving that the nature of injustice is such that it must rank with lack of knowledge and with evil; second, by refuting the claim that injustice is "stronger"; and third, by refuting the claim that it is productive of eudaemonia. On the second level of the *Gorgias*, Socrates conducts a threefold struggle against an oratory devoid of "justice": first (as we have just seen), by classifying it among the arts of flattery that aim at pleasure; second, by refuting the claim that oratory has power; third, by refuting the claim that it is productive of eudaemonia. The parallelism along general lines is unmistakable. The differences are just as significant. In the first place, the struggle against "injustice," here as elsewhere in this later dialogue, is expanded more explicitly into an attack upon the cultural system itself in which this form of immoralism is embodied —i.e., political oratory. In the second place, we must not overlook the modification in the structural plan. In this dialogue, as we saw, the initial attack upon the nature of injustice is not made in dialectical terms; hence, it is not delivered in full force. Why not? Because this aspect is taken over into the third stage of the dialogue, the conversation with Kallikles, where it is developed independently and with heightened tension. Thus, by dividing the two themes, which in the *Thrasymachus* appear together on the same level, between the second and third levels of the *Gorgias*, Plato drives the decisive struggle over the nature of rhetoric to its highest development.

II 2a
466A–468E
In the *Thrasymachus* (351A), it was suggested that the claim to power can be refuted by showing that "power" in the true sense of the word would require understanding. This is now demonstrated here in the *Gorgias*. The power of the political orator, it seems, is very great. Polos compares it to that of the tyrants (ὥσπερ οἱ τύραννοι, 466B), and Socrates constantly combines "orators and tyrants" in the same phrase so that the characteristic type of man may be seen as sharply as possible. Then

Socrates shows that the reason, or goal, of any action is something good, a "good"; and that this goal is the object of "willing" in the true sense. Thus, he who does something harmful may perhaps act as he "pleases" or do what "appears" (good) to him (ἃ δοκεῖ αὐτῷ)—we note the contrast between appearance and reality—but not "what he wills" (ἃ βούλεται). Hence, he does not have power. This paradox which seems to be splitting hairs is designed to make us see the good as the goal of every genuine, rational act of willing.

The second objective is to refute Polos' claim that oratory is productive of happiness—an oratory devoid of justice and, in fact, virtually identical, during a long stretch of the dialogue, with injustice and tyranny as such. Socrates himself says (472c) that we are approaching the moment of decision where "knowledge is most honorable and ignorance most disgraceful." Thesis and antithesis are sharpened in ever new attempts, until both are clearly formulated and the dialectical refutation begins.

II 2b
468E–481B

Socrates and Polos present a portrait of the tyrannical man, Socrates using the case of some political orator in the democratic regime of Athens, Polos citing the case of Archelaos, the tyrant of Macedonia. (Plato wants us to see the unmistakable connection between these two types. The tyrant practices what the politician in a democracy rarely can admit to being so openly.) In their judgment, however, the two partners sharply differ. For Socrates the criterion of happiness is based on a standard of right and wrong. Thus, happiness is not success, but consists in the intrinsic nature of the act and the agent. Socrates goes even further by declaring that wrongdoing is the greatest evil and by advancing the famous thesis that, judged from the perspective of happiness, he would rather—if he were called upon to choose —suffer wrong than do wrong. Socrates, the reader should realize, was true to this principle both in life and in death. To Polos, however, all this is incomprehensible; after all, he had just announced that rhetoric has nothing to do with right and wrong. He cannot see what difference right and wrong possibly can make and must regard, with astonishment, the radical Socratic rejection of the "tyrannical ideal" as incredibly paradoxical. He is willing to concede only that success and failure are legitimate

b1
468E–474c

criteria beyond the act itself. In this respect, he departs from his original principle. It no longer is the exercise of power as such that is good. "Great power" (τὸ μέγα δύνασθαι) becomes "something bad" or a "small power" if success does not correspond to one's own advantage. These concessions are forced upon him by the dialectics of Socrates, which easily could be extended here into genuine Socratic depths but is used only to expand and sharpen the original statement of Polos by drawing out its consequences.[10]

Socrates conducts the struggle in two dialectical moves leading to the defeat of Polos. He explicitly rejects, at the outset, any appeal to present company or to people in general, so that the *logos* itself may shine forth all the more clearly.

b2
474c–476a
The critical point in the first move is the assertion (agreed to by the opponent) that while wrongdoing might be "uglier" or "more disgraceful" (αἴσχιον), suffering wrong (ἀδικεῖσθαι) is "worse" (κάκιον). This distinction shows that there are no standards to which we can refer (εἰς οὐδὲν ἀποβλέπων, 474D) for judging. The predicate "ugly" or "disgraceful" obviously corresponds to the judgment of the many (ὑπὸ τῶν πολλῶν ἀνθρώπων καὶ ὑπὸ σοῦ, 475D) that Socrates previously had expressly repudiated. (The procedure here is somewhat analogous to the way in which, in the *Hippias Major*, the first serious definition equates the beautiful with the "fitting" or πρέπον.) But the predicate "bad," too, is used in the customary sense (not further clarified) of weakness or cowardice; i.e., "bad" is something harmful to the power of the person who suffers wrong. The radical view later expounded by Kallikles will clarify these matters that here remain in a state of confusion.

For the time being, Socrates attacks the confusion by inquiring into the meaning of beautiful and ugly. Beautiful is what is useful and pleasant; ugly is the opposite. Thus, good in the sense of useful and bad in the sense of harmful are subsumed, as component parts, under the concepts of the beautiful and the ugly. We have overcome the distinction (introduced by Polos) between the good and the beautiful. This way of defining the concept of the beautiful is not without risks from Plato's point of view, as we may infer from the enthusiastic assent expressed by the Sophist (475A).[11] He is evidently delighted by the hedonistic and utilitarian overtones of this analysis without suspecting the depths where, as far as Socrates is concerned, pleasure and utility, on the one hand, merge with beauty, goodness, and understanding, on the other.[12] But it cannot be denied that at this point in the discussion we might, with a little determination, construct an argument leading to the opposite conclusion. If wrongdoing is "better," or "good," and the good is included in the concept of the beautiful, then wrongdoing would also be "beautiful." Polos, however, does not have such determination; if he did, he would be Kallikles. Nor does Socrates fall back upon his ultimate resources. It is true that the concepts of the good and the beautiful are unified, but this unity is not carried into those depths where Socrates would confront the nature of real being.

Later (482DE) Kallikles will criticize this controversy. Polos was not consistent and this logical inconsistency was due to his being afraid. Socrates, Kallikles will say, took advantage of this inconsistency by intentionally confusing the different spheres of *nomos* and *physis*, convention and nature. As a matter of fact, Polos from his own point of view should have kept these two perspectives separate. At the same time, what Socrates concedes, as it were—namely, that wrongdoing is not painful—is also false in a deeper sense, for from the Socratic point of view, what could be a more radical opposite to pleasure than doing wrong? Thus, this dialectical section is peculiar in that it is not conducted, strictly speaking, according to the rules either of Polos or of Socrates. This makes it "sophistic," but it is also seductive in the sense of leading us on to the profoundly Socratic view according to which the conflict between *nomos* and *physis* is resolved through the *Idea* of the *Agathon*.

The first move, then, proved that to do wrong is worse than to suffer it. The second move proves that to escape punishment is worse than to suffer it. We must give attention to something in the meaning of the Greek phrase for "paying the penalty" (δίκην διδόναι) which is not included in our "being punished": namely, the active element, and the relationship to "justice" and "right." It is "right justice" and, at the same time, "right punishment" (δίκη ὀρθή), as we read in the *Critias* (106B), "when we lead someone who has gone astray, back to the right path."[13] Thus, in contrast to Polos (*Gorgias* 476D), Socrates does not

b3
476A–481B

mean the passive acceptance of punishment; he means that, by our own action, we reinstate the dignity of the law that has been violated. Nevertheless, we must not fail to feel the paradox here advanced as an extreme antithesis to the popular thesis, which Polos defends, that avoiding punishment is preferable to being punished. How far we are moving in a paradoxical world is shown by the conclusion (480c) that we should accuse ourselves and relatives or friends, to uncover their offenses—yet we know how the author of the *Euthyphro* condemned the charge brought by a son against his father when this actually happened before a court in Athens.

The paradox is carried to grotesque dimensions. If we wish to harm a criminal we must protect him against being punished; immortality would be the worst fate for him; to live as long as possible, the next worse. To Polos this sounds strange, but logical. When Kallikles interrupts expressing his astonishment, Chairephon confirms that Socrates is completely in earnest. And so he is despite the paradox. For he is here hinting at a completely different system of language, opposed to the prevailing system of sophistic rhetoric which makes might triumph and then protects the victory. This different language would be a system in the service of the good as practiced by Plato's Socrates. It is a system alluded to, at the end of the *Gorgias* (517A), by the iridescent name of a "genuine art of rhetoric." It is elaborated, in the second part of the *Phaedrus*, into a philosophical rhetoric, and, according to the *Statesman* (304A), it is a "rhetoric allied with the royal art of government."

The various steps of the argument are as follows. The first assumption is that "what is just is beautiful" (476B). Polos immediately agrees, despite a warning by Socrates. As before, he obviously means "beautiful" as it is commonly understood. Justice, if it takes the form of punishment, would not commonly be called "beautiful." He does not suspect—as the reader should—how correct his agreement is in a deeper sense.

The second assumption deals with the invariant correspondence between activity and passivity. The way in which the agent acts determines the way in which the object suffers (οἷον ἂν ποιῇ τὸ ποιοῦν, τοιοῦτον τὸ πάσχον πάσχειν, 476D). Perhaps we might object to this general formulation on the basis of experience[14]—

but even then, only those cases would be excluded where it is a matter of subjective impressions so that the question, "For whom?" would be justified. In the case of justice, however, as an objective state of affairs in the sense of Socrates, this question would be meaningless. Thus—in a sublime balance—punishing justly and suffering just punishment correspond to each other. According to the foregoing, therefore, both alike are "beautiful" and hence "good." The person who is punished or "pays the penalty" experiences something good (477A).

Finally, there is a brief discussion—we know the subject from the *Alcibiades Major* (see ch. XVII, III 2)—about the ordered structure of the self or the soul, what belongs to the soul and what belongs to the body, what is part of the soul and what are goods and possessions of the body. Each sphere has its own badness or defect (πονηρία) that is worse in proportion to the values of each sphere and, therefore, worst in the case of the soul. For each sphere there is a corresponding art or power that delivers it from its badness. In the case of the soul, this is right or justice. These analogies lead to a scale of happiness depending upon whether there is no evil in the soul, whether the soul is delivered from the evil present in it, or whether it is not so delivered. We are reminded of the *Thrasymachus* in its concluding part, to which we referred earlier as being similar to the second level of the *Gorgias*. There we learn about the "proper excellence" (οἰκεία ἀρετή, *Republic* I 353c) of each thing and, ultimately, of the soul. Justice is its intrinsic excellence and happiness is the condition of the soul in which this proper excellence is exercised. The *Gorgias* provides, despite a more negative twist, a richer development of the same thought, in the end leading the moral problem back to a discussion of the nature of oratory from which it arose. We see how the two problems are connected. Rhetoric in the ordinary sense fails to develop the proper *arete* of the soul; a different art of rhetoric, therefore, is needed to develop it.

The results we have gained so far must withstand the most severe attack that is now launched by a consistent immoralism, or, to put it differently, by the arrogant thesis that might makes right. Both speakers indicate that the moment of decision has come. Kallikles says at the outset: "If you are serious and if what you say is true, then the life of people like us is turned

III
481B–527E
III 1
481B–492C
III 1a
481B–488B

upside down" (481c). Socrates replies in a tone of serious playfulness. Kallikles is dealing not just with some individual, but
with a power transcending the individual—i.e., philosophy. If
he cannot refute this power, he always will be in conflict with
himself, and that is the worst thing for any human being. Later
(487A *et seq.*), after Kallikles has delivered his great program-
matic speech, Socrates commends him on three counts: understanding, good will, and candor (παρρησία). Thus, if Kallikles
should come to agree with him, then the subject they are discussing will have had its most thorough test.[15] It cannot be stated
more clearly that this is the moment of decision.

In between these comments by Socrates, there is the great
speech of Kallikles.[16] It begins with a critique of the halfhearted-
ness displayed by Gorgias and Polos, both of whom were trapped
into subscribing to the prevailing morality, and with a critique
of Socrates who exploited their confusion in order to refute them.
Kallikles distinguishes sharply between *physis* and *nomos*, nature
and convention, as two separate levels between which the other
speakers wavered in their judgment and discussion. There is a
morality by nature, genuine, original, and founded upon true
being—a morality of powerful men to whom suffering wrong is
not only worse, but also more disgraceful, than doing wrong.
A genealogy of morals shows that the many, who are weak,
have introduced the prevailing, counterfeit system of moral rules
into law and language.[17] Yet, it takes but a man sufficiently endowed by "nature" and "inner strength" to let the law of nature
(τὸ τῆς φύσεως δίκαιον) shine forth again.

Thrasymachos had talked in the same spirit of the strong man
or tyrant. What is new in this statement by Kallikles is the contrast between nature and convention. This makes the argument
sharper and also more seductive. For Thrasymachos still admitted
that the will-to-power was unjust and merely characterized this
injustice by giving it another prefix, as it were; Kallikles, however, calls this will-to-power "justice according to nature," which
bestows a higher rank upon it and makes it still more attractive.
As its mythical prototype, he cites Herakles who ran off with
the cattle of the giant Geryon. Moreover, in a bold move, he
converts a saying of Pindar dealing with this myth into its oppo-

site. Pindar said: "Law makes right out of might" (νόμος δικαιῶν τὸ βιαιότατον), which was new and bold enough. Kallikles says: "Law disposes with might over what is right" (νόμος βιαιῶν τὸ δικαιότατον).[18]

The other difference from the *Thrasymachus*, as we have emphasized before, is that the earlier dialogue deals with a conflict of moral principles. In the *Gorgias*, these principles are presented as different ways of life (βίοι). Kallikles adopts the distinction (introduced by Socrates) between the political man and the philosopher, expanding it into a distinction between the practical and theoretical types of men. This is depicted, on the level of myth, in the debate between the twin brothers, Amphion and Zethos, in the *Antiope* of Euripides.[19] The contrast between these two types of men is the concrete expression of the clash between two different systems. Kallikles, to be sure, does not completely do away with philosophy. He does not recognize it as a way of life, but he does grant that it has a place in the education of the young. This indicates a certain concession on his part, as does the fact that he consents to talk with Socrates at all. Men who really are in actual life what Kallikles would like to be would and should not do this; for by entering into a discussion, they acknowledge the validity of a law that must, ultimately, cause their downfall. Kallikles, however, is well disposed toward Socrates in other respects and would like to win Socrates over to his own side by an argument *ad hominem*: if you are attacked, you will not be able to defend yourself. Thus, the trial of Socrates emerges as the crucial test in the background of this controversy. We realize that Kallikles' speech confronts us with a matter of life and death. Three separate issues converge upon a single focus—the struggle between immoralism and justice, the struggle between practical politics and philosophy, and the struggle between the Athenians and Socrates.

The decisive attack, as usual, is preceded by a clarification and amplification of the enemy's position, and some light skirmishes. What, then, does it mean to say that we have justice in the true sense of nature when the superior person has more than the inferior and rules over him? Are better (βελτίων), stronger (κρείττων), and more powerful (ἰσχυρότερος) all synonymous? Kalli-

III 1b
488B–492c

kles says yes, thus using the concept of "good" in its primitive, unclear state where it may mean any kind of superiority or distinction. Socrates sets out to clarify this concept. In the *Thrasymachus*, we find that Socrates replies to the definition that justice is the same as the advantage of the stronger with a malicious interpretation that compels the Sophist to make his meaning more specific. Here we find something similar, only in more pointed form. If we define superiority or power in numerical terms exercised by a majority, so that the individual would be the weaker as against a large number of people, then the law of the stronger would be identical with the slave morality of the many. This kind of sophistry shows that the concept is still quite vague.

Finally, the two men agree, or seem to agree, that the superior should mean the "more intelligent" (489E *et seq.*). But what does "intelligent" mean, and what is the meaning of such expressions as "wanting to have more" and "wanting to be superior"? These phrases can be misunderstood amusingly if we take the case of specialized branches of knowledge and the specific advantages enjoyed by the specialist in each of them. Kallikles, however, means by "intelligent" to be "knowledgeable in political affairs," and he adds—evidently lest knowledge be misunderstood as nothing but passive "theory"—the characteristic of "brave" (ἀνδρεῖοι), which he connects with "ruling" and "having more." These additions make us suspect Kallikles' formula about the rule of the intelligent, which as such is quite close to the Socratic view. To elicit the full meaning of the other's view, Socrates asks the decisive question: Must the ruler also be capable of "ruling himself" (σώφρων)? This is the criterion of judging the words "intelligence" and "courage" in the Socratic sense, rather than intelligence as practiced in a specific field or courage as a natural disposition. Now we see that for Kallikles, ultimately, the life of pleasure has the highest value. Self-mastery and justice are but restrictions imposed upon the pleasure principle, and courage and intelligence are only means to satisfy this principle. Socrates aims at unifying the virtues in one single virtue. (Again, we recognize the significance of the main problem in the *Protagoras*.) Kallikles, however, chooses among the virtues according to the standard of pleasure. "What pleases is permissible," he might say with Goethe's Tasso.

What is at stake is a decision on "how one should live." These are Socrates' words to open the real struggle itself. But even here the means by which this struggle is conducted are subject to improvement. The first thrust does not score. It cites the analogy, derived from Orphic-Pythagorean sources, comparing the life of the pleasure seeker to a leaky vessel and the life of the rational man to a pitcher without holes. This analogy does indeed express clearly, although in a symbolic context, the difference between the two types of lives that will be elaborated in the subsequent demonstration, but the comparison is no substitute for proof. Socrates himself does not ascribe such power to it. Precisely because these images fail to convince the opponent, they make clear what dialectics can and must do and where myth has its place in Plato's thought.[20] On the other hand, they bring out the opponent's resistance all the more forcefully; for Kallikles, the life of self-discipline is that of the stone or the dead. Finally, these similes are significant for the work as a whole, if only because they prepare, at an early stage, what will later enter into the dialogue with intensified power in the great myth at the end.[21]

Myths are not a sharp weapon; only dialectic is. Socrates sets out to make the representative of the pleasure principle acknowledge that shameful pleasures are shameful. He does not hesitate to cite the case of the man who scratches himself because of an itch, or the sexual tickle of the catamite. We feel that Kallikles would like to exclude these pleasures as base; nevertheless, he sticks to his thesis so as "not to contradict himself" (495A), although he does not quite subscribe to it any longer. To put it differently, the hedonist, in order to be consistent, cannot admit that there are qualitative differences among pleasures and he must thus accept even the basest pleasures as being of equal value. Otherwise he would acknowledge a standard of value beyond pleasure. Moreover, itching and scratching are a mixture of pleasure and pain (*Philebus* 46D). It could be shown, therefore, that what is desired here is not pleasure at all, but a mixture—which reminds us of the first words of Socrates in the *Phaedo*.

Thus, the assault, though repulsed, has shaken the enemy's

III 2
492D–500A
III 2a
492D–494B

III 2b
494B–495c

position. Now follows the decisive attack. Plato shows that we are approaching a decision because, as it is imminent, Kallikles tries in vain to wriggle out from under the force of the argument (497A *et seq.*).

To begin with, the views of Kallikles are restated. He holds that "good" and "pleasure" are the same. (We may add that he already had indicated that he would distinguish between pleasures that are "better" and those that are "worse." His position is here stated in its extreme form. If this is overthrown, it will be easy to deal with the qualified version as well.) Yet, Kallikles admits that "knowledge" and "courage" are different from each other and that both, in turn, are different from pleasure and the good. (For him, different concepts of value may run side by side and against each other, whereas for Socrates they all find their common center in the *Idea* of the Good.)

Two skillfully constructed proofs refute Kallikles' position. First (495E), well-being and misfortune, good and evil, happiness and unhappiness are opposites that exclude each other. Pleasure and pain, however, may be mixed. Moreover, not only may pain change into pleasure as happiness may change into unhappiness, but in the act of quenching one's thirst, both the pain of being thirsty and the pleasure of quenching one's thirst disappear at the same time. It follows that good and pleasure must be different. What is unchanging and fixed is opposed to what is constantly changing.

Second (497E), someone is good if the "presence of good" (ἀγαθῶν παρουσίᾳ) is in him. If good and pleasure were really the same, then we would be good because of the presence of pleasure. Yet, Socrates and Kallikles had agreed earlier that the intelligent and courageous man is good, the cowardly and stupid man bad. Even though the two men did not quite mean the same thing, Kallikles did commit himself through this definition to a standard of the good different from pleasure. Thus, Socrates can now easily refute him by a *reductio ad absurdum*. Since the good (i.e., the intelligent and brave man) can experience as much pleasure or pain as the bad (i.e., the cowardly and stupid man), or since the good may, in fact, experience more pain than the bad and the bad more pleasure than the good, we have reached the absurd consequence that the good may be evil and the bad good, or the good man may, in fact, be worse than the bad and the bad man better than the good.

These consequences are as absurd as the view that good and pleasure are the same. The two concepts are quite different, and the good is by no means included in the concept of pleasure. (It is immaterial, for the moment, whether Socrates does not also regard the good and pleasure as in some sense converging upon each other.) This conclusion is reinforced when we realize that the "presence" of goodness by virtue of which someone is good only *seems* to be identical with the "presence" of pleasure or pain by virtue of which someone enjoys himself or suffers. If someone is either good or bad, but if both the good and the bad man may experience pleasure or pain, it is clear that the "presence of goodness or of evil" refers to objective realities, not interchangeable and never changing, whereas the "presence of pleasure or of pain" refers to changing conditions which, like the shadows of a cloud, fall upon and blur the absolute opposites of good and evil.[22]

Let us consider a few details that show how often one would have to reply differently from Kallikles. Socrates asks (496D): "Shall I go on with further questions or do you agree that every state of want and desire is painful?" Kallikles replies, "I agree"; yet, through this ready assent, Plato gives the reader a hint pointing in a different direction. For is there not a great difference between the painful desire of a man dying of thirst, on the one hand, and, on the other, the "desire for the whole" (*Symposium* 192DE), the "desire for the most beautiful life" (*Letter VII* 327D), or the desire aiming at perfect knowledge which is both "a desire and a joy" (*Republic* I 328D)? Later in the *Gorgias* (497B), Socrates asks Kallikles whether it is not true that in the case of a thirsty or a hungry man, satisfaction of the desire causes a cessation both of pleasure and of pain. Kallikles finally says yes, after first protesting strongly against such unworthy questions. Does not this resistance again convey some hint of a joy that does not cease, as pleasure does after drinking, but may increase—even to the happiness of the highest knowledge?

Kallikles has talked himself into a radical position that he does not, in fact, hold. He already had acknowledged, at least as a matter of feeling, that there is a difference between pleasures

III 2d
499B–500A

that are better and those that are worse (see III 2b above). Now he says explicitly that no one would deny this difference, and that he did not mean to say that good and pleasure are the same. This is more true than he suspects; yet, he fails to see that after the radical thesis has been defeated, the more moderate version cannot be maintained either. If pleasures may be both good and bad, it is clear that we must desire those that are good. Once we know the difference between good and pleasure, there can be no doubt as to which should rule. Thus, it is enough for Socrates to refer back to what has been agreed upon in the conversation with Polos (468B), that actions invariably aim at the good. Moreover, it is no accident that, while previously the sphere of the good often had been referred to in the plural (τὰ ἀγαθά), it is now put into the singular as a sign of the uniqueness and identity of its nature determining the course of human action.

We have pointed out repeatedly that the discussion in the *Gorgias* moves on two levels—a discussion of moral principles and a discussion of different ways of life. Kallikles, too, at first played political oratory off against philosophy. Then the struggle shifted from this human conflict in everyday reality to the level of conceptual analysis. On this level, the incompatibility of modes of being is translated into the form of a logical contradiction. The practical way of life represented by Kallikles as an aspiring politician of the market place is not yet overthrown by this refutation of its conceptual foundations. Hence, there follows a struggle over what is the proper vocation or way of life. It is introduced by Socrates at the point where he secures the admission that if the good is the measure of all things, it cannot be anybody's business to decide what is good. It must be a matter for the expert (τεχνικός).[23]

In this last struggle here beginning, there will be no turning back for Kallikles. He has committed himself too far to the kind of life he has chosen. As a matter of fact, he concedes (513c) that there is something in what Socrates is saying when the latter demonstrates the superiority of the just life even at the risk of death. But Kallikles cannot appropriate this conclusion for his own life, and Socrates knows why: love of the demos (ὁ δήμου ἔρως) lures him, counteracting the influence of Socrates.

Here, in condensed form, is the portrait of a typical fate—which, with greater human intensity, is developed in the *Alcibiades Major*. Kallikles has just begun to embark upon the career in public life which Alkibiades is still planning (*Gorgias* 515A; *Alcibiades* 106c). Both wish to rule or govern (510A; 106c). Both are told that they should first learn something themselves (514AB; 109D). As for the *Gorgias*, Socrates, at the end, is resigned to Kallikles' love of the demos; in the other dialogue, however, he expresses a deep concern lest Alkibiades be weaned away from him by the same love (δημεραστὴς γενόμενος).[24]

The debate over the right way of life is conducted in three great movements which, though not sharply separated from each other, may be distinguished clearly by the behavior of the antagonist. In the first section, the resistance of Kallikles grows to the point where he openly withdraws from the conversation. In the second section, Socrates is virtually alone once more, outlining the principles on which he acts. This continues until the major principle that to suffer wrong innocently is better than to do wrong successfully has emerged as a conclusion "bound fast by a chain of arguments as strong as iron and steel." In the last section, then, we witness the victory of the Socratic form of life as the right way of life for the individual in the state. Socrates makes it clear at the outset, with great seriousness (500CD), that the decisive and most important question is at stake. Which of the two ways of life should a man choose?

III 3
500A–522E

Socrates recalls the distinction between genuine arts and pseudo-arts of flattery that he had introduced previously in the conversation with Polos (463A *et seq.*). At that time, the classification of rhetoric alongside of cooking and cosmetics struck a blow which did not penetrate, because we did not as yet have a principle for the classification. Now we do have a twofold principle, in the distinction between "good" and "pleasure," by means of which we can construct the two systems of classification. Thus, the difference in value is unshakably fixed, and we can add a number of other arts to the system of pleasure or pseudo-arts— contemporary instrumental music, dithyrambic poetry, and tragedy. Looking ahead to the *Republic* where this blueprint of the *Gorgias* is expanded, we can see that in order to construct a state

III 3a
500A–505c

in the image of the good, as against a state based on the principle of pleasure, Plato must purge the former of the pseudo-arts of flattery. He will be able to do this because he is conscious of creating a dramatic and dithyrambic poetry entirely different from the old forms.

In the *Gorgias*, however, the subject is oratory, which shares with these pseudo-arts the aim of providing pleasure to the public. This is the kind of rhetoric that is actually practiced. Perhaps there is still another kind, an educational rhetoric, we might say, because its aim is "to make the citizens as good as possible" (502E). This kind of oratory—to the astonishment of Kallikles and the shock of the reader (he is supposed to be shocked!)— was not practiced even by the great statesmen of Athens, for they, too, aimed at satisfying their own desires or those of the public. He who practices the genuine art of oratory will not talk just at random (οὐκ εἰκῆ ἐρεῖ) but will "look at something definite" to give his speech a form, just as a craftsman keeps his eye on a definite form to give his work a specific "shape" and to make a well-wrought object (τεταγμένον τε καὶ κεκοσμημένον πρᾶγμα). Thus, the "something definite" must be a shape or a well-ordered form.[25] Again, we are reminded of the *Republic* (VI 500c) where the philosopher keeps his eye on something well-ordered (τεταγμένα) and unchanging, or of the carpenter in the *Cratylus* (389A *et seq.*) who looks toward the prototype of the weaver's shuttle. After the model of any good handicraft, therefore, a good art of oratory must remove "injustice" or excess (ἀκολασία) from the soul and must produce order, i.e., *arete* in the soul, by imposing moderation (κολάζει). What emerged as a paradox at the end of the conversation with Polos is now given a secure conceptual foundation because the *Eidos*, the *Agathon*, has become the guiding principle. And we suspect that Socrates is the only representative of this true art of oratory. At this moment, then, when lack of discipline is overcome by the *Idea* of the Good, and the prevailing pseudo-art of rhetoric is confronted by the true art, Kallikles withdraws from the commitment to conduct a conversation. By this act he reveals the same lack of discipline in matters of the *logos* that his theory proclaims to be valid in life (οὐχ ὑπομένει . . . κολαζόμενος, 505c 3).

The second movement begins once more "at the beginning." It starts with the distinction between "good" and "pleasure"; it makes clear again that the true aim of every action is the good; and then it shows that "virtue" is the realization of the good in man and that, in concrete terms, virtue refers to an order in the soul. This order goes with the unity of the virtues. We recall that Kallikles earlier (III 1 above) had advocated arbitrary distinctions among them. In the *Protagoras*, Socrates defends this unity of the virtues against the Sophists. In the aporetic dialogues in search of a definition, he shows how the virtues converge toward such a unifying concept. In the *Republic*, this unified system becomes the cornerstone for the education of the individual as well as for the structure of the state. The good man does good things only; hence—in Greek this correlation is shown by using the same verbal expression—he is well off or "does well" (εὖ τε καὶ καλῶς πράττει, 507c 3); in short, he is "eudaemonic" or happy. The bad man does evil things; hence, he does not "do well," but is miserable.

We may recall that a similar scale is set up in the *Charmides* (172A) and in the *Alcibiades Major* (133E *et seq.*).[26] Here in the *Gorgias*, the conclusion is that we must practice *sophrosyne* or self-discipline and that we must avoid the lack of discipline so highly extolled by Kallikles. The value gained through this "taming" by means of self-discipline shines forth once again. The cosmos, or the universe as an ordered structure, becomes the comprehensive model for the "cosmos" or order of the soul. The greed-for-more or will-to-power reveals an ignorance of geometric proportion, a neglect of the study of geometry. (This is an ironic, paradoxical reference to the educational principle of Plato's *Republic* and of the Academy.) Then we return to some matters carried over from earlier parts of the dialogue where they were left as paradoxes, or remained incomplete and controversial; e.g., the statement, in the conversation with Polos, that oratory is designed to punish wrong and that to suffer wrong innocently is better than to do wrong; or the statement, in the conversation with Gorgias, that the true orator (ὀρθῶς ῥητορικός) must possess the knowledge of justice. Even the argument *ad hominem* by which Kallikles, at the end of his first great speech, tried to frighten Socrates (486A *et seq.*) is brought up again that it may be rejected solemnly and decisively (508D *et seq.*). "Bound fast by a chain of arguments as strong as iron and steel"—so Socrates describes the conclusions reached. Yet, even such a conclusion is not meant as a dogma, but as something that, in true Socratic spirit, he would submit to genuine critical examination.

III 3c
509A–522E   The discussion of moral principles, then, has turned again into a struggle of two opposing ways of life. This struggle is now fought through, for the last time, on the firm basis of the conclusions reached so far. Kallikles still holds fast to the following convictions: that, for the sake of one's own protection, one must be either a ruler himself (ἄρχειν ἢ καὶ τυραννεῖν) or a friend of the ruling regime (510A); moreover, that the great statesmen of Athens, though they did not aim at the education of the citizens in the Socratic sense, nevertheless increased the power of the *polis* (515CD); that it is a disgrace if a man cannot defend himself (522C); and that Socrates, for the sake of his own safety, should adapt himself to the powers that be and protect himself against possible dangers (511A, 521AB).

Socrates, however, draws his conclusions from his own system of moral values unshakably founded upon the *Agathon*. He shows once more that it is more important to avoid wrongdoing than to protect oneself against the wrongdoing of others. He transposes the clash of moral principles into the new dimension of political realities and the two competing ways of life. Thus, he defeats the claim made by a political oratory that avoids suffering wrong but, in doing so, commits wrongs, and, ultimately, rests upon an exaggerated estimate of the value of mere living as compared with the value of leading the good life (εὖ ζῆν, 510A–512E). He defeats the claim made by the politicians—most clearly expressed in the extreme case of the four greatest statesmen of Athens—that they increased the power of the state since, in truth, their actions only produced a state swollen and festering, and since the fate they suffered refutes them in that it would not have happened to them had they, in fact, improved the citizens (515C–519C).[27] Finally, he defeats the claim made by sophistic, the sister-art of rhetoric, with regard to education of the young; for this claim is voided by the mere fact that the Sophist takes money for his services and even complains about recalcitrant clients' refusing to pay, whereas, if his claim were justified, he should have awakened in his pupil a desire to do good in return for the benefits received (519c–520e).

In this struggle there emerges as the proper function of the political man the task of rendering a true service to his fellow men; i.e., to make them as good as possible (513e). There emerges the demand that he who wants to be a ruler must first have learned something—from whom, we may wonder?—and that he must show proof of his ability to "improve" matters on a small scale so as not "to learn pottery by first trying his hand on a wine jar" (514a–515b). As against the counterfeit product, there emerges the "true art of oratory" (ἀληθινὴ ῥητορική, 517a 5). Finally, in a proud paradox, Socrates proclaims that he is "one of the few Athenians—not to say the only one—who is studying the true art of politics and the only man now living who is practicing it" (521d). According to the charge of Meletos in the *Apology* (25a), Socrates is the only man who is corrupting the Athenians. The paradoxical claim made here in the *Gorgias* is the most radical reply to this charge.

Thus, the struggle with Kallikles culminates in Socrates' bearing witness to his life's work or his "existence." Philosophy is a matter of life and death. Socrates is so completely clear about the fate awaiting him in his own city that he predicts, in almost the exact words, the charges that will be brought against him (521e *et seq.*). But he has no doubts that the aim of his speech and his education must be the good, not pleasure. He takes his place beside the physician and the architect, not beside the cook. Therefore, as he predicts, his defense appealing to the cause of "justice" he has served will be of no avail to him. For this is the kind of service the others in the city do not want and do not understand; yet, for Socrates it is precisely this question of justice that renders worthless any concern over possible dangers to his life. The decision as to worth or unworth is made on the grounds not *whether* he can "defend" himself, but *how* he can. The question, whether life or death, recedes before the question, whether a just or unjust life. The commitment to the *Agathon* decides his calling—or has decided it long ago.

We see at the end, then, these several strands gathered together: the struggle between pleasure and the good; the struggle between a false sophistic rhetoric and true philosophy (which, at the same time, is the true art of rhetoric and the true art of government); and finally, the struggle between the Athenians and Socrates. The *Agathon*, philosophy, and Socrates are victorious, but they do not prevail in the sense that the struggle is won forever. On the contrary, this struggle is always alive. It is, indeed, necessary for the cause of the *Agathon* itself on whose behalf even Kallikles—especially Kallikles—fights as a rebel against a legal system grown rigid and feeble.[28]

III 4
522E–527E
In the concluding myth of the dialogue, the trial of Socrates is reviewed before the tribunal of eternity and the results of the dialectical arguments are consecrated in a world beyond.[29] Here we have, for the first time in the works of Plato, a Socratic myth. And here Socrates says, for the first time, that "the *logos* stands firm" (527B), a goal that was, in the *Euthyphro* (11D), still but a wish. For the first time, the dialogue not only leads the way; it also gathers up, as in a book of laws, what we have discovered on this way and, filtered through a myth, puts the stamp of the eternal upon it.[30] Yet even these firm foundations are not meant as dogma, but would be subject, at any time, to further critical inquiry in a dialectical conversation. For now, however, this is the *logos* that has come to light. According to it one must live— and die, we must say, remembering Socrates.

NINETEEN

Meno

MENON, an aristocratic landowner from Thessaly, comes to Athens with a large number of retainers (82AB). In an outwardly democratic society, such a display arouses comment. As Gorgias or Protagoras when they visit Athens stay with Kallikles or Kallias, so Menon, following an old family custom, is staying with Anytos (*Meno* 90B, 92D), the politician whom everybody knows as the prosecutor of Socrates. The major part of the conversation is between Menon and Socrates. A young boy, part of Menon's retinue, is called upon once to answer. Anytos, sitting down with the speakers "at the right time" (89E *et seq.*) is drawn into the conversation at the tense moment when the much-discussed question, Is virtue teachable?, is being analyzed, and when Socrates is pursuing the paradox that the politicians of Athens are incapable of making good citizens out of their sons.[1] Anytos is forced to discuss this incompatibility between politics and education just as he represents it in his own person. He drops out of the conversation as soon as this subject is over; yet, he remains to the end and shows his anger by the only other words he says (99E 3): "That's not my business."[2] Thus, the hostility between Socrates and the politicians that is mentioned in the *Apology* comes to life here. The threats of Anytos are realized in the indictment of Socrates—only a few years away.[3] It is natural that the host should sit down by the side of his guest, but this does not mislead us about Plato's dramatic intentions. The sudden appearance and the silent presence of Anytos have the quality of the uncanny.

Menon was known to every reader at the time as one of the

most notable mercenary generals in the service of the Persian prince, Cyrus, insurgent and pretender. If we may believe Xenophon (*Anabasis* II 6 21), who looked at him from close proximity with eyes of hatred, Menon's was a base nature. A will-to-power and ambition served his avarice; he was a man without conscience, without loyalty, and without a capacity for friendship; he wasted his physical assets in debaucheries and exploited them for his ambition, i.e., for his avarice. Plato looks at Menon from a distance and, for this reason alone, sees him as a more resplendent and greater person, more the type of an Alkibiades or Kallikles, youthfully handsome and sensual, proud and greedy for power.[4] His desire for dialogue, which he must show in order to qualify as a partner in the conversation, also reflects the basic traits of his nature. Plato says he was a pupil of Gorgias, and he may have been. We are reminded of another mercenary captain in the service of Cyrus, Proxenos of Boiotia, of whom Xenophon writes (*Anabasis* II 6 16) that even as a mere boy, he had the desire to make a place in the sun for himself, and this was the reason he took lessons from Gorgias.

We may now guess why Plato chose Menon as the partner. In Thessaly, "ruling" has more conspicuous aspects than in the democratic Athens. This becomes evident when Menon appears with a large retinue. But being a mercenary and suffering violent death are obvious associations as well. A striving for power and a bold break with civic norms—this is what is hidden behind the concept of *arete* as far as Menon is concerned. "Whether virtue is teachable or not" is the kind of question he has copied from his teacher Gorgias. He boasts of "having talked about *arete* hundreds of times, and to large audiences, and very well too, as I thought" (80B). We begin to understand why Plato lets him talk again about this subject which he has talked to death, and we recognize how much sarcasm there is in making him the spokesman for *arete*. We can plumb the distance that divides Menon's conception of *arete* from that of Socrates.

Perhaps there is another reason why Plato chose a man from Thessaly as the partner in this dialogue. "Here among us," says Socrates (71A), "there is a kind of intellectual dearth; it seems as if wisdom had migrated from our part of the country to yours."

In Athens (he continues) people are not racking their brains over the question whether *arete* can be taught. They do not even know what *arete* is. This irony is Janus-faced: first, it is directed against Anytos, the representative of the ordinary politician, who indeed does not know, and who acts from this ignorance; second, it refers to Socrates himself who *does not know* in an entirely different sense, i.e., as a person who knows that he does not know. Athens is destined, as it were, to generate opposites of the highest intensity and to make them collide in the mortal encounter of the trial of Socrates. Thessaly is the ironic counterpart of Athens, a city without civic discipline, just as Thrace is in the *Charmides* or the Persian court is in the *Alcibiades Major*. We may recall that in the *Crito* (53D), the laws threaten Socrates that if he should escape, he would have to go to Thessaly—a country of greatest disorder and lack of discipline. Or we may recall that according to the *Hippias Major* (284A), Thessaly is known for the art of breeding horses; according to the *Parmenides* (126C), Antiphon, the reporter of the conversation, has abandoned philosophy in order to take up horse breeding. These allusions must be kept in mind if we would understand what it means to say that wisdom has migrated from Athens to Thessaly.

The dialogue moves between two poles. First, there is the question that Menon puts bluntly at the opening, evidently because he has had it on the tip of his tongue and also because this is not his first meeting with Socrates (76E). The question is whether *arete* can be taught. The other pole is the statement by Socrates in the end that we would have better knowledge if we had first inquired into the question of "what *arete* is in and by itself" (αὐτὸ καθ' αὑτὸ ζητεῖν τί ποτ' ἐστὶν ἀρετή). This is the same polarity we find in the *Protagoras*. There the question of whether virtue can be taught arises as soon as the conversation between Socrates and Protagoras begins (319AB); and, at the end (361C) we learn, in almost the same words, that we might have cleared up the problem on which there was no agreement if we had made clear "what *arete* is in itself" (τί ποτ' ἐστὶν αὐτὸ ἡ ἀρετή). Although this is the same contrast as here in the *Meno*, the *Protagoras* does not pursue the question of the nature of *arete* explicitly, but alludes to it in the discussion of unity *versus* multiplicity (329c *et seq.*). In the *Laches*, the problem of *paideia* raises the question of the nature of virtue expressly (ὅ τι ποτ' ἐστὶν ἀρετή, 190B), but the discussion is confined to one virtue. Similarly, the other aporetic dialogues inquire into the nature of particular virtues, with results that are known. In the *Meno*, the question reappears in the general form of the *Protagoras*. We also find, as in the *Charmides* group of dialogues, a series of definitions ending in a confession of ignorance; yet, the *Meno* is a riper and richer work. It is not a dialogue that consists of nothing more than a series of definitions. Such defining is found only in the first of its three parts. Moreover, the confession of *aporia* does not come at the end of the work; instead, it assumes a special significance in the central part and introduces the basic characteristic of the dialogue, which we may designate provisionally by the word "anamnesis." The third part, then, presents the real struggle of opposing principles of *paideia*, the struggle between Socrates and the Sophists and politicians, concluding with a new order of knowledge and being.

I

71B–79E

The first part, concerned with the search for a definition, moves in four stages. The *Laches* begins by saying that we first must know what courage is, and only then can we see how a young man may partake in it. Before venturing upon a definition, Laches expresses his self-confidence by saying that the question is "not hard" to answer. Correspondingly, in the *Meno*, the question of whether virtue is teachable leads to the question, what is virtue? This is "not hard" to answer, Menon thinks, only to be shown very quickly that he had underestimated the difficulty.[5] In the *Laches*, the *Thrasymachus*, and the *Euthyphro*, the first move toward a definition is to make the interlocutor mistake a random feature derived from his own experience for the essence of the thing to be defined. In the *Hippias Major*, after two rather silly attempts of this type, Plato adds another variety. Hippias tries to define "beauty" by means of a lengthy enumeration of things that are "beautiful."

I 1

71B–73C

Menon starts out with such an enumeration of various "virtues," instead of grasping the "concept" of virtue. These "virtues" he lists are as different as the people who practice them. Socrates points out the fallacy in this procedure by refer-

ring to the "one form, or characteristic, itself" (ἕν τι εἶδος ταὐτόν)
"which the respondent must keep in view." Similarly, he demands of Euthyphron—in the critique of the first definition in
that dialogue (*Euthyphro* 6DE)—that he "keep in view and use
as a model the form itself (εἶδος and ἰδέα) by virtue of which
every individual act of piety is pious." Thus, we have here another
structural affinity between the *Meno* and the earlier, aporetic
group.[6]

There is no doubt that Aristotle has this passage of the *Meno*
in mind when, in *Politics* I, he discusses two opposing views on
the subject of "virtues or capacities."[7] He sides with "those who,
like Gorgias, enumerate the virtues" and is opposed to "Socrates" who recognized only one kind of temperance, courage,
and justice. But does not Aristotle here oversimplify matters?
In the *Republic* (I 335A *et seq.*), it is the objective of Socrates to
discover the "specific capacities" of each person assigned to a
specific task.[8] In this passage of the *Republic*, moreover, we learn
about the capacities of the eyes, ears, horses, and dogs; whereas,
in the *Gorgias* (479B, 504C) and again in the *Republic* (III 403D),
Socrates refers to "health and other kinds of fitness of the body."
Furthermore, the distinction between badness and goodness
(ἀρετή) as applied to the land or soil was as familiar to Plato,
from the time of his early works through his old age, as it was
to his fellow countrymen. Perhaps the contrast, then, between
"Gorgias" and "Socrates" (or Plato) is not so rigid as Aristotle
makes it appear in the passage of his *Politics*.[9] Plato always
recognized, as was quite natural, the most diverse "capacities."
It is only over and out of this diversity that he set up a system of
five or four "virtues" and, above these, the one "virtue" in
which they converge. Out of this convergence of different capacities grows the structure of Plato's city. As a pupil of the Sophists, Menon cannot think beyond diversity. That is not the case
with Aristotle. We need not worry that he would agree with
Menon. This becomes clear when we look at the substance of
"manly virtue" as understood by Menon.

For him, manly virtue is the capacity to manage the affairs of
the city, to do good to one's friends and harm to one's enemies,
and to take care that no harm come to oneself. This is self-evident

for Menon, just as he believes it is a woman's virtue to keep a good house and obey her husband. Manly virtue as defined by Menon agrees, in the actual wording, with what Polemarchos (*Republic* I 334BC) calls "justice." Thus, the enumeration of the many virtues—instead of a synoptic vision and a unifying definition—corresponds, in the formal, logical context, to the lack of that "communal sense" which, according to the *Republic*, must prevail lest the natural differences among human beings cause social disintegration.

12
73C–73D

After insisting that *arete* be one, Socrates asks what it is. From his previous list, Menon picks out what he called manly virtue—i.e., his own strength and intention—and defines it as the "capacity to rule over men." This goes beyond the previous multiplicity; but the unitary concept is bought at the price of validity and at the risk of converting virtue into its opposite. (Menon's naïveté here is like Euthyphron's in the first definition of piety. Both claim universal validity for their own personal cases.) Menon's thesis has its foundation in life—in his imperious character as shown in the dialogue (76AB) and in his historical existence as known from Xenophon's *Anabasis* (II 6 21). He is the same type of man as Theages, Alkibiades, and Kallikles, who also admit freely that a will-to-power is the most natural drive. And just as Kallikles is a follower of Gorgias, so Socrates imputes to Menon that his thesis agrees with Gorgias: rhetoric and the will-to-power go together.[10]

13
73D–77A

It takes one question by Socrates to point out that "virtue" cannot mean the capacity to rule, but only the capacity to rule "justly." Thus, Menon is led to equate virtue with "justice." This is the more correct path, and the leap from ruling as such to ruling with justice seems to cut short the long route pursued in the *Alcibiades* and in the debate with Kallikles. But we soon learn that this is not a true insight for Menon. In reply to the critical prodding by Socrates, he adds that there are other virtues as well, and once more he enumerates them. Again we have the same multiplicity as in the first definition. As far as the substance of the enumeration is concerned, it is instructive to see that Menon, in addition to the four Socratic virtues, includes "magnificence" (μεγαλοπρέπεια)—for Plato elsewhere as well a char-

acteristic trait of the born ruler (*Republic* 536A and *Laws* 709E)
—"and many other things." Socrates points out the old fallacy.
Menon admits he cannot grasp the single concept of virtue cov-
ering them all. "Of course not," Socrates replies. We realize
that, according to Plato, one cannot grasp what one is not himself.

Yet, Socrates now embarks upon an exercise (μελέτη, 75A).
He tries to clarify the meaning of what is the "same in all par-
ticulars" (ταὐτὸν ἐπὶ πᾶσιν) by means of the concepts of "shape"
and "color," first making the mistake, intentional, to be sure,
of defining shape in terms of color, i.e., an x in terms of a y that
is not known either. Menon rightly protests against this procedure. (The Pythagoreans used the word "color" for what was
later called "surface"; here and in what follows we catch glimpses
of discussions conducted in the Academy.)[11] Things now grow
more serious. Twice Socrates employs the word "dialectic"
(75D) referring to a method according to which the person questioned, at each step, must understand and agree with what is
being said. Since the discussion soon turns toward mathematics,
we may wonder whether Plato here did not have more in mind
in using the word "dialectic." Is not the dialectical path of the
Republic beginning to come into view?

"Shape—meaning here *surface*—is the limit of a solid" is the
first definition. In a somewhat stricter formulation, this recurs
almost verbatim in Aristotle and, again with a slight variation,
in Euclid.[12] From mathematics we move to physics. The nature
of color is defined in terms of the physical theory of Empedokles.
The former definition of shape is "better," says Socrates; he
does not for the moment explain why, but instead makes an
ironic allusion to Menon's plans to leave "before the mysteries"
and without "being initiated." Later, Plato himself incorporated
this theory of color into the myth of the *Timaeus*. If he calls it
here, not without mockery, "impressive as a stage play" (τραγική)
and if he prefers the earlier definition of shape, this indicates
that the mathematical definition can be understood immediately,
whereas the physical definition presupposes a theory on which
there may not necessarily be agreement. "But you like it better
because it smacks of the theater." This is the criterion of prefer-

ence employed by the pupil of the rhetorician. Socrates is anxious to teach him to choose what is clear and precise in preference to what is impressive and high-sounding. (This passage of the *Meno* tells us much about the methods used in the Academy, although neither this dialogue nor any other must be singled out as conveying the "program of the Academy.")

We may ask whether the lesson in method conceals something else just as the definition of angling does in the *Sophist* and, in the *Statesman*, the case of weaving. The methodological inquiry serves to clarify matters of substance. The Sophist turns out to be an angler, the statesman a weaver. Does not *arete* itself come into view in the definition of shape as a limit? Looking ahead to the ontology of the *Philebus*, may we not say that *arete* is subordinated, as is stereometric shape, to the mode of the limit, whereas color and pleasure go with the dimension of the indefinite and limitless? Must we not keep the methodological and substantial aspect of this illustration together, inasmuch as Socrates pursues true *arete* as well as form, limit, and conceptual unity—and Menon the opposite?

14
77A–79E

In the case of the fourth definition, Socrates insists, even more urgently than in the case of the second, that it must be a unifying concept and that Menon must stop breaking the unity of *arete* into separate parts. The fourth definition is: Virtue is to desire beautiful things and to be able to acquire them (ἐπιθυμοῦντα τῶν καλῶν δυνατὸν εἶναι πορίζεσθαι, 77B). At bottom, this again comes down to a matter of "power" and "ruling"; yet, it appears that Menon has learned that a definition must somehow have two parts. The critique of Socrates consists in discarding the first part as something that is self-understood and needs no justification. Nobody can desire bad or harmful things, because nobody would want to be unhappy. This is opposed to the common view according to which we may desire both the good and the bad. But Socratic education consists in revealing to men what is hidden to them in their own nature. Thus, Socrates shows, in the *Lysis*, that desire always aims at the beautiful, and, in the *Gorgias*, that we cannot help but "will" the good. In formal terms this is a tautology. In the light of the substance at stake, it means that man is such that he can but choose the good.

We said that the fourth definition, at bottom, amounts to the same thing as the first and second. This is evident from the critique of the second part of this definition: *arete* is the capacity to acquire good things (78B). Again, the acquisition of the good is for Menon a form of "power" or "ruling." Socrates asks the same question as before, whether we must not add the word "just" in order to qualify acquisition (78D; cf. 73D). In short, *arete* would not be the act of acquisition itself; it might indeed be the opposite, provided that it be done with "justice." Thus, we are back at the individual virtues, i.e., back at the third definition, and the critique is repeated that we are breaking *arete* up into separate parts instead of grasping it as a unity. In formal terms, the fallacy is to define a thing in terms of its parts which are known just as little as the thing to be defined is known. In substantial terms, this means that as long as men judge and act arbitrarily, they do not catch sight of *arete*. Socrates insists that the discussants find a new answer, starting from "the beginning" (ἐξ ἀρχῆς). A completely different approach is needed to break out of the vicious circle. Whereas the *Euthyphro* breaks off at this impasse, the *Meno* moves beyond and makes this the turning point.

One makes progress only by making the *aporia* conscious. That Socrates has done for Menon. Now, in the middle part of the dialogue, this situation is clarified and a way out is shown. Menon makes a comparison. Comparisons are, of course, part of ordinary conversation (whose highest form, we may note, is reached by Alkibiades in the *Symposium*). Menon here compares Socrates to a sting ray not only in appearance—the protruding eyes and the flattened nose—but especially in the paralyzing effect. This image catches the impression, but not the true nature of Socrates. The latter counters, first, by explaining that he not only infects others with *aporia*, but feels it himself. Socratic "ignorance" is a presupposition for his *paideia*. Secondly, he adds that his effect is not paralyzing only; he also is ready to help in joint inquiry (συζητῆσαι).

Thus, the nature of Socratic education is made transparent by means of the comparison. This is like the use of an image at a similarly critical point in the *Theaetetus* where Socrates compares

II
79E–86C

II 1
79E–80D

himself to a midwife.[13] In each case, the revelation about the nature of Socrates takes us back to the problem itself: in the *Theaetetus*, to the problem of knowledge; here, to the problem of virtue, i.e., "what it really is" (ὅτι ποτ' ἔστιν, *Theaetetus* 151D; *Meno* 80D).

II 2
80D–82A

In the *Meno*, however, we do not at first follow this question. Instead, we deal—a preliminary step leading to Plato's own level—with a piece of eristic, familiar from the *Euthydemus*. Menon, a pupil of the Sophists, challenges the very possibility of the joint inquiry proposed by Socrates. The challenge is based on the argument that a man cannot search for something that he does not know; conversely, he need not search for what he does know. This argument is here the means by which Plato finds his way to the myth of the soul—a powerful symbol from an entirely different world removing any eristic doubt about the possibility of inquiring into the truth. Socrates has heard the story from wise men and women that the soul of man is immortal and has been born many times. It has learned everything "both here and in Hades"; hence, by recalling a particular thing, it can discover everything else since "all nature is akin." Thus, learning is "recollection." Eristic doubt about knowledge, Socrates continues, is music in the ears of the sluggish and weak. The defense of knowledge as in the myth makes men active and inquiring.[14]

The myth turns toward Hades, i.e., to a world that cannot be seen with earthly eyes (ἀιδές), to a realm of perfect knowledge according to the etymology of the *Cratylus* (404B). Thus, perhaps the path from myth to mathematics is not as long as it may appear at first sight. There was an earlier exercise in geometry

II 3
82A–85B

(*Meno* 75A, 76A). Now we are shown, in the famous lesson, how a young boy—provided he knows Greek, so that we can talk to him—"remembers" under the guidance of Socrates. In the *Alcibiades*, Socrates also shows that it is the pupil, not the teacher, the respondent, not the questioner, who "brings forth what is said." This insight, which is the simplest possible formulation of the dialectical method as practiced by Plato's Socrates, is elicited by an illustration taken from arithmetic (112E *et seq.*). Here it is the young boy of Menon who is taught the lesson.

We need not follow the detailed steps by which the pupil is led
to the solution of the problem of doubling a square. Suffice it to
say that the demonstration proceeds in three stages. First, Socrates establishes the fact that the pupil wrongly thinks he knows
the answer (82E). Second, he shows that *aporia* is a necessary
turning point (84A–C). Third, he leads the boy to the correct
solution, or, in the language of the myth, he awakens recollection (86c).[15]

Mathematics is propaedeutic, as will be shown in the *Republic*. Yet, does not the "lesson" in the *Meno* have a symbolic
significance, over and above its formal meaning, analogous perhaps to the lesson in the *Gorgias* according to which a will-to-
power is ignorance of proportion? On the first level of the *Meno*,
geometrical "shape" appeared as a symbol for *arete*. But the
inquiry into the nature of *arete* led to *aporia*. Now we are suddenly lifted up into the sphere of that ultimate reality which,
according to the *Republic*, culminates in what is "beyond being,"
i.e., in the "ineffable." Is it an accident, or is it rather a signpost
pointing toward these heights that the geometrical task of doubling a square contains the problem of the irrational, i.e., again
the "ineffable" (ἄρρητον)?[16]

At the end of this section, the soul is envisaged once more as
the carrier of this ultimate reality, and hence, as immortal. Even
though this mythical formulation is presently abandoned, lest
anybody take it in a dogmatic spirit, Socrates nonetheless is
ready to defend, with word and act, the thesis that we shall become better and braver men if we go on inquiring than if we
let ourselves be persuaded, by sophistic arguments, that it is impossible to do so. Myth is not a detour into dreamland, but a
call to action. That is Socratic-Platonic "pragmatism."

In this central part of the dialogue, we breathe an air different
from that in the previous and subsequent sections. Later, the
Phaedo (72E) will introduce the problem of "recollection" as
something "frequently" discussed by Socrates, thus referring
back to the *Meno* in so far as we may say that any dialogue refers
to another. Conversely, we may say that the doctrine here advanced in the *Meno*—the indissoluble link between the immortal
soul and the knowledge of forms, cast in the mythical atmosphere

II 4
85B–86C

of "Orphic" poetry—is a first version of what is expanded in the *Phaedo*. Perhaps the interpenetration of *logos* and *mythos*, similar in the two dialogues, is shown as follows. We find, almost verbatim, the same statement by which Socrates first admits that he would not vouch for the complete truth of the story (οὐκ ἂν πάνυ διισχυρισαίμην), only to cling all the more firmly to its consequences (*Meno* 86B; *Phaedo* 63C, 114D).[17] In the *Phaedo*, we have a much more differentiated and expanded treatment of the whole complex of problems, not to mention the fact that it is directly linked with the fate of Socrates. By contrast, the episode with the servant boy who "remembers" the Pythagorean theorem occupies a comparatively large amount of space in the *Meno*. Here the immortality of the soul is used to defend the possibility of inquiry, learning, and knowledge against sophistic doubt; conversely, in the *Phaedo*, the immortality of the soul is justified on the basis of our knowledge of eternal being. If we keep these differences in mind, the structural affinity between the two dialogues is unmistakable, as is the intermediate position of the *Meno* between the aporetic dialogues and the *Phaedo*.

III
86c–100c

In the third part of the dialogue, Menon and Socrates return to the original question about the nature of *arete*. It might seem as if the middle part were a digression beyond the limits set by the problem itself. The last words in this part, "We shall become better," show that this is not so. If we think in Greek terms and remember that the word "good" is the adjective of *arete*, we know that we have remained within the limits of our problem. But we have seen it, with a jerk, as it were, in a different depth— in the relationship between "existence" and "transcendence," to use the terms of Jaspers. The soul has come into view in its proper activity, the search for ultimate reality; and this experience serves as the foundation for the moral task, which is to become better. It is in this dimension of depth that we must seek an answer to the questions, what is the nature of *arete*, and is it teachable?

In its formal aspect, the third part takes us back to the first. There the two problems, "whether *arete* can be taught," and "what it really is," were presented, one after the other, in a perspective view, as it were. Now they are shown in a peculiarly

ironic interconnection. Socrates again asks what *arete* is. Menon again goes back to the practical question of whether it can
be taught. Socrates follows this up—but in such a way that he
first gives a provisional answer by means of a "hypothesis" (in
the manner of the geometers[18]) to the question about the essential nature of *arete* in order to reach a decision, if only condition-
ally, with regard to the other question of whether it is teachable.
It cannot be made more clear how closely these two problems
belong together. They stand as a symbol of the unity of wisdom
and teaching, "philosophy" and "pedagogy," in Socrates-Plato.

The two questions, then, are firmly joined together. If *arete*
is knowledge (ἐπιστήμη), it must be teachable; if it is not knowledge, it cannot be taught. The decisive question is whether *arete*
is a form of knowledge. The presupposition for the ensuing discussion, however, is this: *arete* is something good, it is a good—
which would be taken for granted by every Greek because of the
close connection between the two words. Thus, if we can show
that there is no good outside of knowledge, then *arete* must be a
form of knowledge, and so teachable.

III 1
86c–89c

The method adopted by Socrates is to analyze the nature of
various "goods," and "the good." Back in the fourth definition
of Part I, Menon enumerated "goods" according to the popular
conception. Socrates showed that the true criterion for deciding
whether they were really good, i.e., beneficial or advantageous,
lay elsewhere, namely in the manner in which they were pro-
cured, whether justly or unjustly. Now he presents a much more
systematic order of values. "Goods" of the body, such as good
looks, strength, or health, and "goods" in a more general sense,
such as wealth, upon closer scrutiny are sometimes beneficial
and sometimes harmful. Whether they are good things depends
upon the "right use" (ὀρθὴ χρῆσις) to which the individual, i.e.,
the soul, puts them.[19] Again, the virtues of the soul, as they are
commonly called and as they were cited earlier by Menon (cf.
74A with 88A), are sometimes advantageous and sometimes
harmful. This is shown by referring to the case of "courage" as
popularly, but not Socratically, understood. What raises these
qualities to the status of values, what orients them toward the
goal of eudaemonia, is knowledge or understanding (φρόνησις).

Phronesis is what makes them "advantageous"; *arete* is "something advantageous" too; hence, the two kinds of being either are identical or *arete* is, at least, a part of *phronesis*.

This is by no means the final clarification of the nature of *arete*. We might ask what is the object of this as yet empty "knowledge," and would discover that it is "the good" as we learn in the *Republic* (VI 505B) in a related, but much more profound discussion of this subject. In the *Meno* we remain in a provisional frame, as we are explicitly told (as also in the *Alcibiades*) at the end of the dialogue.[20] But we do not need anything else to decide the question whether virtue can be taught. And Menon, rash as he is and focusing upon this single question, asserts, it can. This kind of reply, however, in the context of shallow, ordinary linguistic usage and even in the dangerous context of a will-to-power, falsifies the very thing represented by Socrates—and only by him—in his own existence. Thus, Socrates is also present in order to prevent this kind of premature freezing of the dialogue. That is a characteristic feature of his (and only his) way of teaching *arete*.

III 2
89c–97c
III 2a
89c–95A

As soon as he has made his countermove, Socrates draws Anytos into the debate, for he just had sat down beside them "at the right time." We must take a comprehensive view to see how this part of the dialogue is rooted in the whole of Plato's work. In the *Apology*, Socrates shows how he has practiced his office of examining others first on the politicians, then on the poets, and always with the same results: he found that they were ignorant, and he incurred their hatred (21B *et seq.*). In the *Ion*, Plato depicts one such encounter, not with the poet himself, but with the derivative figure of the rhapsode. In this episode of the *Meno*, Socrates cross-examines a politician, who is, in fact, one of the prosecutors to whom he replies in the *Apology*. For the symbolic meaning of these connections, it is significant that in the *Ion* (534 CD), in the *Apology* (22c), and in the *Meno* (99c), sometimes the poets and sometimes the politicians are cited in the company of "divine prophets and tellers of oracles." All of them do their work not because they possess knowledge in the Socratic-Platonic sense, but because they have enthusiasm or a share in divine inspiration—as is said more or less ironically.

The specific subject, however, in which Socrates examines the politician here in the *Meno* and thereby incurs his enmity, is the question—particularly important to Plato—why the famous statesmen of Athens have not been able to pass their skill on to anybody else by way of education. The same question is discussed, in various perspectives and with ever greater intensity, in the *Protagoras*, *Alcibiades*, and *Gorgias*.[21] Here on the stage of the *Meno*, it is presented in the form of a live examination of a politician who "was properly educated by his father, as the majority of the Athenian people would acknowledge" (90B).[22] Now, what if it should turn out that statesmen cannot educate their sons, that "virtue cannot be taught" (94E)? Anytos feels that he is himself a target in this "slandering" (κακῶς λέγειν) of the statesmen, among whom he counts himself, whereas Socrates indicates ironically that there is a great difference between them and Anytos. We sense how the anger of Anytos rises, and we know what mortal combat is here taking shape. Anybody who has not previously noticed what is at stake must see now that this is not a matter of words, but a matter of life and death.

Yet, Anytos is hit not only as a person; he also represents a system according to which practical statesmanship, political virtue, or kalokagathia is acquired by means of a firm tradition passed on from one generation to another. Meletos puts it similarly, though in a more democratic or rather demagogic context, during his cross-examination in the *Apology* (24D *et seq.*), when he cites as the guardians of political education first "custom," then "all Athenians"—with the only exception of Socrates! The same thesis has a more aristocratic ring in the *Meno*. It is clear that it aims at the educational system of closely knit aristocracies, which we find as historical fact, say, in Rome at the time of the older Republic, but which in the Athens of Perikles or even of Themistokles was without foundation in reality. Yet, this tradition is defended all the more vehemently for being a product of the imagination. From this comes the extreme hostility shown by Anytos against the "Sophists" who call the traditional educational system into question both by their existence and by their teaching. Socrates is his special enemy. We must note that Anytos does not distinguish between "this Sophist" and the

others any more than the strange Somebody does at the end of
the *Euthydemus*. He is quite right in sensing that the opposition
of this man Socrates is more dangerous than that of all the others.
For the seemingly skeptical question posed by Socrates reveals
the fatal crack in the educational system—or system of noneduc-
ation—represented by Anytos.

III 2b
95A–97C

After Anytos has withdrawn, the two main speakers finish the
topic by themselves. There seems to be no consistency anywhere,
as is said in continuation of the conversation with Anytos. The
politicians are not sure whether they are teachers of civic virtue.
As far as the Sophists are concerned, not even all of them claim to
be such teachers. Menon's teacher Gorgias, for example, professes to teach nothing but rhetoric. Menon himself wavers.
Socrates quotes the poet Theognis as showing the same kind of
vacillation on the subject. Yet, among artisans and craftsmen,
to whose work Plato so often appeals as the standard for activities that rest on firm foundations, there is no such wavering and
uncertainty. Only with regard to *arete*, there seem to be no acknowledged teachers; hence, there are no pupils either. In short,
arete cannot be taught.

The third part of the dialogue first proves dialectically that
arete is a form of knowledge, and hence teachable. There follows
a countermove. The evidence of real life shows that there is no
education, and hence that *arete* cannot be taught. It is now the
task of the concluding section to resolve this antinomy.

III 3
97c–100c

The antinomy is due to the fact that we have looked at the
problem in terms of a radical antithesis of knowledge and ignorance. But life shows that there is a third possibility between
knowledge and ignorance: right opinion (ὀρθὴ δόξα). Thus, the
inflexible "either–or" (which was the cause of all sorts of eristic
confusion in the *Euthydemus*) is now abandoned. A hierarchically
ordered system of forms of knowledge is envisaged for the first
time. Right opinion, i.e., the characteristically human domain,
occupies a place between the ideal limits of pure knowledge
and pure ignorance. (Diotima will have more to say on this
subject in the *Symposium*.) Menon tries to define the difference
between knowledge and right opinion by ascribing to knowledge the attribute of "always" or permanence (97c). Socrates
wrests this argument from him, by means of a slightly sophis-

tic move, only to appropriate it himself all the more firmly. He
defines the difference between right opinion and knowledge by
saying that the former, in order to become knowledge, must
be tied down "by an account of the reason" (αἰτίας λογισμῷ,
98Α). This is quite provisional, as both speakers intimate (ἔοικεν,
εἰκάζων) and as the third part of the *Theaetetus* will show explicitly. Thus, a vast field is opening up, and the reference back to
the myth of the soul (*Meno* 98Α) indicates the direction in which
we are moving—toward the theory of knowledge in the *Republic*.

After "right opinion" has thus found a place among the stages
of knowledge, the politicians of Athens are assigned to this stage
as "divine men." With the deep irony inherent in this desig-
nation and in the comparison with "tellers of oracles and divine
prophets," they are now set free of the curse which the *Gorgias*
had pronounced upon them.[23] In the end, there rises, as a premonition, the vision of the kind of "political man" who can create
others like himself—this the Athenian politicians could not do—
and who, like Homer's Teiresias, is the only one who keeps his
sense among the shades in the underworld. Again, we discern
a movement in the direction of the *Republic*, where the one political man builds the true state to create the conditions in which
others will become political men as well. Here in the *Meno*, however, we are dismissed with a reference to the provisional nature
of our results, and with the demand that we must first "inquire
into what virtue is in and by itself" (αὐτὸ καθ' αὐτὸ ζητεῖν τί ποτ'
ἔστιν ἀρετή). We know who is the only true statesman; for we
have caught sight of him. The myth revealing the essential cognitive relationship between the soul and the "truth of being" provides a means for approaching this sphere of "being-in-itself."
Socrates and *Eidos*, existence and true being: these two perspectives, which ultimately converge upon each other, bring the
dialogue to a close.

Let us review once more the peculiar structure of the whole
work, particularly with regard to the participants. An arrogant
pupil of the rhetoricians, inclined toward a tyrannical nature both
in his conduct and on the basis of his historical record, wants to
talk about the trite question of whether men can acquire "virtue."
But this time he cannot simply indulge in idle talk, for he is facing Socrates. In the presence of this man of knowledge who

claims to be ignorant and in the presence of this educator who does not educate, the topic of conversation (behind which are hidden, ultimately, the ambitions of power politics) is transformed into a profoundly serious search. The question of whether virtue can be taught becomes the question, What is the essential nature of *arete*?, and the examination of the substantive points at issue becomes a test of the human being himself. The first part of the dialogue ends as the aporetic dialogues end. Essential nature cannot be compressed into a definition. But the various attempts at a definition open certain paths and block off others, and the person himself who is pursuing the inquiry becomes transparent in the presence of Socrates. Then the middle part of the dialogue suddenly soars above the level of *aporia* into the dimension of myth, and this vision of a domain beyond all experience is linked with geometry, i.e., with something seemingly altogether different. Secretly nourished by this central section, the concluding part of the dialogue seeks an answer to the question posed at the beginning. It seeks an answer not in terms of a simple yes or no, but in terms of a dialectical to and fro. The most characteristic aspect of this last part is the accent it puts on Anytos. He suddenly is drawn into the conversation, he withdraws from it just as suddenly and remains present to the end as an angry observer. And meanwhile Menon quietly talks the subject through with Socrates.

A number of things in this unusual curve of the dialogue become more clear if we think of the cave simile in the *Republic*. In the middle part of the *Meno*, the soul breaks through into the light and perceives ultimate reality. In this break-through, geometry provides indispensable aid. We recall that in the simile of the cave, it is said: suppose somebody—the very somebody who has made the ascent to the light, i.e., Socrates—would come down and back again to those "forever in chains" and "would set out to deliver them and lead them upward. They would kill him if they could lay their hands on him." In the *Meno*, Socrates returns to the cave, as it were, after viewing the beyond, and he shows men—especially those "statesmen" who are proudest of themselves—what they lack. One of those "in chains" is Anytos. His encounter with Socrates generates the hatred that is vented in the threat upon the life of the unwanted deliverer.

NOTES AND ABBREVIATIONS

ABBREVIATIONS

Books and Periodicals Cited

AbhBerl = *Abhandlungen der Preussischen Akademie*, Phil.-hist. Kl. Berlin.

AbhLeipz = *Abhandlungen der Sächsischen Akademie*. Leipzig.

AbhMun = *Abhandlungen der Bayerischen Akademie*. Munich.

AeR = *Atene e Roma*. Florence.

AfP = *Archiv für Philosophie*. Berlin.

AJP = *American Journal of Philology*. Baltimore.

Apelt = Otto Apelt, *Platonische Aufsätze*. Leipzig and Berlin, 1912.

Arnim = Hans von Arnim, *Platos Jugenddialoge und die Entstehungszeit des Phaidros*. Leipzig, 1914.

Arnim, *Sprachliche Forschungen* = Hans von Arnim, *Sprachliche Forschungen zur Chronologie der platonischen Dialoge*. Sitzungsberichte der Wiener Akademie, 1911.

Ast = Friedrich Ast, *Platons Leben und Schriften*. Leipzig, 1816.

BAB = *Bulletin de la Classe des Lettres de l'Académie de Belgique*. Brussels.

Barth = Heinrich Barth, *Die Seele in der Philosophie Platons*. Tübingen, 1921.

BCH = *Bulletin de Correspondance Hellénique* (École française d'Athènes). Athens.

Bonitz = Hermann Bonitz, *Platonische Studien*. Berlin, 1886.

Bruns = Ivo Bruns, *Das literarische Porträt der Griechen*. Berlin, 1896.

Buccellato = Manlio Buccellato, *La Retorica sofistica negli Scritti di Platone*. Rome and Milan, 1953.

Bull. Budé = *Bulletin de l'Association Guillaume Budé*. Paris.

CB = *Classical Bulletin*. St. Louis, Mo.

Cherniss = Harold Cherniss, *Aristotle's Criticism of Plato and the Academy*. Baltimore, 1944.

Cherniss, *Lustrum* = Harold Cherniss, "Plato 1950–1957," *Lustrum*, IV (1959); V (1960). Göttingen, 1960–61.

CJ = *Classical Journal*. Bloomington, Ind.

Classen = C. Joachim Classen, "Sprachliche Deutung als Triebkraft platonischen und sokratischen Philosophierens," *Zetemata*, XXII (1959).

Cousin = *Œuvres de Platon*, tr. Victor Cousin. Paris, 1822–39. 13 vols.

CP = *Classical Philology*. Chicago.

CQ = *Classical Quarterly.* London and Boston.

CR = *Classical Review.* London.

CW = *Classical Weekly.* Pittsburgh.

de Vries = G. J. de Vries, *Spel bij Plato.* Amsterdam, 1949.

DGrA = Paul Friedländer, *Der Grosse Alcibiades.* Bonn, 1921–23. 2 pts.

Diès = Auguste Diès, *Autour de Platon.* Paris, 1927. 2 vols.

Dioniso = *Bollettino del Istituto Nazionale del Dramma Antico.* Syracuse, Italy.

Eckert = Wilhelm Eckert, *Dialektischer Scherz in den früheren Gesprächen Platons.* Nürnberg, 1911.

Festugière = A.-J. Festugière, *Contemplation et vie contemplative selon Platon.* 2d edn., Paris, 1950.

Frank = Erich Frank, *Plato und die sogenannten Pythagoreer.* Halle, 1923.

Frank, *WWG* = Erich Frank, *Wissen, Wollen, Glauben.* Zurich and Stuttgart, 1955.

Freymann = Walther Freymann, *Platons Suchen nach einer Grundlegung aller Philosophie.* Leipzig, 1930.

Gauss = Hermann Gauss, *Philosophischer Handkommentar zu den Dialogen Platons.* Bern, 1952–61. 3 vols., 6 pts. (References are to pages, not to paragraphs.)

Geffcken = Johannes Geffcken, *Griechische Literaturgeschichte.* Vol. II. Heidelberg, 1934.

GGA = *Göttingische gelehrte Anzeigen.* Göttingen.

Goldschmidt = Victor Goldschmidt, *Les Dialogues de Platon.* Paris, 1947.

Gomperz = Theodor Gomperz, *Greek Thinkers,* tr. Laurie Magnus and G. G. Berry. New York and London, 1901–12. 4 vols.

Greene = William Chase Greene, "Plato's View of Poetry," *Harvard Studies in Classical Philology*, XXIX (1918).

Grote = George Grote, *Plato and the Other Companions of Socrates.* London, 1865. 3 vols.

Grube = Georges M. A. Grube, *Plato's Thought.* London, 1935.

Hermann = Karl Friedrich Hermann, *Geschichte und System der platonischen Philosophie.* Heidelberg, 1839.

Hildebrandt = Kurt Hildebrandt, *Platon.* Berlin, 1933.

Hoffmann = Ernst Hoffmann, *Platon.* Zurich, 1950.

Jachmann = Günther Jachmann, *Der Platontext.* Nachrichten der Akademie der Wissenschaften in Göttingen, 1941.

Jaeger = Werner Jaeger, *Paideia,* tr. Gilbert Highet. Oxford, 1939–45. 3 vols.

Jaeger, *Aristotle* = Werner Jaeger, *Aristotle,* tr. Richard Robinson. 2d edn., Oxford, 1948.

JAesA = *Journal of Aesthetics and Art Criticism.* Cleveland.

Jaspers = Karl Jaspers, *Die Grossen Philosophen.* Vol. I. Munich, 1957.

JHS = *Journal of Hellenic Studies.* London.

Joël = Karl Joël, *Geschichte der antiken Philosophie.* Tübingen, 1921.

Jowett = *The Dialogues of Plato*, tr. Benjamin Jowett. Oxford, 1924. 4 vols.

JPhilos = *Journal of Philosophy*. New York.

Koyré = Alexandre Koyré, *Introduction à la lecture de Platon*. New York and Paris, 1945.

Leisegang = Hans Leisegang, "Platon," in *Real-Encyclopädie der classischen Altertumswissenschaft*, August Pauly, Georg Wissowa, Wilhelm Kroll, eds. Vol. XX, Stuttgart, 1950. Cols. 2341ff.

Levinson = Ronald Bartlett Levinson, *In Defense of Plato*. Cambridge, Mass., 1953.

Lodge = Rupert C. Lodge, *The Philosophy of Plato*. London, 1956.

Loeb = Loeb Classical Library. London and Cambridge, Mass.

Łutoslawski = Wincenty Łutoslawski, *The Origin and Growth of Plato's Logic*. London and New York, 1897.

MusHelv = *Museum Helveticum*. Basel.

Natorp = Paul Natorp, *Platos Ideenlehre*. Leipzig, 1903. (2d edn., 1921; unless otherwise indicated, the first edition is cited.)

Neue Jahrbücher = *Neue Jahrbücher für das klassische Altertum*. Leipzig.

Neue phil. Unters. = *Neue philologische Untersuchungen*. Berlin.

NGG = *Nachrichten der Göttinger Gelehrten Gesellschaft* (*der Wissenschaft*). Göttingen.

ParPass = *La Parola del Passato*. Naples.

Pearson = Alfred C. Pearson, *The Fragments of Sophocles*. Cambridge, 1917. 3 vols.

Perls = Hugo Perls, *Platon. Sa Conception du Kosmos*. New York, 1945.

PhB = Philosophische Bibliothek. Leipzig.

PhilolQ = *Philological Quarterly*. Iowa City.

Plato 1 = Paul Friedländer, *Plato: An Introduction*, tr. Hans Meyerhoff. New York (Bollingen Series LIX:1) and London, 1958.

Platon Budé = *Platon*, Collection des Universités de France, publiée sous le patronage de l'Association Guillaume Budé. Paris, 1920– .

Pohlenz = Max Pohlenz, *Aus Platos Werdezeit*. Berlin, 1913.

PPR = *Philosophical and Phenomenological Research*. New York.

Raeder = Hans Raeder, *Platons philosophische Entwicklung*. Leipzig, 1905.

RBP = *Revue Belge de Philologie et d'Histoire*. Brussels.

R-E = August Pauly, Georg Wissowa, Wilhelm Kroll, eds., *Real-Encyclopädie der classischen Altertumswissenschaft*. Stuttgart, 1894– .

Reinhardt = Karl Reinhardt, *Platons Mythen*. Bonn, 1927.

Reinhardt, *Vermächtnis* = Karl Reinhardt, *Vermächtnis der Antike*. Göttingen, 1960.

RevÉtGr = *Revue des Études Grecques*. Paris.

RevInPh = *Revue Internationale de Philosophie*. Brussels.

RevPhil = *Revue de Philologie*. Paris.

RFIC = *Rivista di Filologia e d'Istruzione Classica*. Turin.

RhM = *Rheinisches Museum*. Frankfurt a. M.

RHR = *Revue de l'Histoire des Religions*. Paris.

RIFD = *Rivista Internazionale di Filosofia del Diritto*. Rome.

Ritter = Constantin Ritter, *Platon*. Munich, 1910, 1923. 2 vols.

Robin = Léon Robin, *Platon*. Paris, 1935.

Robin, *Théorie de l'amour* = Léon Robin, *La Théorie platonicienne de l'amour*. Paris, 1908.

Robinson = Richard Robinson, *Plato's Earlier Dialectic*. Ithaca, N. Y., 1941. (2d edn., Oxford, 1953.)

Rosenmeyer = T. G. Rosenmeyer, "Platonic Scholarship: 1945–55," *Classical Weekly*, Vol. L, Nos. 13–15 (1956).

Ross = Sir David Ross, *Plato's Theory of Ideas*. Oxford, 1951.

RSF = *Rivista Critica di Storia della Filosofia*. Florence.

Salin = Edgar Salin, *Platon und die griechische Utopie*. Munich and Leipzig, 1921.

SBBerl = *Sitzungsberichte der Preussischen Akademie der Wissenschaften*. Berlin.

SBWien = *Sitzungsberichte der Akademie der Wissenschaften in Wien*, Phil.-hist. Kl. Vienna.

Schaarschmidt = Karl Max Wilhelm Schaarschmidt, *Die Sammlung der platonischen Schriften*. Bonn, 1866.

Schaerer = René Schaerer, *La Question platonicienne. Étude sur les rapports de la pensée et de l'expression dans les Dialogues*. Neuchâtel, 1938.

Schleiermacher = Friedrich Schleiermacher, *Platos Werke*. 2d edn., Berlin, 1817–28. 6 vols.

Shorey = Paul Shorey, *What Plato Said*. Chicago, 1933.

Shorey, *Unity* = Paul Shorey, *The Unity of Plato's Thought*. Chicago, 1903.

Singer = Kurt Singer, *Platon der Gründer*. Munich, 1927.

SO = *Symbolae Osloenses*. Oslo.

Socher = Joseph Socher, *Über Platons Schriften*. Munich, 1820.

Stefanini = Luigi Stefanini, *Platone*. Padua, 1932. 2 vols. (2d edn., 1949; unless otherwise indicated, the first edition is cited.)

Steinhart = Karl Steinhart, *Platons sämtliche Werke*, tr. Hieronymus Müller, with introduction by Karl Steinhart. Leipzig, 1850–73. 9 vols.

Stenzel = Julius Stenzel, *Platon der Erzieher*. Leipzig, 1928.

Stenzel, *Studien* = Julius Stenzel, *Studien zur Entwicklung der platonischen Dialektik von Sokrates zu Aristoteles*. 2d edn., Leipzig, 1931.

Stenzel, *Zahl und Gestalt* = Julius Stenzel, *Zahl und Gestalt bei Platon und Aristoteles*. 2d edn., Leipzig, 1933.

Stenzel, *Kleine Schriften* = Julius Stenzel, *Kleine Schriften zur griechischen Philosophie*. Darmstadt, 1956.

Susemihl = Franz Susemihl, *Die genetische Entwicklung der platonischen Philosophie*. Leipzig, 1855–60. 2 vols.

TAPA = *Transactions of the American Philological Association*. Hartford.

Taylor = Alfred Edward Taylor, *Plato, the Man and His Work*. 2d edn., New York, 1927.

Ueberweg-Praechter = Friedrich Ueberweg and Karl Praechter, *Grundriss der Geschichte der Philosophie*. Vol. I, *Altertum*. 12th edn., Berlin, 1926.

Vorsokr. = Hermann Diels, *Die Fragmente der Vorsokratiker*. 6th edn., ed. Walther Kranz. Berlin, 1951–52. 3 vols.

WienStud = *Wiener Studien*. Vienna.

Wilamowitz = Ulrich von Wilamowitz-Moellendorff, *Platon*. Berlin, 1919. 2 vols. (2d edn., 1920; unless otherwise indicated, the first edition is cited.)

Zeller = Eduard Zeller, *Die Philosophie der Griechen*, Pt. II, Vol. 1. 4th edn., Leipzig, 1889. 3 pts. (In some cases, reference is made to the 5th edition supervised by Ernst Hoffmann [1922].)

ZPhF = *Zeitschrift für philosophische Forschung*. Meisenheim a. G.

NOTES

with Bibliography

A bracketed reference of the style [I²] indicates a previous note where the citation in question is given fully. See also the foregoing list of abbreviations.

I : *Protagoras*

RECENT EDITIONS AND TRANSLATIONS: L. Robin, *Platon Budé*, III/1 (1923); W. R. M. Lamb, Loeb IV (1924); K. Preisendanz (Jena, 1925); W. Nestle (7th edn., Leipzig, 1931); G. Faggin (Turin, 1952); O. Apelt, PhB 175 (3d edn., 1956); M. Ostwald and G. Vlastos (New York, 1956); G. Calogero (3d edn., Florence, 1958).

RECENT INTERPRETATIONS: Singer, pp. 28ff.; R. Hackforth, "Hedonism in Plato's *Protagoras*," *CQ*, XXII (1928), 39ff.; Hildebrandt, pp. 25ff.; G. M. A. Grube, "The Structural Unity of the *Protagoras*," *CQ*, XXVII (1933), 203ff.; J. Moreau, *La Construction de l'idéalisme platonicien* (Paris, 1939), pp. 34ff.; A. Levi, "The Ethical and Social Thought of Protagoras," *Mind*, IL (1940), 284ff.; Jaeger, II, 107ff.; J. S. Morrison, "The Place of Protagoras in Athenian Public Life," *CQ*, XXXV (1941), 1ff.; O. Gigon, "Studien zu Platons *Protagoras*," *Phyllobolia für Peter von der Mühll* (Basel, 1946), pp. 91ff.; P. Zenoni Politeo, "Intorno al significato del *Protagora* platonico," *Sophia*, XVI (1948), 362ff.; J. G. Clapp, "Some Notes on Plato's *Protagoras*," *PPR*, X (1949/50), 486ff.; W. Kirk, "*Protagoras* and *Phaedrus*: Literary Techniques," *Studies Presented to D. M. Robinson*, II (St. Louis, 1953), pp. 593ff.; G. Rudberg, "*Protagoras–Gorgias–Menon*: eine platonische Übergangszeit," *SO*, XXX (1953), 30ff.; G. B. Kerferd, "Protagoras' Doctrine of Justice and Virtue in the *Protagoras* of Plato," *JHS*, LXXIII (1953), 42ff.

ADDITIONAL BIBLIOGRAPHY: Shorey, p. 492; Geffcken, Notes, p. 42; Rosenmeyer, p. 188; Cherniss, *Lustrum*, pp. 149ff.

1. *Plato* 1, p. 159. / My interpretation is criticized by de Vries, p. 66. This is the contrast between a naturalistic and a more symbolic point of view.

2. See also *Theaetetus* 173C: ἕκαστος αὐτῶν (i.e., τῶν λόγων) περιμένει ἀποτελεσθῆναι.

3. The captious remarks of earlier interpreters are opposed by Johannes Vahlen, *Opuscula Academica* (Leipzig, 1907–1908), I, 479ff. He, however, goes too far in the other direction when he denies the slightest significance to the picture of Hades. That is the way naturalism sees things.

4. Cf. Bruns, pp. 501ff.

5. *Protagoras* 327E; *Alcibiades Major* 111A; Δισσοὶ Λόγοι (*Dialexeis*), *Vorsokr.* 90 [83], ch. 6, §§ 11, 12.

6. Thus, Plato's intention is not met by Jowett's relativism either (I, 20): "There is quite as much truth on the side of Protagoras as of Socrates. . . ." Cf. Koyré, p. 55: "*La thèse de Protagoras est celle d'un sociologisme conséquent.*"

7. Euripides reflects this discussion (Ferdinand Dümmler, *Kleine Schriften* [3 vols., Leipzig, 1901], I, 172, puts it this way: he uses a socio-political treatise), *Supplices* 913 *et seq.*: ἡ δ' ἰευανδρία διδακτός. *Dialexeis*, *Vorsokr.* 90 [83], ch. 6: περὶ τᾶς σοφίας καὶ τᾶς ἀρετᾶς, αἱ διδακτόν. Eupolis, *Demoi* frag. 4. Cf. Pohlenz, p. 85.

8. *Dialexeis* ch. 6, § 4. / On the textual reading: I should be reluctant to give up the words τὰ αὐτῶν τέκνα ἐδίδαξαν. Cf., e.g., *Protagoras* 324D 4: τοὺς αὐτῶν ὑεῖς διδάσκουσιν. Similarly, see 325B 3, 325B 6. Cf. also *Alcibiades Major* 118D 11.

9. See *Plato* 1, ch. VII.

10. *Plato* 1, ch. IX.

11. The contrast is between the specialization of the *techne* and the necessary universality of political *arete*. The fact that some lack this *arete* is no contradiction. Still, we do not have to recognize a "mythical expression for the presupposition of an instinctive or innate moral sense," as Gomperz (II, 310) says. This also disposes of his proof of internal contradictions. / Olof Gigon, "Studien zu Platons *Protagoras*," *Phyllobolia für Peter von der Mühll* (Basel, 1946), pp. 91ff., sets out to prove such contradictions throughout the structure of the dialogue. Cf. comment by H. Cherniss, *AJP*, LXXI (1950), 85ff.; G. B. Kerferd, *JHS*, LXXIII (1953), 42ff.

12. Cf. Apelt, pp. 189ff.

13. Alfred Gercke, "Eine Niederlage des Sokrates," *Neue Jahrbücher*, XLI (1918), 184, observed correctly—as Steinhart (I, 413) did earlier—that this Parmenidean-sounding thesis is the teaching of the Megarian school (Diogenes Laërtius VII 161). / Gigon, op. cit. [I¹¹], pp. 100f., calls the idea of identity "wholly un-Platonic." In this case "Platonic" seems to stand for the rigidity of a textbook—something that is so un-Platonic! Cf. what will be said in commenting on *Republic*

IV 427D–445E concerning the "provisional character" of the system of the four virtues.

14. The examples "face" and "wax," instead of Plato's "face" and "gold," are employed by Aristotle, in order to make clear the contrast of ἀνομοιομερῆ and ὁμοιομερῆ (e.g., *Meteorology* IV 10, *De partibus animalium* II 1, *Historia animalium* 486ᵃ 5). The ὁμοιομερῆ are ὕλη for the ἀνομοιομερῆ (*De generatione animalium* 715ᵃ 9). Face is a ὅλον, a gold lump a πᾶν (*Metaphysics* V 26). It is the ὅλον at which Plato is aiming.

15. On these intentional fallacies, see Bonitz, p. 265, who defends his view against Zeller. For a penetrating analysis in detail, see Eckert, pp. 98ff. He also makes the appropriate objections to Gomperz (II, 314; III, 316), who assumes "unintended paralogisms on Plato's part." Gigon, op. cit. [I¹¹], pp. 139ff., again has taken up the cudgels for unintentionality. Jaeger (II, 117) is too casual with his "few inaccuracies in Socrates' inferences." Alfred Croiset, *Platon Budé*, III/1, 12, seems to find no difficulty at all when he speaks of *"une rigueur et une précision remarquables."* This very *"rigueur"* leads astray with *"précision."*

16. Gomperz (II, 309) oversimplifies in saying that Protagoras merely represents the prevailing opinion.

17. 336D 5: ὡς ἐγῷμαι cannot be understood as Schleiermacher, Ast, and Jowett translate it and Wilamowitz (I, 138) interprets it: that Socrates is no longer quite certain who the speaker was. The words fit Kritias perfectly; Prodikos (337A 2) replies expressly to him. Nor can the sequence (μετὰ τὸν Ἀλκιβιάδην) be questioned. The speech is appropriate only here. Thus, we must follow Shorey, *CP*, XV (1920), 201, in thinking of cases where οἶμαι, ὡς ἐγῷμαι is the expression of a somewhat ironic assertion: "Can you imagine!" The two belong together, just as they have entered together (316A). Erich Frank called my attention to *Republic* 392c 6 and *Sophist* 218A 7 (ὡς ἔοικε). In all these cases it must be a question of an easily understood arrangement (μετά). / On the following passage, cf. F. Heinimann, *Nomos und Physis* (Basel, 1945), pp. 42, 142; W. Kranz, "Das Gesetz des Herzens," *RhM*, XCIV (1951), 229f.

18. Cf. Wilamowitz, *Sappho und Simonides* (Berlin, 1913), pp. 159ff.; C. M. Bowra, *Greek Lyrical Poetry* (Oxford, 1936), pp. 341ff.; H. Fränkel, *Dichtung und Philosophie des frühen Griechentums* (New York, 1951), pp. 396ff.; H. Gundert, "Die Simonides-Interpretation in Platons *Protagoras*," *Festschrift Otto Regenbogen* (Heidelberg, 1952), pp. 71ff.; L. Woodbury, "Simonides on Ἀρετή," *TAPA*, LXXXIV (1953), 135ff.; Lodge, p. 313; A. E. Raubitschek, *WienStud*, LXXI (1958), 171f.

19. This has been pointed out especially by Eckert, p. 53.

20. Cf. Isokrates, *Nicocles* 43: ὅτι τῆς μὲν ἀνδρείας καὶ τῆς δεινότητος ... ἑώρων καὶ τῶν κακῶν ἀνδρῶν πολλοὺς μετέχοντας, τὴν δὲ δικαιοσύνην

καὶ τὴν σωφροσύνην ἴδια κτήματα τῶν καλῶν κἀγαθῶν ὄντα.

21. Cf. J. Stenzel, *GGA*, 1926, p. 201: "Because all *arete* is political, and hence *arete* is supposed to be chiefly manly virtue, ἀνδρεία, we must expect here the sharpest collision between the archaic, emotion-charged, courageous soul and the modern epistemological mind." Taylor, p. 64, refers pertinently to the Socratic "paradox" of the unity of virtue.

22. It goes without saying that neither the Roman *honestum* nor the German *sittlich gut* nor the English "noble, honorable" corresponds to the Greek καλόν. The French *beau, beauté* probably comes closest to the richness of the Greek word.

23. Cf. Eckert, pp. 125ff. Schleiermacher (I/1, 416) is opposed to the view that Socrates makes use of an illegitimate trick. See A.-J. Festugière, "Sur un passage difficile du *Protagoras*," *BCH*, LXXVI (1946), 179ff.

24. It is an old dispute among students of Plato—a dispute in which the perceptive chapter in Gellius, *Noctes Atticae* VIII 5, has not been duly appreciated—whether the hedonistic thesis in the *Protagoras* is meant seriously, and hence whether we must assume a "hedonistic phase" in Plato's development. Hermann, p. 462, proposed this view and has had a strong following: Zeller; Ueberweg-Praechter; R. Hackforth in *CQ*, XXII (1928), 39ff.; E. R. Dodds, *The Greeks and the Irrational* (Berkeley, 1951), p. 208. Steinhart, I, 419; Bonitz, p. 264; Arnim, p. 14, have been at pains to prove the opposite. In the live dramatic structure of the dialogue, the passage must be so understood that Socrates enters this plane of discussion provisionally. Gomperz (II, 323) is instructive: he carries through the comparison with *Laws* V 733 and thus makes hedonism a permanent undercurrent in Plato. In the *Protagoras*, according to Gomperz, there is a lack of the "mediating proof" and the "ideal background." Surely this means that in the *Protagoras* the discussion takes place on the plane of the πολλοί, which is designated in the *Laws* as τὰ ἀνθρώπινα. / Against the putative hedonism of the *Protagoras* are Taylor, pp. 235, 260; Shorey, p. 131; Jaeger, II, 118; Grube, p. 51. / Arnim, p. 14, claims that the "hedonistic theory" is derived from another philosopher. (R. Philippson, *Hermes*, LIX [1924], 399, thinks this is Demokritos.) But that is not a necessary assumption. Cf. A. Mauersberger, *Hermes*, LXI (1926), 307ff.

25. Cf. Hermann Siebeck, *Untersuchungen zur Philosophie der Griechen* (Freiburg, 1888), p. 120.

26. Shorey, p. 500.

27. On Gercke's view in *Neue Jahrbücher* [I¹³], 164, it is to be said that certainly at this point there is an "epigrammatic pointing up by the reporter," but that beyond this report no fact in itself exists. It is also correct that Socrates "is reporter, judge, and partisan in one per-

son" and all at once. But this very fact should preclude our thinking here of anyone other than Plato's Protagoras and also any reading of a defeat of Socrates into the report of the Platonic Socrates. One should not confuse the planes of historic reality and of the work of art.

28. A widespread view sees in the initial position Socrates' "irony," in the final position his serious attitude. But this conception of irony is too shallow. Natorp, p. 13, has rightly spoken out against this interpretation. He thinks that we have here an unsolved problem in Socratic philosophy which was left for Plato to solve, and that the solution was not yet stated in the *Protagoras*. This means that Natorp is assuming here a separate "Socratic philosophy" later to be overcome by Plato. But there is no such thing in Plato; there is only a Platonic way of philosophizing. Natorp's judgment on *Apology* 19CD and *Meno* 89E *et seq.* is not correct either. There, too, it is a question not of dogmatic statements made by Socrates but of an ironic position against the Sophists. / Bonitz, p. 267, sees a part of the correct interpretation.

29. This is expressed most plainly in *Dialexeis, Vorsokr.* 90 [83], ch. 6. Cf. Pohlenz, pp. 90f. Plato himself puts the matter most sharply in *Republic* VI 488B.

30. See *Plato* 1, pp. 86f.

31. Ibid., pp. 60ff.

32. Schleiermacher puts the discussion of method in the center, and even so with the restriction inherent in the term "scientific method," together with a "scoffing belittlement of the ethical content" (Bonitz). Wilamowitz sees the dialogue as a satire in which Socrates is a Sophist among Sophists. Bonitz realizes that the defeat of sophistics and the criticism of its methods are inseparable. Strangely enough, however, he regards the "insight into Plato's ethics and dialectics," which he himself has worked out well, as not ultimately "determining the composition of the whole." Steinhart (I, 410), on the other hand, considers the task of the dialogue to be the "development of the concept of virtue in its various aspects." Jowett's view (I, 123) is similar: "The aim of the dialogue is to show the unity of virtue." According to Eduard Zeller, *Platonische Studien* (Tübingen, 1839), p. 161, the *Protagoras* proposes to "lay the subjective foundation of philosophy, by presenting, on the one hand, the true philosophic method as opposed to the sophistic one, and on the other hand the doctrine concerning virtue as a knowledge." Gomperz (II, 321) thinks that "the dialectic superiority of Socrates prevails together with the inner concatenation of his system." Stefanini (I, 171) finds the solution in this: ". . . *che nel Protagora non è Socrate che gioca d'ironia sui sofisti, ma Platone che gioca d'ironia su Socrate stesso.*" Jaeger (II, 107ff.) entitles his *Protagoras* chapter, "Sophistic or Socratic *Paideia?*" / For other earlier views, see Susemihl, I, 55ff. Cf. Leisegang, cols. 2386ff.

33. See *Plato* 1, pp. 144ff.

II : *Laches*

RECENT EDITIONS AND TRANSLATIONS: A. Croiset, *Platon Budé*, II (1921);
J. Crexells (Barcelona, 1924); W. R. M. Lamb, Loeb IV (1924);
K. Preisendanz (Jena, 1925); G. Ammendola (2d edn., Naples, 1933);
O. Apelt, PhB 178 (3d edn., 1945); E. Salin (Basel, 1950).

RECENT INTERPRETATIONS: R. Meister, "Thema und Ergebnis des platonischen *Laches*," *WienStud*, XLII (1921), 9ff., 103ff.; Hildebrandt,
pp. 83ff.; W. Steidle, "Der Dialog *Laches* und Platons Verhältnis zu
Athen in den Frühdialogen," *MusHelv*, VII (1950), 129ff.; P. Grenet,
"Note sur la structure du *Lachès*," *Mélanges Auguste Diès* (Paris,
1956), pp. 121ff.; Gallo Galli, *Socrate ed alcuni dialoghi platonici*
(Turin, 1958), pp. 153ff.

ADDITIONAL BIBLIOGRAPHY: Shorey, p. 483; Geffcken, Notes, p. 45; Rosenmeyer, p. 180; Cherniss, *Lustrum*, pp. 103ff.

1. 181c 7 *et seq.* The reading: τί φατε; τί δοκεῖ; τὸ μάθημα . . . is rightly
    criticized by Wilamowitz (II, 366). But the reading should probably
    be: τί φατε; ἦ (or ἦ τι) δοκεῖ τὸ μάθημα. . . . Cf. *Gorgias* 452a 7:
    τί οὖν λέγεις; ἦ. . . . *Republic* 374b 1 *et seq.* and 609b 9 *et seq.*: τί οὖν;
    . . . ἦ οὖν τι. . . . *Phaedo* 74d 4: τί δέ; ἦ πάσχομέν τι . . . .
2. Cf. with 188b 6 *et seq.* the statement of Socrates himself in *Protagoras*
    333c 7: τὸν γὰρ λόγον ἔγωγε μάλιστα ἐξετάζω, συμβαίνει μέντοι ἴσως
    καὶ ἐμὲ τὸν ἐρωτῶντα καὶ τὸν ἀποκρινόμενον ἐξετάζεσθαι.
3. Ast, p. 454, noted that Lysimachos (*Laches* 181bc) and Kephalos
    (*Republic* I 328cd) show the same amicably reproachful manner in
    addressing Socrates—to the point of verbal agreement. Ast, however,
    censures the *Laches* unjustly. Bonitz, p. 223, rightly rejecting the
    censure of Ast (and Schaarschmidt), in turn minimizes the agreement
    of the dialogues. Lysimachos and Kephalos, despite their different
    ages and individualities, belong on the same level.
4. This diversion was facilitated by the verbal usage founded on custom.
    See Eduard Schwartz, *Das Geschichtswerk des Thukydides* (Bonn, 1919),
    p. 352, on ἀρετή and ἀνδρία.
5. John Dewey sees the contrast between the two generals differently
    in "The Socratic Dialogues of Plato," *Studies in the History of Ideas*,
    II (New York, 1925), 10ff.: "Laches is, so to speak, a Cynic without
    knowing it. Nicias stands where the Cyrenaics stood."
6. In this respect, I believe, I can sharpen the analysis of Arnim, pp. 30ff.,
    to which I refer in general. In the other cases as well, one must take

into consideration the different reasoning of Socrates and Laches, even where they agree in their rejection.

7. In spite of Arnim, pp. 24f., it is an open question how far the greater simplicity of the *Protagoras* in this respect can be used for the purpose of dating.

8. This distinction is nothing new (Pohlenz, p. 27, compares Thucydides II 40 3), and certainly Prodikos did not let it escape him. What is done with the distinction, however, is Socratic-Platonic.

9. Natorp, pp. 19, 22f.

10. Bonitz, p. 226.

11. Socher (p. 105) and Wilamowitz (I, 183 = I², 185) underestimate it. Pohlenz, pp. 32ff., overemphasizing the apologetic trend of the frame dialogue, tends to neglect the inner relationship of the parts.

III : *Thrasymachus*

RECENT EDITIONS AND TRANSLATIONS: See *Plato 3*, ch. XXII.

RECENT INTERPRETATIONS: H. D. Verdam, "De Platonis dialogo *Thrasymachus* qui vocatur," *Mnemosyne*, LV (1927), 340ff.; H. von Arnim, *Platons Dialog "Thrasymachus"* (Akademie van Wetenschappen, Amsterdam, 1927); G. Rudberg, "Zum platonischen *Thrasymachos*," *SO*, XXIII (1944), 1ff.; A. R. Henderickx, "Eerste Boek van Platoons *Staat* of Dialoog *Thrasymachos*," *RBP*, XXIV (1945), 5ff.; Goldschmidt, pp. 129ff.; Gauss, I/2, 117ff.; G. Giannantoni, "Il primo libro della *Repubblica* di Platone," *RSF*, XII (1957), 123ff.; K. Vretska, "Platonica III," *WienStud*, LXXI (1958), 30ff., 76ff.

ADDITIONAL BIBLIOGRAPHY: Rosenmeyer, p. 188; Cherniss, *Lustrum*, pp. 154ff.

1. Cf. Wilamowitz, I, 206ff. = I², 209ff. / After Schleiermacher (III/1, 7ff.) had made the decisive observations and Hermann (p. 538) had drawn from them the conclusion as to the early origin of Book I, Dümmler, "Zur Komposition des platonischen *Staates*," *Kleine Schriften* [I⁷], I, 229ff., set forth the relationship in detail. From him derives the name for this dialogue: *Thrasymachus*. But what is really new in his hypothesis is false: that *Republic* X 608c–611A was part of the *Thrasymachus*, so that the dialogue concluded with an eschatological myth. (A view similar to Dümmler's is held, more cautiously, by Wilamowitz, I, 208.) For a dialogue of the aporetic group, a concluding myth would be impossible. See *Plato 1*, pp. 177f. / Verbal statistics: C. Ritter, *Untersuchungen über Platon* (Munich, 1888),

pp. 35ff.; Łutoslawski, p. 319ff.; Arnim, *Sprachliche Forschungen*, pp. 70, 211, 223. Taylor, p. 264, ignores all these findings. He is right in saying that "the first book serves its present purpose as an introduction to the whole work perfectly," but this does not disprove Hermann's theory; nor does Bruns, pp. 320ff., succeed in shaking it. Shorey, p. 215, calls "Duemmler's reconstruction . . . an ingenious conjecture merely" and expresses himself similarly in Plato, *The Republic* (Loeb edn.), pp. x, xxv. Jaeger (II, 95) says that this view, held today by many, is nothing more than a brilliant hypothesis. But this is not quite in keeping with his comments that precede and follow. Auguste Diès, *Platon Budé*, VI/1, xviiiff., gives a careful discussion. He accepts the result of the stylistic research, but he is averse to the thesis that the *Thrasymachus* was a separate dialogue. When Plato wrote the first book (he says), he already could have had the plan of the whole work in mind. Admittedly, various intermediate views between the opposing theories are possible. But even in Diès, and likewise in Shorey and Taylor, the formal element does not receive its due. Book I of the *Republic* has in all essentials the form of a dialogue of the aporetic group. Nor is there any question of "inferiority" of this first book to the *Gorgias*. What we have are morphological levels within Plato's creative work. Cf. R. Preiswerk, *Neue philologische Untersuchungen zum 1. Buch des platonischen "Staates"* (Zurich diss., 1939). Here the "secondary passages" are examined; then the *Thrasymachus* is analyzed as an early dialogue. According to Gauss (I/2, 119), the *Thrasymachus* does not begin until 331c, but then "runs on without later interpolation" to the end of the book. The first theory is very improbable, and the second cannot be correct. See Leisegang, col. 2405.

2. Similar is the judgment of G. M. A. Grube, *CP*, XXVI (1931), 302ff.; Theiler, *MusHelv*, IX (1952), 68. Grube takes the *Clitophon* to be Platonic; J. Stenzel calls it "perhaps Platonic," in *R-E*, III A, col. 839; Geffcken, p. 186, calls it "one of the most puzzling products of the Platonic period." I cannot see that the *Clitophon* is related to the *Phaedrus* (Wilamowitz, I, 485, n. 4 = I², 490, n. 5). See Leisegang, col. 2367.

3. Cf. *Clitophon* 409c with *Republic* 336D; cf. *Clitophon* 410B with *Republic* 335D, and 410D 8 with 331A *et seq.* See Grube, pp. 304f. This demonstration is independent of the question whether the *Clitophon* was written by Plato or by a member of his circle. / Stefanini (I², 201ff., 292ff.) considers the *Clitophon* as written by Plato before the *Thrasymachus*.

4. Arnim, p. 73. In general, Arnim's whole section about the *Thrasymachus* should be consulted.

5. Arnold Toynbee, *A Study of History* (abridged edn., New York and London, 1946), p. 479. / About the festival of Bendis in the Piraeus,

see E. R. Curtius, *Kritische Essays zur europäischen Literatur* (Bern, 1950), p. 372.

6. This function justifies their existence. One hardly has a right to say (with Bruns, p. 322) that they were brought into Book I in order to play the role of interlocutors in Book II. Rather they are used in Book II as a consequence of their necessary presence in Book I.

7. Cicero, *Epistolarum ad Atticum* IV 16, 3 : . . . *deus ille noster Plato*. . . . *Credo Platonem vix putasse satis consonum fore, si hominem id aetatis in tam longo sermone diutius retinuisset*. Cf. J. T. Kakrides, "The Part of Cephalus in Plato's *Republic*," *Eranos*, XLVI (1948), 35ff.

8. *Republic* 421E ; *Laws* 679B, 728E. On what follows see Aristotle, *Politics* VII 4 1325b 37, VII 11 1331b 41.

9. Cf. Arnim, p. 101.

10. James Adam (*The "Republic" of Plato* [Cambridge, 1902]), commenting on 335B, writes : "This chapter contains the only element of permanent ethical interest and value in the discussion with Polemarchus." This judgment is based on the confusion of a Platonic dialogue with a manual.

11. τοῦ ἀγαθοῦ in 335D 7 is the genitive of ὁ ἀγαθός (cf. 335D 1 and 9), not of τὸ ἀγαθόν, as Arnim, p. 102, seems to assume. And yet he was quite correct in detecting the nearness of the *Agathon*.

12. Cf. G. M. A. Grube, "Thrasymachus . . ." in *AJP*, LXXIII (1952), 251. The judgment that "Plato's . . . unforgettable picture has remained unchallenged" must be restricted when we think of the Plato-hostile criticism in Athenaeus XI 505CD : διαβάλλει δὲ ὁ Πλάτων καὶ Θρασύμαχον τὸν Χαλκηδόνιον σοφιστὴν ὅμοιον εἶναι τῷ ὀνόματι. How Plato often plays a serious game with proper names is shown, for example, in *Protagoras* 316A, *Phaedo* 80D *et seq.*, *Theages* 122D, and in many passages of the *Cratylus*. On this see also p. 67, above, and *Platon, Gastmahl, Phaidros*, translated with an introduction by E. Salin (Basel, 1952), pp. 22ff. In this respect Plato follows a widespread Greek tradition : in Aristotle, *Rhetoric* II 23 1400b 16 *et seq.*, such a word play is a form of the enthymeme.

13. Aristotle, *Nicomachean Ethics* V 3–4, defines the ways of using the word δικαιοσύνη. In the broader sense (he says) δικαιοσύνη = ἀρετή. In the narrower sense its field is περὶ τιμὴν ἢ χρήματα ἢ σωτηρίαν . . . καὶ δι' ἡδονὴν τὴν ἀπὸ τοῦ κέρδους. The broader usage is almost that of the Platonic Socrates; the narrower one is the only sense known to Polemarchos.

14. *Republic* 420B : οὐ μὴν πρὸς τοῦτο βλέποντες τὴν πόλιν οἰκίζομεν, ὅπως ἕν τι ἡμῖν ἔθνος ἔσται διαφερόντως εὔδαιμον, ἀλλ' ὅπως ὅτι μάλιστα ὅλη ἡ πόλις. The difference between usefulness and eudaemonia may here be ignored.

15. Wilamowitz (II, 182ff.) has shown that the intervention of Glaukon (347A–348B) is part of the revision, because the thesis concerning

the compulsion to rule neither grows out of the discussion nor finds its completion in the *Thrasymachus*. It is introduced only by the contrast of the rule-loving tyrant and is not picked up again until Book VII, to which specific reference is made. Here, too, is the only hint at the founding of the ideal state: 347D. But this is not enough. The whole section, at least from 345E on, is a unit. The motif οὐδεὶς ἐθέλει ἄρχειν ἑκών already emerges. Whether or not the beginning of this speech of Socrates is part of the original dialogue is uncertain. He does, to be sure, refer to the beginning of the speech of Thrasymachos; he says nothing new, however, as is expressly noted (ἔτι γὰρ τὰ ἔμπροσθεν ἐπισκεψώμεθα, 345BC), but merely repeats what was discussed previously. So the whole section 345B–348B must be assigned to the revision; yet, it must remain doubtful whether there are still pieces of the original construction at the beginning and the end of this section—which is marked off clearly. One such piece is perhaps the remark in 348AB: that there is no point in setting one speech against the other; that a decision can be achieved only dialectically—ἀνομολογούμενοι σκοπῶμεν.

16. The correspondence with *Protagoras* 333D is still closer than that with *Gorgias* 474C. This agrees with the view—widely accepted today—of the place the *Thrasymachus* has in Plato's work.

17. It is possible that this passage was only introduced into the great work of the *Republic*, i.e., following the *Gorgias*. It is just as possible, however, that starting from here the figure of Polos in the *Gorgias* was developed.

18. When Zeller (II/1, 605) says that the lucidity of the thought, correct in itself, is impaired by the ambiguous use of πλεονεκτεῖν, the standard of judgment is the lucidity of the textbook. Plato, however, understood how to probe much deeper with such ambiguity than he could have done with lucidity.

19. In this section which leads to the correspondence between *polis* and individual soul, several things might be part of the revision. There can be no proof of it. Cf. the general remark of Wilamowitz, II, 184. On the subject matter, see H. Fuchs, *Augustin und der antike Friedensgedanke* (Berlin, 1926), pp. 117ff.

20. On the whole, the precise structure of the dialogue and the way its conclusion corresponds to the conclusions of the aporetic dialogues make it difficult to think, as Wilamowitz (II, 185) does, that at its ending any amount might have been cut off or altered.

iv: *Charmides*

RECENT EDITIONS AND TRANSLATIONS: A. Croiset, *Platon Budé*, II (1921);
O. Apelt, PhB 177 (2d edn., 1922); H. N. Fowler and W. R. M.
Lamb, Loeb VIII (1927); G. Ammendola (Naples, 1930); E. Tu-
rolla (Venice, 1945); E. Salin (Basel, 1950).

RECENT INTERPRETATIONS: H. Rick, "Der Dialog *Charmides*," *Archiv für
Geschichte der Philosophie*, XXIV (1916), 211ff.; G. M. Sciacca,
"Il *Carmide* e la ricerca d'un oggetto per la filosofia," *RSF*, V (1950),
103ff.; A. Masaracchia, "Il *Carmide* di Platone," *Maia*, III (1950),
161ff.; T. G. Tuckey, *Plato's "Charmides"* (Cambridge, 1951), pp.
35ff., Appen. II, III.

ADDITIONAL BIBLIOGRAPHY: Shorey, p. 478; Geffcken, Notes, p. 48; Rosenmeyer, p. 178; Cherniss, *Lustrum*, pp. 74f.

1. This perfect endowment, then, is not "quite unessential" to the dialogue, as Pohlenz says (p. 43). But Plato, much as he condemned the
   domestic policy of 404, undoubtedly took the side of his uncle by
   making him a speaker.
2. G. J. de Vries, "Σωφροσύνη en Grec classique," *Mnemosyne*, n.s., XI
   (1943), 81ff.
3. It is possible but not necessary that Kritias himself said so in one of
   his writings (*Vorsokr.* 88 [81] B 41a).
4. Cf. V. Ehrenberg, "Polypragmosyne: A Study in Greek Politics,"
   JHS, LXVII (1947), 46ff. Cf. J. Mehwaldt, *Tübinger Beiträge*, V
   (1929), 86ff. / A. E. Raubitschek, "Ein neues Pittakeion," *WienStud*,
   LXXI (1958), 70ff.
5. E.g., *Phaedo* 82B, *Protagoras* 323B. Cf. Pavlu, *Dissertationes Vindo-
   bonenses*, VIII (1905), 35; *DGrA*, II, 21. Cf. also Gomperz (II, 307)
   who, however, reads into τὰ ἑαυτοῦ πράττειν our economic concept
   of the division of labor.
6. Cf. Eckert, p. 75. It is doubtful how far John Dewey, "The Socratic
   Dialogues of Plato" [II⁵], 19, is right in seeing "a kinship of Critias
   with the Cyrenaic School."
7. At the end of our discussion it will be evident why ἡ τῶν ἀγαθῶν πρᾶξις
   must not be counted as a new definition.
8. Cf. 165E 1 with 166c 3. Pohlenz, p. 53, calls this a fallacy. Arnim
   speaks of the perplexing identification of two entirely different things
   (p. 111) and of a crude fallacy (p. 117). Stenzel, *Studien*, p. 11, thinks
   it is "logically dubious." Yet there is no intentional deception here—
   just as this difference is nowhere cleared up, not even by a hint—and
   still less is there any unintentional deception. We must set aside our

present-day concept of self-knowledge and instead think of an insight
into the objective structure of the soul and the order of rank within it.
Then, when Socrates knows himself (ἑαυτόν), it is at the same time
the knowledge which makes itself (ἑαυτήν) its own object. Cf. Schleiermacher, I/2, 6.

9. Cf. P. Friedländer, *GGA*, 1931, pp. 250ff.

10. Arnim, pp. 123ff., has called particular attention to the relationship
with the *Euthydemus*.

11. The contrast between Bonitz, pp. 243ff., who thinks that the concept
of self-knowledge is definitively refuted in the *Charmides*, and Natorp,
p. 24, who does not take this refutation seriously, is not as sharp as
it appears: self-knowledge is both overcome and integrated into the
knowledge of the good. Pohlenz, pp. 48ff., emphasizes that the negative outcome of the dialogue must be explained in terms of the criticism of somebody else's view. Now it is possible that the definition
of *sophrosyne* as some form of self-knowledge was proposed by someone else, say, in the group around Socrates. Yet for Plato the concept
of self-knowledge was important enough to be put forth by himself
as well, and integrated into something higher. One must, to be sure,
accept the *Alcibiades Major* as genuine in order to see the concept
with the degree of clarity Plato intends—quite remote from what
people today call self-knowledge in subjective terms. Only this
modern kind of self-knowledge is affected by Goethe's well-known
opposition ("Gespräche mit Eckermann" [April 10 and 12, 1829];
"Gespräche mit Kanzler Müller" [March 8, 1824]).

12. Cf. *Meno* 84B 5 *et seq.* and 85c 6 *et seq.*

13. Natorp, p. 23: "the last definition, the only one treated seriously. . . ."
Bonitz pays attention to nothing but this part. Arnim, p. 111: "the
main weight of the entire dialogue, the principal intention. . . ."

14. Cf. Stenzel, *Studien*, pp. 11f.

15. *Alcibiades Major* 131A *et seq.* makes it clear that in the *Charmides* it is
not enough to connect πράττειν τὰ ἑαυτοῦ and γνῶναι ἑαυτόν, but that
γνῶναι has as its objects both ἑαυτόν and τὰ ἑαυτοῦ. For in the *Alcibiades* the steps are: ἑαυτόν, τὰ ἑαυτοῦ, τὰ τῶν ἑαυτοῦ. So in *Timaeus* 72A,
to be sure, only πράττειν belongs with τὰ ἑαυτοῦ, but both objects
belong with γνῶναι. Natorp, p. 23, calls attention to the *Timaeus*
passage (and to *Theaetetus* 210c: σωφρόνως οὐκ οἰόμενος εἰδέναι ἃ μὴ
οἶσθα).

16. E.g., *Gorgias* 491D; *Phaedo* 68c; *Symposium* 196c; *Republic* IV 430E;
Phaedrus 237D *et seq.* Especially notable is *Laws* IV 710A: a contrast
is expressly made between the δημώδης σωφροσύνη and that of
the *Charmides*, ἥν τις σεμνύνων ἂν λέγοι, φρόνησιν προσαναγκάζων εἶναι τὸ σωφρονεῖν.

17. Socher, p. 133, observed the fact and used it to reject the *Charmides*
as spurious.

v : *Euthyphro*

RECENT EDITIONS AND TRANSLATIONS : M. Croiset, *Platon Budé*, I (1920);
H. N. Fowler, Loeb I (1923); J. Burnet (Oxford, 1924); J. Adam
(Cambridge, 1934); R. Guardini (Bern, 1945); G. Schneider, PhB
178 (3d edn., 1945); R. Rufener and G. Krüger (Zurich, 1948);
E. Salin (Basel, 1950); L. G. van der Wal (Groningen, 1951); P.
Rossi (Milan, 1951); G. C. Field and W. D. Woodhead (Edinburgh,
1953).

RECENT INTERPRETATIONS : Hildebrandt, pp. 116ff.; R. Guardini, *Der Tod
des Sokrates* (Bern, 1945; 4th edn., Munich, 1952); R. Stark, "Platons
Dialog *Euthyphron*," *Ann. Univ. Saraviensis*, I (1952), 144ff.; O.
Gigon, *Platons "Euthyphron"* (Westöstliche Abhandlungen, Wies-
baden, 1954), pp. 6ff.; M. Fox, "The Trials of Socrates: An Interpretation of the First Tetralogy," *AfP*, VI (1956), 226ff.; M. Phili-
bert, "Euthyphron," *Revue d'histoire et de philosophie religieuses*, XXXVI
(1956), 136ff.; Gallo Galli, "Saggio sull' *Eutifrone* di Platone," *Estudios . . . al Prof. R. Mondolfo* (Tucuman, 1957), pp. 169ff.; R. G.
Hoerber, "Plato's *Euthyphro*," *Phronesis*, III (1958), 95ff.; W. G.
Rabinowitz, "Platonic Piety: An Essay towards the Solution of an
Enigma," *Phronesis*, III (1958), 108ff.

ADDITIONAL BIBLIOGRAPHY : Shorey, p. 456; Geffcken, Notes, p. 50; Rosenmeyer, p. 179; Cherniss, *Lustrum*, pp. 96f.

1. Before the loss of Naxos in 404 B.C. Cf. Martin Schanz, *Erklärende
    Ausgabe des "Euthyphron"* (Leipzig, 1887), p. 10; Wilamowitz, II,
    76. / Olof Gigon, *Platons "Euthyphron"* (Wiesbaden, 1954), p. 22:
    "The crime of Euthyphron's father shrinks to a minimum." "The
    father did not care any more for him [the laborer], and it was not his
    duty. For, according to antique custom convicts had to be taken care
    of by their own relatives." But how are matters if the laborer who
    had been brought over from Attica had no relatives on the island of
    Naxos ? And was it permissible for the father to throw the prisoner
    into a ditch and there abandon him with hands and feet tied—and in
    the meanwhile to inquire in Athens how he should handle the prisoner ?
    Plato wants to make clear: the laborer commits a crime; Euthyphron's
    father acts criminally, though seemingly according to law; and Eu-
    thyphron does something that is in contrast to all morals. This one
    case suffices to show that a detailed debate with Gigon would fill
    many pages.

2. The view that the apologetic purpose begot the dialogue (Wilamowitz, I, 205 = I², 208) or that it swallowed up, to a high degree, the ethic-dialectic design (Schleiermacher, I/2, 53) does not hit the mark. Apologetics, for Socrates, is everywhere or nowhere, and to single out this purpose disturbs the wholeness of the philosophic work of art. It is not even certain that the *Apology* is apologetic.

3. Gigon, op. cit., p. 14: "Socrates hardly knows what kind of lawsuit is in question here." On the contrary, Socrates knows exactly that Euthyphron wrongly calls the lawsuit a δίκη, that it is in fact a γραφή.

4. Cf. Singer, p. 28.

5. Gigon, op. cit., p. 15, finds here "an inconsistency that can hardly be denied"; in his opinion, Plato has Meletos and Euthyphron both appear as youthful ἀλαζόνες lacking respect for old age; still Euthyphron is Socrates' sincere and understanding friend. But does not Plato want to characterize just the unsteadiness of the apparently so steady Euthyphron?

6. Zeller, II/1, 525; Bonitz, p. 241; Wilamowitz, I, 205 = I², 208; II, 79f. If Socrates wants to use the ἰδέα of the ὅσιον as a παράδειγμα in order to determine what should be called a ὅσιον, then the single ὅσιον must be determined by that prototype and must be "similar" to it. So much against Zeller. Wilamowitz claims that the ἰδέα "is not detached from the single phenomenon, does not belong to another sphere." But the confrontation is unmistakable all the same, if we are to measure the one by the other. What is lacking is at bottom only the mythical speech of the τόπος νοητός. Cf. Shorey, *Unity*, p. 32: "The realistic language used in the definition of the *Euthyphro* must be presumed to imply what a similar terminology does elsewhere." Cf. also Freymann, pp. 42ff.; Grube, p. 8; Robin, p. 101; Arnim, p. 142; Galli, "Saggio sull' *Eutifrone* di Platone," *Estudios . . . Mondolfo* (Tucuman, 1957), pp. 188f.; Classen, pp. 43ff.

7. Bonitz, p. 241; Natorp, p. 38, n. 1.

8. Cf. Grube, p. 152.

9. Gomperz (II, 365) claims to see a logical violence in this subordination. One will not master the difficulty if one follows Bonitz in translating δικαιοσύνη by a rather colorless "morality"; one should look sharply at the politico-legal factor.

10. Schanz, *Erklärende Ausgabe des "Euthyphron"* [V¹], p. 8, emphasizes the "captiousness." There is, then, all the more cause for inquiring into the reason.

11. Bonitz, p. 234, is right in referring here to the *Timaeus* and the *Republic* and in suggesting that it is ultimately the ἰδέα τοῦ ἀγαθοῦ that is aimed at. But the whole matter is treated in a moralizing manner if piety is equated with "perfect morality." This fails to see the sublimity of the *Agathon* and its *epekeina*. Cf. also Wilamowitz, II, 78f.: here the regime of the gods in the *Euthyphro* is opposed with too much

theology and dogmatism to the "neutral *Idea* of the Good" in the *Republic*, as if the latter had supplanted the former.

12. 15E 7, τῆς πρὸς Μέλητον γραφῆς, repeats the phrase τῆς γραφῆς τῆς πρὸς Μέλητον at 5A 4. Strictly speaking, this must be distinguished from ἡ Μελήτου γραφή. It is "the brief *against* Meletos" in which Socrates must defend himself against "the written indictment *of* Meletos." Here, too, the emphasis is on Socrates as an active agent.

VI : *Lysis*

RECENT EDITIONS AND TRANSLATIONS : A. Croiset, *Platon Budé*, II (1921); O. Apelt, PhB 177 (2d edn., 1922); H. N. Fowler and W. R. M. Lamb, Loeb V (1925); J. Crexells (Barcelona, 1926); K. A. Matthews (London, 1930); C. Diano (Bari, 1934); G. Ammendola (Naples, 1936); E. Turolla (Venice, 1945); E. Salin (Basel, 1950); M. Verbruggen (Antwerp, 1954); X. de Win (Antwerp, 1955).

RECENT INTERPRETATIONS : H. von Arnim, "Platons *Lysis*," *RhM*, LXXI (1916), 364ff.; Hildebrandt, pp. 105ff.; K. Glaser, "Gang und Ergebnis des platonischen *Lysis*," *WienStud*, LIII (1935), 47ff.; R. G. Hoerber, "Character Portrayal in Plato's *Lysis*," *CJ*, XLI (1945/46), 271ff.; Gallo Galli, *Due studi di filosofia greca* (Turin, 1950); A. Levi, "La teoria della *philia* nel *Liside*," *Giorn. di Metafisica*, V (1950), 285ff.; A. W. Begemann, *Platons "Lysis"* (Amsterdam, 1960).

ADDITIONAL BIBLIOGRAPHY : Shorey, p. 487; Geffcken, Notes, p. 46; Rosenmeyer, p. 182; Cherniss, *Lustrum*, p. 114.

1. See *Plato* 1, pp. 159f.
2. Cf. K. Glaser, "Gang und Ergebnis des platonischen *Lysis*," *WienStud*, LIII (1935), 47ff. Arnim, pp. 65ff., denies that this protreptic conversation has any special significance for the main part of the dialogue. A similar view is found in Taylor, p. 67. This seems as little acceptable as when the description of the environment is detached as "accoutrement" and the claim is made "that it has no necessary inner connection with the philosophic content of the dialogue" (Arnim, p. 69). Is it not the task of interpretation to seek these connections? Pohlenz, *GGA*, 1916, p. 259, is right. / If this chapter is full of polemical remarks against Arnim, this means that it is especially instructive to debate with him, the most sagacious among the more recent interpreters of Plato. See also Arnim, "Platons *Lysis*," *RhM*, LXXI (1916), 364ff.
3. Cf. Steinhart, I, 224; Eckert, pp. 85ff.; Arnim, pp. 42ff.; Glaser, op. cit. [VI²], pp. 50ff.

4. In order to appreciate the paradox of the statement that the "bad ones" can have no friendship, one should read Herodotus III 82, where he says of democracy: ἔχθεα μὲν οὐκ ἐγγίνεται τοῖσι κακοῖσι, φιλίαι δὲ ἰσχυραί· οἱ γὰρ κακοῦντες τὰ κοινὰ συγκύψαντες ποιεῦσι.

5. Stenzel, p. 240—without mentioning the *Lysis* but alluding to it— speaks of "coming to an understanding with *one's like*, who yet are *others.*"

6. Arnim sees here the germ of the doctrine of the *parousia* of the *Idea*. See also Steinhart, I, 267, n. 28. It is primarily a phenomenological analysis of παρουσία.

7. Arnim, p. 52, says it is not proved but assumed as obvious that a final cause must be present. True, it is no proof, but it is no assumption either. The φίλον is seen in the actual fullness of its relations. Hence, the prior question (218D): πότερόν ἐστίν τῷ φίλος ἢ οὔ;

8. The debate as to whether the "doctrine of *Ideas*" is developed here, or whether it is presented in its germinal state, or whether it is not yet present at all, has no meaning for one who cannot work with these expressions of a dogmatizing interpretation of Plato. Nobody can fail to recognize that Plato, when he wrote this, knew the way and the goal. Cf. Arnim, p. 53; Freymann, p. 61.

9. Arnim's view, p. 53, that Plato regarded this formula as "monstrous," as is shown by the mocking manner with which it is introduced, is only half correct. With Plato, irony does not exclude but rather points to the fact that "there is something to this." And even if one accepts the word "monstrous," that still does not entail a value judgment. In this kind of discussion, the fact that something "is proved to be inconclusive" does not mean it is worthless. When Arnim, p. 50, concludes that, because both *causa efficiens* and *causa finalis* "are shown by the further inquiry to be meaningless," these amplifications were not approved by Plato himself, but instead stemmed from the view of another philosopher whom Plato wants to refute, that seems to me to rest upon a fundamental misunderstanding of this dialectic. It is not a question of statements that Plato approves and others that he disapproves. A thesis shows something, and for that reason it is introduced. But it shows too much or too little, and for that reason it is refuted. Nor is it correct to see in the "refuted" statements "love-theories of Plato's philosophic colleagues." On this matter Singer, p. 34, is sound.

10. Incidentally, it is another sophistic trick, when (220E 4) ἐχθροῦ ἕνεκα takes the place of the previously demonstrated διά τι. Cf. Steinhart, I, 268, n. 31.

11. Cf. *Plato* 1, ch. II.

12. Here Arnim, p. 59, finds "the only place in the *Lysis* where (apart from the introduction, which is merely dramatic setting) reference is made to the love of boys. It is outside the inquiry proper and is merely a casual jest, justified by the dramatic setting." But such a mere set-

ting simply does not exist in Plato. This passage, far from standing outside the inquiry proper, touches upon the most important matter— as is shown by the reference to the γνήσιος ἐραστής, i.e., Socrates himself.

13. Arnim, p. 60, puts a gap before 222c 3, because the *Agathon* should not emerge too suddenly and hence must previously "be introduced into the inquiry." But the ἀγαθός and the ἀγαθόν have been in the center of vision since the beginning of the third conversation, and with increasing emphasis. The word οἰκεῖον may mean both "fitting" and "related to" something, of whatever kind. Both possibilities are tried out; neither one needs to be prepared for. To show that οἰκεῖον could have the meaning of the fitting, the lexicons cite Herodotus III 81: οὔτε εἶδε καλὸν οὐδὲν οὐδ' οἰκήιον. So the equation οἰκεῖον = ἀγαθόν was most easily derived from linguistic usage. For this reason alone Arnim's attempt (p. 64) to take the passage from the *Charmides* (163cD) as a quotation from the *Lysis* must be rejected.

14. Arnim's reference to φόμεθα ἐξελέγξαι deserves serious consideration. If then two "dogmas" are presented as the philosophic "yield" of the inquiry carried on in the second part of the *Lysis*, there certainly is something valid in all that; in the very word "dogmas," however, there is something that threatens to destroy the dialectic movement of the dialogue.

15. This kinship is emphasized by Schleiermacher (I/1, 173ff.) with the chronological sequence *Phaedrus, Lysis, Symposium,* and later by Pohlenz, pp. 370f. The *Lysis* is seen as satellite of the *Symposium* by Gomperz (II, 383). The *Lysis* contains the critical complement of the *Symposium* for the doctrine of the φίλον: Ferdinand Dümmler, *Akademika* (Giessen, 1889), p. 187. The correct arrangement, with considerable lapse of time between the *Lysis* and the *Symposium*, is arrived at by Robin, *Théorie de l'amour,* p. 55. The *Lysis* is seen as a prelude to the Eros-doctrine of the *Symposium* by Barth, p. 25, n. 1.

16. "Brotherly resemblance": Hermann, p. 443. "Twin brothers": Arnim, pp. 69ff. "Twin dialogue": Wilamowitz, I, 187 = I[2], 189. Any questioning of Arnim's dating would have to be supported by reasons entirely different from the alleged "development" of Platonic "doctrines."

17. Similarly, Ueberweg-Praechter, pp. 238f. Cf. also Robin, *Théorie de l'amour,* p. 55, and Taylor, p. 64.

18. Cf. Steinhart, I, 232, *contra* Hermann, who designates the friendship of the *Lysis* as something basically different from the love in the *Phaedrus*. The discussion that follows here in the text is directed primarily against Arnim.

19. Cf. Raeder, pp. 153ff.; Barth, p. 25; Robin, *Théorie de l'amour,* pp. 49f.; Guido Calogero, *Il Simposio*[2] (Bari, 1946), pp. 24ff.; Glaser, "Gang und Ergebnis des platonischen *Lysis*" [VI[2]], pp. 53ff.; Grube, pp. 90ff.

VII : *Hippias Major*

RECENT EDITIONS AND TRANSLATIONS: O. Apelt, PhB 172a (2d edn., 1921);
A. Croiset, *Platon Budé*, II (1921); H. N. Fowler, Loeb VI (1926);
D. Tarrant (Cambridge, 1928); J. D. García Bacca (Mexico, 1945).

RECENT INTERPRETATIONS: Apelt, pp. 203ff.; D. Tarrant, "On the *Hippias
Maior*," *JPhilos*, XXXV (1920), 319ff.; G. M. A. Grube, "On the
Authenticity of the *Hippias Major*," *CQ*, XX (1926), 134ff.; D. Tar-
rant, "The Authorship of *Hippias Major*," *CQ*, XXI (1927), 82ff.;
G. M. A. Grube, "The Logic and Language of the *Hippias Major*,"
CP (1929), 369ff.; J. Moreau, "Le Platonisme de l'*Hippias Majeur*,"
RevÉtGr, LIV (1941), 19ff.; J. Pavlu, "Der pseudoplatonische *Grös-
sere Hippias*," *WienStud*, LIX (1941), 35ff.; É. de Strycker, "De Irra-
tionalen in den *Hippias Maior*," *Antiquité Classique*, X (1941), 25ff.;
M. Soreth, *Der platonische Dialog "Hippias Major"* (Munich, 1953);
O. Gigon, *Gnomon*, XXVII (1955), 14ff.; R. G. Hoerber, "Plato's
Hippias Major," *CJ*, L (1955), 183ff.; Annemarie Capelle, "Plato-
nisches im *Grösseren Hippias*," *RhM*, IC (1956), 178ff.; G. E. Mueller,
"Unity of the Platonic *Hippias Major*," *CB*, XXXII (1956), 37ff.

ADDITIONAL BIBLIOGRAPHY: Shorey, p. 472; Geffcken, Notes, p. 40; Rosenmeyer, p. 180; Cherniss, *Lustrum*, p. 100.

1. See the survey in D. Tarrant, *The "Hippias Major" Attributed to Plato*
(Cambridge, 1928), pp. xff. This book is the most extensive attempt
to prove the dialogue as un-Platonic. Genuineness of the dialogue is
recently affirmed by G. M. A. Grube, *CQ*, XX (1926), 134ff.; *CP*,
XXIV (1929), 369ff.; Freymann, pp. 49ff.; Goldschmidt, pp. 36ff.;
Ross, p. 3; M. Soreth, *Der platonische Dialog "Hippias Major"* (Munich, 1953); A. Capelle, *RhM*, IC (1956), 178ff.; Shorey, p. 91 (with
reservations). Its genuineness is denied by Pohlenz, *Gnomon*, VII
(1931), 300ff.; A. K. Rogers, *The Socratic Problem* (New Haven,
Conn., 1933), Appen. B; H. N. Fowler (Loeb edn.); J. Pavlu, *Wien-
Stud*, LIX (1941), 35ff.; O. Gigon, *Sokrates. Sein Bild in Dichtung
und Geschichte* (Bern, 1947), p. 264; Hoffmann, pp. 126ff.; Gauss, I/2,
207f. (in the *Hippias Major* "any reasonable logical sequence is lacking"). Wilamowitz (II, p. 325, n. 1) considers the use of the word
μέρμερος in 290E 4 to be "an unmistakable stigma." Jachmann, p. 276,
agrees. Is it not rather a very appropriate, and forcible, word from
poetry? The ill-fated κρήγυος in *Alcibiades* 111E is a suitable analogy;
see *DGrA*, II, 6ff. See Gigon's careful analysis and comments on the

question of genuineness in *Gnomon*, XXVII (1955), 14ff. / Note-worthy is the edition by Juan David García Bacca, *Obras completas de Platón*, "*Hipias Mayor*," "*Fedro*" (Mexico, 1945). In the "Intro-ducción Filosófica" to the *Hippias*, the "*plan ontológico*" of Socrates and the "*plan óntico concreto*" of Hippias are contrasted, whereupon this strange judgment is given (p. xxv): "*Sócrates—non calumniemos, dígase Platón—no entendió jamás estotro plan finito y plurál*" (i.e., of Hippias).

2. Bruns, pp. 348f., misjudges the meaning of the introductory scene, considering it a contribution to "cultural history." He also misses the organic connection between "scenery" and "scientific content."

3. Pohlenz (p. 125; and *Gnomon*, VII [1931], 305) sees a sign of late origin in the fact that Anaxagoras is named among the παλαιοί. But the words καὶ ἔτι τῶν ὕστερον μέχρι Ἀναξαγόρου show clearly that Anaxagoras is *not* considered by the author to be one of the "old ones." Nor is this affected by 283A, where Anaxagoras is one of the πρότεροι but (despite καὶ περὶ ἄλλων τῶν παλαιῶν) not one of the παλαιοί. / R. Walzer, "Magna Moralia," *Neue phil. Unters.*, VII (1929), 190, tries to fit the passage of the "pseudo-Platonic Hippias" into his construction of the historical changes of the Seven Sages. But what if the *Hippias* is genuine and belongs to Plato's earlier period?

4. This lecture then (ὑποτιθέμενος, 286B 3) belongs in the series of the "Hypothekai," which has been discussed in *Hermes*, XLVIII (1913), 558ff. With the poetic productions of this kind it shares their mytho-logical dress, and with the works of Demokritos and Isokrates their prose form.

5. At the beginning of this critique (288A 6), the personal distribution in the text must be altered thus: ΣΩ. Εἶεν. ΙΠ. Πάνυ μὲν οὖν. ΣΩ. Φέρε δή. ... This follows from a comparison with *Symposium* 206E 6–7 and *Hip-pias Major* 289A 1, 289A 7–8. Εἶεν is a somewhat hesitant assent, πάνυ μὲν οὖν a very animated one.

6. "A kind of anticipation of the doctrine of *Ideas*," Apelt, p. 230; Ross, p. 17. For an opposite view, see G. M. A. Grube, "Plato's Theory of Beauty," *The Monist*, XXXVII (1927), 272; the *Hippias Major* (he says) makes no use of the theory of *Ideas*. In agreement with the *Euthy-phro* is not only the *Eidos* terminology but also the contrast of οὐσία and πάθος (*Euthyphro* 11A, *Hippias Major* 301B); Pohlenz, p. 127, and *Gnomon*, VII (1931), 306; Tarrant, op. cit. [VII¹], p. LXI. Even earlier, R. Hirzel, "Οὐσία," *Philologus* (1913), 57, uses this contrast as an argument—probably not justified—for the late origin of the *Hippias Major*. Diès, pp. 289f., is correct. It is usually not observed that the muddle-headed Hippias says ἢ πάθος ἢ οὐσίαν (301B 8), as if there were no distinction. One is supposed to notice that he has picked up these technical terms somewhere or other. Socrates, on the other

hand, distinguishes between the two concepts: οὐσία is the essence of the beautiful (302c 5); πάθος is the manifestation of the beautiful (302ε 6).

7. On the textual criticism of this passage, see the chapter on the *Phaedo* in *Plato 3*.

8. This is a current meaning of προσγίγνεσθαι. *Republic* I 346D 7: ἐὰν μισθὸς προσγίγνηται. *Letter VI* 322D 2: χρυσοῦ προσγενομένου.

9. Apelt, p. 212. One must consider the *Alcibiades* spurious (see 135B 13) in order to prove as Pohlenz does (p. 126) that this correlation between καλόν and πρέπον is unique in Plato's early writings.

10. In contrast, e.g., to Apelt, I do not count these two definitions as two separate sections of the dialogue, since in 296DE one is clearly given as a more precise version of the other.

11. "A reminiscence": Tarrant, *The "Hippias Major" Attributed to Plato* [VII¹], p. 69, on *Hippias Major* 297B.

12. On the concept of the αἴτιον and this entire passage Apelt, p. 214, is illuminating.

13. Cf. Apelt, p. 218, n. 2. (But when Apelt says that in the *Hippias* "the beautiful" is to be taken throughout in an ethical sense, that is narrowing the concept in an un-Greek and un-Platonic sense.) Olof Gigon, *Gnomon*, XXVII (1955), 20, thinks it is "crass arbitrariness" when in 298D 3–5 an essential objection is thrust aside. Is it not evident, on the contrary, that the objection fulfills its function by making us see that the definition is criticized because it is much too narrow?

14. *Topics* VI 146ᵃ 21 *et seq*. The fact that Aristotle does not expressly mention the *Hippias Major* is regarded by Pohlenz, p. 126, and Tarrant, op. cit. [VII¹], p. IX, as an argument for its spuriousness. It will be more correct to assume that Aristotle—as often is the case—does not quote the title of a Platonic dialogue that he has before him. The small formal deviation (ἤ instead of τε καί) is no argument against it. Cf. Cherniss, 25, n. 19; Ross, p. 4.

15. According to Apelt, pp. 216, 221, the second definition is the positively Platonic one, a view which he finds confirmed because the definition recurs at the end of the dialogue. One should, instead, find the answer hovering dialectically between all the fixed points set down by Plato.

16. Dümmler, *Akademika* [VI¹⁵], p. 204, rightly referring to *Sophist* 246BC, makes the reading σώματα certain—which probably means the robust and palpable objects (the "beautiful girl" and the "gold") and not, as Dümmler thinks, "the continuous, god-inspired matter of Ionian physics." Apelt, p. 231, on the other hand, who scores this weakness of Dümmler's interpretation, has destroyed the crude physical sense of Plato's expression by conjecturing σχήματα for σώματα. To be sure, διανεκεῖ λόγῳ τῆς οὐσίας καθ' Ἱππίαν (301ε 3) does refer back to it, but it means "the corporeal, coarsely material concept of

being"; διανεκής in this case pertains not only to λόγῳ but to λόγῳ τῆς οὐσίας (cf. Wilamowitz' commentary on verse 468, in *Euripides' Herakles*[2] [2 vols., Berlin, 1895], II). / The construction proposed by Grube, *CQ*, XX (1926), 147, "that such large bodies of being are also by nature continuous," separates the two closely connected adjectives. / On this section of the dialogue, cf. Diès, pp. 187ff. / According to Gigon, *Gnomon*, XXVII (1955), 20, the criticism of Hippias in 301B 2–7 and 304A 4–6 is understandable only if Plato " 'is quoting' something or other." Let us emphasize once more that the reference to an *x* outside the dialogue never can take the place of an interpretation from within the dialogue itself.

17. Schleiermacher, II/3, 409.

18. Dümmler, *Akademika*, p. 51, asserting that the *Hippias Major* is "a most valuable critical supplement to the speech of Diotima," tries to bring out the same correspondences to which we have frequently referred. / Bruns, p. 347, objects to the "un-Platonic" feature that Socrates concludes with mild irony, without humiliating the opponent. For a similar view, see Wilamowitz, II, 327. Has not the *Alcibiades Major* been rejected just because of Socrates' rudeness (*DGrA*, II, 33f.)? And what of the humbling of Euthyphron or Thrasymachos, for example, at the end of those dialogues? And is not the certain Somebody in the *Hippias* rude enough?

VIII: *Hipparchus*

RECENT EDITIONS AND TRANSLATIONS: H. N. Fowler and W. R. M. Lamb, Loeb VIII (1927); G. Calogero (Florence, 1938); F. Novotny (Prague, 1938).

RECENT INTERPRETATIONS: J. Pavlu, *Die pseudoplatonischen Zwillingsdialoge "Minos" und "Hipparch"* (Vienna, 1910); E. Azzolini, *Ricerche sull' "Ipparco" attribuito a Platone* (Modena, 1916); M. Hirsch, "Die athenischen Tyrannenmörder in Geschichtsschreibung und Volkslegende," *Klio*, XX, n.f. II (1926), 129ff.; J. Papp, *Die Echtheit des Dialogs "Hipparchos"* (Szeged, 1936); G. Calogero, "L'autenticità dell' *Ipparco* platonico," *Annali della Scuola Normale di Pisa*, VII (1938), 13ff.

ADDITIONAL BIBLIOGRAPHY: Shorey, p. 660; Geffcken, Notes, p. 158; Cherniss, *Lustrum*, p. 99.

1. The genuineness of the *Hipparchus* has been defended strongly by Guido Calogero, "L'autenticità dell' *Ipparco* platonico," *Annali della*

Scuola Normale di Pisa, VII (1938), 13ff. and *Platone*, *"L'Ipparco"* (with introduction and commentary, Florence, 1938). Prior to him almost no one but Eckert, pp. 46ff., took this view. See also M. Hirsch in *Klio*, XX (1926), 155ff. The verbal and material arguments advanced against the genuineness of the *Hipparchus* have no compelling force. What Ast, p. 499 (partly following Schleiermacher), puts together follows the usual type of argumentation, according to which any agreements with writings of Plato are put down as "awkward borrowings," and any expressions that ostensibly or actually do not occur in Plato are called "un-Platonic." I have shown the value of this kind of criticism—which puts the author into a hopeless seesaw— by means of a lengthy example in *DGrA*, II, and I shall pay no further attention to it. The attempt of Wilamowitz (II, 415; cf. his commentary on *Menander's Schiedsgericht* [Berlin, 1925], p. 52) to assign the dialogue to the period of the New Comedy because of the form of address ὦ γλυκύτατε (227D) is based upon an error. For in the *Hipparchus* it is by no means that "widespread flattering address" of the New Comedy (where, incidentally, and probably with good reason, we find only the form γλυκύτατε without ὦ). Instead, it has a very specific sense quite like ὦ ἥδιστε in *Republic* I 348C, to which it is related, as is ὡς γλυκύς εἶ (*Hippias Major* 288B) to ὡς ἡδὺς εἶ (*Gorgias* 491E, *Euthydemus* 300A), or as is τὸ αὑτοῦ γλυκύ in *Phaedrus* 240A to the piled-up ἡδύ ἥδιστον ἡδονή which precede in a discussion where the ἡδονή is thematic. / Addressed to women, γλυκυτάτη and ὦ γλυκύτατον have a different ring, as in Aristophanes: T. Wendel, *Gesprächsanrede im griechischen Epos und Drama* (Stuttgart, 1929), p. 21. A similar case is ἁδίστα in Theocritus. / ὦ γλυκύτατε *Hipparchus*: γλυκύτατε Menander = ὦ ἥδιστε *Republic*: Τερεντιανὲ ἥδιστε in Περὶ ὕψους.

2. The view of Ast, p. 498.

3. Calogero, in his commentary to *L'Ipparco* [VIII¹], p. 3, agrees.

4. As to the *Hipparchus*, Eckert and M. Hirsch, op. cit. [VIII¹], have seen the main point correctly. As to the *Alcibiades*, see ch. XVII, pp. 236f., below.

5. *Topics* 146b 20 *et seq.*, *Politics* II 1263b 2 *et seq.* One thinks of *Hipparchus* 227C 7, πάντες αὖ φιλοκερδεῖς φαίνονται. An analogous consideration is found in Xenophon, *Memorabilia* III 14 2, regarding the word ὀψοφάγος with verbal suggestion of Plato and Aristotle: ἐσθίουσι μὲν γὰρ δὴ πάντες ἐπὶ τῷ σίτῳ ὄψον.

6. Thucydides II 44 (Perikles); Kritias, *Vorsokr.* 88 [81] B 15; Xenophon, *Oikonomikos* 14 10. Aristotle defines both human types as to similarity and difference: *Politics* V 1315ª 16, *Rhetoric* I 1361ª 39. In Xenophon's *Hieron* 7 3, φιλοτιμία is that which no animals possess and not even all men, but that which makes a human being truly a man.

7. For a dialogue of Herakleides Pontikos (frag. 88 Wehrli = Cicero,

Tusculanae Disputationes V 3), the Platonic view of three stages was put in the mouth of Pythagoras. It is mistaken to be Pythagorean by John Burnet, *Greek Philosophy* (London, 1914), I, 42. The right view is taken by Jaeger, *Aristotle*, p. 97, and *Paideia*, II, 268, 412.

8. How thoroughly the companion expresses the usual, psychologically justified view is shown by the agreement of ἥττους τοῦ κέρδους (225в 1) with Demokritos, *Vorsokr.* 68 [55] в 50: ὁ χρημάτων παντελῶς ἥσσων οὐκ ἄν ποτε εἴη δίκαιος.

9. κέρδος ... ζημία also in Demokritos, *Vorsokr.* 68 [55] в 220; Plato, *Laws* VIII 835в. This, then, was current usage. For the concept of ζημία as "damage" in general, not "atonement" in particular, see Anon. Jamblichi, *Vorsokr.* 89 [82] ch. 4, §3.

10. The sentence, Ἔστιν οὖν ὅτῳ ἀγαθόν ἐστι ζημιοῦσθαι (227A 2), might make us think for a moment of the paradox in the *Gorgias*, according to which ζημία in the sense of "punishment" is said to be useful to a person. But it cannot be proved that such an allusion is made here.

11. It is the ταυτότης of which Aristotle, *Metaphysics* V 9 1018ᵃ 7, says that it ἑνότης τίς ἐστιν πλειόνων τοῦ εἶναι.

12. 228D 4: ἦν τ' ἔμαθεν καὶ ἦν αὐτὸς ἐξηῦρεν. On this cf. *Protagoras* 320в 7: πολλὰ δὲ μεμαθηκέναι, τὰ δὲ αὐτὸν ἐξηυρηκέναι. *Cratylus* 428в 2: δοκεῖς γάρ μοι αὐτός τε ἐσκέφθαι τὰ τοιαῦτα καὶ παρ' ἄλλων μεμαθηκέναι. *Cratylus* 438в: ἢ ... μαθόντας ἢ αὐτοὺς ἐξευρόντας. *Alcibiades I* 106D 4: οὐκοῦν ταῦτα μόνον οἶσθα, ἃ παρ' ἄλλων ἔμαθες ἢ αὐτὸς ἐξηῦρες.

13. On the hermae of Hipparchos, see P. Friedländer and H. B. Hoffleit, *Epigrammata: Greek Inscriptions in Verse* (Berkeley, Los Angeles, 1948), pp. 139ff.

14. So in Schleiermacher (I/2, 323), where in general the path is correctly seen which Schleiermacher then blocked off for himself by "many-sided and lengthy deliberation." Pavlu, *Die pseudoplatonischen Zwillingsdialoge "Minos" und "Hipparch"* (Vienna, 1910), suspects behind the κέρδος of our dialogue the προηγμένα of the Stoics, just as he is reminded of the Stoic sage by the description of the ruler. Yet, there is nothing Stoic that goes beyond the Socratic foundations of Stoicism.

15. "Put together from reminiscences of Platonic passages," says Ast, p. 498, thus basing his rejection on the exact opposite of Schleiermacher's argument.

16. The questioning of the Platonic origin by Aelian, *Varia historia* VIII 2, has no binding force, since neither the origin of the thesis nor any argument is given. In other places as well, Aelian rather prides himself upon such critical remarks. The arguments of Pavlu, op. cit. [VIII¹⁴], pp. 11ff., will not bear scrutiny. The historic interest, as well as the desensualization of the erotic element, is thought to point to the second half of the fourth century. But there is no question of history, and not everyone will be made to see the desensualization. / Against the contention (H. Usener, *Vorträge und Aufsätze* [Leipzig,

1907], p. 95; Pavlu, op. cit., pp. 33ff.) that the dialogue is dependent on Aristotle's *Politeia Athenaiōn*, cf. also Wilamowitz, *Aristoteles und Athen* (Berlin, 1893), I, 119; M. Hirsch, *Klio*, XX (1926), 162. In response to what Pavlu, p. 24, says in principle about connections with Platonic dialogues that are "recognized as genuine," we may say that these connections as such can be applied *in utramque partem*. It is something else, however, to compare structures of form and thought, which we consider to be the task of the interpreter. / Let us add expressly that the dialogue *Minos* does not become Platonic simply because the *Hipparchus* is or is believed to be. The two—despite some connections (see Pavlu) about which opinions can differ—are in truth not "twin dialogues," as Eckert, p. 47, rightly observes in opposition to the formula repeated over and over since Ast (p. 500) and Socher (p. 122). What distinguishes the *Minos* sharply is (1) the constant play with τὸ ὄν and τὰ ὄντα (315A, 316B, 317D, 321B), which does not point to the time around 400; (2) the abrupt conclusion which (according to Pavlu, p. 13) is supposed to preserve the illusion of *aporia* in the conversation that is really ended.

17. J. Souilhé, *Platon Budé*, XIII/2, 57, dates the dialogue, which he regards as spurious, before the publication of the historic work of Thucydides, since the author of the dialogue regards Hipparchos as the oldest son and successor of Peisistratos, whereas Thucydides (I 20 2 and VI 54 2) contests this view sharply.

18. Marsiglio Ficino begins his work of translation with the *Hipparchus* (*Divi Platonis opera*, Venice, 1561). Ficino's *Argumenta* would deserve examination.

IX: *Ion*

RECENT EDITIONS AND TRANSLATIONS: O. Apelt, PhB 172a (1918); E. Chambry (Paris, 1919); W. R. M. Lamb, Loeb III (1925); L. Méridier, *Platon Budé*, V/1 (1931); G. La Magna (Naples, 1933); F. Bosi (Lanciano, 1936); L. Cooper (London, New York, 1938); R. Nihaud (Liége, 1939); A. Ghiselli (Milan, 1941); J. D. García Bacca (Mexico, 1944–45); A. Annaratone (3d edn., Naples, 1952).

RECENT INTERPRETATIONS: M. Delcourt, "Socrate, Ion, et la poésie: La structure dialectique de l'*Ion* de Platon," *Bull. Budé*, LV (1937), 4ff.; J. Moreau, "Les Thèmes platoniciens de l'*Ion*," *Rev ÉtGr*, LII (1939), 419ff.; W. J. Verdenius, "L'*Ion* de Platon," *Mnemosyne*, n.s., XI (1943), 233ff.; E. Grassi, *Von der Dichtung im platonischen Dialog "Ion"* (Bern, 1946), pp. 45f.; F. Wehrli, "Der erhabene und der schlichte Stil," *Phyllobolia für Peter von der Mühll* (Basel, 1946), pp. 9ff.; L. Roussel, *Pan: Sur l'Ion de Platon* (Paris, 1949); C. La Drière, "The

Problem of Plato's *Ion*," *JAesA*, X (1951), 26ff.; H. Diller, "Probleme des platonischen *Ion*," *Hermes*, LXXXIII (1955), 171ff.; E. A. Wyller, "Platons *Ion*: Versuch einer Interpretation," *SO*, XXXIV (1958), 19ff.; H. Flashar, *Der Dialog "Ion" als Zeugnis platonischer Philosophie* (Berlin, 1958); E. Lledó Iñigo, *El concepto "Poíesis" en la filosofía griega* (Madrid, 1961), ch. 4.

ADDITIONAL BIBLIOGRAPHY: Shorey, p. 475; Geffcken, Notes, p. 38; Rosenmeyer, p. 180; Cherniss, *Lustrum*, pp. 101ff.

1. On the rhapsodes, see L. Méridier in *Platon Budé*, V/1, 7ff.; but one must not misjudge the new style of the rhetors, as mocked by Plato and Xenophon, when compared with the old ῥαπτῶν ἐπέων ἀοιδοί. The dating of the *Ion* soon after 394 (Méridier, p. 23) is supported by the fact that the beginning of the dialogue refers to the newly founded festal games in Epidauros. See M. S. Ruipérez, "Sobre la cronología del *Ión* de Platón," *Aegyptus*, XXXIII (1953), 241ff.

2. Schleiermacher (I/2, 449) did not understand the irony, and in this passage he sees "rather a poor imitation of diverse passages than overhaste on Plato's own part." But it is neither the one nor the other, and this kind of jesting recurs in 536D.

3. Schleiermacher (I/2, 449) scores this anticipation of a thought which (he says) is not brought out until the second part of the dialogue and leads nowhere at this point. The reproach fails to do justice to the live course of the conversation. Neither must one overlook the fact that what is shown, in the beginning, in its correct proportions is exaggerated in the concluding part: namely, that poetry has a specific factual content.

4. *Plato als Mitgenosse einer christlichen Offenbarung* (1796). Wilamowitz is influenced by Goethe in seeing a "satire" in the dialogue. The characterization of Ion is too rich: one cannot brush him aside with the predicate "incredibly stupid," as Bruns (p. 355) shows.

5. W. J. Verdenius, "L'*Ion* de Platon," *Mnemosyne*, n.s., XI (1943), 262: "*En réfutant la compétence des rhapsodes il les prive, en même temps, de leurs prétentions pédagogiques. . . .*"

6. τἀληθῆ λέγω is bracketed by Wilamowitz, *Hermes*, XLIV (1909), 458. This is at first quite plausible, until one observes that here we have a typical phraseology of the Platonic Socrates: *Hippias Major* 288D 5, *Symposium* 198D 3. See H. Flashar, *Der Dialog "Ion" als Zeugnis platonischer Philosophie* (Berlin, 1958), p. 48. A detailed refutation of the rejection is made by H. Diller, "Probleme des platonischen *Ion*," *Hermes*, LXXXIII (1955), 179.

7. Schleiermacher calls the remark "odd and rather poor"; Wilamowitz (II, 38) calls it "heedless." But if something taken seriously is sense-

less, yet as a jest has a meaningful and most witty effect, may we not take it as a jest instead of criticizing it? See de Vries, pp. 278f.

8. The strength of the positive value assigned to the poet in the *Ion* is misjudged by Wilamowitz, I, 130f. = I², 132f.; II, 43. It is misjudged too by Méridier, *Platon Budé*, V/1, 16: "*Il semble ... que l'auteur de l'Ion n'ait pour l'inspiration poétique, comparée à la science, qu'une estime assez médiocre.*" One must not, of course, miss the irony—nor the genuine features of the poet's self-appraisal. Schleiermacher, who regarded the *Phaedrus* as the earliest Platonic dialogue, imagined that the author of the *Ion* "must have thought himself completely into that speech" from the *Phaedrus* (see I/2, 451). Steinhart, pp. 7ff., is closer to the sense of our interpretation. Cf. Greene, pp. 9, 15f. / Demokritos' statement about the "enthusiasm" of the poet was put beside that of Plato even in ancient times: *Vorsokr.* 68 [55] B 17, 18. Today there is a tendency to regard Demokritos as Plato's "source." See F. Wehrli, in *Phyllobolia für Peter von der Mühll* (Basel, 1946), pp. 11ff.; W. Kranz, "Kosmos," *Archiv für Begriffsgeschichte*, II 1 (1955), 43; Flashar, op. cit. [IX⁶], pp. 56ff. But one must not forget the graphic arts! The Orpheus jug in Berlin and the Musaios amphora in London (Ernst Buschor, *Griechische Vasenmalerei²* [Munich, 1914], figs. 143, 144) illustrate around the middle of the fifth century what Demokritos and Plato will say some decades later. Nor must one fail to hear that Plato himself refers expressly to poets for this self-appraisal of poetic enthusiasm: *Ion* 534A 6 *et seq.* Perhaps in poems that went under the names of Orpheus and Musaios (*Vorsokr.* 1 [66] and 2 [67]) poetic enthusiasm had become conscious of itself, so that Demokritos and Plato draw from the same "source." And perhaps prior to both is the art of monumental painting, on which in turn those vases depend.

9. Schleiermacher (I/2, 452) rejects the relationship. More correct is Steinhart, p. 14.

10. Cf. Cousin, IV, 230ff.; Raeder, p. 92.

11. Wilamowitz (II, 43), correctly noting the agreement of the *Ion* and the *Apology*, infers that the young Plato took this "doctrine" over from Socrates. A similar view is held by Ueberweg-Praechter, p. 224. But it is not permissible to ascribe without proof any utterance in the *Apology* to the historic Socrates, who incidentally is unlikely to have taught anything regarding the enthusiasm of the poet. If we are looking for a sign of how the historic Socrates felt about poetry, the beginning of the *Phaedo* still provides the most reliable evidence.

12. "The true intermediary is art. Speaking about art means to be a mediator of the intermediary, and yet much that is precious has come to us in that way." Goethe, "Maximen und Reflexionen," *Schriften der Goethe-Gesellschaft* (Weimar), XXI (1907), 413.

13. H. Diller, op. cit. [IX⁶], pp. 178f., rejects 531A 5–531B 10, but is sufficiently self-critical virtually to take back the rejection (pp. 186f.).

Of Diller's lesser rejections, Schanz' deletion of κεκοσμῆσθαι in 530β 6 is demonstrably false. This would destroy the precise symmetry of the sentence: ἅμα μὲν πρέπον εἶναι (*A*), ἅμα δὲ ἀναγκαῖον εἶναι (*B*); dependent on *A* is τὸ σῶμα κεκοσμῆσθαι (*a*) καὶ ὡς καλλίστοις φαίνεσθαι (*b*); dependent on *B* is ἔν τ' ἄλλοις ποιηταῖς διατρίβειν (*a*) καὶ τὴν τούτων διάνοιαν ἐκμανθάνειν (*b*). / κεκοσμῆσθαι is not a gloss to πρέπον εἶναι.

14. I find a reference to the interpretation developed here in Jowett, I, 496: "The old quarrel between philosophy and poetry . . . is already working in the mind of Plato, and is embodied by him in the contrast between Socrates and Ion." / Whether Diller, p. 171, is justified in calling my interpretation "more psychological than substantial" may be passed over. At any rate, what I endeavor to show is something other than "Abreaktion des Zwiespalts zwischen Dichter und Denker." Cf. Geffcken, Notes, p. 39; Leisegang, col. 2377. / Apelt (pp. 65f. and introd. to the translation p. 16) sees in the *Ion* Plato's farewell to poetry. But Plato is just beginning his poetic mission. Stefanini (I, 111f.) says: "*L'espressione Ciceroniana per cui Platone in oratoribus irridendis ipse esse orator summus videbatur (De Oratore I 47) può essere completata: in poetis irridendis ipse summus poeta.*" / It should now be clear how little the *Ion* can be regarded—with Bruns, p. 355—as merely a "harmless play" without any "serious reverse side." / L. Roussel's *Pan: Sur l'Ion de Platon* (Paris, 1949) is known to me only from the notice of it by D. Tarrant, *JHS*, LXXI (1951), 267; but that seems to suffice. See Cherniss, *Lustrum*, p. 102. / J. Moreau, "Les thèmes platoniciens de l'*Ion*," *RevÉtGr*, LVII (1939), 419ff., regards the *Ion* as a pupil's work. Diller also points in that direction. / Remarkable for the precision of its conceptual construction is Juan García Bacca's "Introducción al diálogo Platónico *Ión*," in *Obras completas de Platón*, "*Banquete*," "*Ión*" (Mexico, 1944).

x: *Hippias Minor*

RECENT EDITIONS AND TRANSLATIONS: O. Apelt, PhB 172a (2d edn., 1921); M. Croiset, *Platon Budé*, I (1920); G. Modugno (Perugia-Florence, 1930–31); T. Ciresola (Turin, 1937); G. Calogero (Florence, 1948); J. B. Bergua (4th edn., Madrid, 1957).

RECENT INTERPRETATIONS: Apelt, pp. 203ff.; B. J. H. Ovink, *Philosophische Erklärungen der platonischen Dialoge "Meno" und "Hippias Minor"* (Amsterdam, 1931); W. Schneidewin, *Platons zweiter "Hippias" Dialog* (Paderborn, 1931); Hildebrandt, pp. 54ff.; G. M. Sciacca, "Ippia Minore," *Giorn. di Metafisica*, VIII (1953), 670ff.

ADDITIONAL BIBLIOGRAPHY: Shorey, p. 470; Geffcken, Notes, p. 40; Rosenmeyer, p. 180; Cherniss, *Lustrum*, p. 101.

1. Since in *Hippias Major* 286B the Sophist announces a lecture, which Eudikos has induced him to deliver, ἐν τῷ Φειδοστράτου διδασκαλείῳ, here too we may well think of something similar. / On the scene setting, see *Plato* 1, pp. 158ff.
2. See Apelt, pp. 223f.
3. The criticism is found in Aristotle, *Nicomachean Ethics* 1140b 22: καὶ ἐν μὲν τέχνῃ ὁ ἑκὼν ἁμαρτάνων αἱρετώτερος, περὶ δὲ φρόνησιν ἧττον ὥσπερ καὶ περὶ τὰς ἀρετάς (cited by Apelt on the translation, p. 47). Other hints in Aristotle: Apelt, p. 235.
4. In general only this hint is picked up by the interpreters.
5. Wilamowitz, I, 135, n. 1 = I², 137, n. 1. See Apelt, p. 204, n. 1, regarding other passages where Aristotle's formulation, τῶν ἐναντίων μία ἐπιστήμη, is given.
6. Despite the quotation by Aristotle, *Metaphysics* V 29 1025ᵃ 6, the dialogue is regarded as un-Platonic by Schleiermacher and Ast (against them is Hermann, p. 432), and by A. K. Rogers, *The Socratic Problem* [VII¹], Appen. B.
7. Gomperz, II, 291; Eckert, p. 28.
8. On the fundamentally different interpretations of the *Hippias Minor*, see Leisegang, cols. 2381f. These conflicting views run strangely parallel in Wilamowitz, I, 136f. = I², 138f. The dialogue (he says) is a satire against Hippias—that is all. But just before, Wilamowitz had referred to 376B 5, the passage where "the followers of Socrates were bound to find a hint for an understanding of the whole work." / The correct dating is given by Wilamowitz, I, 136 = I², 138.

XI: *Theages*

RECENT EDITIONS AND TRANSLATIONS: J. Souilhé, *Platon Budé*, XIII/2 (1926); H. N. Fowler and W. R. M. Lamb, Loeb VIII (1927); G. Carugno (2d edn., Naples, 1952); G. Amplo (Rome, 1957).

RECENT INTERPRETATIONS: J. Pavlu, "Der pseudoplatonische Dialog *Theages*," *WienStud*, XXXI (1909), 13ff.; H. Gomperz, "Plato on Personality," *The Personalist*, XXII (1941/42), 28ff.; K. J. Vourveris, *Platon II* (Athens, 1951), pp. 1ff.; Gauss, I/2, 208ff.

ADDITIONAL BIBLIOGRAPHY: Shorey, p. 661; Geffcken, Notes, p. 157; Rosenmeyer, p. 190; Cherniss, *Lustrum*, pp. 207ff.

1. "Plato could hardly have written the intolerably clumsy and scholastic

first two sentences of the *Theages*" : Shorey, p. 429. But what if the author *intentionally* put this courteously stiff address in the mouth of Demodokos?

2. Cf. Rudolf Hirzel, "Der Name," *AbhLeipz*, XXXVI, ii (1918–21), 7.

3. On the *Theages*, cf. *Plato* 1, pp. 34ff.; J. Souilhé in *Platon Budé*, XIII/2, 130ff.: "La 'Voix démonique.' " In our critical judgments we are far apart.

4. Pavlu, "Der pseudoplatonische Dialog *Theages*," *WienStud*, XXXI (1909), 26ff. Cf. *DGrA*, I, 46. The detailed comparison there makes it probable to me that the *Theages* is to be dated before the *Alcibiades*.

5. Kurt von Fritz, *R-E*, V A, col. 1350, thinks that "the pseudo-Platonic dialogue *Theages* undoubtedly refers to this passage of the *Republic*."

6. Sophocles frag. 13 N² = Pearson 14, in *Theages* 125B and *Republic* 568A falsely ascribed to Euripides. Ast, p. 496, has the author of the *Theages* borrow from the *Republic*. If the *Theages* is Platonic, then Plato had this verse in mind as Euripidean. In agreement is Grote, I, 431. See also W. Janell, *Hermes*, XXXVI (1901), 432, and Pearson, I, 12f.

7. Cf. *DGrA*, pp. 31ff.

8. The remarkably precise agreement of *Apology* 19E with *Theages* 127E *et seq.* has been noted frequently; see, e.g., Pavlu, op. cit. [XI⁴], p. 28, and Souilhé in *Platon Budé*, XIII/2, 139. In the *Apology* the motif is extended to take in the Euenos episode, and then the verbal parallel goes on a bit further (20BC): ἐγὼ τὸν Εὔηνον ἐμακάρισα ... ἐγὼ γοῦν καὶ αὐτὸς ἐκαλλυνόμην ... ἄν εἰ ἠπιστάμην ταῦτα· ἀλλ' οὐ γὰρ ἐπίσταμαι. ... *Theages* 128B: οὐδὲν γὰρ τούτων ἐπίσταμαι τῶν μακαρίων τε καὶ καλῶν μαθημάτων—ἐπεὶ ἐβουλόμην ἄν. (I should like—with due reservations—to consider this enlargement of the motif as an indication that the *Apology* is to be dated later than the *Theages*.)

9. Pavlu, loc. cit., claims that the author of the *Theages* misunderstood the *Theaetetus*. But he supports this thesis by coarsening the *Theages*. Actually, the two dialogues are in harmony with each other. Only, in the *Theages* ἐπίδοσις means what μαθεῖν ἤ τεκεῖν means in the *Theaetetus*.

10. These words will make one think of *Symposium* 175C. Agathon speaks much more in a jesting and detached manner, and Socrates goes on in that tone. / See also D. Tarrant, "The Touch of Socrates," *CQ*, VIII (1958), 95ff.

11. See R. Boehringer, *Mein Bild von Stefan George* (Munich and Düsseldorf, 1951), p. 147.

12. Cf. e.g., Stallbaum, *Comm.* 222: "*Socratem vaticidae anus partes agere*," and Bruns, p. 346, who speaks of "a genuine little private oracle" (". . . this private oracle which can be consulted even by his friends," Shorey, p. 430—quite incorrect). But the meaning that all these stories convey is not grasped, and when Bruns finally speaks of "a certain Aristides," it seems as if he had completely forgotten the *Laches* and *Theaetetus*. The dissertation of Willing, "De Socratis Daemonio"

(*Comm. Jenenses VIII*), once more hits the wrong nail on the head ("*quae deliratio!*"). / For Schleiermacher (II/3, 508), with whom Cousin (V, 425) agrees, ἡ φωνὴ ἡ τοῦ δαιμονίου (128E 5) is proof of spuriousness, because at this point "τὸ δαιμόνιον is regarded as a person. But in vain will one look in the speech of defense or elsewhere . . . for anything similar." Schleiermacher must have forgotten that the wording of *Apology* 40A 4, ἡ γὰρ εἰωθυῖά μοι μαντικὴ [ἡ τοῦ δαιμο-νίου], is based on his own rejection. "The long and boastful discussion of the divine gift": Hermann, p. 430. Similarly, see Jaspers, p. 125.

13. Johannes Kirchner, *Prosopographia Attica* I (Berlin, 1901), 6536, 3584.

14. A comment on πολλοῖς δὲ συνεῖναι μὲν οὐ διακωλύει (129E 6) because Pavlu, op. cit. [XI⁴], considers the words to have been senselessly copied from *Theaetetus* 151A 3: ἐνίοις μὲν τὸ γιγνόμενόν μοι δαιμόνιον ἀποκωλύει συνεῖναι. But it is not correct to expect πολλούς in the *Theages*. The supplied object is of course με. / The fact that in the *Theages* the daimonion decides as to the first meeting, and in the *Theaetetus* as to the renewed acceptance of a disaffected pupil, may in no case be interpreted with Schleiermacher to indicate that the author of the *Theages* misunderstood the *Theaetetus*. There is no reason at all why the one should not be as right as the other, and the *Alcibiades* bears witness (no matter how one may regard its authorship) that in this case no individual misunderstanding on the part of the author of the *Theages* is to be assumed. / In the *Theages* the "force of the demonic" is said on occasion "to assist" (129E 7); see *Plato* 1, p. 34. Certainly this is a shading which Plato avoids elsewhere. Hence, this deviation is employed as an argument against the genuineness of the *Theages*; cf. Gerhard Krüger, *Der Dialog "Theages"* (Greifswald diss., 1935), pp. 19ff. Assuming the *Theages* to have been a youthful work of Plato, the inference would be that later on Plato avoided this shading. / Cf. Grote, I, 440.

15. The question of Platonic repetitions—a special burden in the discussion of whether the *Theages* is genuine—has been treated by Walter Eberhardt in his Leipzig dissertation, "De iteratis apud Platonem," 1923 (unpublished).

16. So says Wilamowitz, II, 324. His conclusion, that the ancients themselves rejected the *Theages*, is a conclusion *e silentio*. Even as such it is not correct. At least Plutarch and Albinus used the *Theages*. Plutarch, *De genio Socratis* ch. 10—προποδηγὸν ἐξ ἀρχῆς τινα—most probably had *Theages* 128D before him or in his head: παρεπόμενον ἐκ παιδὸς ἀρξάμενον. Similarly, Plutarch, *Nikias* 13 9 goes back to *Theages* 129 CD: Socrates' premonition of the Sicilian catastrophe. (G. Soury, *La Démonologie de Plutarque* [Paris, 1942], pp. 118, 122, is right.) Albinus (*Eisagoge* ch. 4) reports, without the slightest critical doubt, that "some" begin the reading of Plato with the *Theages*. Cf. Diogenes Laërtius III 62.

17. Souilhé (*Platon Budé*, XIII/2, 142) would like to shift the dialogue to the second or third century, because Theages wishes "to become God." Does that not mean a complete failure to recognize the boyishness of the wish? And what of the style of the whole? / Gauss (I/2, 209) calls the dialogue "a wretched bit of hackwork," the stories of the daimonion "quite out of line." If he objects to the "assurance that the daimonion can be appeased with sacrifices and prayers," he is forgetting that in this case (131A) the "youngster" Theages is speaking. Krüger, *Der Dialog "Theages"* [XI¹⁴], points rightly to the fact that in the discussion of tyranny some things "are designed for a boy." 131A: εὐχαῖσί τε καὶ θυσίαις. "This one iota (εὐχαῖσι) reveals" the spuriousness: C. Ritter, *Neue Untersuchungen über Platon*² (Munich, 1910), p. 94. Actually one should hear the dactylic rhythm: the boy is practicing what he learned at school. / The only recent critic to recognize the value of the *Theages* and believe in its Platonic origin is Heinrich Gomperz, "Plato on Personality," *The Personalist*, XXII (1941/42), 30ff. On *Theages* 130B *et seq.*, Gomperz comments that "it is hardly possible to depict in a simpler and more convincing manner what today we might style the charm and the spell of a great and inspiring personality."

XII: *Apology*

RECENT EDITIONS AND TRANSLATIONS: In the last fifty years, more than seventy-five editions and translations have been published. Some of these are: H. N. Fowler, Loeb I (1914); M. Croiset, *Platon Budé*, I (1920); J. Burnet (Oxford, 1924); L. Cooper (Ithaca, N. Y., 1941); E. Salin (Basel, 1945); L. G. van der Wal (Groningen, 1946); M. Claudius (Hamburg, 1947); O. Apelt, PhB 180 (3d edn., 1951); W. D. Woodhead (Edinburgh, 1953); H. Tredennick (London, 1954); N. Casini (Florence, 1957); H. Williamson (London, 1958); V. Stazzone (Brescia, 1959).

RECENT INTERPRETATIONS: E. Horneffer, *Der junge Platon*, I (Giessen, 1922); J. Morr, *Die Entstehung der platonischen "Apologie"* (Reichenberg, 1929); Erwin Wolff, "Platos *Apologie*," *Neue Phil. Unters.*, VI (1929); Hildebrandt, pp. 57ff.; C. Coulter, "The Tragic Structure of Plato's *Apology*," *PhilolQ*, XII (1933), 137ff.; R. Hackforth, *The Composition of Plato's "Apology"* (Cambridge, 1933); E. Turolla, "Una prima crisi spirituale di Platone riflessa nell'*Apologia*," *AeR*, V (1937), 102ff.; R. Guardini, *Der Tod des Sokrates* (Bern, 1945), pp. 67ff.; H. Schmalenbach, "Macht und Recht: Platons Absage an die Politik," *Natur und Geist* (Zurich, 1946), pp. 183ff.; I. Düring, "Socrates' Valedictory Words to his Judges," *Eranos* XLIV (1946), 90ff.; Gallo Galli, "L'*Apologia* di Socrate," *Paideia*, II (1947), 273ff.;

A. Delatte, "La Figure de Socrate dans l'*Apologie* de Platon," *BAB*, XXXVI (1950), 213ff.; É. de Strycker, "Platonica II," *Études Classiques*, XVIII (1950), 269ff.; E. A. Havelock, "Why Was Socrates Tried?" *Studies Norwood* (Toronto, 1952), pp. 95ff.; Erik Wolf, *Griechisches Rechtsdenken* (Frankfurt a. M., 1954), III/1, 38ff.; M. Fox, "The Trials of Socrates: An Interpretation of the First Tetralogy," *AfP*, VI (1956), 226ff.

ADDITIONAL BIBLIOGRAPHY: Shorey, p. 461; Geffcken, Notes, p. 34; Rosenmeyer, p. 178; Cherniss, *Lustrum*, pp. 72ff.

1. We put an incomparably greater value on the formative labor of Plato, in this work as well, than Burnet and Taylor were inclined to do. At the same time it is obvious that we too do not ascribe to Plato any "falsification of fundamental facts" (Taylor, p. 156). / W. A. Oldfather, "Socrates in Court," *CW*, XXXI (1937/38), 203ff., evokes with comprehensive sweep and a strong sense of reality the "confusion, hugger-mugger" of the actual trial.

2. For literature on the genuineness of Xenophon's *Apology*, see Shorey, p. 462.

3. Heinrich Gomperz, "Sokrates' Haltung vor seinen Richtern," *WienStud*, LIV (1936), 32ff.; Oldfather, op. cit. [XII¹]; A. D. Winspear, *Who Was Socrates?* (New York, 1939), pp. 72ff.

4. Arnim, *Xenophons Memorabilien und die "Apologie" des Sokrates* (Det kongelige Danske Videnskabernes Selskab, Copenhagen, 1923), p. 68, is rightly opposed to the customary view (Zeller, II/1, 529, n. 2; Ueberweg-Praechter, p. 218; Ritter, I, 368; etc.) that the Platonic *Apology* must have been written soon after 399 B.C. Diès, p. 291, dates it around 396; Arnim says 392, at the earliest. Our arrangement is intended to be much more typological than chronological. It must remain doubtful how far one may draw chronological inferences (1) from the relationship to the group of aporetic dialogues (the problem of the unity of the virtues); (2) from the relationship in particular to the *Euthyphro*, which is among the latest writings in that group (the problem of the ὅσιον against the background of the trial); and (3) from the relationship to the *Alcibiades Major* and the *Gorgias*, to which the *Crito*, hardly separable from the *Apology*, is closely related as well. Verbal statistics fail to help in this case. But the *communis opinio* must be sharply questioned. / Erwin Wolff, "Platos *Apologie*," *Neue phil. Unters.*, VI (1929), 85, sees in the *Apology* "Plato's first work." So do Geffcken, pp. 40f.; Gauss, I/2, 18. But no proof of this is possible.

5. In opposition to this see, e.g., Martin Schanz, *Sammlung ausgewählter Dialoge* (Leipzig, 1893), III, 101: the purpose of the *Apology* is "the

justification of the master in the eyes of the educated." Socher, p. 70, says, "a eulogy of Socrates addressed to all Hellas, to posterity." Socher refers to Pseudo-Dionysius, *Techne* VIII 8, where the *Apology* is cited as συμπλοκή of defense, attack, panegyric, and at its best φιλόσοφος θεωρία. ἔστι γὰρ τὸ βυβλίον παράγγελμα ὁποῖον εἶναι δεῖ τὸν φιλόσοφον. Almost all modern commentators lag far behind this judgment. An exception is Erwin Wolff, op. cit. [XII⁴], p. 87. Reginald Hackforth, *The Composition of Plato's "Apology"* (Cambridge, 1933), p. 46, calls the *Apology* "non-philosophical" and immediately afterwards quotes Pseudo-Dionysius with approval.

6. Cf. Schanz, op. cit. [XII⁵], Introd., §§ 16ff. The disposition tentatively set up by Wolff is less adequate.

7. On the juridical problems, see A. Menzel, "Untersuchungen zum Sokrates-Prozesse," *SBWien*, CXLV (1903), Abh. 2; R. J. Bonner, "The Legal Setting of Plato's *Apology*," *CP*, III (1908), 168ff. On the "elastic nature" of the concept ἀσέβεια, see Moritz H. E. Meier, G. F. Schömann, and J. H. Lipsius, *Der attische Prozess* (2 vols., Leipzig, 1883–87), II, 366ff.

8. Originally, νομίζειν θεούς meant "to honor according to custom"; in that age, which combined skepticism with intolerance, it had drifted over into νομίζειν εἶναι θεούς. (This, too, is still different from πιστεύειν εἰς θεόν or ἐν θεῷ, hence preferably not to be translated "to believe in.") A copious collection of materials is to be found in J. Tate, *CR*, L (1936), 3ff.; LI (1937), 3ff. The interpretation of B. Snell, *Die Entdeckung des Geistes*³ (Hamburg, 1955), pp. 46f., seems to me decidedly superior; I follow him. On Tate, this further comment: the language of the *Laws* is no certain proof for that in the *Apology*. / On νομίζειν and πιστεύειν, cf. also R. Bultmann in *Theologisches Wörterbuch zum Neuen Testament* (Stuttgart, 1955), IV, 174ff., esp. 179.

9. I was mistaken in the first edition when I considered this passage of the *Apology* as "sophistically overrefined in the highest degree." Ast had thought so and used this as an argument in favor of spuriousness. In comparison he calls Xenophon's arguments "simple and sufficient." And in fact the latter are more fitting—if it is a question of pleading for acquittal. From this it follows, however, that something quite different is at stake in Plato's Socrates. / According to the jurist Menzel, op. cit. [XII⁷], p. 52, the refutation of the accusation "is simpler and more effective in Xenophon." More sweeping is Cousin, I, 56: "*Comme plaidoyer, comme défense régulière, on ne peut nier que l'Apologie de Socrate ne soit très faible.*"

10. Cf. Emma Edelstein, *Xenophontisches und Platonisches Bild des Sokrates* (Berlin, 1935), pp. 17f., 141f.

11. Erwin Wolff, "Platos *Apologie*" [XII⁴], pp. 37f.

12. μύωψ means "gadfly," not "spur." (Aeschylus in the story of Io calls μύωψ what is otherwise called οἶστρος: *Prometheus 675, Supplices*

305.) Now it happens that "gadfly" also means a "spur" to a Greek, so that in δεομένῳ ἐγείρεσθαι ὑπὸ μύωπός τινος the reader could also be aware of the metaphorical meaning. But the living animal—Ἥρα τῇ βοΐ οἶστρον ἐμβάλλει (Apollodorus II 7) and Δία οἶστρον ἐμβαλεῖν τῷ Πηγάσῳ (Schol. to *Iliad* VI 155)—is a more striking and original image than the lifeless instrument. This is in opposition to the interpretations of Schanz and Burnet. Schanz is wrong in taking προσκείμενον to indicate the rider; actually, the gadfly is already hinted at. The rejection of ὑπὸ τοῦ θεοῦ (30E 3) also is wrong.

13. On the text of 34E 5: evidently we must not start out from τῷ Σωκράτει in B, since it is fitted to δεδογμένον ἐστί. Hence, δεδογμένον γ' ἐστὶ τὸν Σωκράτη διαφέρειν τινὶ τῶν πολλῶν ἀνθρώπων. τὸν is more expressive than τό.

14. Arnim, *Xenophons Memorabilien . . .* [XII⁴], wants to interpret away the contrast between Xenophon and Plato: it is (he says) only the difference between a summary and a detailed report. But οὔτε τοὺς φίλους εἴασεν in Xenophon looks exactly like an opposition to the tradition recorded in Plato. Cf. Oldfather, "Socrates in Court" [XII¹], p. 209; Hackforth, *The Composition of Plato's "Apology"* [XII⁵], p. 17.

15. 36C: μὴ πρότερον μήτε τῶν ἑαυτοῦ μηδενὸς ἐπιμελεῖσθαι πρὶν ἑαυτοῦ ἐπιμεληθείη ὅπως ὡς βέλτιστος καὶ φρονιμώτατος ἔσοιτο. *Alcibiades I* 127E: τί ἐστι τὸ ἑαυτοῦ ἐπιμελεῖσθαι . . . καὶ πότ' ἄρ' αὐτὸ ποιεῖ ἄνθρωπος; ἆρ' ὅταν τῶν αὐτοῦ ἐπιμελῆται, τότε καὶ αὐτοῦ;

16. Others (e.g., Joël, *Der echte und der xenophontische Sokrates* [Berlin, 1893–1901], 439, n. 1; and Schanz, op. cit. [XII⁵], p. 98) consider the proposal of a money fine fictitious. But it is not credible that Plato invented this in order to confront voices in the public which charged a lack of help. For if it was a fiction, then those very voices were right! And it is unthinkable that Plato should have intended to suggest "that the proposal of a fine was merely a blind and an artifice." Menzel, op. cit. [XII⁷], p. 57, calls the version in Xenophon "more dignified and consistent." On this point see also Hackforth, op. cit. [XII⁵], pp. 16, 137.

17. So says, e.g., Wilamowitz, I, 163=I², 165. Against this view are Schanz, op. cit. [XII⁵], p. 99; Arnim, op. cit. [XII⁴], p. 77; Taylor, p. 157; Menzel, p. 50; Hackforth, p. 138. Our text attempts to show that Wilamowitz' thesis must be preserved to some extent.

18. Jowett (II, 107): "It has been remarked, that the prophecy . . . was, as far as we know, never fulfilled." But Plato evidently means himself and those whom he will educate. / Cf. Hildebrandt, p. 76.

19. Schanz, op. cit. [XII⁵], p. 100, narrows the perspective by making this proud confession of Plato's Socrates serve as answer to the weak ones who thought he should have appealed to the mercy of the judges.

XIII: *Crito*

RECENT EDITIONS AND TRANSLATIONS: In the last fifty years, more than fifty editions and translations have been published. Some of these are: H. N. Fowler, Loeb I (1914); M. Croiset, *Platon Budé*, I (1920); J. Burnet (Oxford, 1924); R. Harder (Berlin, 1934); U. E. Paoli (Florence, 1934); G. Calogero (Florence, 1937); E. Salin (Basel, 1945); L. G. van der Wal (Groningen, 1946); O. Apelt, PhB 180 (3d edn., 1951); W. D. Woodhead (Edinburgh, 1953); H. Tredennick (London, 1954); N. Casini (Florence, 1957); G. di Napoli (Milan, 1959).

RECENT INTERPRETATIONS: U. E. Paoli, "Problemi di diritto pubblico nel *Critone* platonico," *RIFD*, XII (1932), 605ff.; R. Guardini, *Der Tod des Sokrates* (Bern, 1945), pp. 144ff.; H. Schmalenbach, "Macht und Recht: Platons Absage an die Politik," *Natur und Geist* (Zurich, 1946), pp. 183ff.; P. Piovani, *Per una interpretazione unitaria del "Critone"* (Rome, 1947); Erik Wolf, *Griechisches Rechtsdenken* (Frankfurt a. M., 1954), III/1, 38ff.; M. Fox, "The Trials of Socrates: An Interpretation of the First Tetralogy," *AfP*, VI (1956), 226ff.; A. W. Gomme, "The Structure of Plato's *Crito*," *Greece and Rome*, 2d ser., V (1958), 45ff.

ADDITIONAL BIBLIOGRAPHY: Shorey, p. 467; Geffcken, Notes, p. 37; Rosenmeyer, p. 178; Cherniss, *Lustrum*, pp. 83f.

1. Xenophon, *Apology* 23; Diogenes Laërtius II 35, 60; III 36 (from Idomeneus the Epicurean). Cf. Martin Schanz, "Einleitung zur kommentierten Ausgabe" (Leipzig, 1887), p. 10.
2. Socher, p. 66: "The dialogue *Crito* is an apology of Socrates' friends." Wilamowitz, II, 55: "It is clear that his sole intention is to justify the way in which Socrates acted." Jowett (II, 141) is similar, but with the addition "... the defense ... not to the Athenians of his day, but to posterity and the world at large." It is seen as a defense of Socrates and his friends by Zeller, II/1, 529, n. 2. Richard Harder, *Platos "Kriton"* (Berlin, 1934), p. 48: "The dialogue is not apologetic; it is ... polemic"; Kriton is "the foe in the friend." "In this judgment a correct feeling is exaggerated": Max Pohlenz, *GGA*, 1935, p. 234. Harder's "Nachwort," pp. 42ff., should be consulted in connection with ch. XIII.
3. Does not this opening of the dialogue speak against Harder's view (op. cit., pp. 51f.) that the Socrates of the *Crito* lacks individual features?

4. This intention of Plato is blurred if one follows Schanz, op. cit. [XIII¹], p. 9, in arranging neatly the arguments of the *Crito* in such a way that the Kriton-section appears as tripartite, like the Socrates-section. The fact is that the ἀταξία on Kriton's part contrasts with the τάξις on Socrates' part, even in the formal structure of the argumentation.

5. Once one has recognized how important is this reference from 49A back to 47E, he will not be able to consider as un-Platonic the words ὅπερ καὶ ἄρτι ἐλέγετο (49A 7), despite the harsh phrasing: "Which was also stated just now [*implicite*] when we agreed that injustice is the specific damage of the soul." Cf. also 48c 7.

6. If G. Sarton, *A History of Science* (Cambridge, Mass., 1952), I, 408ff., had paid attention to this one passage only, he would have seen some things differently in his chapter, "Politics, The Great Betrayal," written with fanatical antipathy to Plato. Levinson, writing in 1953, could not yet deal with Sarton's charges.

7. Cf. G. Bornkamm, "ΟΜΟΛΟΓΙΑ," *Hermes*, LXXI (1936), 377ff. / The words ὅτι μὴ ἅπαξ εἰς ᾿Ισθμόν (52B 5) cannot be a subsequent addition (Harder, op. cit. [XIII²], p. 32; Jachmann, pp. 314ff.), not even an addition of Plato's own: see Wilamowitz, II, 343; E. Bickel, *RhM*, XCII (1949), 145. For only these words explain why previously just the phrase ἐπὶ θεωρίαν is used, and they are presupposed in the spatial adverbs ἄλλοσε οὐδαμόσε, which are justified completely only by εἰς ᾿Ισθμόν, not by ἐπὶ θεωρίαν. If the words had been lacking originally, then the sentence would have read simply οὐ πώποτ᾿ ἐκ τῆς πόλεως ἐξῆλθες εἰ μή ποι στρατευόμενος. One should also note the rhythmical parallelism of the clauses:

(a¹) οὔτ᾿ ἐπὶ θεωρίαν . . .   (b¹) ὅτι μὴ ἅπαξ εἰς ᾿Ισθμόν
(a²) οὔτ᾿ ἄλλοσε . . .   (b²) εἰ μή ποι στρατευσόμενος
(a³) οὔτ᾿ ἄλλην . . .   (b³) ὥσπερ οἱ ἄλλοι ἄνθρωποι

Each of the clauses (b¹), (b²), and (b³) has eight syllables. Is that an accident? / The condition of the mss., to be sure, calls for an explanation. Should this not be found in an ancient rejection, made in order to remove the contradiction of the testimony of Aristotle: καὶ Πυθῶδε ἐλθεῖν [i.e., τὸν Σωκράτη] ᾿Αριστοτέλης φησίν (Diogenes Laërtius II 23)? / The prevailing tendency to rid the Platonic text of expansions is justified but one-sided. By shortening as much as possible, one does not always achieve the Platonic form.

8. See Schanz, op. cit. [XIII¹] on this passage.

9. Cf. W. Kranz, "Das Gesetz des Herzens" [I¹⁷], 225f.; U. Galli, *Platone e il* ΝΟΜΟΣ (Turin, 1937), 76ff.

10. For example, see Jowett, II, 139: "The *Crito* seems intended to exhibit the character of Socrates in one light only, not as the philosopher . . . but simply as the citizen. . . ." For comment, see Shorey, p. 469.

XIV: *Euthydemus*

RECENT EDITIONS AND TRANSLATIONS: W. R. M. Lamb, Loeb IV (1924);
J. Crexells (Barcelona, 1928); E. Martini (Turin, 1929); L. Méri-
dier, *Platon Budé*, V/1 (1931); G. J. de Vries (Groningen, 1951);
P. Papanikolaos (Athens, 1952); O. Apelt, PhB 176 (3d edn., 1955);
J. B. Bergua (4th edn., Madrid, 1957).

RECENT INTERPRETATIONS: K. Praechter, "Platon und Euthydemus," *Philologus*, LXXXVII (1932), 121ff.; G. Hinrichs, "The *Euthydemus* as
a Locus of the Socratic Elenchus," *New Scholasticism*, XXV (1951),
178ff.; Buccellato, ch. 5; Gauss, II/1, 158ff.

ADDITIONAL BIBLIOGRAPHY: Shorey, p. 158; Geffcken, Notes, p. 76; Rosenmeyer, p. 179; Cherniss, *Lustrum*, p. 95.

1. Schleiermacher, II/1, 545.
2. L. Méridier, *Platon Budé*, V/1, 119: *"L'Euthydème est une comédie,
   avec son décor et ses acteurs."*
3. Cf. Wilamowitz, I, 300, n. 1 = I², 303, n. 1. The judgment, however,
   that we have here a "perfecting of Plato's art as compared with his
   youthful work . . . an advance as from Goethe's *Satyros* to his *Urfaust*"
   seems to me an astonishing exaggeration. The *Lysis* is richer in the
   presentation of the poetic space as well as in the development of the
   problem. There is much less distance in time between the two dialogues than Wilamowitz assumes. The *Euthydemus* fits in artistic form
   and philosophic content the place to which Arnim's verbal statistics
   assign it. Taylor, pp. 75ff., concurs. This dialogue, which is essentially
   aporetic, protreptic, and polemic, seems to be hardly thinkable after
   the *Gorgias*. It is placed after *Gorgias* and *Meno* by Hildebrandt, pp.
   165ff.; Shorey, pp. 160ff.; Méridier, op. cit., pp. 139ff.; Leisegang,
   cols. 2425ff.
4. Some relations between the *Euthydemus* and the *Protagoras* already
   had been pointed out by Ast (p. 415) and used to reject the *Euthydemus*. He was followed by Schaarschmidt, pp. 327ff. That has long
   since been settled (see Bonitz, pp. 145ff.), but the relationship with
   the *Protagoras* calls for a positive evaluation.
5. Aristotle, *De sophisticis elenchis* 11, 171b 25, makes (somewhat arbitrarily) a distinction: οἱ μὲν οὖν τῆς νίκης αὐτῆς χάριν τοιοῦτοι ἐριστι-
   κοὶ ἄνθρωποι καὶ φιλέριδες δοκοῦσιν εἶναι, οἱ δὲ δόξης χάριν τῆς εἰς χρη-
   ματισμὸν σοφιστικοί. This is not the place to deal with the historic
   origin of this eristic. The influence of Zeno (Taylor, p. 92) and Protagoras (*Euthydemus* 286c; Joël, p. 709) is certainly most significant.

Still more important is the presence of these tendencies in Plato's immediate environment. One should think of the Megarian and the Cynical logic. See E. S. Thompson, *The "Meno" of Plato* (London, 1901), Excursus V.

6. For the spatial setting, see *Plato* 1, p. 160. / On the following discussion, see Wilamowitz, I, 299 = I², 301.

7. Wilamowitz (I, 306 = I², 309) seems rather to blur one's view of this structure by dividing the whole work, including the conversational frame, into five acts and by putting the first two pairs of the five conversations into one act each.

8. Bonitz, p. 106. For the logical fallacies, see also Bonitz and Gifford, *The "Euthydemus" of Plato* (London, 1905), pp. 35ff.; L. Méridier, *Platon Budé*, V/1, 214ff. It cannot be doubted that in Σοφιστικοὶ Ἔλεγχοι Aristotle is largely focusing on Plato's *Euthydemus*. Anyone who would question this reference (as does Bonitz, p. 135) must logically have to do the same for the *Rhetoric* and the *Phaedrus*, the *Nicomachean Ethics* and the *Lysis*. The relationship in those pairs is analogous. Cf. Cousin, IV, 357: *"L'ouvrage d'Aristote intitulé De la Réfutation des sophismes n'est pas autre chose que l'Euthydème réduit en formules générales."* See also Grote, I, 543f.

9. In order to obviate misunderstandings as far as possible, the following may be added. Bonitz (p. 114) is correct when he says that the first ten sophisms deal with the concepts of learning and knowing, but he goes astray in saying that these express the "convictions of the Sophists" that there is no knowledge; for the two jugglers have no convictions. Bonitz is half correct in opposing Steinhart, who claims to find "a certain truth" in the sophisms themselves. What was vaguely seen by Steinhart (as his reference to the *Meno* shows) is lifted up in our text to a clarity which does not blur the sharp distinction between eristic and dialectic. / In this connection, a word on Steinhart's introductions. Today they are as good as forgotten, unjustly so. Wilamowitz (*Erinnerungen* [Leipzig, 1928], p. 78) calls them confused. But despite frequent vagueness and prolixity, it was their merit that they did not confine themselves to conceptual systematization as the allegedly sole concern of philosophy. Bonitz, who opposes Steinhart with particular frequency, was incomparably keener, but he was also incomparably drier and more narrow.

10. In connection with the concept εὐτυχία, there is a first insight into what is subsequently demonstrated in the case of the other "goods." So even if there *is* a reference to "a philosophical opponent of Plato who had included the εὐτυχία among the ἀγαθά" (Arnim, p. 124), that says nothing about the meaning of εὐτυχία in this connection. For the rest, the view that luck or success is a good is so universal that one must search for the person who does *not* share it. / εὐτυχία contains a genuinely Platonic intensification of the usual sense of the

word as a result of listening to the original meaning of τυχεῖν. Cf. the comment of Bonitz, pp. 96f. / Taylor (p. 93) and Shorey (p. 162) understand by εὐτυχία simply "good luck" and thus remain on the surface.

11. E.g., *Euthydemus* 282B: οὐδὲν αἰσχρὸν οὐδὲ νεμεσητὸν ἕνεκα τούτου ὑπηρετεῖν καὶ δουλεύειν. *Symposium* 184c: αὕτη ἡ ἐθελοδουλεία οὐκ αἰσχρὰ εἶναι οὐδὲ κολακεία. The agreement goes even further.

12. It is not correct that the *Meno* is presupposed here (Schleiermacher II/1, 400f.; Gomperz, III, 148; Apelt, "Einleitung zur Übersetzung" [Leipzig, 1922], p. 22; Wilamowitz, I, 301 = I², 303; II, 151; Méridier, *Platon Budé*, V/1, 140). For (1) the verbal statistics place the *Meno* later, and the analysis of form and content leads to the same conclusion; (2) the "teachableness of virtue" in the *Meno* is decided (100B) only ἐξ ὑποθέσεως (86E); (3) in the *Euthydemus*, the "teachableness" is not taken for granted, but the discussion is also conducted on the assumption that such a "teachableness" exists. / The views of Arnim (p. 126) and Shorey (p. 520) are correct.

13. Shorey, *Unity*, pp. 54f., says about the *Cratylus*—and this applies for him (and for us) to the *Euthydemus* as well: "It is obvious 1. that the fallacy is none to Plato; 2. that he feels himself able to carry the analysis farther; 3. that he does not do so because he wishes to write the *Cratylus*, not the *Sophist*." Cf. H. Cherniss, *JHS*, LXXVII (1957), 19.

14. 288A: ἔοικεν . . . ὁ λόγος . . . καταβαλὼν πίπτειν, surely with an allusion to Protagoras' work Καταβάλλοντες. Cf. 286c: τούς τε ἄλλους ἀνατρέπων καὶ αὐτὸς αὑτόν.

15. Wilamowitz (I, 303 = I², 306) tries to prove that that is "not an entirely honest continuation." But his arguments are not plausible.

16. It is by no means as certain as Arnim, p. 129, assumes that this passage is aimed at the same speechmaker as at the close of the dialogue (304D). To take the polemic intent as the principal matter, instead of looking for the artistic and systematic relations, always leads one astray. That an extensive polemic is here directed against the λογοποιοί is probably due to the fact that Plato envisages and practices a different art of the *logoi*, in which there is no distinction between ἡ τοῦ ποιεῖν τέχνη and ἡ τοῦ χρῆσθαι.

17. Here, too, Arnim looks for a polemic against an unknown opponent (a "Pythagorean"). Without entirely excluding this interpretation, I find that it does not get at what is essential; and if one puts it first, instead of inquiring into the connection, one neglects an understanding of the latter.

18. This transition from the related conversation to the frame conversation is one of the best examples of Plato's formative irony (see *Plato* 1, pp. 145ff.). Arnim says it is "an external indication from which the reader is supposed to conclude that it is no longer a question of

protreptic. . . ." I should not say so. For here too it *is*, in a certain sense, a question of protreptic. But no one can fail to see that this penetration of the "frame" by the "image" indicates the decisive moment in the situation. In the *Phaedo* there is a similar formal motif (88c *et seq.*).

19. Arnim (pp. 135, 140) thinks that Eukleides is attacked here, since he is said to have declared φρόνησις, among other things, to be the ἀγαθόν (Diogenes Laërtius II 106). Apart from the fact that we cannot gain a live image of Eukleides from such meager doxographic sources, and even admitting the fact that this connection may have been in Plato's mind, we must not allow such an external reference to blur our understanding of the inner dialectic with which Plato mounts by stages. The identification of ἀγαθόν and ἐπιστήμη is such a stage. And Plato does not require another person above and beyond whom he would advance at a point where he supersedes himself. / The same is true in still greater degree as to the alleged reference to Antisthenes (Arnim, p. 140).

20. Cf. Arnim, p. 127.

21. Cf. pp. 108f., above.

22. E.g., Bonitz, p. 137.

23. *Plato* 1, pp. 145ff.

24. Stefanini, I, 193: *"Il dubbio di Critone è il dubbio di Platone."* The reverse is true. Plato does not doubt, but he has his Crito doubt.

25. For Isokrates: Schleiermacher, II/1, 408; Spengel, *AbhMun*, 1853, pp. 763ff.; Méridier, *Platon Budé*, V/1, 133ff.; Shorey, pp. 34, 167 ("Isocrates or a disciple of Isocrates"); G. Mathieu, "Les premiers conflits entre Platon et Isocrate . . .," *Mélanges Gustave Glotz*, II, 1932, 55ff. (quoted by de Vries, p. 241); H. Raeder, *Platon und die Sophisten* (Det kongelige Danske Videnskabernes Selskab, Copenhagen, 1956), pp. 21ff. For other older assumptions see Hermann, p. 629, whose guess is Polykrates. For Antisthenes: Schleiermacher, II/1, 404; Arnim, p. 129. See Kurt von Fritz, "Zur Antisthenischen Erkenntnistheorie und Logik," *Hermes*, LXII (1927), 456, n. 1. / Taylor, pp. 101f., guessing Antiphon the Sophist, touches briefly upon the general meaning of that Someone. / It is not Plato who "forsakes the scenic frame of the dialogue at that moment" (Bruns, p. 315); it is the interpreters who do so.

26. Cf. Wilamowitz, I, 301 = I², 304.

xv : *Cratylus*

RECENT EDITIONS AND TRANSLATIONS: O. Apelt, PhB 174 (2d edn., 1922);
H. N. Fowler, Loeb VI (1926); E. Martini (Turin, 1930); L. Méri-
dier, *Platon Budé*, V/2 (1931); A. Manzoni (Turin, 1936); J. Olives
Canals (Barcelona, 1952); M. Buccellato (Turin, 1958).

RECENT INTERPRETATIONS: M. Leky, *Plato als Sprachphilosoph* (Paderborn,
1919); J. van Ijzeren, "De Cratylo Heracliteo et de Platonis Cratylo," *Mnemosyne*, XLIX (1921), 174ff.; K. von Fritz, "Zur Antisthenischen Erkenntnistheorie und Logik," *Hermes*, LXII (1927),
453ff.; I. Abramczyk, *Platons Dialog "Kratylos" und das Problem der
Sprachphilosophie* (Breslau, 1928); M. Warburg, *Zwei Fragen zum
"Kratylos"* (Berlin, 1929); E. Haag, *Platons "Kratylos"* (Stuttgart,
1933); K. Büchner, *Platons "Kratylos" und die moderne Sprachphilosophie* (Berlin, 1936); B. Unterberger, *Platons Etymologien im "Kratylos"* (Graz, 1935–37); V. Goldschmidt, *Essai sur le "Cratyle"*
(Paris, 1940); P. Boyancé, "La 'Doctrine d'Euthyphron' dans le
Cratyle," *RevÉtGr*, LIV (1941), 141ff.; A. Nehring, "Plato and the
Theory of Language," *Traditio*, III (1945), 13ff.; Goldschmidt, pp.
112ff.; G. S. Kirk, "The Problem of Cratylus," *AJP*, LXXII (1951),
225ff.; A. Pagliaro, "Il *Cratilo* di Platone," *Dioniso*, n.s., XV (1952),
178ff.; Buccellato, ch. 7; J. Derbolav, *Der Dialog "Kratylos" im Rah-
men der platonischen Sprach- und Erkenntnisphilosophie* (Saarbrücken,
1953); J. Lohmann, *Gnomon*, XXVI (1954), 449ff.; D. J. Allan,
"The Problem of Cratylus," *AJP*, LXXV (1954), 271ff.; F. Sontag,
"The Platonist's Conception of Language," *JPhilos*, LI (1954), 823ff.;
Sir David Ross, "The Date of Plato's *Cratylus*," *RevInPh*, IX (1955),
187ff.; V. Goldschmidt, *Revue Philosophique*, CXLVI (1956), 145ff.;
É. Amado-Lévy-Valensi, "Le Problème du *Cratyle*," *Revue Philoso-
phique*, CXLVI (1956), 16ff.; H.-G. Gadamer, *Wahrheit und Methode*
(Tübingen, 1960), pp. 383ff.

ADDITIONAL BIBLIOGRAPHY: Shorey, p. 565; Geffcken, Notes, p. 78; Rosenmeyer, p. 178; Cherniss, *Lustrum*, pp. 75ff.

1. Strongly expressed by H. Steinthal, *Geschichte der Sprachwissenschaft*[2]
   (Berlin, 1890), pp. 80ff. Nevertheless, it has often been forgotten
   again, as by Ueberweg-Praechter (p. 256) and by Apelt in the introduction to his translation. φύσει in Kratylos' statement does not refer
   to the nature of man (Apelt, "Einleitung zur Übersetzung des *Kratylos*," 2d edn., 1922, p. 6) but to the relation of word to thing. Cf.

Ernst Hoffmann, "Die Sprache und die archaische Logik," *Heidel-berger Abhandlungen zur Philosophie und ihrer Geschichte*, III (Tübin-gen, 1925), 15ff.; J. H. Dahlmann, *De philosophorum Graecorum sen-tentiis ad loquellae origines pertinentes* (Leipzig diss., 1928), pp. 41ff.; Stenzel, "Sokrates," in *R-E*, III A, cols. 821ff.; Perls, I, 44ff.; Leise-gang, cols. 2328ff.

2. We are accustomed to place the contrast upon the words *physis* and *nomos*, or *physis* and *thesis*. Plato intentionally uses νόμος only as one word among several. And indeed it is ambiguous, since the νόμος and the νομο-θέτης (388DE) can transmit words to usage, which φύσει co-incide with the thing. The interpreters of Plato over and again dis-cuss the question of how Plato decides between the φύσει and νόμῳ ὀρθότης (φύσει and θέσει, as Proklos says, or even Gellius, *Noctes Atticae* X 4: *Quaeri enim solitum apud philosophos*, φύσει τὰ ὀνόματα sint ἢ θέσει). Whether the one or the other is thought to be Platonic, or the two are reconciled ("a mediating view," Ritter, I, 474), we merely draw Plato down to the level of sophistic chatter until we see how he anchors the concepts of *physis* and *nomos* in an entirely new depth. See M. Pohlenz, "Nomos und Physis," *Hermes*, LXXXI (1953), 418ff.; F. Heinimann, *Nomos und Physis* [I¹⁷]. / Richard Robinson, "The Theory of Names in Plato's *Cratylus*," *RevInPhil*, IX (1955), 221ff. "The *Cratylus* is solely about the correctness of names, it is not about the origin of names" (p. 224) is much too narrow.

3. 384D 2, 385A 2. 385A 2 must read, essentially as in the Bodleian: ὃ ἂν (for ἐὰν is only an orthographical variant) θῇ καλεῖν τις ἕκαστον, τοῦτ' ἔστιν ἑκάστῳ ὄνομα. The proof is provided by the parallel pas-sages cited. In the θεῖναι there is already the sound of the νομοθέτης. ἔστιν is necessary. The name with which, in a given case, someone decrees that each person and thing is to be named—that is the name which each person and thing has. (See also Euripides, *Ion* 75: ὄνομα κεκλῆσθαι θήσεται.) The view of L. Méridier (*Platon Budé*, V/2) is correct; he is also right, at other points, in not yielding to the "Cobe-tism" that is widely prevalent in the textual criticism of Plato's works.

4. The contrast is similarly formulated by Ernst Cassirer, *Philosophie der symbolischen Formen* (Berlin, 1923–29), I, 62.

5. Cf. Steinthal, *Sprachwissenschaft* [XV¹], pp. 80ff. "No one takes the pains to criticize a view unless he has some inner relation to it" (p. 85).

6. Diogenes Laërtius III 6: [Πλάτων] προσεῖχε Κρατύλῳ τε τῷ Ἡρακλειτείῳ καὶ Ἑρμογένει τῷ τὰ Παρμενίδου φιλοσοφοῦντι. In the Προλεγόμενα τῆς Πλάτωνος φιλοσοφίας, ch. 4 (Hermann, p. 199), there is instead Ἑρ-μίππῳ τῷ Παρμενιδείῳ, evidently as the result of an error, as already observed by Ast, p. 20, and Hermann, p. 106. It is surely not un-natural to follow Ast (who names Tennemann as his predecessor), Hermann (p. 47), Zeller (p. 397), and Natorp (*R-E*, s.v. "Hermog-enes") in assuming that the Eleaticism of Hermogenes is spun out

of the contrast between Hermogenes and Kratylos in the Platonic dialogue. But that is by no means certain, and one may perhaps find a certain confirmation in the words of Parmenides himself, πάντ' ὄνομ' ἐστίν, ὅσσα βροτοὶ κατέθεντο (*Vorsokr.* 28 [18] B 8, 38f.), if one compares them with the thesis of Hermogenes in general and with the formulation ὅτι ἄν τις τῷ θῆται ὄνομα τοῦτο εἶναι τὸ ὀρθόν (384D).

7. The polemic against Antisthenes was set forth principally by Schleiermacher (II/2, 12ff.), that against the Megarians by Hermann (489ff.). Schleiermacher already exaggerated the Antisthenes-thesis, which later (in Dümmler and Joël) has been carried to the extreme that Kratylos appears as a mere mask of Antisthenes. / Against this thesis are: Taylor, p. 86, n. 1; Dahlmann, *De philosophorum Graecorum sententiis* [XV¹], pp. 44ff.; Méridier, *Platon Budé*, V/2, 38ff. See the thorough discussion by K. von Fritz in *Hermes*, LXXII (1927), 457ff. / Dümmler, *Akademika* [VI¹⁵], 158f., sees in Prodikos a forerunner of the etymological "wisdom" combatted in the *Cratylus*. According to M. Warburg, *Zwei Fragen zum "Kratylos"* (Neue Philol. Unters. V, Berlin, 1929), the dialogue is directed against Herakleides Pontikos and should therefore be assigned to Plato's late period. Against this view is Hans von Arnim, "Die sprachliche Forschung als Grundlage der Chronologie der platonischen Dialoge und der *Kratylos*," *SBWien*, 1929. According to E. Haag, *Platons "Kratylos"* (Tübinger Beiträge, Stuttgart, 1933), the *Cratylus*, *Theaetetus*, and *Sophist* constitute a unity, a view concurred in by E. Hoffmann, *Gnomon*, XV (1939), 477. Cf. also D. J. Allan, "The Problem of Cratylus," *AJP* LXXV (1954), 273f. Arnim's verbal statistics place the *Cratylus* after the *Gorgias* and *Meno*. Our own arrangement deviates somewhat from this order; again, however, this deviation is not intended in a strictly chronological sense, for the groups may overlap in their dates.

8. On the structure of the dialogue see Victor Goldschmidt, *Essai sur le "Cratyle"* (Paris, 1940), pp. 37ff. Max Leky, *Plato als Sprachphilosoph* (Paderborn, 1919), divides the dialogue into four main parts of equal order—three of which go to the conversation with Hermogenes.

9. See Aristotle, Περὶ ἑρμηνείας, ch. 1: περὶ γὰρ σύνθεσιν καὶ διαίρεσίν ἐστι τὸ ψεῦδος καὶ τὸ ἀληθές. Steinthal, *Sprachwissenschaft* [XV¹], p. 86, calls attention to the "paralogism" and says (p. 108) that "the assumed connection of λόγος and ὄνομα is false and must be retracted," i.e., in the light of the final result. Put in such terms, to be sure, it is un-Platonic; for if there is true and false in ὀνομάζειν, then a false ὀνομάζειν cannot become a correct λέγειν. But Plato conceals the question in what sense an ὄνομα can be true and false. / In *Letter VII* 343AB, firmness (βέβαιον) is denied to the ὄνομα. Hence, it has the element of arbitrariness.

10. In 389D Codex *W* has ὀνοματοθέτης, *BT* have ὁ νομοθέτης. *Charmides* 175B 4 has νομοθέτης in *BTW*, ὀνοματοθέτης in "*recc.*" Goldschmidt,

Essai sur le "Cratyle" [XV⁸], p. 66, decides in both places on νομοθέτης, with good reason. In the *Cratylus*-passage, only νομοθέτης has the shade of meaning that is important here. In the *Charmides*-passage, νομοθέτης would probably point to the fact that at that time Plato already had in mind the question posed in the *Cratylus*. Giorgio Pasquali, in the index to Proklos, *In Platonis "Cratylum" Commentarii* (Leipzig, 1918), lists four occurrences of ὀνοματοθέτης, so that there might be a Neoplatonic, clarifying variant in the Platonic text. / Whether the figure of the lawgiver who gave things their names derives from the Pythagoreans (Goldschmidt, *Essai*, p. 63) remains uncertain, considering the indefiniteness of the concept "so-called Pythagoreans."

11. See Steinthal, *Sprachwissenschaft* [XV¹], p. 91. To this extent, one could accept the view of E. Hoffmann, "Die Sprache und die archaische Logik" [XV¹], p. 61, that, according to Plato, language is τέχνη, and therefore (if I understand correctly) neither νόμῳ nor φύσει. But is this not also too dogmatic? Is the "speech-creator" not taken too literally? Is not the antithesis νόμῳ-φύσει incorrectly transferred to language instead of the ὀρθότης? Finally, is not the contrast of φύσις and τέχνη conceived in Aristotelian terms, and are not *techne, nomos,* and *physis* in Plato practically synonymous? / Cf. Goldschmidt, *Essai sur le "Cratyle"* [XV⁸], pp. 61ff.

12. Proklos, *In Platonis "Cratylum" Comm.* (Pasquali edn. [XV¹⁰]), ch. 51, p. 19, 24: καί μοι δοκεῖ τὸν νομοθέτην ὁ Πλάτων ἀνάλογον ἱδρύων τῷ ὅλῳ δημιουργῷ. The connection with the *Timaeus* is a constant theme in Proklos' interpretation of the *Cratylus*: see Pasquali's index, p. 124. /Among the moderns, Karl Lehrs, *RhM*, XXII (1867), 438, has pointed with particular emphasis to these last thoughts or surmises of the Platonic *Cratylus*. Theodor Benfey, *Abh. d. Gött. Ges.*, XII (1866), 318ff., turns the Platonic surmise into a theory, which he expands by saying that it is the task of the dialectician to form an ideal language. This is ingeniously thought out, and it is, at any rate, rewarding to reflect why, in the work of Plato, such an ideal language was *not* devised. See Goldschmidt, *Essai sur le "Cratyle"* [XV⁸], pp. 199f. / For reference to the *Timaeus*, see E. Hoffmann, "Die Sprache und die archaische Logik" [XV¹], p. 58. *Timaeus* 78E (τὸν γὰρ τὰς ἐπωνυμίας θέμενον) is a reference back to the *Cratylus*; a very significant one occurs also in 83c.

13. The discussion as to whether the εἶδος refers to the "doctrine of *Ideas*" derives from the doctrinaire conception of the *Idea* which we are seeking everywhere to overcome. / See Freymann, p. 119ff.

14. 396D, 399A, 400A, 407D, 409D, 428c.

15. 400D: περὶ θεῶν οὐδὲν ἴσμεν οὔτε περὶ αὐτῶν οὔτε περὶ τῶν ὀνομάτων ἅττα ποτὲ ἑαυτοὺς καλοῦσιν. Cf. Protagoras, frag. 4: περὶ μὲν θεῶν οὐκ ἔχω εἰδέναι οὔθ' ὡς εἰσὶν οὔθ' ὡς οὐκ εἰσὶν οὔθ' ὁποῖοί τινες ἰδέαν.

16. According to Dümmler, *Akademika* [VI¹⁵], pp. 129ff., this entire section is a polemic of Plato against a monotheistic-pantheistic-materialistic theory, which he associates with Antisthenes. True, Plato must have encountered a multitude of such etymologies, more or less dangerous, and philosophical notions that he particularly disliked readily combined with such etymologizing. But this view underestimates Plato's power to create enemies for himself out of diverse tendencies. The weakness of Dümmler's theory can be taken up here only in so far as the *Cratylus* is concerned. For Hestia (401c) and Pan (408B *et seq.*) Dümmler would like to assume that Plato suppressed such etymologizing interpretations as the reference to the "all" in the case of Pan. Apart from the fact that this cannot be proven, one does not understand how such a suppression can be the right way of polemics. Dümmler, moreover, has misunderstood the etymology of Poseidon (402E). Here the ὀνομάσας must not be deleted from the text. For it is he who is meant by αὐτόν, not at all Poseidon, who, on the contrary, is the ποσίδεσμος for him who walks on solid ground. Méridier is right, but we should write, with Codex *W*, ὑπὸ τοῦ πρώτου.

17. 393D 3: ἕως ἂν ἐγκρατὴς ᾖ ἡ οὐσία τοῦ πράγματος δηλουμένη ἐν τῷ ὀνόματι. Wilamowitz (II, 349) praises Dümmler's conjecture ἐναργής. It is plausible, but not correct. "The essence prevails." Beside δηλουμένη, ἐναργής would be tautological. The wording of the manuscripts is supported by 393E 2: ἕως ἂν αὐτοῦ δηλουμένην τὴν δύναμιν [!] ἐντιθῶμεν. In 393C 2, μόσχον should probably be deleted, as Ast proposes; cf. 394D 8.

18. 399A 4, 399E 4; 400B 4; 401E 1; 402D 3; 406B 5, 406C 1; 407C 8.

19. 421B 1 should be written ἡ δ' ἀλήθεια, καὶ τοῦτο τοῖς ἄλλοις (ὁμοίως) ἔοικε συγκεκροτῆσθαι, unless one prefers to follow Heindorf in substituting κατὰ ταὐτὰ τοῖς ἄλλοις.

20. See, e.g., Jakob Grimm, *Über den Ursprung der Sprache* (Berlin, 1852), pp. 39ff.; Grote, II, 531; H. Paul, *Prinzipien der Sprachgeschichte* (Halle, 1920), ch. 9; E. Cassirer, *Philosophie der symbolischen Formen* [XV⁴], I, 138ff.; Wilamowitz, I, 292 = I², 294: "So far as I can see, we have not become wiser." See also Méridier, *Platon Budé*, V/2, 26; Gilbert Highet, *A Clerk of Oxenford* (New York, 1954), p. 137.

21. See *Plato* 1, ch. II.

22. Cf. Dümmler, *Akademika* [VI¹⁵], p. 136. Walther Kranz's Index (Vol. III) to *Vorsokr.* makes it easy to increase the number of comparable passages. With 412D: διὰ δὲ τούτου παντὸς εἶναί τι διεξιόν, δι' οὗ πάντα τὰ γιγνόμενα γίγνεσθαι, εἶναι δὲ τάχιστον τοῦτο καὶ λεπτότατον cf., e.g., the following: Empedokles, *Vorsokr.* 21 A 86; B 84: "Air and fire go clear through the other elements," διιέναι λεπτὸν ὄν. Anaxagoras, *Vorsokr.* 46 B 12, regarding νοῦς: ἔστι γὰρ λεπτότατόν τε πάντων χρημάτων. Demokritos, *Vorsokr.* 55 A 101, regarding πῦρ = νοῦς = ψυχή: λεπτομερέστατόν τε καὶ μάλιστα τῶν στοιχείων ἀσώματον. Diog-

enes of Apollonia, *Vorsokr.* 51 A 20, regarding ἀήρ = ψυχή : λεπτομερέστατον. We may leave it an open question whether the etymological jest καλόν = καλοῦν (416в *et seq.*) conceals a deeper meaning. Without deciding this matter, we merely point out that the course of proof goes thus: It is to be proven that καλόν = καλοῦν. To that end it must be shown, first, διάνοια = καλοῦν, and second, διάνοια = καλόν. The first is done in 416c 1–6: διάνοια is αἴτιον κληθῆναι. The second is done in 416c 7–D 7 by way of the analogical conclusion, which guarantees the equality of what effects and what is effected. Hence this playful proof, formally quite strict, is impaired if one follows Badham in writing τὸ καλοῦν in 416c 7, instead of recognizing τὸ καλόν as the object of καλέσαν. For what is to be shown, of course, is the equality of subject and object. It was just as wrong—and that led to Badham's emendation—to take τὸ καλόν as nominative. Marsiglio Ficino and Schleiermacher do so in their translations. Burnet completes the misunderstanding when, in 416D 4, he writes καλοῦν instead of καλόν.

23. Concerning the passage on Apollo (404E–406A) see P. Boyancé, "Note sur la Tétractys," *Antiquité Classique*, XX (1951), 421ff.

24. ἡ ὀρθότης τοιαύτη τις ἐβούλετο εἶναι, οἵα δηλοῦν οἷον ἕκαστόν ἐστι τῶν ὄντων (422D). αὕτη μοι φαίνεται . . . βούλεσθαι εἶναι ἡ τῶν ὀνομάτων ὀρθότης (427cD).

25. Wilamowitz, *Griechische Verskunst* (Berlin, 1921), pp. 59ff.; H. Ryffel, "Eukosmia," *MusHelv*, IV (1947), 23ff.; Warren D. Anderson, "The Importance of Damonian Theory in Plato's Thought," *TAPA*, LXXXVI (1955), 88ff.

26. εἰ ἔστιν εἰς ἃ ἀναφέρεται πάντα ὥσπερ τὰ στοιχεῖα (424D 2). Difficult as the text is at this point, at least it is certain that here it is not a question (as E. Hoffmann, "Die Sprache und die archaische Logik" [XV¹], p. 55, thinks it is) of the relationship between the reality of the words and that of the objects (which is only mentioned in the following section with ἐπιφέρειν). On the contrary, here it must be a matter of the simplest ὄντα like "tree" or "circle" or "just," to which the immense abundance of living reality is "reduced," as the infinitude of speech sounds is reduced to the letters of the alphabet. If this is the correct interpretation, one cannot give up τὰ ὄντα in D 1 as the proper opposite of ταῦτα, i.e., the γράμματα as a whole. But then the question arises how Plato in writing prevented the reader from making the most natural connection ταῦτα διελώμεθα τὰ ὄντα. It seems to me that he could do so only if a word followed τὰ ὄντα which necessarily occupied the second position in the sentence. That word is not εὖ, which also seems strange in other respects. But it might well be αὖ. I conjecture, therefore, τὰ ὄντα αὖ πάντα [αὖ] οἷς δεῖ. . . .

27. E. Hoffmann, "Die Sprache . . ." [XV¹], p. 25, thinks he finds here a derived theory to be traced back to Demokritos, "since this conception rests upon the assumption of an atomistically structured matter."

It is, however, a question not of matter and atoms, but of general structures of being. Similarly, one cannot agree with what Hoffmann further says (pp. 54f.) about this "theory" and its "cessation." Cf. Goldschmidt, *Essai sur le "Cratyle"* [XV⁸], p. 150.

28. Schleiermacher (II/2, 9f.) had already pointed to the system, briefly, but emphatically. See also Shorey, *Unity*, p. 51; Apelt, "Einleitung zur Übersetzung" [XV¹], pp. 25ff., although the latter's discussion of Plato's "logical mysticism," to be sure, must be ruled out. / Perhaps the passage about the τέμνειν κατὰ τὴν φύσιν (*Cratylus* 387Α) should also be considered in this context. Here τέμνειν gets a medical shading from κάειν which follows, whereas, to start with, τέμνειν is to be understood generally. Then, however, it agreés with διατέμνειν κατ' ἄρθρα ᾗ πέφυκεν (*Phaedrus* 265Ε) and the similar passages cited by Stenzel, *Studien*, p. 59, and is part of the undercurrent of the *Cratylus*, which is characterized by the words εἶδος, διαλεκτικός, διαίρεσις, and, lastly, αὐτὸ τὸ καλόν.

29. *Letter VII* 343ΑΒ is also reminiscent of the *Cratylus*, even as to verbal parallels. There the view regarding ὄνομα and λόγος is closer to the thesis of Hermogenes (cf. the close correspondence with *Cratylus* 433Ε). But it is hardly necessary to point out that skeptical abuse is precluded by the structure of different stages leading from ὄνομα and λόγος to ἐπιστήμη and up to the εἶδος. Nor can we possibly claim that Plato changed his mind. Just because he believed in absolutes he is a "relativist" with regard to each stage. / Aristotle, Περὶ ἑρμηνείας, ch. 2, simply sides with the thesis of Hermogenes.

30. See *Plato* 1, pp. 25ff.

31. δι' ὀνομάτων ... δι' αὐτῶν (439Α), and also πλὴν ὀνομάτων and ἄνευ ὀνομάτων (438D 6), taken strictly, point to the second. But all the same it is noteworthy that nowhere does Plato say ἄνευ λόγου.

32. "The proof as brief as it is radical": Natorp, p. 125. The discussion of the interpreters as to whether and how far the dialogue aims at the so-called "theory of *Ideas*" is put together by H. Kirchner in four "programs" of the Brieg Gymnasium, especially III b (1897), 24f. See Freymann, pp. 119ff.; Shorey, pp. 267f.; Grube, pp. 13f.

33. In this light one may ask himself whether Leky (*Plato als Sprach-philosoph* [XV⁸], p. 84) and Derbolav are right in saying that the main purpose of the dialogue is the philosophy of language, and that "all the other issues, such as the metaphysical-epistemological chapter of the last part, are subordinate to this main purpose." The same objection may be made to Sir David Ross, "The Date of Plato's *Cratylus*," *RevInPh*, IX (1955), p. 191: "The dialogue is about etymology and in the main about nothing else." Plato rejects such dissection.

XVI: *Menexenus*

RECENT EDITIONS AND TRANSLATIONS: O. Apelt, PhB 177 (2d edn., 1922);
R. G. Bury, Loeb VII (1929); L. Méridier, *Platon Budé*, V/1 (1931);
G. La Magna (Milan, 1934); K. Hildebrandt (Leipzig, 1936); J.
Olives Canals (Barcelona, 1952); N. Scholl (Rome, 1959).

RECENT INTERPRETATIONS: Singer, pp. 169ff.; A. Momigliano, "Il Menesseno," *RFIC*, VIII (1930), 40ff.; Hildebrandt, pp. 139ff.; K. Oppenheimer, *Zwei attische Epitaphien* (Berlin, 1933); R. Harder, "Plato
und Athen" in *Kleine Schriften* (Munich, 1940), pp. 212ff.; K. Vourveris, Συμβολὴ εἰς τὴν ἑρμηνείαν τοῦ Μενεξένου τοῦ Πλάτωνος (Salon-
ica, 1947); de Vries, pp. 256ff.; G. M. Lattanzi, "Il significato e
l'autenticità del *Menesseno*," *ParPass*, VIII (1953), 303ff.; Gauss,
II/1, 223ff.; P. M. Huby, "The *Menexenus* Reconsidered," *Phronesis*,
II (1957), 104ff.; M. Pavan, *La grecità politica da Tucidide ad
Aristotele* (Rome, 1958), pp. 67ff.; Ilse von Loewenclau, *Der platonische Menexenos* (Tübinger Beiträge, 1961).

ADDITIONAL BIBLIOGRAPHY: Shorey, p. 538; Geffcken, Notes, p. 70; Rosenmeyer, p. 182; Cherniss, *Lustrum*, pp. 114f.

1. Cf. Eduard Schwartz, *Hermes*, XXXV (1900), 124 (following Ast,
   pp. 448ff.). On modern criticism, see Stefanini, II², 69f.
2. Especially P. Wendland, "Die Tendenz des platonischen *Menexenos*,"
   Hermes, XXV (1890), 171ff. Pohlenz, pp. 244ff., and Wilamowitz,
   II, 126ff., have done much for the elucidation of the work. The first
   two look upon it as a satire (as do Taylor, pp. 41ff.; de Vries, pp.
   256ff.) whereas Wilamowitz considers it a competitive work. None
   has faced as a problem the inconsistency into which his interpretation
   forced him. What happens if every sentence is read as a satire is
   shown by Trendelenburg's interpretation, *Jahresbericht des Friedrichs-
   Gymnasiums* (Berlin, 1905). The dialogue is seen as a battle against
   the prevailing rhetoric by: Schleiermacher, II/3, 373ff.; Hermann,
   pp. 520f.; Grote, III, 8ff.; Méridier, *Platon Budé*, V/1, 77; Robin,
   p. 41. A deeper view is taken by Schaerer, pp. 76, 175ff. / Cf. Leisegang, cols. 2417ff.; Levinson, pp. 609ff.
3. Suggested even before Pohlenz and Wilamowitz by Bruns, p. 359.
   Heinrich Dittmar, *Aischines von Sphettos* (Berlin, 1912), pp. 19ff.,
   tried in vain to justify this thesis.
4. The comparison with Shakespeare's *Troilus and Cressida* which Taylor
   (p. 45) suggests is ingenious, little as Taylor's conception of the

work as a satire on patriotic eloquence exhausts the content of his own comparison. See Gundolf, *Shakespeare* (Berlin, 1928), II, 188: *Troilus and Cressida* "unites hostile states of mind and derives its charm from their juxtaposition and opposition." Idem, p. 190: "Astonishing, almost moving, and equally perplexing for pure dogmatists, excitables, and skeptics remains Shakespeare's power of keeping alive, even to the point of parody, the sweet and painful stirrings which he smiles at or bewails, and more than that, the high seriousness and the festive dignity which he ridicules. What distinguishes him from the scoffers is that he does not have to step out of the state which he intends to abolish—like Lucian, Swift, Shaw, and even Aristophanes and Cervantes—but that he can incorporate his irony in his pathos and his ethos, that he simultaneously, not before or after, laughs and suffers and, like the Creator, along with his annihilating knowledge is still master of undivided life."

5. The paradox may be found as early as Herodotus VII 104, where Demaratos says to Xerxes (concerning the Athenians): ἐλεύθεροι γὰρ ἐόντες οὐ πάντα ἐλεύθεροί εἰσι· ἔπεστι γάρ σφι δεσπότης νόμος.

6. Wilamowitz (I, 185 = I², 188) doubts that this Menexenos is the same one as in the *Lysis*. He does not doubt that the Ktesippos of the *Lysis* is the same one as in the *Euthydemus*. In the *Phaedo*, Ktesippos and Menexenos are present at the death of Socrates; Plato—like Balzac—used the same name to evoke the same person.

7. See also Diels, "Über das dritte Buch der aristotelischen Rhetorik," *AbhBerl*, 1886, p. 21; Wendland, "Die Tendenz des platonischen *Menexenos*" [XVI²], p. 179; K. Oppenheimer, *Zwei attische Epitaphien* (Berlin, 1933), p. 70.

8. Cobet's rejection of the one word πολιτικούς (249E 4) deprives the conclusion of the dialogue—in fact, ultimately, the whole dialogue—of its meaning.

9. Cf. *Plato* 1, p. 148.

10. Ameipsias, Konnos, *Fragm. Com. Graec.*, ed. Meineke (Berlin, 1839–57), I, 201ff.; II, 703ff.; *editio minor*, I, 403f. Cf. Bruns, pp. 317, 358; Wilamowitz, II, 139.

11. Cf. Pohlenz, pp. 268ff. To be sure, the view that Plato wanted to "ridicule the adaptation of the encomium to the *epitaphios*" ascribes to him an intention belonging to the school of rhetoric. Since the *epitaphios* is an encomium, the separation of the two types is an abstraction.

12. Anaximenes 82, 2: ἐπιτιμᾶν δὲ καὶ τοῖς ἄλλοις, ὅσοι τοὺς προγόνους ἐπαινοῦσι, λέγων, ὅτι πολλοὶ προγόνων ἐνδόξων τυχόντες ἀνάξιοι γεγόνασι.

13. See Pohlenz, pp. 273f.

14. See Wilamowitz, II, 131.

15. With ἰσονομία Plato picks up the favorite slogan of democracy. See B.

Keil in Alfred Gercke and Eduard Norden, *Einleitung in die Alter-tumswissenschaften*[2] (3 vols., Leipzig, 1933), III, 368; E. Weiss, *Griechisches Privatrecht* (Leipzig, 1923), I, 71f. ἰσογονία is perhaps a Platonic coinage. Liddell-Scott lists the word nowhere else except in Dio Cassius 52, 4, where Agrippa delivers a speech on constitutional forms combining ἰσονομία, ἰσογονία, ἰσομοιρία.

16. The verbal coincidence of *Menexenus* 240BC and *Laws* 698C–E is no proof of spuriousness (Zeller, *Platonische Studien* [I[32]], p. 149). This should be kept in mind in other cases of extensive verbal agreement, as, for example, in the *Theages*. Cf. above, ch. XI, n. 15.

17. Pohlenz, p. 292.

18. Ibid., p. 293.

19. Ibid., p. 295.

20. Ibid., p. 296.

21. E.g., Ritter, II, 867. Only the *Menexenus* (he claims) is as poor as the *Critias* in philosophical content, among all the writings of Plato, apart from that youthful jest or hoax the *Hippias Minor* (i.e., the dialogue containing the germ of the *Sophist*!). "Eine taube Nuss": Diels, as quoted by K. Hude, *Les Oraisons funèbres de Lysias et de Platon* (Det kongelige Danske Videnskabernes Selskab, Copenhagen, 1917), p. 13.

XVII: *Alcibiades Major*

RECENT EDITIONS AND TRANSLATIONS: O. Apelt, PhB 172b (2d edn., 1921); M. Croiset, *Platon Budé*, I (1920); H. N. Fowler and W. R. M. Lamb, Loeb VIII (1927); G. Ammendola (Naples, 1929); F. Novotny (Prague, 1938); E. Turolla (Venice, 1945); J. Olives Canals (Barcelona, 1956).

RECENT INTERPRETATIONS: P. Friedländer, *DGrA*, I (1921); II, *Kritische Erörterung* (1923); C. Vink, *Plato's "Eerste Alcibiades"* (Amsterdam, 1939); É. de Strycker, "Platonica I: L'authenticité du *Premier Alcibiade*," *Études Classiques*, XI (1942), 135ff.; A.-J. Festugière, "Grecs et sages orientaux," *RHR*, CXXX (1945), pp. 29ff.; E. Delcominette, *Sur l'authenticité du "Premier Alcibiade" de Platon* (Liége, 1949); cf. *RBP*, XXIX (1950), 771; R. S. Bluck, "The Origin of the *Greater Alcibiades*," *CQ*, n.s., III (1953), 46ff.; P. M. Clark, "The Greater Alcibiades," *CQ*, n.s., V (1955), 231ff.

ADDITIONAL BIBLIOGRAPHY: Shorey, p. 652; Geffcken, Notes, p. 156; Rosenmeyer, p. 177; Cherniss, *Lustrum*, pp. 71f.

1. See *DGrA*, I (1921); II, *Kritische Erörterung* (1923). It goes without

saying that the question of genuineness is not reargued here in all its details (including the κρήγυος argument, in spite of Jachmann, p. 276). / See Leisegang, cols. 2367f. / Plato's authorship is supported more recently by Apelt, 131ff.; Stefanini, I, 78ff.; Grube, p. 8; C. Vink, *Plato's "Eerste Alcibiades"* (Amsterdam, 1939), with detailed discussion of the arguments; Goldschmidt, pp. 316ff.; Festugière, p. 67. Against it, among others, are Jachmann, pp. 308ff. ("inferior, schoolboy product," "imbecile scribbler"); Joseph Bidez, *Eos, ou Platon et l'Orient* (Brussels, 1945), ch. 13 (written, for the most part, by É. de Strycker); Jula Kerschensteiner, *Platon und der Orient* (Stuttgart, 1945), pp. 202ff.; E. Dupréel, *Les Sophistes* (Paris, 1949), pp. 151ff.; Ross, p. 3 ("almost universally rejected"); Hoffmann, p. 126; W. J. W. Koster, *Le Mythe de Platon, de Zarathoustra et des Chaldéens* (Leiden, 1951), pp. 23f.; R. S. Bluck, "The Origin of the *Greater Alcibiades*," *CQ*, n.s., III (1953), 46ff.; H. Gundert, "Platon und das Daimonion des Sokrates," *Gymnasium*, LXI (1954), 521; Gauss, I/2, 205ff. / P. M. Clark, "The Greater Alcibiades," *CQ*, n.s., V (1955), 230ff., ascribes the first two-thirds to a pupil of Plato, the last third to Plato himself. / Gauss (I/2, 204ff.) criticizes the dialogue with an excess especially inappropriate for a "philosophical commentary." For an example of serious misunderstanding in detail, see Gauss, p. 206, regarding ὅλον τε καὶ πᾶν (109B). / Classen, p. 145, believes that he has a new argument against genuineness. He quite correctly points out that the Platonic Socrates never uses ἀρετή for a δημιουργική. When he takes *Alcibiades I* 135A 6 *et seq.*, however, as a confirmation of the spuriousness of the dialogue, he draws a wrong conclusion. For the steering of a ship is no more a δημιουργική than the art of a physician is, or the science of mathematics. Cf. *Republic* VI 488A–489D; *Statesman* 297E–299E. / Alain (Émile Chartier), *Idées* (Paris, 1932), p. 69, shows how the dialogue can affect a superior mind untouched by the discussion of whether the work is genuine or not: ". . . je conseille de lire d'abord [Alain is speaking of the *Symposium*] le "*Premier Alcibiade*," toujours neuf pour tous, toutefois assez familier aussi, puisqu'on y voit la plus brillante vertu tourner à mal. . . ." Still worth reading is H. Taine, "Les Jeunes Gens de Platon," in *Essais de critique et d'histoire*[8] (Paris, 1900), pp. 180ff.: "*Un de ces portraits est développé avec plus de soin que les autres, celui d'Alcibiade. . . .*"

2. See E. R. Dodds, *Gnomon*, XXVII (1955), 164.

3. The Lindskog-Ziegler edition notes our dialogue in the flute story of ch. 2, but does not say that much in chs. 4–6 goes back to it. The conclusion of ch. 6, derived from *Lysis* 210E, shows how completely Plutarch takes it as one of the series of Plato's educational dialogues.

4. Note the most important coincidences of Persius IV and the *Alcibiades*: v. 1 ∼ 105A 4, 106C 4; v. 3 ∼ 106C 8, 104B 4–5; v. 5 ∼ 106C 4; v. 8 ∼ 106C 7; v. 9 ∼ 109B 5, 109C 5, 109C 11; v. 10 ∼ 109D 2;

vv. 14–16 ∼ 104A 5–6, 113B 8–113C 7; v. 20 ∼ 105D 2, 123C 6; v. 23 ∼ 127E 1 *et seq.*; 128E 10 *et seq.* From these correspondences it follows: (a) The paragraph before v. 23 is not in Persius' sense. (b) In v. 2, Persius probably wrote *tollet*, not *tollit*. Should he not have been aware, with the dialogue *Alcibiades* so clearly before his eyes, that the death of Socrates is a generation away in the future? *Tollit* can hardly be "historical present" (see Gildersleeve [*The Satires of Persius*, New York, 1875] on this); and *tollet . . . cicuta* is actually the reading in Horace, *Satire* II 1 56, in the verse which Persius had in mind when writing IV 3 (cited by Conington-Nettleship [Oxford, 1893]).

5. See *Plato* 1, ch. XVIII.

6. Paul Friedländer, "Socrates Enters Rome," *AJP*, LXVI (1945), 248ff.

7. Xenophon, *Memorabilia* I 2 40 and III 6 1 ∼ Plato, *Alcibiades* 123D. III 7 4 ∼ 114BC. IV 2 22 ∼ 135C. Cf. *DGrA*, II, 46ff. See also *Aeschinis Socratici Reliquiae*, ed. H. Krauss (Leipzig, 1911), pp. 32ff.; H. Dittmar, *Aischines von Sphettos* [XVI³], pp. 97ff. Cf. *DGrA*, II, 41ff.; G. C. Field, *Plato and his Contemporaries* (London, 1930), pp. 146ff. / The new fragments of Aischines' *Alcibiades*, in *Oxyrhynchus Papyri* XIII (1919) 1680, do not contribute anything to the question under discussion.

8. *Geschichte des Altertums*, V, § 752. Bluck, "The Origin of the *Greater Alcibiades*" [XVII¹], dates the dialogue 343/342 B.C.

9. Hermann, p. 439. The opposite view is the most widespread. According to Taylor, "the character-drawing is far too vague and shadowy for Plato even in his latest and least dramatic phase." Similar views are held by de Strycker (Bidez, *Eos* [XVII¹]), p. 108; Dupréel, *Les Sophistes* [XVII¹]; and even among those who believe it genuine: Apelt, "Einleitung zur Übersetzung" (*Der Grosse Alkibiades* [2d edn., Leipzig, 1921]), p. 135; Maurice Croiset, *Platon Budé*, I, 50. The opposite view is held by Hermann; Taine; Vink, *Plato's "Eerste Alcibiades"* [XVII¹], pp. 91ff. Quite apart from the question of genuineness, the conflict of views poses a problem: Do we read the same work so differently? Or do we mean something different by "portrait of character"?

10. See *Plato* 1, pp. 35, 40, 345, n. 8.

11. M. Croiset, *Platon Budé*, I, 50, to be sure, does not see that: *"on n'y trouve point de péripéties proprement dites."* Croiset considers the dialogue genuine. But his dating (*"au temps du séjour à Mégare"*) is arbitrary and his interpretation not exactly profound. His remarks on the Persian speech are disappointing, coming from the land of the *Lettres Persanes*.

12. The references to Persia associated by Jaeger, *Aristotle*, pp. 131f., with the oriental tendencies of the later Academy would be just as possible in the period shortly after the march of Cyrus. There is

really no question of "oriental influence." Persian conditions are depicted with a graceful play for which the remark about "the parallel
of Plato's four virtues with the ethic of Zoroaster" is much too bur-
dened with the history of ideas and of dogmas. For a correct comment,
see Bidez, *Eos* [XVII¹], p. 125; Kerschensteiner, *Platon und der Orient*
[XVII¹], pp. 202ff.; Bluck, "The Origin of the *Greater Alcibiades*"
[XVII¹], p. 47. / Cf. K. J. Vourveris, Αἱ ἱστορικαὶ γνώσεις τοῦ Πλάτωνος
(Athens, 1938), pp. 76ff.

13. Bluck, op. cit., p. 46, takes this αὐτὸ τὸ αὐτό as "mind" and finds
essential support in this interpretation for the rejection of the dialogue. But cf. *DGrA*, II, 17f.

14. The (Neoplatonic?) expansion of the genuine text (133c), referring
to the mirror of the Godhead, has had a particularly far-reaching effect.
Cf. H. Leisegang, "Dieu au miroir de l'âme et de la nature," *Revue
d'histoire et de philosophie religieuses*, XVII (1937), 145ff. / Jaeger,
Aristotle, p. 165, n. 1, essentially on the basis of this textual expansion, considers the *Alcibiades* an attempt by a pupil of Plato "to anchor
the problems of Plato's early period in a dogmatically firm principle:
in the mysticism of the late-Platonic theory of the *nous*." E. des Places,
RevÉtGr, XLIV (1931), 164, rejects this view. / Wiggers, *Berliner
philologische Wochenschrift*, LII (1932), pp. 702ff., and Bluck, op. cit.,
p. 46, again have tried to prove that the lines added to the text of
the mss. of Plato by Eusebius and Stobaeus were originally part of
the dialogue. See W. Beierwalter, *Lux intelligibilis* (Munich diss.,
1957), p. 82. But the analogy of the mirroring eye is enough to
justify λαμπρόν in 134D 5; it need be no back reference to λαμπρότερα
in 133c 9. Schleiermacher saw this. Indeed, the arguments for and
against the inclusion of the questionable lines in the text were discussed long ago. See I. Bekker, *Platonis . . . Scripta Graece Omnia*
(London, 1826), VI, 127ff. / One argument perhaps deserves to be
considered: in the mss. of the Plato text, κάτοπτρον occurs twice,
whereas the expansion shifts from one occurrence of κάτοπτρον to two
of ἔνοπτρον. Plato (according to Ast, *Lexicon Platonicum* [Leipzig,
1835–38]) uses only κάτοπτρον, never ἔνοπτρον. / Again, 128A 13–
128B 1 is probably an addition (though less important). The words
are found only in Stobaeus, derive probably from *Gorgias* 517D, and
seem rather disturbing in the concise discussion.

15. E. Hoffmann, *Platonismus und Mittelalter*, Vorträge der Bibliothek
Warburg (Leipzig, 1923/24), pp. 56f. = *Platonismus und christliche
Philosophie* (Zurich, Stuttgart, 1960), pp. 284f., thinks this simile and
the demand connected with it is sufficient to show that the dialogue
is not Platonic. "Look into a friend's soul, then you look into your
own soul, and therewith you see God. . . . That is as simple as to look
into the pupil of another's eye." It seems to me a basic defect of this
interpretation that it does not see the persons behind the words. To

look into Socrates' soul is not easy, but it demands precisely that: ἐπιμέλειαν ἑαυτοῦ. I would not call attention again to these different ways of interpreting Plato had not R. S. Bluck, "The Origin of the *Greater Alcibiades*" [XVII¹], p. 49, expressly opposed me: "I can see no justification for the claim 'that it is not a question of Tom, Dick, or Harry, but of Socrates, into whose soul one must look.'" May I refer Bluck to Shakespeare, *Julius Caesar*, Act I, scene 2, lines 67ff.? See W. Kranz, "Shakespeare und die Antike," *Englische Studien*, LXXIII (1938), 33ff.

16. The treatment of the important passage 133BC by L. Havet, *RevPhil*, XLV (1921), 87ff., is untenable: (1) νοερώτερον is a Neoplatonic interpretation for θειότερον. The word is not Platonic. (2) τε καί makes a unity of θεόν τε καὶ φρόνησιν. Hence, just the opposite of "décomposé" is true. (3) The judgment "*sans préparation aucune*" would apply to θέαν (proposed by Havet for θεόν). (4) Havet concedes that the addition found in Eusebius and Stobaeus does not fit clearly into the context. But he assumes there must be a big gap in order to find a place for this addition. In support of this hypothesis he claims (5) that even according to the Plato mss. "*le lecteur saute brusquement à la σωφροσύνη sans comprendre pourquoi*," suggesting that this alone justifies the assumption of a gap. The reply is that σωφροσύνη entered into the discussion back in 131B and is taken up again here. / *Contra* Schanz and Burnet, followed by Wilamowitz (II, 362) and Jachmann, p. 310, it may be said that Olympiodoros (Creuzer edn., p. 217) interprets in detail the words θεόν τε καὶ φρόνησιν.

XVIII : *Gorgias*

RECENT EDITIONS AND TRANSLATIONS: A. Croiset–L. Bodin, *Platon Budé*, III (1923); W. R. M. Lamb, Loeb V (1925); K. Preisendanz (Jena, 1925); C. O. Zurretti (Palermo, 1927); E. Martini (Turin, 1929); B. Stumpo (Palermo, 1931); G. Modugno (Florence, 1936); L. Cooper (London, New York, 1938); W. Theiler (Bern, 1943); J. C. Bruyn (Amsterdam, 1944); R. van Pottelbergh (Antwerp, 1948); R. Rufener and G. Krüger (Zurich, 1948); J. Calonge Ruíz (Madrid, 1951); W. C. Helmbold (New York, 1952); W. D. Woodhead and G. C. Field (Edinburgh, 1953); O. Apelt, PhB 148 (4th edn., 1955); N. Sabbatucci (3d edn., Bari, 1956); J. B. Bergua (4th edn., Madrid, 1957); E. R. Dodds (Oxford, 1959).

RECENT INTERPRETATIONS: J. Geffcken, "Studien zu Platons *Gorgias*," *Hermes*, LXV (1930), 14ff.; J. Humbert, *Polycratès: L'accusation de Socrate et le "Gorgias"* (Paris, 1930); Hildebrandt, pp. 121ff.; W. Schneidewin, *Das sittliche Bewusstsein. Eine Gorgiasanalyse* (Paderborn, 1937); J. Duchemin, "Remarques sur la construction du *Gorgias*," *RevÉtGr*, LVI (1943), 265ff.; I. M. Linforth "Soul and Sieve in Plato's *Gorgias*," *Univ. Calif. Publ. Class. Philology*, XII (1944), 295ff.; A. Rivier, *Les Horizons métaphysiques du Gorgias de Platon* (Lausanne, 1948); E. Voegelin, "The Philosophy of Existence: Plato's *Gorgias*," *Review of Politics*, XI (1949), 477ff.; G. Rudberg, *"Protagoras–Gorgias–Menon*: eine platonische Übergangszeit," *SO*, XXX (1953), 30ff.; Gauss, II/1, 24ff.; F. Zucker, "Der Stil des *Gorgias* nach seiner inneren Form," *SBBerl*, 1956; M. Vanhoutte, *La Notion de liberté dans le "Gorgias" de Platon* (Leopoldville, Congo, 1957); H. Reiner, "Unrechttun ist schlimmer als Unrechtleiden," *ZPhF*, XI (1957), 548ff.

ADDITIONAL BIBLIOGRAPHY: Shorey, p. 501; Geffcken, Notes, p. 65; Rosenmeyer, p. 180; Cherniss, *Lustrum*, pp. 97ff.

1. The answers of antiquity to the question of the σκοπός of the dialogue will be found in Olympiodoros' *Commentary to the "Gorgias*," ed. Norvin (Leipzig, 1936), Prooem., p. 2: (1) οἱ μὲν γάρ φασιν ὅτι σκοπὸς αὐτῷ περὶ ῥητορικῆς διαλεχθῆναι. (2) ἄλλοι δέ φασιν ὅτι περὶ δικαιοσύνης καὶ ἀδικίας διαλέγεται. (3) ἄλλοι δὲ λέγουσιν ὅτι σκοπὸν ἔχει περὶ τοῦ δημιουργοῦ διαλεχθῆναι (on account of the myth). (4) Olympiodoros censures all these interpretations because they ἀπὸ μέρους τὸν σκοπὸν ἐκλαμβάνουσι and says himself: ὅτι σκοπὸς αὐτῷ περὶ τῶν ἀρχῶν τῶν ἠθικῶν διαλεχθῆναι τῶν φερουσῶν ἡμᾶς ἐπὶ τὴν πολιτικὴν εὐδαιμονίαν.

2. Bonitz, p. 1.

3. Schleiermacher, II/1, 8: ". . . the opening of the *Protagoras* is resumed here—one might say almost literally. . . ." The coincidences are listed in Pohlenz, pp. 129ff. / Jaeger (II, 127) calls the *Protagoras* and the *Gorgias* "next of kin," which must be considerably qualified by what precedes and follows in Jaeger's own text. Grube, p. 58, also brings "those two great dialogues of Plato's youth" much too close to each other.

4. That this is not at all a definition of the real Gorgias but a stage in Plato's strategy is correctly stated by Hermann Mutschmann, *Hermes*, LIII (1918), 440. He also notes that the form occurs previously in the *Charmides* where medicine is defined as ὑγιείας δημιουργός.

5. Following Bonitz, ταῦτα ὅπη ποτὲ ἔχει is to be referred to the as yet unresolved contradiction.

6. Cf. Wilamowitz, II, 372f.; L. Reinhard, *Die Anakoluthe bei Platon* (Berlin, 1920), pp. 86f.

7. In 462D 9–11, the distribution of persons as corrected by Hirschig is given in the editions of Schanz (Leipzig, 1880), Sauppe-Gercke

(Berlin, 1897), and Theiler (Bern, 1943). Theiler, Appen. crit. 136, has shown it as given in Olympiodoros, p. 67, 27.

8. Bonitz is certainly right in opposing those who did not distinguish between the Gorgias-stage and the Polos-stage (see, especially, Bonitz, pp. 41ff.). Yet his own over-rigid schema must also be modified.

9. The system according to which rhetoric is given a regular place is based upon the diaeretic procedure that largely prevails in the *Sophist* and the *Statesman*. See Lukas, *Einteilung bei Platon* (Halle, 1888), pp. 125ff.; Shorey, *Unity*, p. 51; Stenzel, *Zahl und Gestalt*, pp. 10ff.; Leisegang, cols. 2412ff. Especially akin is *Sophist* 227c *et seq*. The division περὶ σῶμα—περὶ ψυχήν is quite analogous. Even the four τέχναι are similar. Again, what matters here is the classification of sophistic as there the classification of rhetoric. The word formations in –ικός already play a special role in the *Gorgias*, as noted by Shorey. I add the following motif: there are groups which have no name in common (*Gorgias* 464b ∼ *Statesman* 260e). Proportion (ὥσπερ οἱ γεωμέτραι, *Gorgias* 465b) has its analogy in *Republic* VI 509 *et seq*. See Pierre-Maxime Schuhl, *Études sur la fabulation platonicienne* (Paris, 1947), pp. 41ff. ("Mythe et proportion"). / A similar division, only much simpler, is found in Isokrates, Περὶ ἀντιδόσεως, 180. / On the concept of the *techne*, see Jaeger, II, 129.

10. On 470a Bonitz comments justly: "Led to it by Socrates himself, Polos gives his statement a more definite formulation." The sharpness of this dialectic is blunted if one agrees with Sauppe (commenting on this passage), Thompson, and Wilamowitz (II, 373) in deleting the words τὸ μέγα δύνασθαι in 470a 9 and καὶ μικρὸν δύνασθαι in 470a 12. (Croiset-Bodin is correct.) Actually, the preserved reading means: "So the great capability seems to you now, in contrast to your former opinion (πάλιν αὖ), only then to be good when it is to the advantage of him who acts according to his arbitrary will, and hence this is really (ἔστι) the great capability; in any other case however (it seems to you) something bad and a poor capability." The real point is that by Polos' own admission the previously unrestricted μέγα δύνασθαι becomes under some circumstances a μικρὸν δύνασθαι.

11. Gomperz (II, 345) considers the "fallacy" to be unintentional. Gomperz' section on the "defects of the Socratic-Platonic conceptual philosophy" in the *Gorgias* is useful even for him who is convinced that Plato knew all about the "logical weaknesses" when he wrote the *Gorgias*.

12. See *Republic* 457b, 580d *et seq*., and the comment by Apelt, pp. 216f. The proof in the *Gorgias* has a forerunner in the *Alcibiades*, as was shown in ch. XVII, above.

13. In *Laws* 728b, δίκη and τιμωρία are expressly distinguished. On the problem of punishment, see Apelt, pp. 189ff.

14. Cf. Gomperz, II, 346f., who, however, does not get beyond these subjective objections.

15. G. Bornkamm, "ΟΜΟΛΟΓΙΑ" [XIII⁷], pp. 377ff.

16. "The most eloquent statement of the immoralist's case in European literature is put into his mouth": Shorey, p. 154.

17. Aristotle, *De sophisticis elenchis* 173ᵃ 13: ἦν δὲ τὸ μὲν κατὰ φύσιν αὐτοῖς τὸ ἀληθές, τὸ δὲ κατὰ νόμον τὸ τοῖς πολλοῖς δοκοῦν. / See F. Heinimann, *Nomos und Physis* [I¹⁷], pp. 110ff.; W. Kranz, "Das Gesetz des Herzens" [I¹⁷], pp. 222ff.

18. Cf. Wilamowitz, I, 218 = I² 221; II, 95ff. The only improbability is that Plato's reversal of Pindar's words is "a failure of memory." Surely he twisted them around very sarcastically ("*consulto*" A. Turyn, *Pindari Carmina* [Cracoviae, 1948], p. 351), the more so since "βιαιῶν is by no means a usual word."

19. See B. Snell, *Die Entdeckung des Geistes*³ [XII⁸], pp. 405f.; H. von Arnim, *Supplementum Euripideum* (Bonn, 1913), pp. 11ff.

20. See *Plato* 1, ch. IX. / See Frank, pp. 90f., 298ff.; Ivan Mortimer Linforth, "Soul and Sieve in Plato's *Gorgias*," *University of California Publications in Classical Philology*, XII, no. 17 (1944), 295ff.; E. R. Dodds, *The Greeks and the Irrational* [I²⁴], pp. 209, 225.

21. See Schleiermacher, II/1, 11: "The experiments which Socrates conducts with Kallikles may easily be the most skillful part of this work." Cf. also the sentences which follow.

22. The commentators disagree as to whether the "theory of *Ideas*" is meant here or not. Those who say yes are surprised that Plato says "inexactly" ἀγαθῶν instead of ἀγαθοῦ (thus Sauppe-Gercke's commentary). That is a dogmatic quarrel over words. ἀγαθῶν is a somewhat looser form of expression. The strict form, in which the *Agathon* is not capable of pluralization, is not chosen because the discussion remains in the area of the provisional. But it seems very doubtful to say (with Ueberweg-Praechter, p. 243) that the choice of the plural is the point of departure for an intentional paralogism. Could this proof, or rather, this *reductio ad absurdum*, not be carried through as well (or even better) if ἀγαθοῦ were in the text?

23. Bonitz, pp. 13f., considers our second part as belonging to what follows. Our disposition agrees with Sauppe-Gercke [XVIII⁷], p. xxiv. One must realize that this section moves over into the third. By still representing the hedonistic thesis without reference to a specific *bios*, it belongs to what precedes. But by representing this thesis in a form that permits Socrates to call for the τεχνικός, the transition to what follows is made at the same time.

24. The motif is prepared for by 481D *et seq.* δήμου and Δήμου will likewise be understood in 513c.

25. The anacoluthic sentence ὥσπερ καὶ οἱ ἄλλοι. . . (503DE) is correctly printed in Croiset-Bodin. On this, cf. L. Reinhard, *Observationes criticae in Platonem* (Berlin diss., 1916), pp. 51ff.; *Die Anakoluthe bei Platon* [XVIII⁶], p. 146. αὐτῶν is more probable than αὐτοῦ.

26. On the apparent double meaning of εὖ (κακῶς) πράττειν, see *DGrA*,

II, 20f. πράττειν means to live actively. See Aristotle, *Nicomachean Ethics* 1098b 15–22. Our "multilingual age" (J. Bernays, *Die Dialoge des Aristoteles* [Berlin, 1863], p. 80) finds it difficult to accept such an argument as shown by Grote, II, 126f., n. 9 ("equivocal," "fallacious").

27. The attack upon the great statesmen of Athens is not to be understood polemically as an answer to the polemic treatise of Polykrates (thus Gomperz, II, 343f.). With Plato, polemic is probably never an adequate explanation; besides, Polykrates' treatise is most likely later than the *Gorgias* (Wilamowitz, II, 98f.). A biographic interpretation—"renunciation of the world" (Wilamowitz, I, 230ff. = I², 233ff.) —is not convincing either. The *Gorgias* could at most be a renunciation in the thoroughly ambivalent sense in which, according to Festugière, pp. 381ff., the wise man withdraws into contemplation; but *"telle vie contemplative est essentiellement politique."*

28. One may ask whether K. Schilling, *Platon* (Wurzach, 1948), pp. 92f., is right in saying that Kallikles is "incurably wicked." Cf. *Plato* 1, pp. 166f.

29. On this myth, see *Plato* 1, pp. 184ff.

30. The new form of speech in the last part of the *Gorgias* ("Confession") is discussed by F. Solmsen, *Die Entwicklung der aristotelischen Logik und Rhetorik* (Berlin, 1929), pp. 266f. / The "consistently positive attitude" of the *Gorgias*, as Natorp (p. 41) puts it, has often been emphasized in contrast to the aporetic dialogues. All the same, the view with which E. Hoffmann begins his *Platonismus und Mittelalter* [XVII¹⁵] is surely erroneous. There he calls our dialogue the first of Plato's writings "which aims at expounding a philosophical doctrine of its own and no longer merely portraying Socrates." Even the aporetic dialogues aimed at something more than this. Cf. also Hoffmann, *Platon* (Zurich, 1950), ch. 11. / When Taylor (p. 103) ascribes to the *Protagoras* "a riper mastery of dramatic art" and calls the *Gorgias* "an early work and probably a work dating not many years after the death of Socrates," he confuses two things: the *Protagoras* has a greater abundance of characters, more varied color in its happenings, more animation in its dialogical course. The *Gorgias* is much more economical in its means; it is, however, incomparably more tense, profound, closer to tragedy, advancing toward the *epekeina*.

XIX: *Meno*

RECENT EDITIONS AND TRANSLATIONS: F. Zambaldi (Bari, 1917); B. Stumpo
(Palermo, 1922); A. Croiset and L. Bodin, *Platon Budé*, III (1923);
W. R. M. Lamb, Loeb IV (1924); K. Preisendanz (Jena, 1925);
F. Acri and A. Guzzo (Florence, 1927); F. Galli (Lanciano, 1929);
G. Modugno (Perugia-Florence, 1930–31); E. Martini (Turin,
1932); O. Apelt, PhB 153 (3d edn., 1944); R. Rufener and G. Krüger
(Zurich, 1948); W. K. C. Guthrie (West Drayton, 1956); J. Olives
Canals (Barcelona, 1956); A. Ruiz de Elvira (Madrid, 1958).

RECENT INTERPRETATIONS: Stenzel, 147ff.; B. J. H. Ovink, *Philosophische
Erklärungen der platonischen Dialoge "Meno" und "Hippias Minor"*
(Amsterdam, 1931); Hildebrandt, pp. 152ff.; K. Buchmann, "Die
Stellung des *Menon* in der platonischen Philosophie," *Philologus*,
Suppl. XXIX (1936); Jaeger, II, 160ff.; Koyré, pp. 7ff.; Goldschmidt,
pp. 117ff.; Robinson, pp. 118ff. = 2d edn., pp. 114ff.; Stefanini, I²,
96ff.; G. Rudberg, "*Protagoras–Gorgias–Menon*: eine platonische
Übergangszeit," *SO*, XXX (1953), 30ff.; Buccellato, pp. 159ff.;
Gallo Galli, *Da Talete al "Menone" di Platone* (Turin, 1956), pp. 116ff.;
Gauss, II/1, 104ff.; W. J. Verdenius, "Notes on Plato's *Meno*,"
Mnemosyne, IV, 10 (1957), 289ff.; E. Lledó Iñigo, "La *anámnesis*
dialéctica en Platón," *Emerita*, XXIX (1961), 219ff.

ADDITIONAL BIBLIOGRAPHY: Shorey, p. 511; Geffcken, Notes, p. 73; Rosenmeyer, p. 182; Cherniss, *Lustrum*, pp. 115ff.

1. "Anytos, who in response to the not very artistic command of the
    author is immediately at hand": Wilamowitz, I, 277 = I², 279. "This
    sudden appearance [is] probably the worst piece of dramatic technique
    in Plato": Grube, p. 231. But if one feels the deep irony of εἰς καλὸν
    ἡμῖν ᾽Ανυτος ὅδε παρεκαθέζετο (89E 10), and if one also realizes how
    Anytos suddenly quits the conversation again, only to rejoin it once
    more by a sharp word of rejection, one will recognize in his sudden
    entrance artistic wisdom rather than artistic weakness. Would it not
    have been easy for Plato to introduce Anytos, Menon's host, in the
    very first words of the dialogue, as he does Kallikles in the *Gorgias*?
    Schleiermacher (II/1, 336) translates παρεκαθέζετο "is sitting here
    with us" and interprets the scene as if Anytos had been present from
    the beginning. This false interpretation leads to misjudging the art
    of the dialogue; a correct interpretation is given by Thompson, *The
    Meno* [XIV⁵], p. 170. / See de Vries, pp. 102ff.

2. The best comment on the distribution of persons in 99ᴇ 1–3 was made by P. Maas, *Hermes*, LX (1925), 492, before *Plato Latinus*, ed. R. Klibansky (London, 1944), I, 44, showed the following distribution: Socrates. *At forsan Anitus hic tibi molestatur dicenti.* / Meno. *Nichil cura est michi.* / Socrates. *Super hoc, o Menon.* . . . Here it is correct that καίτοι ἴσως belongs to Socrates. Menon is too passive for such a contradiction, whereas here, as in 89ᴇ 10 *et seq.*, Socrates uses the sharply pointed ῎Ανυτος ὅδε to establish a connection with the foe, which is a challenge. Over against ὅδε stands the distancing word τούτῳ, with which Socrates turns away from Anytos and back to Menon, much as in 95ᴀ (οὗτος, ᴀ 5). But οὐδὲν μέλει ἔμοιγε would hardly fit Menon, for whom such a discourtesy toward his guest would be without precedent. The three words do fit Anytos as an answer to the rejoinder of Socrates. They are ascribed to Anytos in the *Codex Parisinus*, 1811 (*"supra scripto rc ἄνυτος"*) according to I. Bekker, *Platonis . . . Scripta Graece Omnia* [XVII¹⁴], IV, 86. (Correspondence with P. Maas has helped me clarify this matter.)

3. According to Taylor, p. 128, the dialogue takes place in the year 402; according to Croiset-Bodin, *Platon Budé*, III/2, 231ff., it is in the last years of the Peloponnesian War. Plato probably does not set a definite year. But the names Menon and Anytos must make everyone think of the campaign of Cyrus and the trial of Socrates: both are imminent.

4. On the figure of Menon, see E. Bruhn in Χάριτες *F. Leo dargebracht* (Berlin, 1911), pp. 1ff. Wilamowitz, II, 145: "Plato does not characterize the man Menon at all." Is this not another case of the problem which was indicated in ch. XVII, n. 9, above?

5. *Laches* 190ᴅ: ἀνδρεία τί ποτ' ἐστίν. ἔπειτα μετὰ τοῦτο σκεψόμεθα καὶ ὅτῳ ἂν τρόπῳ τοῖς νεανίσκοις παραγένοιτο . . . οὐ μὰ τὸν Δία, ὦ Σώκρατες, οὐ χαλεπὸν εἰπεῖν. *Meno* 71ᴀ: . . . εἴθ' ὅτῳ τρόπῳ παραγίγνεται. . . . ὅ τι ποτ' ἐστὶ τὸ παράπαν ἀρετή. . . . *Meno* 71ᴇ: ἀλλ' οὐ χαλεπόν, ὦ Σώκρατες, εἰπεῖν.

6. Natorp, p. 38, n. 1, calls attention to the coincidence. Cf. Ueberweg-Praechter, pp. 246ff. / On the subject of the faulty definitions in the *Meno*, see F. Solmsen, *Die Entwicklung . . .* [XVIII³⁰], pp. 161f.

7. *Vorsokr.* 82 [76] ʙ 18, 19; Aristotle, *Politics* I 13, 1260ᵃ 20 *et seq.* For comment see Hermann, p. 485 (and n. 434); Pohlenz, p. 168; W. L. Newman, *The Politics of Aristotle* (4 vols., Oxford, 1887–1902), II, 219 (it is more than doubtful that Aristotle meant the historic and not the Platonic Socrates); III, 172, 324. Cf. Eduard Schwartz, *Das Geschichtswerk des Thukydides* [II⁴], p. 353, where a part of the history of the concept ἀρετή is instructively sketched.

8. *Republic* I 353ʙ: οὐκοῦν καὶ ἀρετὴ δοκεῖ σοι εἶναι ἑκάστῳ ᾧπερ καὶ ἔργον τι προστέτακται. 353ᴀ: ἑκάστου . . . ἔργου. *Meno* 72ᴀ: πρὸς ἕκαστον ἔργον ἑκάστῳ ἡμῶν ἡ ἀρετή ἐστιν. The problem involved here is de-

veloped by Aristotle, *Politics* III 4, in the discussion regarding the ἴδιος and the κοινὸς λόγος of the ἀρεταί.

9. Fritz Wehrli, "Ethik und Medizin," *MusHelv*, VIII (1951), 46, sees in Aristotle, *Politics* I 13, 1260ᵃ 27 *et seq.*, "an unequivocal assent to the way of thought of Gorgias and the Sophists."

10. Is it logical that in *Vorsokr.* 82 [76] B 19, the passage *Meno* 71E is referred back to an "undefined work" of Gorgias, but not 73C and 76B ? The same irony of Socrates-Plato is at work in all three places. That makes B 18 also doubtful, since Aristotle refers to the *Meno*. One might almost be tempted to propose a Group D in the *Vorsokratiker*: "Half in jest referred back to Gorgias."

11. Aristotle, Περὶ αἰσθήσεως, 439ᵃ 31. For comment on this and the following, see J. Stenzel, "Anschauung und Denken in der klassischen Theorie der griechischen Mathematik," *Die Antike*, IX (1933), 145ff. = *Kleine Schriften*, pp. 322ff.

12. στερεοῦ πέρας σχῆμα, *Meno* 76A. ἐπίπεδον πέρας στερεοῦ, Aristotle, *Topics* IV 141b 22. στερεοῦ πέρας ἐπιφάνεια, Euclid XI, Def. 2. On Empedokles, see *Vorsokr.* 31 [21] A 92. Cf. E. Bignone, *Empedocle* (Turin, 1916), pp. 102ff.

13. Similarly, Socrates as snake-charmer: *Republic* II 358B, in a corresponding passage, only that room was lacking there to develop the systematic meaning of the image.

14. Cf. *Plato* 1, pp. 181f.; 370, n. 14. Cf. Gauss, II/1, 124ff.

15. K. Buchmann, "Die Stellung des *Menon* in der platonischen Philosophie," *Philologus*, Suppl., XXIX (1936), 64ff., and C. Mugler, *Platon et la recherche mathématique* (Strasbourg, 1948), ch. 6, conceive of the experience of the earlier existence as sense perception. Against this view, and rightly, are H. Cherniss, *AJP*, LVIII (1937), 497ff.; *Review of Metaphysics*, IV (1951), 421; N. Gulley, *CQ*, n.s., IV (1954), 194ff. On mathematics in the *Meno*, see Maria Timpanaro Cardini, "Sull' ipotesi geometrica del *Menone*," *ParPass*, VI (1951), 401ff.; Robert S. Brumbaugh, *Plato's Mathematical Imagination* (Bloomington, 1954), pp. 21ff. / Plato's "doctrine of recollection" made a strong impression on Leibniz; see "Metaphysische Abhandlung" (Discours de Métaphysique) in *Hauptschriften zur Grundlegung der Philosophie*, ed. A. Buchenau and E. Cassirer (Leipzig, 1924), II, 171ff. Leibniz refers to it as "a doctrine which is well-founded provided it be correctly understood and cleansed of the mistaken notion of pre-existence. . . ." In other words, he wants to eliminate the mythical component. Should not he then, strictly speaking, also have objected to the term "recollection" ? Cassirer remarks that *Meno* 82c *et seq.* is "a common point of reference among the founders of modern philosophy and science, Nicholas of Cusa and Descartes, Kepler and Galileo."

16. Reference by Erich Frank. Cf. the general suggestion of Schleiermacher, II/1, 330.

17. Cf. *Plato* 1, p. 189. / Cf. Léon Ross, "Sur la doctrine de la rémini-
scence," in *La Pensée Hellénique* (Paris, 1942), p. 337. The very word
"doctrine" indicates the too doctrinal point of view.

18. Whether the geometric example of the triangle enclosed in a circle
has a symbolic meaning over and above the methodological one—
as is probably the case in the mathematical examples of the first two
parts of the dialogue—is not possible for me to decide. The attempt
of Dümmler, *Akademika* [VI[15]], pp. 260ff., is ingenious but probably
fantastic. In comparison, see Paul Tannery, *Mémoires scientifiques*
(Toulouse, 1876–1913), II, 401ff.; Thomas Heath, *A History of Greek
Mathematics* (Oxford, 1921), I, 298ff. On the "hypothetical method,"
see Robinson, pp. 118ff. = 2d edn., pp. 114ff.; Classen, pp. 72ff.

19. "The individual, i.e., the soul" is inserted here from *Alcibiades* 130D
because it clarifies what is briefly stated in the *Meno*.

20. Cf. 100B with *Alcibiades* 130C and the comment in *DGrA*, I, 23.

21. *DGrA*, I, 31ff.

22. Wilamowitz (I, 279 = I[2], 281) failed to hear the scorn in these words.
Strange also is his view (II, 147) that Plato "now as before wants to
spare Anytos."

23. Schleiermacher (II/1, 332) regards the judgment as ironic, i.e., not
seriously meant, as Zeller (II/1, 542, n. 2) also denies that in the
Meno Plato wanted to save the reputation of the old politicians.
Gomperz (II, 376) protests against the view that "vindication" was
"only ironically" meant. A shallow concept of irony is to blame for
this verbal dispute. / To us it seems most important to lay bare the
systematic root of this new estimate, or, more correctly, of this new
shade of meaning. ("There is really no 'recantation' in the *Meno*":
Taylor, p. 142.) That Plato here is making a concession to his people
(Wilamowitz, I, 280 = I[2], 282; similarly, Gomperz, II, 376) is at
best an allowable admission. But then one must rule out any thought
of opportunism. We disregard the question of how far any controversy
with Polykrates played a part in this discussion. Was not this, perhaps, far beneath Plato?

INDEX

Abramczyk, I., 339
Academy, 92, 217, 234, 269, 279, 280, 350¹²
Achilles, 138, 139, 165, 177
Acri, F., 357
activity / passivity, 258–59
Adam, J., 307¹⁰, 311
Adeimantos, 52, 225
ἀδικία, see justice; wrongdoing
Adonis-cry, 153
advantageous, see useful, concept of
Aelian, 321¹⁶
Aeschylus, 331¹²
affinities, see dialogues by title
Agamemnon, 76
Agathon, 103, 133, 327¹⁰
Agathon: and fitting, 315¹³; and knowledge, 338¹⁹; and moral values, 270; as origin and goal, 222; as principle, 268; Socrates' commitment to, 271, 272; and soul, 101; sublimity of, 312¹¹; *mentioned*: 124, 125, 144, 145, 191, 257, 307¹¹, 355²²; see also *Eidos | Idea s.v. Idea* of the Good
Aischines (orator), 9
Aischines (Socratic), 173, 216, 232, 350⁷
Alain (Émile Chartier), 349¹
Albinus, 328¹⁶
ALCIBIADES MAJOR, 231–43, 348–52; and aporetic dialogues, 233–34, 239–40, 241; as background for *Symp.*, 242–43; character change in, 234, 236; chronology of, 232, 350⁸ ¹¹ ¹²; genuineness of, 231, 237, 239, 319¹⁸, 349¹, 350⁹ ¹¹, 351¹³ ¹⁴; honored in antiquity, 231–32; impact of, 231, 349¹; ironic history in, 236, 238; participants in, 232; as portrait of human

existence, 239; royal speech in, 232, 235–36, 238–39; and self-knowledge, 310¹¹; setting of, 232; has Socratic education as objective, 239, 240; structure of, 233, 234–35, 238–39; transitional movement from aporetic dialogues to *Gorg.* and *Rep.*, 242;
  and *Apol.*, 169; *Charm.*, 79–80, 232, 233, 236, 239, 310¹⁵; *Euthyd.*, 232; *Euthyph.*, 83; *Gorg.*, 233, 240–41, 259, 267, 269; *Hipparch.*, 238–39; *Hipp. maj.*, 110, 316¹; *Laches*, 233; *Lysis*, 232, 239; *Menex.*, 218, 220, 221; *Meno*, 282, 286, 360¹⁹ ²⁰; *Protag.*, 11, 34, 236; *Rep.*, 241–42, 349¹; *Statesm.*, 349¹; *Symp.*, 242–43, 349¹; *Thrasym.*, 64
Alkibiades: in *Alcib. maj.*, 64, 149–50, 218, 231–43, 350⁹; first meeting with Socrates, 232–33; undergoes inner change, 234, 236; in *Protag.*, 5–6, 9–10, 22–35 *passim*, 67; in *Symp.*, 164, 168, 187, 242–43; Plutarch's biography of, 231, 349³; *mentioned*: 130, 180, 274, 278
Allan, D. J., 339, 341⁷
"all-wise," as Sophists' claim, 106, 146, 182–83, 198, 247
Alopeke, 39, 153
Amado-Lévy-Valensi, É., 339
ambiguities, 96, 101, 139, 225; in Greek terms, 95, 184–85, 308¹⁸; as irony, 31, 214; in *paideia*, 48–49; *see also* ignorance *s.v.* Socratic; irony
Ameipsias, 347¹⁰
Ammendola, G., 304, 309, 313, 348

apologetics, 312[2]; movement
of, 82–83, 90; participants in,
83–84; setting of, 83; structure
of, 84, 90; and theory of *Ideas*,
85, 312[6];
  and *Alcib. maj.*, 83, 88;
Charm., 70, 90; *Crat.*, 203;
Euthyd., 195; *Hipp. maj.*, 83,
114, 115, 317[6]; *Hipp. min.*,
143; *Laches*, 85, 86, 90;
Laws, 88, 91; *Menex.*, 221;
Meno, 85, 91, 281; *Protag.*,
37, 82, 87; *Rep.*, 88, 91,
312[11]; *Symp.*, 83; *Theaet.*, 89;
Thrasym., 50, 53, 88, 90;
Tim., 88, 312[11]
Euthyphron, 82–91, 195, 203, 204,
277, 278, 312[5], 319[18]; crime of
father, 83, 91, 311[1]
εὐτυχία, *see* good fortune
excess, *see* measurement; proportion
exile, 169, 177
existence: dimension of, 37, 41, 49,
69, 91, 115, 143, 166, 168–69,
178, 215, 228, 284; forms of
human, 100, 109–10, 120–21,
131–34, 145, 261, 266–71, 320[6];
Socratic, 115, 144, 145, 159–60,
165, 169, 170, 267, 271, 272,
286; unique portrait of human,
in *Alcib. maj.*, 233–34, 239
experts, 12, 25, 39, 40, 52, 80, 122,
130, 135, 138, 142, 143, 159,
200–2, 249, 355[23]
eye of the soul analogy, 74

Face analogy, 18–19, 20, 26, 301[14]
Faggin, G., 299
fallacies, intentional, 181; in
Euthyd., 186, 207, 210, 336[8 9],
337[13]; *Gorg.*, 354[11]; *Protag.*,
19–20, 26, 301[15]; alleged in
Charm., 309[8]
family, 82, 217
family tree, 220
fathers and sons: in *Euthyd.*, 193,
194; *Euthyph.*, 83; *Laches*,
39–40, 41, 42, 48; *Menex.*, 226;

Meno, 273, 287; *Protag.*, 9, 12–
17 *passim*, 31; *Theages*, 147, 148,
151
faulty definitions, 113, 358[6]
festivals: Bendis, 51, 306[5];
  Epidauros, 323[1]; gymnastic,
227, 228; *see also* religion, popular
Festugière, A.-J., 294, 302[23], 348,
349[1], 356[27]
Ficino, M., 231, 322[18], 344[22]
Field, G. C., 311, 350[7], 352
fine, *see* money fine
fitting, 109, 110, 112, 315[13], 318[9]
Flashar, H., 323[6], 324[8]
flattery, 31, 93, 107; arts of, *see*
arts *s.v.* system of genuine and
pseudo–
flute story, 349[3]
flux, doctrine of eternal, 197–98,
205, 207, 213–15 *passim*
forms, see *Eidos*
Fowler, H. N., 309, 311, 313, 316,
316[1], 319, 326, 329, 333, 339,
348
Fox, M., 311, 330, 333
Frank, E., 294, 301[17], 355[20], 359[16]
Fränkel, H., 23, 301[18]
freedom: in Athens, 223; "complete," 217, 224–25; and law,
217–18; and oratory, 248;
tyrant's view of, 224
Freymann, W., 294, 312[6], 314[8],
316[1], 342[13], 345[32]
Friedländer, P., 294, 310[9], 316[1],
319[18], 320[1], 321[13], 327[4 7], 348,
348[1], 350[6 7], 351[13], 355[26],
360[20 21]
friends and enemies, 56, 58–59,
61, 95, 97, 126, 174, 175
friendship, 92–104; "bad ones"
cannot have, 97, 314[4]; as
centripetal principle in state,
224–26, 237, 241–42; and the
good, 97–98; between like and
unlike, 97–98, 102–3; natural
form of, 94, 96, 102, 239; stages
of, 94, 96, 98, 102; *see also* Eros
Fritz, K. von, 327[5], 338[25], 339, 341[7]

to life in, 82; and Athens, 51,
107, 165, 167, 176, 215, 216–28
passim, 255, 261–73; chooses
death, 170–71, 173; and the
community, 167, 169; death of,
9, 93, 107, 136, 154, 157, 162,
170–73, 176, 227, 271, 272,
347[6], 350[4]; as educational
"consultant," 38, 39, 147–48,
149, 193, 218; existence of,
see under existence; fate of, 195,
271; followers of, 6, 9–10, 146,
164, 167–68, 169, 172–75, 180,
195, 198, 245, 310[11], 326[8],
333[2]; and the gods, 51, 164–65,
168; indictment of, 83, 85, 91,
158, 160, 163–65, 168, 195,
271, 273, 313[12]; as only true
doubter, 235;— lover, 232;
— orator, 268;— statesman,
163,167, 271, 289;— teacher, 34,
183, 235, 290; and opposition to
Sophists, 5–37, 105–7, 114–15,
137, 138–43, 144–46, 157–72,
180–95, 198, 210–11, 233,
244–72, 276, 284–90, 303[28 32];
physical appearance of, 69, 105,
281; and Plato, *see under* Plato;
and poetry, 324[11]; political
education most important life
task for, 83; poverty of, 166;
praised by the young, 39;
presence of, 152, 179; prophetic
power of, 153–54, 170–71,
327[12], 328[16], 332[18]; and religious ritual, 51, 159, 164;
rudeness of, 319[18]; shows no
fear of death, 165–66, 178; as
soldier, 39, 41, 68, 69, 166,
232; sons of, 171, 175; soul of,
and mirroring eye analogy,
351[15]; and Stoicism, 321[14];
strangeness of, 232, 243;
"Socrates tests men," 20, 22,
41, 290; use of sophistic techniques by, 24–25, 28–32, 57,
71, 78, 113, 137–39, 145, 205,
220, 252, 257, 303[32], 314[10];
as teacher, 10, 34, 39, 40, 42,

48, 52, 78, 147–48, 150, 194,
240; trial of, 82, 83, 84,
91, 115, 157–72, 261, 275,
330[1], 358[3]; Xenophon's view
of, 159, 164, 168, 169; *see also*
conversation, Socratic; education *s.v.* Socratic; ignorance
s.v. Socratic
Solmsen, F., 356[30], 358[6]
Solon, 56, 120
Somebody, as anonymous spokesman: in *Euthyd.*, 193–94, 288,
338[19 25]; *Hipparch.*: 119;
Hipp. maj., 105, 107–15
passim, 319[18]; *Menex.*, 219;
Protag., 5
Sontag, F., 339
soothsayers, 46, 84; *see also*
prophecy
SOPHIST: and *Charm.*, 78; *Euthyd.*,
188; *Gorg.*, 354; *Hipp. min.*,
145–46, 348[21]; *Protag.*, 6, 7
Sophists / sophistics: and education, 5–35, 38–40, 106–7,
149, 151, 162–63, 180–95,
198–99, 204, 270, 273–
76, 284–90; followers of,
10, 52, 180, 245; and im-
moralism, 244, 254, 259–72,
289–90; method of, 21–22, 36,
181–86 *passim*, 303[32]; "not all
bad," 11–12; and oratory, 52,
119, 145–46, 160, 161, 219–20,
240, 241, 244–59, 268–72, 278;
and poetry, 72, 129–35 *passim*,
137–39, 286; political aims of,
9–10, 12–17, 106–15 *passim*,
150–51, 180–83, 193–94, 219–
20, 233, 248, *and see* tyranny;
portraits of, 10, 14, 60–61,
85, 90, 105–6, 144–46, 182–83,
198, 217, 336[9], *and see* "all-
wise," Jack-of-all-trades,
peddler; radically different from
philosopher, 105–7, 115, 144;
"Sophists take money," 7, 14,
31, 33, 106, 107, 151, 271;
speeches of, 7, 10, 18, 21–24,
106–16 *passim*, 137–46 *passim*,